T0182808

# Introduction to Privacy Enhancing Technologies

Carlisle Adams

# Introduction to Privacy Enhancing Technologies

## A Classification-Based Approach to Understanding PETs

 Springer

Carlisle Adams
School of Electrical Engineering and Computer Science
University of Ottawa
Ottawa, ON, Canada

ISBN 978-3-030-81042-9      ISBN 978-3-030-81043-6   (eBook)
https://doi.org/10.1007/978-3-030-81043-6

© The Editor(s) (if applicable) and The Author(s), under exclusive license to Springer Nature
Switzerland AG 2021
This work is subject to copyright. All rights are solely and exclusively licensed by the Publisher, whether
the whole or part of the material is concerned, specifically the rights of translation, reprinting, reuse of
illustrations, recitation, broadcasting, reproduction on microfilms or in any other physical way, and
transmission or information storage and retrieval, electronic adaptation, computer software, or by similar
or dissimilar methodology now known or hereafter developed.
The use of general descriptive names, registered names, trademarks, service marks, etc. in this publication
does not imply, even in the absence of a specific statement, that such names are exempt from the relevant
protective laws and regulations and therefore free for general use.
The publisher, the authors, and the editors are safe to assume that the advice and information in this book
are believed to be true and accurate at the date of publication. Neither the publisher nor the authors or the
editors give a warranty, expressed or implied, with respect to the material contained herein or for any
errors or omissions that may have been made. The publisher remains neutral with regard to jurisdictional
claims in published maps and institutional affiliations.

This Springer imprint is published by the registered company Springer Nature Switzerland AG
The registered company address is: Gewerbestrasse 11, 6330 Cham, Switzerland

*I am happy to dedicate this book to my lovely wife Marion, who not only provided endless encouragement throughout this process, but also tangibly helped (in countless big and little ways) to vastly improve this book and bring it to completion. Thank you so much for everything!*

# Preface

This book has been refined and developed in a graduate course that I have taught 15 times at the University of Ottawa since 2004; the classification-based approach that it uses was first published as a research paper in 2006. Like a number of my colleagues around the world, I have for a long time been somewhat frustrated by the absence of a textbook on PETs that I could use for my course. While it is appropriate and reasonable in a graduate course to point students to a set of foundational and recent academic papers on the topic of discussion, I have nevertheless felt that it would be useful to have a single text that can serve as a general introduction to the field. Eventually, since no one else seemed to be doing this (and with the unexpected coincidence of a sabbatical year and a global pandemic removing all other options for things to distract me!), I decided to put this book together.

Consequently, the primary target audience of this book is graduate and upper-year undergraduate students in computer science and software engineering with an interest in technologies that protect and enhance privacy in online environments. However, my hope is that students, researchers, practitioners, and interested parties in many other fields and at many different levels will find this book instructive and helpful. Although privacy is a much bigger field than just PETs, privacy advocates in all areas can benefit from understanding the role that PETs can play in guarding some aspects of privacy in our online interactions.

In terms of organization, I feel that it is essential to begin with the first two chapters, which motivate the need for PETs and describe the classification-based approach that this book uses (the *privacy tree*). The six subsequent chapters (on various example PETs in each of the six leaves of the tree) are mostly standalone and can be read in any order. Chapter 9 discusses how to use the privacy tree in practice, and Chap. 10 maps out a path forward, and so it is fitting that they should be read after a basic understanding of PETs and the privacy tree is in place from the previous eight chapters. For readers that are new to the tools and techniques of cryptography, it will be helpful to read Chap. 11, "Crypto Primer" prior to Chaps. 3, 4, 5, 6, 7, and 8; others may skip this chapter or simply use it to see a description of a particular unfamiliar term or concept. Finally, students and researchers in the field may find Chap. 12 valuable: this chapter collects together all the references at the end of the individual chapters throughout the book, adds a hyperlink to each reference (for easy retrieval), and provides a (short) bibliography of recommended reading in privacy.

I would like to greatly acknowledge the academic system in which we operate: without a year-long sabbatical in which to focus, it would have been far more difficult to complete this book in a reasonable time! I am extremely grateful, too, for the comments and feedback I received from several reviewers on an initial draft of this manuscript; my many thanks go to Mozhgan Nasr Azadani, Ian Goldberg, Marion Rodrigues, and Paul Syverson. Their careful reading and attention to detail significantly improved the clarity, coverage, and correctness of the text in many places. (But note, of course, that any errors remaining in the book are entirely due to the author, not the reviewers!) Finally, I would like to thank the many friends and relatives who encouraged and supported me in this project, as well as Susan Lagerstrom-Fife and the terrific team at Springer who brought this book to publication with dedication, efficiency, and professionalism.

Ottawa, ON, Canada                                              Carlisle Adams

# Contents

1   **The Privacy Minefield**. . . . . . . . . . . . . . . . . . . . . . . . . . . . . . . . . . .   1
    1.1   Threats to Privacy . . . . . . . . . . . . . . . . . . . . . . . . . . . . . . . . . . .   4
    1.2   The Battle for Supremacy Over Personal Data . . . . . . . . . . . . . .   8
        1.2.1   Controlling the Goods and Services Available to Alice. . . .   9
        1.2.2   Controlling the Choices That Alice (Apparently Freely)
               Makes. . . . . . . . . . . . . . . . . . . . . . . . . . . . . . . . . . . . . .   10
        1.2.3   Controlling What Alice Can Say, What She Can Do,
               and Where She Can Go . . . . . . . . . . . . . . . . . . . . . . . . . .   12
    1.3   High-Stakes Hide-and-Seek. . . . . . . . . . . . . . . . . . . . . . . . . . . .   15
    1.4   Summary . . . . . . . . . . . . . . . . . . . . . . . . . . . . . . . . . . . . . . . . .   16
    References. . . . . . . . . . . . . . . . . . . . . . . . . . . . . . . . . . . . . . . . . . . . .   19

2   **A Collection of Tools: The Privacy Tree** . . . . . . . . . . . . . . . . . . . . .   21
    2.1   Many Privacy Enhancing Technologies. . . . . . . . . . . . . . . . . . . .   22
    2.2   Classification (Privacy Tree) . . . . . . . . . . . . . . . . . . . . . . . . . . .   22
    2.3   Previous Work on Classifications for Privacy . . . . . . . . . . . . . . .   23
        2.3.1   Antón et al. (2002). . . . . . . . . . . . . . . . . . . . . . . . . . . . . .   23
        2.3.2   Rezgui et al. (2003) . . . . . . . . . . . . . . . . . . . . . . . . . . . . .   24
        2.3.3   Skinner et al. (2006). . . . . . . . . . . . . . . . . . . . . . . . . . . . .   24
        2.3.4   Adams (2006). . . . . . . . . . . . . . . . . . . . . . . . . . . . . . . . . .   25
        2.3.5   Solove (2008). . . . . . . . . . . . . . . . . . . . . . . . . . . . . . . . . .   25
        2.3.6   Nissenbaum (2009) . . . . . . . . . . . . . . . . . . . . . . . . . . . . .   26
        2.3.7   Pfitzmann and Hansen (2010) . . . . . . . . . . . . . . . . . . . . .   27
        2.3.8   Heurix et al. (2015) . . . . . . . . . . . . . . . . . . . . . . . . . . . . .   27
        2.3.9   OPC (2017) . . . . . . . . . . . . . . . . . . . . . . . . . . . . . . . . . . .   28
    2.4   The Selected Privacy Tree . . . . . . . . . . . . . . . . . . . . . . . . . . . . .   30
    2.5   The Remainder of This Book. . . . . . . . . . . . . . . . . . . . . . . . . . . .   36
    References. . . . . . . . . . . . . . . . . . . . . . . . . . . . . . . . . . . . . . . . . . . . .   38

3   **Limiting Exposure by Hiding the Identity** . . . . . . . . . . . . . . . . . . . .   39
    3.1   Mix Network . . . . . . . . . . . . . . . . . . . . . . . . . . . . . . . . . . . . . . .   39
        3.1.1   The Basic Scheme . . . . . . . . . . . . . . . . . . . . . . . . . . . . . .   40

    3.1.2   Enhancements .....................................   45
    3.1.3   Strengths ........................................   47
    3.1.4   Disadvantages, Limitations, and Weaknesses ..........   48
  3.2   Anonymous Remailer ....................................   49
    3.2.1   The Basic Scheme ..................................   49
    3.2.2   Enhancements .....................................   51
    3.2.3   Strengths ........................................   52
    3.2.4   Disadvantages, Limitations, and Weaknesses ..........   52
  3.3   Onion Routing and Tor .................................   53
    3.3.1   The Basic Scheme ..................................   53
    3.3.2   Enhancements .....................................   59
    3.3.3   Strengths ........................................   60
    3.3.4   Disadvantages, Limitations, and Weaknesses ..........   61
  3.4   Summary ..............................................   63
  References.................................................   66

4  Limiting Exposure by Hiding the Action .......................   69
  4.1   Transport Layer Security (SSL/TLS).......................   70
    4.1.1   The Basic Scheme ..................................   70
    4.1.2   Enhancements .....................................   73
    4.1.3   Strengths ........................................   74
    4.1.4   Disadvantages, Limitations, and Weaknesses ..........   75
  4.2   Network Layer Security (IPsec in Transport Mode) ...........   76
    4.2.1   The Basic Scheme ..................................   77
    4.2.2   Enhancements .....................................   80
    4.2.3   Strengths ........................................   81
    4.2.4   Disadvantages, Limitations, and Weaknesses ..........   81
  4.3   Private Information Retrieval (PIR).......................   82
    4.3.1   The Basic Scheme ..................................   83
    4.3.2   Enhancements .....................................   86
    4.3.3   Strengths ........................................   88
    4.3.4   Disadvantages, Limitations, and Weaknesses ..........   88
  4.4   Summary ..............................................   89
  References.................................................   91

5  Limiting Exposure by Hiding the Identity-Action Pair...........   95
  5.1   Network Layer Security (IPsec in Tunnel Mode) ..............   96
    5.1.1   The Basic Scheme ..................................   96
    5.1.2   Enhancements .....................................   97
    5.1.3   Strengths ........................................   98
    5.1.4   Disadvantages, Limitations, and Weaknesses ..........   98
  5.2   Off-the-Record (OTR) Messaging..........................   98
    5.2.1   The Basic Scheme ..................................   99
    5.2.2   Enhancements .....................................  101
    5.2.3   Strengths ........................................  104
    5.2.4   Disadvantages, Limitations, and Weaknesses ..........  104
  5.3   Summary ..............................................  105
  References.................................................  107

**6   Limiting Disclosure by Hiding the Identity** ..................... 109
   6.1   $k$-Anonymity ......................................... 110
       6.1.1   The Basic Scheme .............................. 112
       6.1.2   Enhancements ................................. 115
       6.1.3   Strengths ...................................... 118
       6.1.4   Disadvantages, Limitations, and Weaknesses .......... 119
   6.2   Credential Systems. ....................................... 120
       6.2.1   The Basic Scheme .............................. 122
       6.2.2   Enhancements ................................. 131
       6.2.3   Strengths ...................................... 135
       6.2.4   Disadvantages, Limitations, and Weaknesses .......... 136
   6.3   Summary ............................................. 137
   References. ................................................ 140

**7   Limiting Disclosure by Hiding the Attribute** ................... 143
   7.1   Database Protection Approaches .......................... 144
       7.1.1   The Basic Scheme .............................. 144
       7.1.2   Enhancements ................................. 148
       7.1.3   Strengths ...................................... 149
       7.1.4   Disadvantages, Limitations, and Weaknesses .......... 150
   7.2   Multi-Party Computation. ................................ 150
       7.2.1   The Basic Scheme .............................. 151
       7.2.2   Enhancements ................................. 155
       7.2.3   Strengths ...................................... 157
       7.2.4   Disadvantages, Limitations, and Weaknesses .......... 157
   7.3   $\varepsilon$-Differential Privacy. ................................ 158
       7.3.1   The Basic Scheme .............................. 159
       7.3.2   Enhancements ................................. 165
       7.3.3   Strengths ...................................... 168
       7.3.4   Disadvantages, Limitations, and Weaknesses .......... 169
   7.4   Summary ............................................. 169
   References. ................................................ 172

**8   Limiting Disclosure by Hiding the Identity-Attribute Pair.** ........ 175
   8.1   Hippocratic Databases (HDB) ........................... 175
       8.1.1   The Basic Scheme .............................. 176
       8.1.2   Enhancements ................................. 179
       8.1.3   Strengths ...................................... 181
       8.1.4   Disadvantages, Limitations, and Weaknesses .......... 182
   8.2   Platform for Privacy Preferences Project (P3P). ............... 182
       8.2.1   The Basic Scheme .............................. 183
       8.2.2   Enhancements ................................. 185
       8.2.3   Strengths ...................................... 188
       8.2.4   Disadvantages, Limitations, and Weaknesses .......... 188
   8.3   Architecture for Privacy Enforcement Using XML (APEX). ..... 189
       8.3.1   The Basic Scheme .............................. 189
       8.3.2   Enhancements ................................. 192

        8.3.3    Strengths . . . . . . . . . . . . . . . . . . . . . . . . . . . . . . . . . .    195
        8.3.4    Disadvantages, Limitations, and Weaknesses . . . . . . . . . .    195
    8.4    Credential Systems Showing Properties of Attributes . . . . . . . . . .    196
        8.4.1    The Basic Scheme . . . . . . . . . . . . . . . . . . . . . . . . . . . .    196
        8.4.2    Enhancements . . . . . . . . . . . . . . . . . . . . . . . . . . . . . .    201
        8.4.3    Strengths . . . . . . . . . . . . . . . . . . . . . . . . . . . . . . . . . .    202
        8.4.4    Disadvantages, Limitations, and Weaknesses . . . . . . . . . .    202
    8.5    Summary . . . . . . . . . . . . . . . . . . . . . . . . . . . . . . . . . . . . . . .    203
    References. . . . . . . . . . . . . . . . . . . . . . . . . . . . . . . . . . . . . . . . . . . .    206

9   **Using the Privacy Tree in Practice**. . . . . . . . . . . . . . . . . . . . . . . . . . .    209
    9.1    In Conjunction with Security Technologies. . . . . . . . . . . . . . . . . .    210
    9.2    In Conjunction with the Legal Infrastructure. . . . . . . . . . . . . . . . .    214
    9.3    In Conjunction with Other Technologies . . . . . . . . . . . . . . . . . . . .    217
        9.3.1    Software Defined Networking (SDN) . . . . . . . . . . . . . . . .    217
        9.3.2    Machine Learning (ML) . . . . . . . . . . . . . . . . . . . . . . . . .    219
    9.4    Summary . . . . . . . . . . . . . . . . . . . . . . . . . . . . . . . . . . . . . . . .    223
    References. . . . . . . . . . . . . . . . . . . . . . . . . . . . . . . . . . . . . . . . . . . .    225

10   **The Path Forward**. . . . . . . . . . . . . . . . . . . . . . . . . . . . . . . . . . . . . .    227
    10.1    The First Step: Decisions. . . . . . . . . . . . . . . . . . . . . . . . . . . . . .    230
        10.1.1    Hide-and-Seek (Revisited). . . . . . . . . . . . . . . . . . . . . . .    230
        10.1.2    Defense-in-Depth. . . . . . . . . . . . . . . . . . . . . . . . . . . . .    231
    10.2    The Next Step: Actions . . . . . . . . . . . . . . . . . . . . . . . . . . . . . . .    232
    10.3    Summary . . . . . . . . . . . . . . . . . . . . . . . . . . . . . . . . . . . . . . . .    235
    References. . . . . . . . . . . . . . . . . . . . . . . . . . . . . . . . . . . . . . . . . . . .    237

**Part I    Supplemental Chapters**

11   **Crypto Primer**. . . . . . . . . . . . . . . . . . . . . . . . . . . . . . . . . . . . . . . . .    241
    11.1    Terminology. . . . . . . . . . . . . . . . . . . . . . . . . . . . . . . . . . . . . . .    241
    11.2    Goals: *Confidentiality, Integrity, Authenticity, Cryptographic
            Strength* . . . . . . . . . . . . . . . . . . . . . . . . . . . . . . . . . . . . . . . . .    243
    11.3    Realizing These Goals in Practice . . . . . . . . . . . . . . . . . . . . . . . .    244
        11.3.1    Confidentiality . . . . . . . . . . . . . . . . . . . . . . . . . . . . . . .    244
        11.3.2    Integrity . . . . . . . . . . . . . . . . . . . . . . . . . . . . . . . . . . . .    253
        11.3.3    Authenticity . . . . . . . . . . . . . . . . . . . . . . . . . . . . . . . . .    255
        11.3.4    Cryptographic Strength . . . . . . . . . . . . . . . . . . . . . . . . .    258
    11.4    Summary . . . . . . . . . . . . . . . . . . . . . . . . . . . . . . . . . . . . . . . .    265
    References. . . . . . . . . . . . . . . . . . . . . . . . . . . . . . . . . . . . . . . . . . . .    266

12   **Source Material**. . . . . . . . . . . . . . . . . . . . . . . . . . . . . . . . . . . . . . .    269
    12.1    Full List of Hyperlinked References . . . . . . . . . . . . . . . . . . . . . .    269
    12.2    Hyperlinked Bibliography . . . . . . . . . . . . . . . . . . . . . . . . . . . . .    301
    12.3    Further Reading on Selected Topics . . . . . . . . . . . . . . . . . . . . . .    302

**Glossary** . . . . . . . . . . . . . . . . . . . . . . . . . . . . . . . . . . . . . . . . . . . . . . . .    305

**Index**. . . . . . . . . . . . . . . . . . . . . . . . . . . . . . . . . . . . . . . . . . . . . . . . . . .    313

# About the Author

**Carlisle Adams** is a professor in the School of Electrical Engineering and Computer Science (EECS) at the University of Ottawa. Prior to his academic appointment in 2003, he worked for 13 years in industry (Nortel, Entrust), in the design and international standardization of a variety of cryptographic and security technologies for the Internet. Dr. Adams' research interests include all aspects of applied cryptography and security. Particular areas of interest and technical contributions include the design and analysis of symmetric encryption algorithms (including the CAST family of symmetric ciphers), the design of large-scale infrastructures for authentication (including secure protocols for authentication and certificate management in Public Key Infrastructure (PKI) environments), and comprehensive architectures and policy languages for access control in electronic networks (including X.509 attribute certificates and the XACML policy language).

Dr. Adams has maintained a long-standing interest in the creation of effective techniques to preserve and enhance privacy on the Internet. His contributions in this area include techniques to add delegation, non-transferability, and multi-show to digital credentials, architectures to enforce privacy in web-browsing environments, and mechanisms to add privacy to location-based services and blockchains. He was co-chair of the international conference Selected Areas in Cryptography (1997, 1999, 2007, and 2017), and was general chair of the 7th International *Privacy Enhancing Technologies Symposium* (2007).

He lives in Ottawa with his wife and children and enjoys music, good food, and classic movies (old and new).

# Chapter 1
# The Privacy Minefield

**Abstract** This chapter discusses why privacy enhancing technologies (PETs) exist and why they are important. It provides a definition of privacy that will be assumed throughout this book and describes a number of threats to privacy in our online world. Finally, it suggests that we are in a *battle for supremacy over our personal data* and argues that unless we increase our awareness and employ suitable tools, there can be serious consequences for our personal lives.

**Keywords** Privacy · Privacy definition · Privacy risks · Personal data · Privacy enhancing technologies · PETs

For much of human existence, the average person was known essentially completely by his or her local group, and was almost completely unknown elsewhere. The people that knew Bob intimately were, in turn, intimately known by Bob (and by everyone else in the local group). In such an environment, there was effectively no privacy (at a local level), but there was relatively little danger that Bob's personal information could be stolen and used against him (someone pretending to be Bob would immediately be recognized as not being Bob!). We might say that the high level of familiarity in the local group actually led to a sense of safety and reassurance for Bob (with respect to his personal information).

The emergence of larger towns and cities, and the corresponding emergence of stored information about citizens, meant that people that were unknown to Bob could know specific things about him. For example, a government office might hold a list of property owners in the city; another government office might have a record of all the military veterans in a region; the department of motor vehicles would know all the drivers and their license numbers; and a town newspaper might publish birth announcements in its "Local News" or "Community" pages. However, even as recently as the 1950s, compiling a dossier about a person was a time-consuming, non-trivial, task: correlating all these various lists and records to determine that *"Bob is a veteran who owns a small two-bedroom house, drives a Buick LeSabre, and has two children under 5 years old"* was laborious and required a significant amount of human effort. In this environment, although there was relatively little

© The Editor(s) (if applicable) and The Author(s), under exclusive license
to Springer Nature Switzerland AG 2021
C. Adams, *Introduction to Privacy Enhancing Technologies*,
https://doi.org/10.1007/978-3-030-81043-6_1

privacy at a municipal or national level, there was still relatively little danger that Bob's personal information would be used against him. We might say that the high level of complexity in aggregating information led to a sense of safety and reassurance for Bob (with respect to his personal information).

In the last several decades it is clear that everything has changed dramatically. Collection and correlation of data – on a very large scale – is not only possible, but is cheap, fast, and almost trivial. Data is collected silently and unobtrusively from anywhere in the world, and data from multiple sources can be merged effortlessly by tools that are ubiquitously deployed and commonly used. Non-identifiable data can become identifiable after being merged with other sources of data. Data collected for one purpose (such as business operations) can quickly and easily be used for entirely different purposes (for example, it may be used as an asset to be sold in bankruptcy filings, or as evidence in legal proceedings). This is the *privacy minefield* in which we live: at any moment, a "landmine" may be triggered (by others, or unintentionally by us) and our privacy will be blown to bits. The "sense of safety and reassurance" that Bob enjoyed in the previous two environments does not exist in our current world.

Today, privacy is no longer free. Privacy no longer happens by default. It used to be the case that if you did nothing at all, you would have privacy (because it was impossible, or too difficult, for strangers to breach your privacy by obtaining your personal information and using it against you). Now, you need to take conscious, deliberate, intentional actions to attain any level of privacy. Now, achieving privacy for your data is up to you.

**This is why Privacy Enhancing Technologies (PETs) exist.**

What about other measures to protect privacy? In modern societies, don't we have privacy laws and regulations, privacy guidelines, publicly-accessible privacy policies, privacy auditors and privacy certification teams, Chief Privacy Officers, provincial and national Privacy Commissioners, and so on? Yes, we do, and these can all be very helpful. But, in general, they <u>cannot prevent privacy breaches</u>. At best, they can *define* what a privacy breach is, and can impose sanctions and remedies after a breach has occurred. This is certainly useful, but we need something more proactive than this.

In our present world, almost everything is digital. Therefore, personal information is generated in digital form, is transmitted digitally, is processed digitally, and is stored digitally. This means that privacy breaches happen through hacking and software-based attacks, possibly enabled or facilitated by some form of social engineering. Privacy violators no longer break into your physical house and search through your drawers and closets; instead, they use a handful of social engineering tools and a wide variety of sophisticated device/network exploit tools. So, if we hope to actually prevent privacy breaches, we need *solid user education* to minimize the effectiveness of social engineering attacks (i.e., attacks that cannot be prevented by technology, such as Bob being tricked by a telephone solicitor into giving away some personal information during the call). But, more than this, we need *technological solutions* that will minimize (or eliminate!) the effectiveness of exploit tools.

*This is why PETs are important.*

## Privacy

What is privacy? Unfortunately, *privacy* is one of those frustratingly "slippery" words: everyone seems confident that they know intuitively what it means, but formal definitions inevitably end up being incomplete and unsatisfying. The reason for this is that privacy is multi-faceted; it means different things to different people, and its meaning depends heavily on circumstances and on the participants in a given situation. Daniel Solove, in his 2008 book *Understanding Privacy* (2008), writes "Currently, privacy is a sweeping concept, encompassing (among other things) freedom of thought, control over one's body, solitude in one's home, control over personal information, freedom from surveillance, protection of one's reputation, and protection from searches and interrogation." He further quotes various scholars who have claimed that privacy is "difficult to define because it is exasperatingly vague and evanescent", that it is "infected with pernicious ambiguities", and that it is "complex" and "entangled in competing and contradictory dimensions."

Nevertheless, it seems self-evident that having a working definition of privacy is a necessary precursor to being able to comprehend and reason about technologies that are designed to enhance privacy!

Solove's book has the goal of developing "a new understanding of privacy that strives to account for privacy's breadth and complexities without dissipating into vagueness." He does a very thorough and impressive job of building a definition (ultimately, a *taxonomy*; see Sect. 2.3 of Chap. 2) of privacy from a comprehensive collection of activities that pose privacy problems (i.e., activities that impinge upon privacy and serve as socially recognized privacy violations). Although this privacy definition is expected to be very helpful for creating law and policy to address privacy issues, it is not suitable for analyzing and comparing different PETs because it was constructed exclusively from a legal perspective.

Among the many technical privacy definitions in the literature, one of the more interesting is the proposal by Ken Barker et al. in 2009 (2009). This proposal treats privacy as a 4-dimensional space, where the dimensions are Purpose (with values of *Single, Reuse Same, Reuse Selected, Reuse Any*, and *Any*), Visibility (with values *Owner, House, Third Party*, and *All/World*), Granularity (with values *Existential, Partial*, and *Specific*), and Retention (with values *Unspecified* and *Date*). A given technology can then be described as a particular point in this space, allowing different technologies to be usefully compared and contrasted. Although this definition is very helpful when considering privacy in the context of data repositories (which is the environment for which it was designed), it is not applicable to other types of PETs, such as anonymous communications or online proof of attribute ownership.

We rely, therefore, on the privacy definition that has historically been the basis for PETs research: *an entity's ability to control how, when, and to what extent personal information about it is communicated to others* (Westin 1967) (see also (Brands 2000)). This definition may not be ideally appropriate for some areas of legal privacy interest (such as freedom of thought, control over one's body, or solitude in one's home), but it does capture the underlying goal of the vast majority of

PETs. Furthermore, while this definition is not as nuanced as the proposal by Barker, et al., it **is** applicable to many PETs (not just PETs for data repositories), while still capturing the essential flavour of the privacy required in a data repository setting.

*(Note that our chosen privacy definition, proposed by Alan Westin in 1967, has not been adopted by all PETs. For a given individual, Bob, Westin's definition addresses a flow of Bob's personal information (held by him or by another holder) <u>outward</u> to other entities. Another view of privacy – often referred to as "the right to be left alone" – considers control over the flow of information <u>into</u> Bob's personal space (e.g., protection from unwanted advertising). There are PETs (such as ad-blockers) that are designed for this notion of privacy, but we have left them as out-of-scope for the purposes of this book. This is for three reasons. First, if the advertisement is generic (i.e., not targeted to or personalized for Bob in any way), then straightforward ad blocking is typically difficult and ineffective: it is somewhat analogous to trying to prevent him from seeing a billboard as he drives along the highway. Second, if the ad is generic but the ad blocking tool is more advanced (providing so-called* privacy preserving targeted advertising*), then the tool typically uses either naïve or sophisticated* private information retrieval *(PIR) techniques that we discuss in* Chap. 4. *Third, if the ad from the ad company is not generic but is specifically targeted to Bob, then this must be based on some of his personal information that the ad company previously acquired, and that prior privacy violation can be addressed by the PETs that we do cover.)*

## 1.1   Threats to Privacy

"Alice" (not her real name) is an individual living her life in our modern society. She is a member of a family; she is an employee of a company; she is a citizen of a country. Like most people, she spends a significant amount of time online (working, playing, shopping, learning, banking, and interacting endlessly with friends and family).

As we have noted, <u>data about Alice gets collected at various places and in various ways</u>. The following are just a few examples.

- Government (this is sometimes referred to as a "womb-to-tomb dossier"):
  - Birth record
  - Social Insurance Number (SIN), Social Security Number (SSN), or similar lifelong identifying number
  - Records about marriages, divorces, and death
  - Accident reports and traffic citation records
  - Voting record
  - Tax record
  - Record of professional affiliation
  - Worker's Compensation record
  - Public employee personnel record
  - Street list record

- Property tax assessment record
- Police arrest record
- Court record
- Record of jurors in court cases
- Records of special civil proceedings (such as bankruptcy)
- Divorce court proceedings
- Criminal court proceedings

– Companies that Alice deals with

- Credit card company
- Cell phone company
- Banking and financial institutions
- Microsoft, Apple, Google, etc.
- Social media (Facebook, Twitter, Instagram, etc., etc., etc.)
- Grocery stores (especially through store loyalty cards)

– Companies that Alice does not deal with (or does not realize she is dealing with)

- Ad companies
- Ad-serving companies (such as DoubleClick (a subsidiary of Google))
- "Information brokering" and data collection companies (such as ChoicePoint, Acxiom)

Some of this data is collected as a result of normal living (getting married, acquiring a mortgage or a loan, making a credit card purchase, and so on). Some is collected as a result of software (her browser giving information to websites, cookies that are stored and later replayed, health monitoring wearables that send readings to a cloud service, spyware installed on her machine). Some comes from Alice willingly giving her information in return for goods, services, convenience, discounts, or notoriety (although of course Alice may give this without a full understanding of what her information may subsequently be used for). Some comes from court or government actions (such as subpoenas). Some comes from business dealings outside of Alice's control (mergers, acquisitions, amalgamation of online and offline data, data mining practices to derive greater insight from existing data, and so on).

Not only is there incessant data collection, but it is also the case that <u>data never gets deleted</u>. Many years ago, people would occasionally do a "clean-up" of their files, sorting them into topics or categories, saving those that were important and discarding the rest. Today, with the ever-decreasing cost of memory and the ever-increasing volume of data, it is much simpler (and ultimately much cheaper because so much time is saved) to simply keep everything. Even if a company makes a determined effort to delete specific data (in order to comply with retention requirements or right-to-be-forgotten obligations in privacy laws, for example), it is impossible to guarantee with absolute certainty that this data has not been copied any number of times and stored in any number of locations anywhere in the world. In short, the safest assumption is always that any piece of data that was ever created still exists somewhere.

This probably goes without saying, but just to be explicit: <u>Alice's data has tangible value</u>. Any entity that stores any data about Alice treats it as an asset. Every piece of personal information about her is worth money to someone and can be sold for actual cash (either individually, or in some kind of collection: *"Here is a list of all the people in this region who own dogs or cats"*).

Furthermore, <u>processing, combining, correlating, organizing, sanitizing, and mining Alice's data gives it greater value</u>. The processing of Alice's data adds meaning and insight; it allows deeper connections to be made or additional facts to be learned. Ultimately, it increases the amount of data about her and, additionally, makes her data more reliable and more actionable. Consequently, it has greater significance and usefulness, and so it is worth more money.

Finally, it is important to recognize that <u>many entities (including Alice!) only see the benefits in all this data collection</u>.

- Alice is quite happy to have companies store information about her because in exchange she can receive personalized service, discounts, and helpful recommendations. She may also be able to build/expand personal and professional contacts (for example, on social media or job-focused networking sites).
- Companies are happy to have Alice's information because they can improve their service to her, which may lead to greater customer loyalty and additional future sales.
- Governments and law enforcement agencies are happy to have citizen information because it helps them to enhance safety and security for society (for example, they may be able to find criminals, detect fraud, dismantle drug distribution rings, locate terrorist cells, and so on, more quickly and more easily).

The result of these five points (data gets collected, it never gets deleted, it has value, it can be processed to give it greater value, and most entities are happy with the status quo) is a set of ***threats to privacy***.

The threat that leaps most quickly to mind for most people is *targeted advertising*. Alice might have a somewhat uncomfortable feeling that "someone is watching her". As soon as she does a search for some item on her search engine, suddenly ads for that item, or very similar items, start showing up when she uses Facebook, YouTube, Gmail, and a variety of other platforms. She may find that she starts getting recommendations for related items in various places (including her physical mailbox!). This might all be fine if this is an item she is really interested in, but it starts to feel more like a privacy violation if she has no interest in this item (for example, she searched for, and purchased, a CD or book for a friend as a gift, and does not like that genre of music or writing herself) or if she no longer has interest in this item (for example, she purchased a washing machine and does not need another one).

Another privacy threat related to the above is *unauthorized dissemination of personal data*. Alice sees that these different applications and platforms (from apparently different companies) all seem to know about the search she did, the transaction she completed, or the data she shared with one of them. Why is her data being given, or sold, to these third parties without her consent or approval?

Privacy threats that do not seem to spring so readily to mind for many people are those connected with use of social media. Many people use social media venues extensively and post a vast amount of highly personal information on these platforms. This can lead to at least five kinds of threats to privacy.

- *Physical danger*. Many people unthinkingly (perhaps naively) post precise current or future location information on social media. Something like *"Every Tuesday at 6:00 a.m. I go alone to the woods near my house and just commune with nature. I really need this!"* or *"I can't wait for the party at Derek's place on Friday night. Of course I'll have to walk there because I won't be in any shape to drive back. ☺ "* allows any malefactor to know exactly where Alice will be at a given time (in the woods by her house, or on a footpath between her place and Derek's place). This, of course, opens her up to a host of potential physical attacks on her person.
- *Risk to personal security*. The opposite of the previous threat is just as dangerous: if the malefactor knows where Alice is, then he also knows where Alice is not. If Alice is at Derek's place on Friday night, then she is clearly not at her own house. This knowledge can lead to a variety of potential attacks related to Alice's personal security, rather than to her own physical danger (such as home break-in, kidnapping of her child, car theft, and so on).
- *Identity theft*. Another major risk for Alice is identity theft. Many people put narratives about themselves on social media (for example, in a blog post) and reveal many things about their upbringing, family, hobbies, pets, interests, heroes, favourite books/movies/characters/songs, and so on. Very often, this type of information is used in the creation of passwords and in the responses to identity verification questions (e.g., mother's maiden name, or last three residential addresses). Consequently, someone familiar with this narrative may have a much easier time stealing Alice's identity and using it to purchase a large item or take out a loan.
- *Loss of data ownership*. When Alice posts data, pictures, and videos on social media, she may not realize that she might no longer own these items. It is essential to read the privacy policies of these various platforms because some of them explicitly take ownership of anything posted on their site, meaning that they can then do anything that they wish with this information. Alice will have no legal recourse to stop them from using her information because she consented to their Terms of Use (likely without reading it) when she created an account on the platform.
- *Human profiling*. There may be serious short-term and long-term privacy implications for Alice, depending on what information she has posted on social media. People will read her posts and profile her (make decisions about what type of person she is in a number of different categories). Based on their judgements (*"she seems like a bit of a gossip"*, *"she's easily bored"*, *"she's pretty immature"*, *"she's a real complainer!"*), she may not get hired into a specific job, or may get passed over for a promotion. Depending on what she has posted, she may not win a nomination for public office many years later. Outcomes like this will occur even if these judgements are completely wrong or if Alice has changed

significantly in the intervening years, but of course Alice may never learn what these incorrect judgements were and how they negatively impacted the opportunities available to her.

The threats to privacy are myriad. The above has outlined a few examples, but there are countless others. A recent whitepaper by Jules Polonetsky and Elizabeth Renieris gives the authors' forecast of ten privacy risks to watch in the next decade (2020). Included in their list are the following:

- Risks to personal physical or behavioural information due to increased use of biometric-based user interface (UI) systems;
- Risks to (unprotected) patient-generated data as it is used to assess the safety and effectiveness of drugs or medical devices;
- Risks due to "intimate" IoT devices (such as smart contact lenses, Bluetooth-enabled "smart pills", and Wi-Fi-enabled pacemakers), as well as further development of brain-machine interfaces (BMI) that allow people to communicate and control devices with their thoughts alone;
- Risks due to increasingly sophisticated artificial intelligence (AI)-based systems (including augmented-reality/virtual-reality systems and collaborative robots), along with their further incorporation into personal spaces such as homes and private offices;
- Risks due to ever-greater precision and accuracy of location information from a wide range of mobile and wearable devices, which can reveal sensitive information about religious beliefs, health issues, mobility patterns, and behaviour;
- Risks due to the emergence of smart communities (smart cities), particularly with respect to the plethora of sensors that will capture data in public spaces; and
- Risks due to the possibility of quantum computers that can potentially break existing cryptographic protections and enable computing that is orders of magnitude faster (providing more advanced computation and better predictive analysis on personal data).

In all these cases there is collection, storage, processing and use of personal data on an ever-expanding scale, leading to a phenomenal rise in the number of privacy threats in every aspect of society.

## 1.2   The Battle for Supremacy Over Personal Data

Section 1.1 describes a set of threats to privacy that may have different levels of importance to Alice, depending on her circumstances. For many people, targeted advertising, and even unauthorized dissemination of their personal information to third parties, are relatively minor annoyances that are easily forgiven and forgotten if the returned benefits are sufficiently high. Some possible consequences of social media indiscretions may resonate (much) more strongly, even if the probabilities are lower, because physical attacks and identity theft can have a serious impact on

Alice's life. Finally, other consequences of a social media presence – particularly human profiling – can affect many areas of her life, and may be disturbing because she may never know whether human profiling (a type of *social sorting*) played a part in her failing to get a job interview, or a promotion to a high-profile position, or a date with a potential romantic partner.

However, over the past number of years (particularly the last decade and a half or so), our society has moved from *privacy threats* to an actual *battle for supremacy over personal data*. As the amount of data collected, stored, and processed has grown exponentially over this time, so has the value of this data to many players across industry and government. Naturally, as the value has grown, so has the tenaciousness with which all entities will try to acquire and retain it, leading to a literal battle if Alice wishes to protect her personal information from these other parties.

What has changed over the years to make this personal data so valuable? I suggest that there has been a subtle (but critically important!) shift from other entities recognizing that <u>if they understand Alice</u> they can derive some benefit from her, to realizing that <u>if they control Alice in some fashion</u> they can derive greater, deeper, or more insidious benefit from her. This control happens in three increasingly powerful ways: controlling the goods and services available to her; controlling the choices she makes; and controlling what she can say, what she can do, and where she can go.

### 1.2.1   Controlling the Goods and Services Available to Alice

The logical step beyond human profiling is automated profiling: software makes decisions about Alice based on data it can gather about her. Increasingly, this software uses AI algorithms and machine learning (ML) models, meaning that the formulas and the weighting of various parameters and criteria are unknown, not only to Alice, but often to the person using the software as well (such as a loan officer at a bank). The specific data used to make the decision may also be unknown to both of them. However, the output of the software is some kind of label (that typically is not communicated to Alice). The label may be something like "credit problem", "security risk", "questionable history", or "potential terrorist". Based on this label, the human user of the profiling software (or possibly other programs that use the profiling software) may choose to modify the goods and services available to Alice. She may get turned down in a credit card application; she may be offered only certain kinds of accounts or products.

There are several problems with this practice, but the most obvious is that *the profiling software may get it wrong*. The AI algorithm or ML model may be flawed, or may have been trained on inadequate or biased data, or the data that is used for Alice may contain errors. (Studies have shown, for example, that a significant percentage of credit reports have errors, with some containing mistakes serious enough that credit can be denied; see (Federal 2013; Rennie 2021).) The software then outputs an incorrect label, which Alice may not be able to challenge (society currently has inordinate faith that AI is smarter than humans, and assumes it must therefore be right!), but this incorrect label could potentially prevent her from buying a house, obtaining a loan, or keeping her job. In fact, many entities may choose to rely on this flawed software or error-ridden data to make decisions about what to offer (or not offer) Alice, including insurance companies, landlords, government agencies, retailers, and health care organizations.

A more fundamental problem with profiling software is that, ultimately, it is making a prediction: it is predicting Alice's future behaviour based on what "other people like Alice" have done in the past. The software (and, therefore, the human user of the software) is treating Alice not as a person with autonomy, but literally only as a member of group $X$, with the assumption that "all members of group $X$ behave in this way".

Entities have come to believe that limiting the goods and services available to Alice, based on the results of automated profiling, will allow them to increase revenues or reduce losses, thus enlarging their overall profits. Controlling what Alice is not able to select (by constraining the set of things shown to her from which she is able to choose) is therefore an effective – and almost imperceptible – technique to *control Alice*, for the ultimate benefit of the entity offering the choices.

### 1.2.2 Controlling the Choices That Alice (Apparently Freely) Makes

This next level of control can bring much greater benefit to other entities (and not only financial rewards), but carries correspondingly greater risk to Alice's personal life. In the previous level, an entity might think "*I can increase my profits if, based on the profile I have derived for Alice, I offer her a choice of (say) these 3 options instead of my full range of 7 options.*" In this enhanced level, the entity might think "*I can increase my benefit much more if I can just influence Alice to pick option #2.*" This benefit might be directly financial (the entity will make more money from a sale of higher-priced option #2 than from a sale of lower-priced options #1 and #3), or it might be indirectly financial (there is a surplus of option #2 inventory and this item needs to be sold before it spoils). However, the benefit may have little to do with money and more to do with prestige, power, or something else of value to the entity. Option #2 might be a particular law or policy that this entity wants to see adopted, for example.

Stephen Baker, in his 2008 book *The Numerati* (2008), discusses this (somewhat terrifying!) topic in fascinating and enlightening detail. The *numerati* are the number-crunchers, the mathematical modellers, the statisticians, the data scientists, who are employed to pore through vast quantities of data to not only understand and categorize individuals, but to find ways to manipulate their choices (with surprising and ever-increasing accuracy). Baker describes the extensive efforts underway in the work world, in shopping, in politics, in law enforcement and anti-terrorism, in healthcare, and in love and dating; this was in 2008 – the list is certain to be much longer and more varied today.

It may be tempting to lump all of this into "targeted advertising" because there is an element of that in the technique. But this is not simply "Oh, I see that Alice clicked on an ad for jackets and so I will show her several more ads for jackets that are on sale." This is laser-focused micro-targeted advertising whose goal is to sway Alice's behaviour in realms well beyond shopping. This is "advertising" in the deepest and most psychological sense: cherry-picking the newspaper articles, blog posts, videos, podcasts, cartoons, memes, and so on that are displayed to Alice; prioritizing and adjusting the responses she gets to web searches; creating disinformation or "fake news" to steer her away from specific choices; manipulating what she is shown with respect to public surveys, opinion polls, reviews, and analyses; suppressing or downplaying "inconvenient" facts and evidence supporting alternate views.

Can this happen? *Does* this happen? The answer is yes: aspects of this have taken place, to a greater or lesser extent, for years. One well-known example is the influence of the company *Cambridge Analytica* on elections in many countries around the world between 2013 and 2018 (see Ingram 2018; Wikipedia 2021). This company (a subsidiary of UK-based *SLC Group*, which advertised itself as a "global election management agency") used demographics, consumer behaviour, Internet activity, general online data, Facebook "likes", and smart phone data (such as physical movements and contacts) to build a detailed psychological picture of each individual. Voters were categorized into over 30 personality types to predict their "needs" and how these might change over time. In addition, online surveys were conducted to acquire data about political, product, and brand preferences, as well as preferred sources of information for making decisions. All of this was utilized to modify the tone used in ad messages or voter contact scripts, or to ensure that issues of importance to the target voters were included and addressed (and issues likely to cause a negative reaction were omitted). The goal, of course, was to induce each individual to vote in a particular way, ultimately influencing the election outcome. (See (Burkell and Regan 2019) for an extended discussion of the use of such techniques in political elections.)

Although experts disagree on the effectiveness of the *Cambridge Analytica* strategies in past elections (some claiming, for example, that many voters are committed partisans who would not have been swayed by such micro-targeting tactics), today organizations of every size are using these and similar methods to influence the choices that people make so that these organizations can ensure some desired outcome (see, for example (Peinado et al. 2018)). Companies, advocacy groups, lobbyists, political parties, and many others take whatever opportunities they can to shape, distort, filter, or otherwise alter Alice's view of the world so that there is a greater likelihood that she will choose the option they want. She is not *forced* to choose in a particular way – she is fully convinced that she has free will in her selection – but through these controlling techniques she has been psychologically manipulated to make the choice that is favoured by the organization (even if, given an undistorted picture of the world, she would very likely have made a different choice).

Shoshana Zuboff, Professor Emerita at Harvard Business School, calls this *surveillance capitalism* and says that surveillance capitalists "want to know how we will behave in order to know how to best intervene in our behaviour". Zuboff states that surveillance capitalists "tune and herd and shape and push us in the direction that creates the highest probability of their business success" and concludes that there is no way "to dress this up as anything but behavioural modification" (Kavenna 2019; Zuboff 2019).

As with the previous level, entities have come to believe that steering Alice toward a specific choice, by making full use of the detailed knowledge they have about her and the technologies they have at their disposal, will allow them to obtain the outcome they desire. Controlling what Alice chooses (by manipulating her view of the world) is therefore an effective technique to *control Alice*, for the ultimate benefit of the entity who wants a particular choice to prevail.

### 1.2.3   Controlling What Alice Can Say, What She Can Do, and Where She Can Go

This third level of control is by far the most invasive to Alice's privacy. In this level, an entity (typically an entity with official authority such as a law enforcement agency or government bureau, but often simply an individual with malicious intent such as someone monitoring or stalking an ex-spouse or partner) uses a combination of technology and knowledge of Alice's personal information to observe or to severely restrict her movements and her interactions with others. Again, the goal is to achieve some perceived benefit for the entity.

Although this level appears to be less frequently used than the previous two levels, it certainly does exist. One recent example is the field of *digital vehicle forensics*.

Modern cars and trucks contain a large number of sensors and onboard computers, and therefore store a surprisingly large amount of data, much of which can qualify as personal information (see, for example, (Solon 2020)). It is possible to recover location data, when doors were opened and closed, whether texts and calls were made while a cellphone was connected, and time-stamped recordings of voice commands to the hands-free system. Sensors can reveal the weight of the occupant(s), and a driver-facing camera (a "smart" feature to detect whether the driver is awake and paying attention to the road) can provide video from inside the vehicle. Sensors monitoring how the driver is controlling the vehicle can determine whether the driver is sober, fatigued, happy, distracted, or under stress, and can deduce which family member (or whether a complete stranger) is currently driving.

Two main systems are the primary targets for forensics investigations: the telematics system and the infotainment system. The former stores detailed travel information, including turn-by-turn navigation, speed, acceleration and deceleration data, and when and where lights were turned on, doors were opened, seat belts were engaged, and airbags were deployed. The infotainment system records call logs, contact lists, text messages, e-mails, pictures, videos, web histories, voice commands, and social media feeds; it can also list the phones that have been connected by USB or Bluetooth, and the apps that were installed on those devices. Note that security on vehicle infotainment systems is typically missing or very minimal (for example, they do not normally require a passcode or fingerprint to unlock them), and so text messages, calls, and files can be extracted from a vehicle much more easily than from a smartphone.

All this data has been extremely helpful in building solid evidence to convict criminals because it can reconstruct a vehicle's journey and paint a picture of driver and passenger behaviour. On the other hand, there are also serious privacy concerns. People may not realize when they rent a car that a significant amount of information about their trips, activities, and personal details (including home and work location, saved Wi-Fi passwords, phone calendar entries, phone call lists and address books, and session cookies) may be readily available to the rental company or to subsequent renters. Furthermore, there has been at least one case (in Australia) where "a man stalked his ex-girlfriend using an app that connected to her high-tech Land Rover and sent him live information about her movements. The app also allowed him to remotely start and stop her vehicle and open and close the windows." (Solon 2020)

Another recent example is COVID-19 tracing apps.

*Channel News Asia* recently reported (Mohan 2021) that the Singapore Police Force can obtain data from a COVID-19 tracing app called *TraceTogether* for criminal investigations. Although the privacy statement on the *TraceTogether* website originally promised that the data would only be used "for contact tracing purposes", the Singapore Police Force stated at the beginning of January, 2021, that they are empowered under the Criminal Procedure Code "to obtain any data, including the *TraceTogether* data, for criminal investigations" and that any such data "may be used in circumstances where citizen safety and security is or has been affected." After this statement was issued, the *TraceTogether* website was updated to clarify that the Criminal Procedure Code applies to all data under Singapore's jurisdiction.

This clearly illustrates that data collected for one purpose (even with a formal privacy policy in place) can be claimed by an authority and used for an entirely different purpose. In this particular case, "criminal investigations" obviously encompass closely observing the movements and interactions of a specific person or set of people.

In both of the above examples, one might be tempted to ask, *"What is the problem with using technology and personal data to find, observe, and apprehend criminals? Isn't that ultimately a good thing?"* The answer is probably "yes" (the newest techniques have been used to help catch criminals in every era throughout history), **unless** the person being found, observed, and apprehended is <u>not</u> actually a criminal. It is not simply that a mistake might be made (although this is also a concern). The problem is that there is a *slippery slope* from targeting the "genuinely guilty", to targeting the "suspected guilty", to targeting the "future guilty", to targeting the "declared guilty". The step from "genuinely guilty" to "suspected guilty" is common and defensible; monitoring suspects is the essence of criminal investigation. On the other hand, the move to "future guilty" (*given this individual's past history, known associates, and current situation, we think he is likely to commit a crime sometime in the future*) starts to have important privacy implications.

The real danger, however, is the slide to "declared guilty." An authority pronouncing someone as guilty, not because what they have done is illegal, but because what they have done (even innocently in the distant past), or who they are, is unpopular, uncomfortable, or contrary to what the authority currently desires. *"Our society does not want these kinds of people, so we will single out all who we decide are unacceptable, and we will deal with them."* The combination of technology and extensive knowledge of personal data will allow an authority to target anyone they wish, at any time. And, of course, given enough data about someone, it may be possible to construct literally any sufficiently compelling case about him/her to convince a third party that this person is "guilty".

Is this just extreme paranoia? Perhaps. But again we ask ourselves, "Can this happen? Does this happen?" The answer is that we do not have to look too far in history to find many examples where exactly this situation *did* happen (think of the midnight Gestapo raids in Nazi Germany where the targets were "groups within German society defined as political opponents, most notably, communists and socialists, religious, dissidents, Jews, and a much broader group of 'racial' enemies, including long-term criminals, prostitutes, homosexuals, Gypsies [*sic*], juvenile gangs and the long-term unemployed" (McDonough 2015)). The power of modern technology and the vast quantities of your personal data currently in the hands of others make it far easier for this to happen again, and much more effectively.

With this third level, entities believe that constraining what Alice can do and where she can go will allow them to obtain an outcome they desire. Controlling Alice's interactions and movements effectively *controls Alice*, for the ultimate benefit of authorities who want to create and enforce a particular vision of society.

The collection, processing, and use of your personal data is very real: it is going on all around you, all the time, and the total worldwide quantity of this activity increases daily, probably hourly. This has led to increased levels of stress and anxiety for many people, stemming from the general impression that they are always being watched (and judged). Security advocate and author Bruce Schneier wrote a book in 2015 entitled *Data and Goliath: The Hidden Battles to Collect Your Data and Control Your World* (2015). The summary description on the dust jacket for this book includes the following text.

> Your cell phone provider tracks your location and knows who's with you. Your online and in-store purchasing patterns are recorded, and reveal if you're unemployed, sick, or pregnant. Your e-mails and texts expose your intimate and casual friends. Google knows what you're thinking because it saves your private searches. Facebook can determine your sexual orientation without you ever mentioning it.
>
> The powers that surveil us do more than simply store this information. Corporations use surveillance to manipulate not only the news articles and advertisements we each see, but also the prices we're offered. Governments use surveillance to discriminate, censor, chill free speech, and put people in danger worldwide. And both sides share this information with each other or, even worse, lose it to cybercriminals in huge data breaches.

Much of your personal information is clearly already in the hands of others, and trying to protect it now is the uncertain province of laws, regulations, and policies. But these other entities are never satisfied; they never feel that they have enough information. If you want to prevent them from acquiring more of your information tomorrow (and thereby regain a sense of empowerment and confidence that you are not completely helpless), you will need to engage in a *battle for supremacy over your personal data*. Every battle requires weapons. This is where PETs enter the picture.

## 1.3   High-Stakes Hide-and-Seek

Given the risks involved and the potential consequences (some of them decidedly life-changing!) of other entities having our data, it is more important than ever before to protect our privacy, to exert some control over our personal information, to constrain unauthorized data dissemination and use.

The **stakes are high** because the consequences can be extreme. The stakes are high because the other entities may be tremendously motivated, very well-funded, and incredibly powerful – they may, in fact, seem like the "good guys" to many external observers. The stakes are high because a misstep or a moment of negligence can have long-lasting negative implications.

We are playing **hide-and-seek**: we try to hide our data, and other (known and unknown) entities try to find it. We may think, "I'll put my data in this secret location", but someone will eventually scour all the nooks and crannies of our machines and transactions to locate it. We may think, "I'll encrypt my data", but someone will inevitably try to break the encryption or (more likely) will install malware to obtain the data before it is encrypted or in the brief moments that it is decrypted for further processing. As the methods we use to protect our data become increasingly sophisticated, so do the techniques that others use to break our protections and get their hands on our data. Certainly do what you can to hide your personal information, but know that others will do <u>everything</u> they can (including the use of illegal means) to find it.

So, yes, this is hide-and-seek. However, this is hide-and-seek with chess-like intricacy in which our mistakes can have serious real-world penalties. We are playing hide-and-seek, but it is definitely not a game.

On our side, we have laws and regulations, privacy advocates, and various friends and associates. However, these may be of limited help (depending on the adversary we are facing). The real "weapons" in our hide-and-seek activity are the PETs at our disposal: these are the tools we have to truly make our personal data unreadable or inaccessible to other entities. But, as with many activities, selecting the right tool for the job is at least half the distance to successfully completing the job.

How can we know what tool is most appropriate for the specific task at hand in any given situation?

James enters his local hardware store. After a few minutes of wandering up and down the aisles looking a bit lost, he is approached by a clerk.

"May I help you, sir?"

"I'm looking for some tools. I have a bit of work to do around the house."

The clerk smiles encouragingly. "Well, we certainly have a lot of tools available. What are you looking for specifically?"

James hesitates slightly. "Several people have told me that a hand saw and a paintbrush can be very useful", he says, "and I do need to do some cutting and painting, so perhaps I should take one of each."

"Very good, sir. Right this way." The clerk takes James to Aisles B and E. "Here you go."

"Thank you very much – these both look perfect!" James pays for his purchases and heads home feeling quite optimistic. Later that day, James finds that the hand saw does a very poor job at trimming his hedges, and the 3″ paintbrush does a painfully slow and uneven job of painting his dining room wall. Disappointed and frustrated, James considers abandoning home improvement altogether.

## 1.4   Summary

We began this chapter by motivating why PETs exist and why they are important. This was followed by a brief discussion of definitions for privacy, ending with the definition that we will assume throughout the book. We presented some threats to privacy and the risks that can arise (including, among other things, physical danger, identity theft, and human profiling).

We then suggested that individuals are now in a battle for supremacy over their personal data: other entities want your data so much that you need to fight to keep it to yourself. Entities want your data so that they can control you in such a way as to derive some benefit for themselves. They may use your personal data to control the goods and services available to you, to control the choices that you make, and ultimately to control what you can say, what you can do, and where you can go.

PETs are an important collection of weapons for our battle. They can be highly effective in our fight to keep our private data out of the hands of others. However, they will only be useful if we have some understanding of what they do and what aspect of privacy each one is designed to protect.

This book is an introduction to the world of PETs. Its objective is to present the topic through the lens of the *privacy goals* that Alice may wish to accomplish, and to describe, as examples, a number of PETs that illustrate these privacy goals and how they can be achieved. This approach will hopefully allow Alice (and you, the reader!) to better understand what needs to be protected and the options available for protecting it.

The following chapter discusses the foundation of our approach, a relatively simple construct we refer to as the *privacy tree*.

**Questions for Personal Reflection and/or Group Discussion**

1. Find three definitions of privacy in the academic literature (other than the one from Westin that we have adopted for this book). For each definition that you find, in what ways is it suitable, and in what ways is it not suitable, for describing what PETs are designed to achieve?
2. Choose two major social media platforms. Read the privacy policy of each platform very carefully. What does each policy say about data ownership, data retention, data use, and sharing of data with third parties? Are there privacy concerns that you feel someone should think about before clicking "OK" to the policy?
3. Select a friend or family member who is quite different from you (perhaps is a different age, has a different educational background, or is interested in different hobbies, for example). Spend some time with that person trying to do identical tasks online (search for the same term in the same search engine, click on the same links in the responses, and so on). How does what is displayed on their device differ from what is displayed on your device? Are you given different response links, shown different ads, or presented with different options/information? Discuss your findings, and its implications, in some detail.

# References

S. Baker, *The Numerati* (Houghton Mifflin Company, 2008)

K. Barker, M. Askari, M. Banerjee, K. Ghazinour, B. Mackas, M. Majedi, S. Pun, A. Williams, A data privacy taxonomy, in *British National Conference on Databases (BNCOD 2009)*, (Springer, LNCS 5588, 2009), pp. 42–54

S. Brands, *Rethinking Public Key Infrastructures and Digital Certificates: Building in Privacy* (The MIT Press, 2000)

J. Burkell, P.M. Regan, Voter preferences, voter manipulation, voter analytics: Policy options for less surveillance and more autonomy. Internet Policy Rev. **8**(4), 22 (2019, Dec 31)

Federal: Federal Trade Commission, In FTC study, five percent of consumers had errors on their credit reports that could result in less favorable terms for loans, *Federal Trade Commission press release* (2013, Feb 11)

D. Ingram, Factbox: Who is Cambridge Analytica and what did it do?, *Reuters*, (2018, Mar 19)

J. Kavenna, Interview: Shoshana Zuboff: 'Surveillance capitalism is an assault on human autonomy', *The Guardian* (2019, Oct 4)

F. McDonough, Careless whispers: How the German public used and abused the Gestapo, *The Irish Times* (2015, Sep 28)

M. Mohan, Singapore Police Force can obtain TraceTogether data for criminal investigations: Desmond Tan, *Channel News Asia* (2021, Jan 4)

F. Peinado, E. Palomo, J. Galán, The distorted online networks of Mexico's election campaign, *El País* (2018, Mar 22)

J. Polonetsky, E. Renieris, Privacy 2020: 10 privacy risks and 10 privacy enhancing technologies to watch in the next decade, *Future of Privacy Forum white paper* (2020, Jan 28)

L. Rennie, Top 5 most common errors that appear on credit reports in Canada, *Loans Canada blog* (2021)

B. Schneier, *Data and Goliath: The Hidden Battles to Collect Your Data and Control Your World* (W. W. Norton and Company, 2015)

O. Solon, Insecure wheels: Police turn to car data to destroy suspects' alibis, *NBC News* (2020, Dec 28)

A.F. Westin, *Privacy and Freedom* (Ig Publishing, 2015). (This is a new printing of the original 1967 edition of this book, which is now out of print)

Wikipedia, *Cambridge Analytica* (2021, Jan 16)

S. Zuboff, *The Age of Surveillance Capitalism: The Fight for a Human Future at the New Frontier of Power* (Public Affairs, 2019)

# Chapter 2
# A Collection of Tools: The Privacy Tree

**Abstract** This chapter highlights the fact that many different PETs have been proposed and used over the past four decades. It suggests that a classification may be a helpful way to compare and contrast these PETs, leading to a greater understanding of which ones are most appropriate for particular privacy goals. A literature review is provided and one selected classification is described in some detail.

**Keywords** Privacy enhancing technologies · PETs · Privacy classification · Privacy taxonomy

The previous chapter tried to paint a (hopefully convincing) picture that personal privacy is at peril in the highly-technological age in which we live. Some will argue – in fact, some *have* argued (Sprenger 1999) – that privacy is not "at peril" at all, but rather is long gone and irreparably lost. There is certainly some justification for this sentiment when so much of our life is conducted online, and when every keystroke and mouse click seemingly leave a digital trail that can be examined by anyone willing to make the minimal effort to take a look.

However, although it may be widely believed that privacy is totally lost, this is not universally accepted. There is a small, but brave (should we rather say "foolhardy"?), community of privacy advocates who believe that privacy is still only "at peril" and that some measure of privacy can be retained by individuals, even in their online activities today. This community includes people from many walks of life: lawyers, policy makers, government workers of various kinds, privacy commissioners, and chief privacy officers, to name a few. It also includes technologists (computer scientists, engineers, IT specialists). The technologists design, build, deploy, configure, and administer tools (typically software tools) that focus on the protection of personal privacy. Such tools are often referred to as Privacy Enhancing Technologies (PETs), and the technologists are typically called PETs researchers. The PETs community (PETs researchers, along with the collection of active PETs users and enthusiastic PETs supporters) is therefore a subset of the overall privacy community: their focus is more on technologies that can help to protect privacy than on laws, policies, and human practices to safeguard privacy in societal interrelationships.

© The Editor(s) (if applicable) and The Author(s), under exclusive license
to Springer Nature Switzerland AG 2021
C. Adams, *Introduction to Privacy Enhancing Technologies*,
https://doi.org/10.1007/978-3-030-81043-6_2

## 2.1   Many Privacy Enhancing Technologies

The PETs community has been active for four decades: the earliest academic paper in this area is generally acknowledged to be David Chaum's ground-breaking work on *Untraceable electronic mail, return addresses, and digital pseudonyms* in 1981 (1981). Since that time, there has been an explosion of papers in this field, leading to a vast and somewhat bewildering array of proposed technologies (see, for example, [https://freehaven.net/anonbib], which is an extensive list of published work, but is a non-exhaustive set of selected papers dealing specifically with anonymity). Some technologies do quite similar jobs; others do completely different jobs. Many share underlying characteristics, but take incompatible technical approaches to achieve these; others use what appear to be the same techniques, but then accomplish distinct goals.

This plethora of technologies leads to difficulties both for PETs researchers and for PETs users. It is hard to make sense of what is "out there" in the literature and in the available tools (both commercial and open-source). How can these various PETs be compared and contrasted? How can their similarities and differences usefully be assessed? How can gaps (missing technologies) and overlaps be discovered? Perhaps most importantly, how can the "right tool for the job" be found when a particular privacy goal has been determined?

## 2.2   Classification (Privacy Tree)

A helpful step in this direction is to create a classification of privacy enhancing technologies. A classification (taxonomy, organization, grouping, or categorization) is exactly the mechanism by which similar things are put together and dissimilar things are kept apart. It typically has multiple layers (allowing for greater and greater levels of similarity) and multiple branches (specifying rules by which separations can be made). The classification structure is normally a tree: more precisely, it is an inverted tree, with the root at the very top and branches extending downward until leaves are found at the very bottom. At each "node" in the tree there will typically be one branch coming in, and multiple branches going out; a generic tree structure is shown in Fig. 2.1.

The items at the leaf of a single branch at the bottom of the tree are most similar in the classification; items at the leaves of different branches are dissimilar in one or more explicitly-defined ways.

A classification for PETs would allow us to compare the various proposals that exist. It would also identify any gaps in this field: a branch with no leaves would highlight the fact that there are no technologies in a particular area, which would allow researchers to either design new proposals with those characteristics, or explore whether that category in the classification is actually useful (or achievable) in real-world environments.

In this book, I refer to such a classification as the "privacy tree". Existing PETs proposals and tools are placed at the leaves of this tree, allowing us to readily see

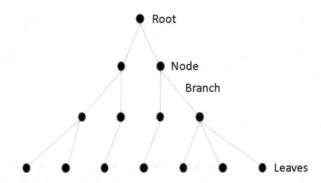

**Fig. 2.1**  Generic tree structure

which ones are suitable for which specific purposes. All the technologies are intended to protect privacy in some sense, but exactly how they achieve this, and exactly what aspect(s) of privacy they protect, becomes much clearer when we see them in the "bigger-picture" context of the privacy tree.

## 2.3   Previous Work on Classifications for Privacy

The idea of a classification for privacy is not new; it has been explored before by several researchers. However, the number of proposals for a classification (often referred to in these papers as a *taxonomy*) is small, especially in comparison to the number of surveys, overviews, critical studies, and discussion papers that have been published in the area of PETs.

### 2.3.1   Antón et al. (2002)

In 2002, Annie Antón, Julia Earp, and Angela Reese used the tools of requirements engineering to analyze the privacy requirements of a collection of e-commerce websites (2002) (see also (Antón and Earp 2001)). In their paper, the authors propose a taxonomy for privacy-related system goals ("privacy protection goals"), which builds on the well-known Fair Information Practices (CFIP 1973). It thus has the following categories (each with their own sub-categories): *notice/awareness*; *choice/ consent*; *access/participation*; *integrity/security*; and *enforcement/redress*. Their taxonomy also includes "vulnerability goals" (practices that may violate consumer privacy; note that this appears to be a subset of Solove's 2008 taxonomy below): *information monitoring*; *information aggregation*; *information storage*; *information transfer*; *information collection*; *information personalization*; and *contact*.

The taxonomy introduced in this paper, and the analysis that it enabled, allowed the authors to find some interesting results for the websites (and the associated privacy policies) that they examined, such as explicitly identifying websites that engage in more vulnerability behaviours than privacy protection behaviours. Although useful, this taxonomy is not a mechanism for categorizing and comparing PETs; a technology-focused taxonomy is needed for such a purpose.

## 2.3.2   Rezgui et al. (2003)

One early attempt at a taxonomy that can be applied to technologies is the work by Abdelmounaam Rezgui, Athman Bouguettaya, and Mohamed Eltoweissy in 2003 (2003). This paper proposes a taxonomy of technology-enabled and regulation-enabled solutions for privacy preservation in the Web and categorizes these solutions based on the primary enablers of privacy. On the technology side of their taxonomy, this results in client-based solutions, server-based solutions, and client-server solutions. As noted in (Adams 2006), there are at least two difficulties with such a taxonomy:

> First, in much of the technology community, designating a node as a "client" implies that some other node will be a "server" and so it seems somewhat counter-intuitive to include peer-to-peer architectures (such as many of the anonymizer architectures) in which there are no clients or servers, just peer nodes, under "client-based solutions." Second, and more importantly, this classification has no further role for the enabler discriminator: technologies are listed without further sub-classification under client-based, server-based, and client-server. Thus, it is difficult to know whether this taxonomy is complete and it is virtually impossible to compare adjacent technologies in any meaningful way.

This early paper broke new ground in proposing a taxonomy that not only categorizes technologies for the purpose of comparison and analysis, but also includes other techniques for addressing privacy (i.e., regulatory-enabled solutions). However, it was quite limited in its ability to usefully discriminate various PETs.

## 2.3.3   Skinner et al. (2006)

Geoff Skinner, Song Han, and Elizabeth Chang in 2006 proposed a taxonomy for information privacy (2006). Their proposal defines three dimensions (time, matter, and space) and three sub-categories within each of these dimensions. The time dimension defines a *computation view* for information privacy (the amount of time and resources that would be required to compromise privacy protection) and is subdivided into "ideal" (or infinite), "computational", and "fragile". The matter dimension defines a *content view* for information privacy (the different types of information that require privacy protection) and is subdivided into "data privacy", "identity privacy", and "meta privacy" (metadata and its implementation details, which the authors refer to as metastructure). The space dimension defines a *structural view* for information privacy (the different entities and entity relationships that require privacy protection) and is subdivided into "individual privacy", "group privacy", and "organizational privacy".

The proposed taxonomy is an interesting way of incorporating different definitions, terminology, and proposed solutions in the privacy field, but it is focused on
information privacy (rather than on PETs), and is explicitly intended for Collaborative
Environments (rather than all online use). It is therefore of limited applicability in
understanding and comparing privacy enhancing technologies.

### 2.3.4   Adams (2006)

In 2006, I published *A Classification for Privacy Techniques* (Adams 2006). Like
Rezgui et al., this paper proposes a classification that encompasses both technological approaches and societal approaches to protecting privacy. This classification
considers two types of personal information in online environments (*actions* that a
user performs, and *attributes* about the user), and three types of entities (the *user*
himself or herself, a legitimate *holder* of personal information about the user, and an
*unintended recipient* (acquirer or observer) of the user's personal information).

In this classification, the user may wish to *perform an action* or *reveal attributes* – in all cases hiding this information from unintended recipients, but perhaps
also hiding it from intended recipients. Similarly, a legitimate holder of the user's
personal information may wish to *use* or *disseminate* this information – in all cases
hiding it from unintended recipients, but perhaps also hiding it from intended recipients. PETs are the tools that can be used in each of these situations to accomplish
the desired protection and are categorized in the classification according to which
specific privacy goal they are designed to achieve.

The proposed classification in this paper is relatively intuitive and appears to
accommodate the wide variety of PETs that currently exist. Furthermore, it provides
a set of discriminators that allows PETs to be analyzed and compared in meaningful ways.

### 2.3.5   Solove (2008)

An extensive and thoughtful treatise on privacy, which includes a detailed proposal
for a taxonomy of privacy, was put forward by Daniel Solove in 2008 (2008).
Solove's taxonomy considers three types of entity (i.e., three roles): the data subject,
the data holder, and a separate third party. Data flowing from the subject to a holder
defines the category "information collection", which has *surveillance* and *interrogation* as sub-categories. Data residing with the holder defines the category "information processing", which has *aggregation, identification, insecurity, secondary
use*, and *exclusion* as sub-categories. Data flowing from a holder to a third party
defines the category "information dissemination", which has *breach of confidentiality, disclosure, exposure, increased accessibility, blackmail, appropriation*, and *dis-
tortion* as sub-categories. Finally, unwanted advances from a third party to the
subject (which may or may not involve a transfer of data) defines the category

"invasion", which has *intrusion* and *decisional interference* as sub-categories. (This taxonomy is summarized nicely in an infographic created by Enterprivacy Consulting Group; see (Enterprivacy 2006).)

As Solove rightly points out, "All taxonomies are generalizations based upon a certain focus, and they are valuable only insofar as they are useful for a particular purpose." Given this, it is important to recognize that Solove's purpose in publishing his taxonomy is not to aid in the understanding and comparison of PETs, but rather to aid in the crafting of law and policy. In particular, he presents long and persuasive arguments as to why it is difficult – and perhaps, ultimately, impossible – to define or conceptualize privacy in a way that properly captures all its nuances and shades of meaning (which are often context-dependent or culturally-delimited). Rather, he puts his attention on tangible, real-world privacy problems that have necessitated (or will necessitate) concrete remedies in laws, policies, cases, constitutions, and guidelines. Thus, for example, *secondary use* is "the use of data for purposes unrelated to the purposes for which the data was initially collected without the data subject's consent". *Secondary use* is in his taxonomy because "the potential for secondary use generates fear and uncertainty over how one's information will be used in the future, creating a sense of powerlessness and vulnerability. ... The harm is a dignitary one that emerges from denying people control over the future use of their data, which can be used in ways that have significant effects on their lives" (Solove 2008). This harm has been explicitly recognized in some US court decisions.

Solove's taxonomy of privacy was an important contribution and it set the stage for much fruitful discussion among lawyers and legal scholars in the privacy arena, but it was not intended to, and does not, provide a good basis for appreciating the subtle differences between various privacy enhancing technologies. A different taxonomy was needed for that purpose.

### 2.3.6   Nissenbaum (2009)

Helen Nissenbaum's 2009 book *Privacy in Context: Technology, Policy, and the Integrity of Social Life* (2009) proposes a framework for understanding privacy issues and identifying potential privacy breaches. Using the concept of *contextual integrity* as a basis, it suggests ways in which individuals and society can assess whether information has flowed appropriately from one entity or location to another, providing an approach for evaluating potential violations of privacy. The author considers *roles*, *activities*, *norms*, and *values*, and how these interact with the topics of *capacity to monitor and track*, *aggregation and analysis*, and *dissemination and publication*. Her goal is to define and examine the context within which privacy violations are often registered.

Nissenbaum's widely-cited work on contextual integrity was initially applied to reasoning about the privacy rules in privacy law (see (Barth et al. 2006)), but it has also been applied to technology design and directly to PETs. However, its focus is on the philosophy of privacy; it is not meant to offer a means to classify and compare various PETs. Thus, a taxonomy for that purpose is still of value.

### 2.3.7  Pfitzmann and Hansen (2010)

Between 2000 and 2010, Andreas Pfitzmann and Marit Hansen successively expanded and refined a proposal for talking about privacy concepts that deal with *data minimization* (this proposal was referred to generally as "the terminology paper"). The final published version, v0.34 (Pfitzmann and Hansen 2010), defines and discusses in detail the terms anonymity, linkability, unlinkability, undetectability, unobservability, pseudonymity, pseudonyms, digital pseudonyms, identity, identifiability, partial identity, digital identity, and identity management. (See (Syverson and Stubblebine 1999) for original and acclaimed work in characterizing anonymity properties formally/rigorously using epistemic logic.) In addition, Pfitzmann and Hansen describe the relationships between these terms, give a rationale for their chosen definitions, and list mechanisms (i.e., PETs) that provide these various concepts.

The goal of this important work was to develop a terminology that is both expressive and precise, with the hope that this will help to clarify the use and meaning of these terms in subsequent academic (and non-academic) discourse. To this end, the authors even provide an appendix that translates the essential terms into ten other languages, including Czech, Japanese, and Russian. This paper is a classification in the area of privacy, but its objective is to be a classification of terms and concepts, not a classification of PETs.

### 2.3.8  Heurix et al. (2015)

Johannes Heurix, Peter Zimmermann, Thomas Neubauer, and Stefen Fenz proposed a detailed and comprehensive structure in their 2015 paper, *A Taxonomy for Privacy Enhancing Technologies* (2015). The top level has seven characteristics (referred to as *dimensions*), several of which are familiar from the information security literature: scenario, aspect, aim, foundation, data, trusted third party, and reversibility. At the next level, scenario has sub-categories *untrusted client*, *untrusted server*, *mutual*, and *external*; aspect has sub-categories *identity*, *content*, and *behaviour*; aim has *indistinguishability*, *unlinkability*, *deniability*, and *confidentiality*; foundation has *security model* and *cryptography*; data has *stored*, *transmitted*, and *processed*; trusted third party has *frequency*, *phase*, and *task*; and reversibility has *cooperation* and *degree*. Three of these dimensions have yet another layer of sub-categories below those given above, and a fourth dimension has three additional layers of sub-categories.

In this paper, the seven proposed *dimensions* are important, but are essentially unrelated to each other. They encompass

- Possible designs of PETs (e.g., Is a trusted third party required? Is the operation that protects privacy reversible?),
- Possible goals of PETs (e.g., Does the PET protect the identity, the content, or the behaviour? Does the PET provide indistinguishability, unlinkability, deniability, or confidentiality?),

– Possible <u>techniques</u> of PETs (e.g., does the PET use symmetric, asymmetric, or no encryption?), and
– Possible <u>attack models</u> of PETs (e.g., is the client, server, an external party, or everyone untrusted?).

Each dimension has a tree under it for all the options available within that dimension. Thus, the overall taxonomy is not one tree with a single root leading to a set of leaves, but rather results in a table with all the dimensions and their various subcategories as columns, and a row for each specific PET filled with check marks and descriptions/comments.

The proposed taxonomy appears to be the most comprehensive of any in the literature thus far for privacy enhancing technologies. It is therefore very valuable for comparing any given number of PETs at a highly detailed level: the features of each PET can be contrasted with the other PETs on a point-by-point basis. However, the taxonomy is also quite complex. There are many columns (it takes several tables in the paper to show all the columns in the classification of PETs); this can make it unwieldy to work with for initial research investigations and may render it difficult to use as a teaching tool to instruct someone who is new to the field. A taxonomy that is simpler and more intuitive may be better suited to these purposes, whereas the taxonomy in this paper may be ideal for deeper levels of comparative analysis.

### 2.3.9   OPC (2017)

In 2017, the Technology Analysis Division of the Office of the Privacy Commissioner of Canada (OPC) published *Privacy Enhancing Technologies – Review of Tools and Techniques*, which focuses on a proposed taxonomy of PETs (OPC 2017). This taxonomy classifies PETs according to the functions or capabilities that they provide to the end user; it thus has the following categories: *informed consent, data minimization, data tracking, anonymity, control, negotiation of terms and conditions, technical enforcement, remote audit of enforcement*, and *use of legal rights*. Within each category, the authors give several (sometimes 10 or more) PETs that provide that particular service.

This report provides an extensive collection of existing PETs, along with a way to organize them. The authors note that some of the included tools and techniques provide more than one of the capabilities listed, "making it somewhat difficult to neatly categorize them". However, it is worth pointing out that this is not necessarily a limitation because it can enhance the ability to compare and contrast the features of different PETs. On the other hand, the authors do highlight an important deficiency: the report only considers technologies that protect information in transit; PETs that protect information at rest are explicitly excluded. Thus, a large number of PETs cannot fit into this proposed taxonomy, which significantly limits its scope.

The above proposals are summarized in Table 2.1.

**Table 2.1**  Summary of previous work on classifications for privacy

| Proposal | Purpose | Scope | Strengths | Limitations |
|---|---|---|---|---|
| Antón et al. (2002) | A taxonomy of privacy protection goals | Classifies privacy goals as well as vulnerability goals | Enables analysis of website privacy and vulnerability behaviours | Not a mechanism for categorizing and comparing PETs |
| Rezgui et al. (2003) | A taxonomy of privacy solutions for the Web (technology and regulation) | Classifies solutions based on the enablers of privacy (i.e., client, server, or client-server) | Encompasses both technology and law techniques for privacy | Difficult to discriminate and compare PETs within a given enabler (e.g., client-based solutions) |
| Skinner et al. (2006) | A taxonomy of personal data (referred to as "information privacy") | Classifies information based on resistance to computational attack, information type, and entity type | Designed for understanding information privacy within collaborative environments | Not designed for understanding and comparing PETs in other online environments |
| Adams (2006) | A classification of privacy techniques (technological and societal) | Classifies techniques based on hiding actions or attributes | Intuitive, while encompassing a wide variety of PETs | Less comprehensive than Heurix et al. |
| Solove (2008) | A taxonomy of privacy definitions | Classifies privacy based on collection, processing, dissemination, and invasion | Designed for crafting law and policy | Not designed for comparing PETs |
| Nissenbaum (2009) | A framework for analyzing information flow | Examines the contextual integrity of flows of information | Designed for assessing potential privacy violations | Not designed for comparing PETs |
| Pfitzmann and Hansen (2010) | A terminology for talking about privacy concepts | Focuses on terms related to privacy by data minimization | Provides expressive and precise definitions of essential terms in privacy | Not designed for comparing PETs |
| Heurix et al. (2015) | A taxonomy of PETs | Classifies PETs according to seven defined dimensions | Very comprehensive; valuable for comparing PETs at a highly-detailed level | Complex and difficult to use for initial research investigations or as a teaching tool |
| OPC (2017) | A taxonomy of PETs | Classifies PETs according to the functions they provide to the user | Designed for organizing PETs that protect information in transit | Does not include PETs that protect information at rest |

## 2.4   The Selected Privacy Tree

In the paper (Adams 2006), I introduce the classification that forms the basis for the exposition presented in this book. Readers are encouraged to consult the paper for additional context and details, but the two central sections of that paper are included in their entirety here in order to give a complete description of the classification as originally published.

**Personal Information and Privacy**

We begin with a definition of personal information. PIPEDA (2000), a Canadian law focusing on the privacy of personal information, defines personal information as *information about an identifiable individual* (PIPEDA 2000, sec. 2). While this definition is suitable for many purposes, it is not sufficiently general in some cases. We therefore clarify and generalize the concept of an "identifiable individual." First, information about a group may be considered to be personal information with respect to a member of that group. For example, the statement "the Jones family is bankrupt" is likely to be regarded as personal information by Alice Jones if she is known to be a member of the Jones family referred to in the statement. Thus, personal information may be about several entities simultaneously without naming any of the individual entities explicitly. Although this may be implied in the notion of "identifiable individual," we make this more precise in the definition given below. Second, there are situations in which an entity may treat some information as his/her personal information even though he/she is not the identifiable individual who is the subject of the information (see below). The following definition also deals with such cases.

Let $E$ be a set of entities (more precisely, the set of identities associated with a set of entities), where $|E| \geq 1$. Let $A$ be the identity of Alice and let $B$ be the identity of Bob. Furthermore, either $A \in E$, or $B \in E$ and Alice $\in$ R(Bob); that is, either Alice's identity is in the set $E$, or Bob's identity is in the set $E$ and Alice is a member of the set of valid *representatives* of Bob (for example, Bob is a minor and Alice is his legal parent or guardian, or Bob is unfit or incapacitated in some way and Alice is his legal power-of-attorney). Finally, let $I$ be some information that contains or implies the subset of $E$ that includes A or B, along with some other data that is associated with this subset of $E$. The information $I$ is then *personal information*. Note that if $A \in E$ then $I$ may be referred to as "Alice's personal information", whereas if Alice $\in$ R(Bob) and $B \in E$ then $I$ is not technically Alice's personal information, but is really "Bob's personal information" (over which Alice has valid legal authority). In some environments the distinction is not critical (in the case of a minor and a legal parent/guardian, for example, the only legally-recognized authoritative voice is that of the parent/guardian and so, for legal purposes,

(continued)

(continued)

there is no distinction); in other environments the distinction may be more important (for example, a manager or agent that represents a client in the entertainment or professional sports industries may have some authority over the client's personal data, but the client will retain ultimate authority over this data). For the purposes of the present discussion, however, the distinction is ignored and $I$ is loosely referred to in both cases as "Alice's personal information."

Given the existence of $I$, there is a group of entities (typically Alice, along with lawmakers and other entities at the regional, national, and international government level) that explicitly or implicitly defines $n \geq 1$ sets of valid recipients for $I$ ($R_j$, $1 \leq j \leq n$) and a set of valid purposes, $P_{Rj}$, for which $I$ may be used by the recipients in $R_j$, for each $j$. Privacy, then, can be understood with respect to the above definition of personal information. Let $r$ be a receiver of $I$ (i.e., $r$ has acquired this information by some means) who uses $I$ for some purpose, $p$. A breach of privacy has occurred if and only if $r \notin R_j$ for any $j$, or $p \notin P_{Rj}$ when $r \in R_j$ for some $j$ (that is, $r$ is not a valid recipient, or $r$ uses $I$ for a purpose that is invalid for his/her recipient set). Avoiding breaches of privacy is the process of exercising control over who receives personal information and how it is used. A privacy technique is a mechanism (that may be employed by Alice or by others) to enable such control; that is, it is a mechanism for restricting the recipients of $I$ and the purposes for which $I$ may be used to defined sets $R_j$ and $P_{Rj}$.

**Classification**

The classification proposed here is shown in Fig. 2.2. This classification is for techniques that encourage, preserve, or enhance privacy in online environments. Thus, activities such as wearing dark sunglasses and a false moustache in public or using cash for purchases at a convenience store, although they are both privacy-preserving techniques, are intentionally outside the scope of this work. Online environments support a variety of activities including electronic communications such as email and other forms of messaging, electronic shopping and auctions, electronic banking and finance, electronic delivery of entertainment and games, electronic learning and education, electronic healthcare, and the use of Web portals and search engines. In all such environments there can be a requirement for privacy, and a wide variety of techniques have been proposed over the years to address this need. As stated above, the goal of the classification proposed here is to organize these techniques in a manner that allows them to be more easily understood, compared, and analyzed.

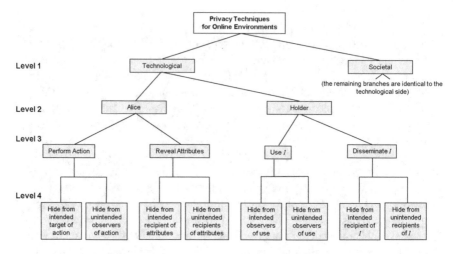

**Fig. 2.2**  Classification of privacy techniques for online environments

We begin with a discussion of the intuition behind each of the levels in the classification.

**Level 1.** The first division in the classification is between *technological* privacy techniques and *societal* privacy techniques. A technique is classified as technological in nature if it is enabled primarily or exclusively by machines (software or hardware running on computing equipment) with minimal intervention by humans once an initial installation and set-up phase has been completed. On the other hand, a technique is classified as societal in nature if it is enabled primarily or exclusively by humans with minimal reliance upon machines. In essence, since privacy has to do with controlling the dissemination and use of Alice's personal information, techniques are distinguished at this first level according to how the control is actually implemented: are computers used to effect this control, or are human means used?

**Levels 2 and 3.** Within each of the above branches, technological and societal, privacy techniques are further classified according to whether Alice is doing something to effectively create new personal information, or a "holder" (an entity other than Alice who is in possession of Alice's personal information) is doing something with that information. More specifically, Alice may perform an action (on her local machine or on some remote machine) that is noticed by another entity Eve. Even if Eve does not know the content of the action (such as the data that was actually transmitted in a communications session between Alice and Bob), new personal information has been created if Eve becomes aware that this action is taking place. This personal information will typically include the participants, type, time, and location of the action in which Alice is engaged. As an alternative way for Alice to create new personal information, Alice may reveal specific attributes about herself (address and credit card information, for example) to another entity. From that entity's point of view, new personal information has been created if the entity did not previously know these attributes about Alice (i.e., even though Alice has only disseminated some of her existing personal information, a new collection of personal information about Alice has been created at the other entity's site that did not exist previously).

Discussions about privacy often use the term "personal information" to refer only to attributes (data) about a subject, such as gender, address, salary, credit card number, political affiliation, health record, and the like. However, in many circumstances (such as corresponding with a specific individual/group, connecting to a certain Web site, or editing a particular file) the mere knowledge that the action was performed by Alice can also be personal information. This "action analysis" aspect of privacy is analogous to the "traffic analysis" aspect of security. This classification, therefore, recognizes both "actions" and "attributes" as valid types of personal information by categorizing privacy techniques according to which type of personal information Alice creates.

With respect to the "holder" (an entity in possession of Alice's personal information), there are also two possibilities. The holder may use this information for his or her own purposes, or may forward (disseminate) this information to some third entity. New personal information about Alice will be created in the latter case if the third entity did not previously know this forwarded information about Alice; but here it is the holder, rather than Alice, that is responsible for this creation.

**Level 4.** Privacy techniques can be further categorized according to the threat model under consideration. In particular, when Alice performs an operation, she may wish to hide this personal information from an intended target of the action (for example, she may wish to make an anonymous connection to a server), or she may wish to hide this personal information from unintended observers of her action (network eavesdroppers). When Alice reveals some personal attributes, again she may wish to hide it from the intended recipients of the data or from unintended recipients of the data. In the same way, a holder of Alice's personal information $I$ may desire to protect against intended or unintended observers of his use of $I$, or against intended or unintended recipients when he disseminates $I$.

The classification up to this point is a balanced binary tree with 16 nodes at Level 4 (only 8 of these nodes are shown in Fig. 2.2, but nodes 9–16 are identical to these).

**Level 5** (See Fig. 2.3.) We use the term "exposure" to refer to the unintentional release of information about the operations of Alice to other entities. Her activities are exposed (they are "brought to light" or "revealed") if an unintended entity can make the link between a particular action and the identity "Alice". That is, when Alice performs an operation, an *operation tuple* is formed: $\omega = (\iota, \alpha)$, where $\iota$ is the identity and $\alpha$ is the action. Private operations exist for Alice when unintended entities are unable to discover or infer the tuple $\omega$.

Analogously, we use the term "disclosure" to refer to the unintentional release of the records of Alice to other entities. (A *record* may be narrowly defined in the sense of a single database record, or may be more broadly defined as a higher-level aggregation of information in a particular domain, such as a health record or a transaction record. In all cases, however, a record is some collection of information about a specific entity.) Alice's data is disclosed (given away or disseminated) if an unintended entity can make the link between one or more particular attributes and the identity "Alice." That is, when a record is created for Alice, a *record tuple* is formed: $\rho = (\iota, \bar{a})$, where $\iota$ is the identity and $\bar{a}$ is a collection of attributes. Private records exist for Alice when unintended entities are unable to discover or infer the tuple $\rho$.

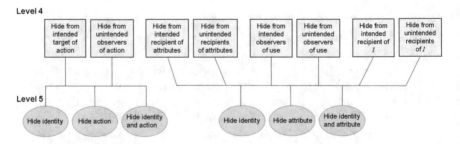

**Fig. 2.3** Level 5 in the classification of privacy techniques

Privacy techniques can be categorized at this level according to what kind of protection they offer for the two tuples $\omega$ and $\rho$. In particular, exposure-reducing transformations may be applied to operational data to increase the difficulty for an unintended party to construct $\omega$, and disclosure-reducing transformations may be applied to record data to increase the difficulty for an unintended party to construct $\rho$. Protecting $\omega$ against exposure can be done in three ways: a transformation $\tau_\omega(\iota)$ may be applied to hide or remove the identity $\iota$; a transformation $\tau_\omega(\alpha)$ may be applied to hide or remove the action $\alpha$; or a transformation $\tau_\omega(\omega)$ may be applied to hide the full tuple $\omega$. Similarly, protecting $\rho$ against disclosure can be done in three ways: a transformation $\tau_\rho(\iota)$ may be applied to hide or remove the identity $\iota$; a transformation $\tau_\rho(\bar{a})$ may be applied to hide or remove the attributes $\bar{a}$; or a transformation $\tau_\rho(\rho)$ may be applied to hide the full tuple $\rho$.

**Classification Summary**

In more intuitive and descriptive terms, the classification proposed above is based on the discriminators that characterize any kind of investigation: who, what, when, where, why, and how.

- The "Why" of the classification is its title, its starting point: the classification's purpose is to categorize privacy techniques for online environments.
- "How" is the discriminator at Level 1: is privacy protected through technological means or through societal means?
- "Who" is the Level 2 discriminator: who is creating or using Alice's personal information $I$ (is it Alice herself, or is it some other holder of $I$)?
- "What" is the Level 3 discriminator: what kind of personal information is being protected (is it the actions that Alice performs, or is it some attribute information about Alice; that is, does the privacy technique protect $\omega$ or does it protect $\rho$)?
- "When" is the Level 4 discriminator: when is the information protected (as it is released to intended recipients, or as it is acquired by unintended recipients)?
- Finally, "Where" is the Level 5 discriminator: where is privacy protection applied (is it applied on the identity data, on the action/attribute data, or on the tuple)?

This set of discriminators makes the classification relatively simple to understand and to use.

The above definitions of *personal information* and *privacy*, and the described structure of the *classification*, will be assumed and used throughout all following chapters.

## 2.5   The Remainder of This Book

This chapter has introduced and discussed the concept of a "privacy tree", a classification for privacy enhancing technologies that allows meaningful analysis and comparison of various PETs so that their relative strengths, weaknesses, and privacy goals can be readily understood. Placing individual PETs in this tree highlights, for each one, what particular aspect of privacy is being addressed. We can see how distinct PETs might complement each other (to provide "privacy-in-depth"); we can study how two given PETs in the same branch might use different underlying techniques to achieve the same privacy purpose; we can discover if there are any specific privacy goals that are not addressed by any existing PETs (and then investigate why this is the case and whether new PETs should be designed to tackle this omission).

A privacy tree is thus useful for many aspects of research and analysis. Beyond this, however, it is also useful simply as a framework to assist those who are new to the field and are eager to learn. For many who are approaching a new field of study, an initial "big picture" of the field can be tremendously helpful for clarifying where things fit, for seeing how different pieces relate to one another, and for answering the question "what is the point?" about a specific fragment of knowledge.

In the remainder of this book we therefore introduce several notable PETs through the lens of the privacy tree. We cover a number of fundamental PETs, and some important emerging PETs, describing how each one works and – in the context of the privacy tree – what aspect of privacy it is intended to address. As we mentioned at the beginning of this chapter, the PETs community has been active for 40 years; consequently, it would be impossible to include every proposed PET in an introductory text. However, this approach of studying a PET through its position in the privacy tree will be useful to the reader as new PETs are encountered (*"Oh, this new PET sits in* this *branch of the tree, so it is in the same class as these three other PETs that I already know. Now let me see what it does to technically achieve this privacy goal and how that compares with the other three PETs..."*).

The next six chapters will introduce PETs that serve as examples of the six main techniques in the tree for protecting privacy: limiting **exposure** of operations by hiding the *identity*, hiding the *action*, and hiding the *identity-action* pair; and limiting **disclosure** of records by hiding the *identity*, hiding the *attribute*, and hiding the *identity-attribute* pair. Each of the six techniques will be illustrated by two, three, or four representative PETs.

We start with *limiting **exposure** by hiding the identity*, and present the privacy enhancing technology that began the entire PETs field, the *mix network*.

(Note that many *privacy enhancing technologies* rely on underlying *cryptographic algorithms, protocols, or techniques*. For readers unfamiliar with the field of cryptography, a *"Crypto Primer"* is provided in Chap. 11 to give a brief introduction to some of the terminology and concepts needed in this book.)

**Questions for Personal Reflection and/or Group Discussion**

1. Several proposed classifications/taxonomies for privacy were discussed in Sect.
   2.3. Choose any of these (other than the one adopted for this book) and read the
   original publication that proposed it. What are the strengths and weaknesses of
   that proposal? Discuss the ways in which it would be suitable, and not suitable,
   for categorizing PETs.
2. Look carefully at Fig. 2.2 (Classification of privacy techniques for online environments). If you were to design your own classification from scratch, how
   would you structure this tree differently? What nodes, branches, and leaves
   would you choose, and why? In what ways would your classification be more
   useful, and in what ways would it be less useful, than the classification given in
   Fig. 2.2?

# References

C. Adams, A classification for privacy techniques. Univ. Ottawa Law Technol. J. **3**(1) (2006)

A. Antón, J. Earp, A taxonomy for website privacy requirements, *NCSU Technical Report TR-2001-14* (2001, Dec 18)

A. Antón, J. Earp, A. Reese, Analyzing website privacy requirements using a privacy goal taxonomy, in *Proceedings of the IEEE Joint International Conference on Requirements Engineering,* (Essen, Germany, 2002, Sep 9–13)

A. Barth, A. Datta, J. Mitchell, H. Nissenbaum, Privacy and contextual integrity: Framework and applications, in *Proceedings of the IEEE Symposium on Security and Privacy,* (2006, May), pp. 184–198

CFIP: The Code of Fair Information Practices, U.S. Department of Health, Education and Welfare, Secretary's Advisory Committee on Automated Personal Data Systems, Records, Computers, and the Rights of Citizens, viii, 1973

D. Chaum, Untraceable electronic mail, return addresses, and digital pseudonyms. Commun. ACM **24**(2) (1981, Feb)

Enterprivacy Consulting Group, A taxonomy of privacy, in *Infographic Based on Daniel Solove's "A Taxonomy of Privacy" Paper.* https://papers.ssrn.com/sol3/papers.cfm?abstract_id=667622 (ca. 2006)

J. Heurix, P. Zimmermann, T. Neubauer, S. Fenz, A taxonomy for privacy enhancing technologies. Comput. Secur. **53**, 1–17 (2015, Sept)

H. Nissenbaum, *Privacy in Context: Technology, Policy, and the Integrity of Social Life* (Stanford Law Books, 2009)

OPC: Office of the Privacy Commissioner of Canada, Technology Analysis Division, Privacy enhancing technologies – A review of tools and techniques, *Research Report* (2017, Nov)

A. Pfitzmann, M. Hansen, A terminology for talking about privacy by data minimization: Anonymity, unlinkability, undetectability, unobservability, pseudonymity, and identity management, *Anonymity Terminology document, version v0.34* (2010, Aug 10)

PIPEDA: Personal Information Protection and Electronic Documents Act, S.C. 2000 c.5. See also Stephanie Perrin *et al., The Personal Information Protection and Electronic Documents Act: An Annotated Guide,* (Irwin Law, Toronto, 2001)

A. Rezgui, A. Bouguettaya, M. Eltoweissy, Privacy on the web: Facts, challenges, and solutions, in *IEEE Security and Privacy,* (2003, Nov–Dec), pp. 40–49

G. Skinner, S. Han, E. Chang, An information privacy taxonomy for collaborative environments. Inf. Manag. Comput. Secur. **14**(4), 382–394 (2006, Aug 1)

D. Solove, *Understanding Privacy* (Harvard University Press, 2008)

P. Sprenger, Sun on privacy: get over it, *Wired* (1999, Jan 26)

P.F. Syverson, S.G. Stubblebine, Group principals and the formalization of anonymity, in *Proceedings of the First World Congress on Formal Methods in the Development of Computing Systems (FM '99), Volume 1,* (Springer, LNCS 1708, Toulouse, France, 1999, Sep 20–24), pp. 814–833

# Chapter 3
# Limiting Exposure by Hiding the Identity

**Abstract** This chapter examines PETs that limit exposure by hiding the user's identity information. As examples of this category, the following PETs are described: mix networks; anonymous remailers; and onion routing networks. For each of these examples, the original scheme is given, enhancements made over the years are presented, and strengths and limitations of the technology are discussed.

**Keywords** Mix network · Anonymous remailer · Cipherpunk remailer · Mixmaster · Mixminion · Onion routing network · Tor

Given the classification described in Chap. 2, we can now discuss various example PETs in terms of their position in the technological branch of the privacy tree (that is, in terms of <u>who</u> would use the PET, <u>what</u> personal information it protects, <u>when</u> the personal information is protected, and <u>where</u> the protection is applied). Ultimately, we are examining each PET with respect to whether it limits *exposure* of information about the actions of the user or *disclosure* of information about the attributes of the user, and whether it achieves this by hiding the user's *identity*, the user's *actions/attributes*, or both pieces in the tuple.

This chapter looks at the first category: PETs that limit *exposure* by hiding the user's *identity* information. Subsequent chapters consider the remaining categories. Three example PETs that will be covered in this chapter are *mix networks, anonymous remailers*, and *onion routing networks*.

## 3.1 Mix Network

The concept of a mix network was first proposed by David Chaum in his pioneering 1981 paper, "*Untraceable electronic mail, return addresses, and digital pseudonyms*" (1981). This is generally acknowledged to be the first academic paper on a technique explicitly designed as a privacy enhancing technology (of course encryption has existed for thousands of years and can readily be used to provide

© The Editor(s) (if applicable) and The Author(s), under exclusive license
to Springer Nature Switzerland AG 2021

C. Adams, *Introduction to Privacy Enhancing Technologies*,
https://doi.org/10.1007/978-3-030-81043-6_3

*confidentiality* for personal information, but encryption is clearly a general technique that can provide confidentiality for arbitrary data content and so encryption itself is not specifically a PET).

Chaum was concerned with the problem of *traffic analysis* in open networks ("the problem of keeping confidential who converses with whom, and when they converse"), particularly in the context of electronic mail use (which was just beginning to see significant growth at that time). A recent critical breakthrough was the invention of public-key cryptography to address the *key distribution problem* (Diffie and Hellman 1976; Merkle 1978; Rivest et al. 1978), and Chaum wanted to use this new cryptographic technique to hide not only the content of communication, but also the identity of an e-mail sender. He proposed the idea of a "mix": a computer in the network that receives an item of mail and processes it before sending it further toward its destination. In a real-world communication system, there may be several such mix nodes (mixes); this gives rise to a "mix network".

Mix networks have been widely studied in the PETs community since 1981 and have been analyzed and discussed in literally scores of papers over the years (in 2020, freehaven.net/anonbib had 68 papers with the word "mix" explicitly in the title, but of course there are others (including Chaum's original paper!) that are about mix networks but do not have "mix" in the title). In this section we will describe the original scheme and then discuss some important enhancements that have been proposed since 1981.

### 3.1.1   The Basic Scheme

The goal of a mix is to hide the correspondence between items that are input to it and items that are output from it. In particular, in an e-mail scenario, a mix will receive several incoming e-mails and will ultimately send these toward their destinations. If the mix acts as a queue (so that items are processed in a *first-in-first-out* (FIFO) fashion), then anyone who observes both the input channels and the output channels of the mix will know an exact correspondence between e-mails. Similarly, if the mix acts as a stack (so that items are processed in a *last-in-first-out* (LIFO) fashion), the correspondence will again be obvious. Thus, the mix is designed to operate such that it waits until it has received exactly $n$ e-mails, at which point it randomly reorders them and then sends them out. This avoids any timing correspondence that can be seen by the external observer.

However, we need to hide more than just the timing of the e-mails. Clearly, if the observer can see the content of the messages, then input-output correspondences will still be obvious. We can use cryptography to help with this. With a cryptographically-strong encryption algorithm, a plaintext and its associated ciphertext appear to be independent bit strings to any computationally-bounded attacker. There are several possible ways to implement this. Examples include the following:

– Input messages are in plaintext, and the ciphertext output messages are their encryptions (using an encryption key known only to the mix node);

- Input messages are in ciphertext, and the plaintext output messages are their decryptions (using a decryption key known only to the mix node);
- Input messages are in ciphertext, and these are decrypted to plaintext and then re-encrypted before being output (here, both the decryption key and the separate encryption key are known only to the mix node).

All of the above options can work, but note that either the external observer or the mix node itself can see the content when it is in plaintext. To avoid this loss of confidentiality, Chaum proposed a clever variation: the input messages are encrypted twice (i.e., the plaintext is encrypted under $key_1$ to $ciphertext_1$, and then $ciphertext_1$ is encrypted under $key_2$ to $ciphertext_2$). Then, $ciphertext_2$ is sent to the mix node; this node knows only $key_2$ and so it decrypts $ciphertext_2$ to $ciphertext_1$ and outputs $ciphertext_1$. This not only prevents correspondence between input and output messages, but also ensures that the actual plaintext is not available to either the external observer or the mix node. *Nice!*

$$E_{key2}( \; E_{key1}(input) \; ) \; \rightarrow \; \boxed{\text{mix node}} \; \rightarrow \; E_{key1}(input)$$

Two other steps must also be taken by the mix node in order to prevent correspondences. Input and output messages (or, at the very least, output messages) must be of the same size; otherwise, a short input message in a batch of long input messages will obviously correspond to the single short output message in the batch of outputs. Thus, either the sender or the mix node itself will need to split long messages into pieces and pad short messages so that all messages are identical in length.

Additionally, any duplicate messages in the input must be removed. Because all encryption or decryption within the mix node is done with a single key, duplicate messages in the input will result in duplicate messages in the output. As a simple example, suppose that Alice submits the same message twice (inadvertently). When an observer sees two identical outputs from the mix node, the observer will know that these are the duplicate messages from Alice. An attacker can exploit this by deliberately replaying a message from Alice (a replay attack) and tracing the corresponding identical outputs, repeating the attack as needed across the path through the network. (Note that even if the mix node uses non-deterministic decryption (so that the decryptions of identical inputs yield different outputs), the attacker can mount an intersection attack: the attacker observes the total set of recipients when Alice's original message was sent and the total set of recipients when the replayed message was sent; the intersection of these two sets narrows down (possibly to one) the set of possible actual recipients of Alice's message.) Removing duplicates in the mix node prior to processing will prevent such attacks. Chaum notes that checking for duplicates must happen not only within a single input batch, but also across all input batches (to protect against an adversary that is present for a long period of time). The mix must therefore keep track of all the input messages it has processed (until it changes its key, at which point the records can be discarded). Alternatively, the system could mandate that all messages contain some additional string – such as an identifier or a timestamp – that is only valid for a particular batch so that the mix would not need to retain records for previous batches.

So, in summary, the mix node must

- Wait until $n$ input messages arrive,
- Remove any duplicate messages,
- Split or pad the input messages to make them all the same length (if needed; note that this may instead be done by the message senders),
- Cryptographically process the messages (i.e., encrypt or decrypt them),
- Rearrange the messages into a random order, and
- Transmit the batch of $n$ output messages.

A mix that faithfully carries out all these steps will prevent an external observer from learning a correspondence between its input and output messages. But what if the attacker has somehow compromised the mix node itself (that is, what if the attacker causes the mix to *not* faithfully carry out the above steps)? To protect against this, Chaum proposed a *cascade*, or a *series of mix nodes*. This can be configured such that everyone in the network uses the same cascade, or such that different users use different cascades. Under appropriate constraints/assumptions (such as independence of the input messages), if even a single mix node in the cascade operates correctly, then the correspondence between input and output of the entire cascade will be effectively hidden.

If the system is set up such that the $m$ mixes in the cascade all have different keys ($mix_1$ uses $key_1$, $mix_2$ uses $key_2$, ..., $mix_m$ uses $key_m$), then Alice can encrypt her message $m$ times using these $m$ keys: the original message is encrypted with $key_m$, then the result is encrypted with $key_{m-1}$, then that result is encrypted with $key_{m-2}$, and so on, until the last encryption is with $key_1$. This final ciphertext is sent to $mix_1$, the first mix in the cascade. $mix_1$ decrypts its batch of input messages with $key_1$ and sends the results out. $mix_2$ decrypts its batch of input messages with $key_2$ and sends the results out. At the end of the cascade, $mix_m$ decrypts its input batch with $key_m$ and sends the results to recipients (so that Alice's message is delivered to Bob). This works well, but note that if the system uses a symmetric encryption algorithm (such as the Data Encryption Standard (DES) or the Advanced Encryption Standard (AES)), then if Alice knows $key_1$, ..., $key_m$, she will be able to trace the messages of other participants who use the same cascade. Chaum prevents this by proposing the use of asymmetric (or public-key) cryptography instead, so that everyone encrypts their messages with public keys $key_1$, ..., $key_m$, but each $mix_i$ decrypts using the corresponding private key $key'_i$, which it alone knows.

When there is a large population of users, it can be problematic to have everyone use the same cascade of mix nodes (since this will be a performance bottleneck). Chaum thus proposed a large number of mix nodes, subsequently called a *mix network*. Alice can choose a random subset of mixes from this network to form her own cascade, and can then send her message through this cascade; see Fig. 3.1. She may choose a different random subset for each message she sends.

Because of the random selection of mixes, Alice will need to include some addressing information with her messages: $mix_i$, once it has decrypted its incoming message from $mix_{i-1}$ in Alice's randomly-formed cascade, will need to know where to send the result (this address might be for some other random mix that will serve

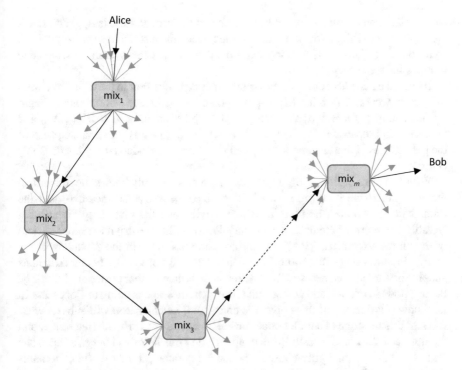

**Fig. 3.1  A Cascade of Mix Nodes Chosen by Alice:** Alice's message goes through $m$ mix nodes before it is finally delivered to her intended recipient, Bob. At each of these nodes, her message is batched with $n$-1 other messages (from up to $n$-1 other senders) and, after processing, is one of $n$ output messages

as $mix_{i+1}$ in the cascade, or it might be the intended recipient, Bob, if $mix_i$ is the last mix in the cascade).

As an example, assume that Alice wants to send a message to Bob through a mix network, and that she chooses $mix_3$, $mix_1$, and $mix_2$ (in that order) to be her cascade. Her original message, $M$, and Bob's address, $A_{Bob}$, will be encrypted with $key_2$ (the encryption key of $mix_2$). This ciphertext will be appended with the address of $mix_2$, ($A_{mix2}$), and the result will be encrypted with $key_1$ (the encryption key of $mix_1$). Then, this new ciphertext will be appended with the address of $mix_1$, ($A_{mix1}$), and the result will be encrypted with $key_3$ (the encryption key of $mix_3$). This final ciphertext is Alice's outgoing message, $M_{Alice}$; it is sent to $mix_3$.

$$M_{Alice} = E_{key3}\left( E_{key1}\left( E_{key2}\left( M, A_{Bob} \right), A_{mix2} \right), A_{mix1} \right)$$

When $mix_3$ receives $M_{Alice}$, it decrypts it using $key'_3$, sees that the next address is $A_{mix1}$, and sends the remaining ciphertext to $mix_1$. Upon receiving this, $mix_1$ decrypts using $key'_1$, sees that the next address is $A_{mix2}$, and sends the remaining ciphertext to

$mix_2$. Finally, $mix_2$ decrypts using $key'_2$, sees that the next address is $A_{Bob}$, and sends the content $M$ to Bob. (Note that at each stage, when the next address is stripped off, some random "junk" bits are appended instead, so that the overall message size remains the same.)

In the given construction, we see that the message $M$ is sent in the clear from $mix_2$ to Bob. However, if Bob has his own public key, $key_{Bob}$, Alice can optionally begin by encrypting $M$ for Bob (that is, she can begin by computing $M' = E_{keyBob}(M)$) and then she can prepare $M'$ for the cascade as above. In this way, the final segment of the path carries ciphertext and the original message $M$ is readable only inside Bob's computer.

With Chaum's design, every mix node in the cascade only knows the immediate previous node (the node from which it received an encrypted message) and the immediate next node (the node to which it will send the remaining ciphertext). Notably, no intermediate node in a cascade knows either the original sender (Alice) or the ultimate recipient (Bob). Furthermore, the first node in the cascade will see that its input message has come from Alice, but will not know whether Alice has simply forwarded this message from some other source further upstream. Similarly, the last node in the cascade will see that its output message is going to Bob, but will not know (particularly if this content is encrypted) whether Bob will subsequently forward this message to another node further downstream. Thus, the true sender and the true receiver are successfully "decoupled", and this holds as long as at least one mix in Alice's randomly-chosen cascade operates correctly (i.e., remains uncompromised).

The mix network provides *anonymity* for Alice. Clearly, Alice knows who Bob is because she needs to prepare her message specifically for delivery to him. However, Bob is unable to trace the message in any way to learn who the sender is. In fact, Alice could send multiple messages to Bob using the mix network, and Bob will be unable to know with any certainty whether those messages are connected to each other at all. However, Alice could choose to create a *pseudonymity* service instead: she could include a specific *pseudonymous identifier* (a *pseudonym*, such as "*12345*" or "*your secret admirer*") in the content of all her messages. If she does this, Bob will know that these messages are all from the same individual, even though he will not be able to determine that the individual is Alice.

The above is the basic operation of the mix network to send an e-mail message anonymously (or pseudonymously) from Alice to Bob. But Chaum provides one more very useful feature. Given that this is an e-mail environment, it is reasonable to expect that Alice might want a response from Bob for some message that she sends him. How can this be achieved without compromising her anonymous/pseudonymous status? Chaum proposes what he calls an *untraceable return address*. Alice chooses a cascade of $m$ mix nodes (independent of the cascade that she chooses for sending her original message to Bob), creates $m + 1$ new random public-private key pairs, and uses these public keys $K_1, \ldots, K_{m+1}$ to form an untraceable return address (*URA*) as follows:

$$URA = E_{key1}( \ldots E_{keym\text{-}2}( \boxed{K_{m\text{-}2}, E_{keym\text{-}1}( \boxed{K_{m\text{-}1}, E_{keym}( \boxed{K_m, A_{Alice}} )} )} ) \ldots )$$

Alice then sends *URA* along with $K_{m+1}$ to Bob in her message to him (e.g., perhaps concatenated with her actual original message, *M*). Note that, in order to keep the notation simple, the addresses of the *m* mix nodes are not shown in the above *URA*, but they would be included in a real *URA* just as they appear in $M_{Alice}$ previously; this is how each node will know where to send the portion it has processed.

When Bob wants to respond to this anonymous (or pseudonymous) message he has received, he will encrypt his response, $R_{Bob}$, with the received public key $K_{m+1}$ and send $\{URA, E_{Km+1}(R_{Bob})\}$ to $mix_1$ (the first mix node in the return cascade that Alice has chosen). $mix_1$ will decrypt *URA* with its own key $key'_1$ to obtain the following:

$$K_1, E_{key2}( \ldots E_{keym-2}( K_{m-2}, E_{keym-1}( K_{m-1}, E_{keym}( K_m, A_{Alice}))) \ldots ) = K_1, URA'$$

$mix_1$ uses $K_1$ to encrypt Bob's response and sends $\{URA', E_{K1}(E_{Km+1}(R_{Bob}))\}$ to $mix_2$. The process continues through the cascade until $mix_m$ decrypts with its own key $key'_m$ to obtain $K_m, A_{Alice}$. $mix_m$ uses $K_m$ to again encrypt Bob's response and sends

$$E_{Km}( E_{Km-1}( \ldots E_{K1}( E_{Km+1}(R_{Bob})) ) \ldots ))$$

to Alice's address (i.e., to $A_{Alice}$). Because Alice knows the private keys that correspond to $K_1, \ldots K_{m+1}$ (since she created all those key pairs), she can recover the plaintext response $R_{Bob}$. Thus, Alice is able to send a message to Bob, and receive a response, while fully retaining her anonymity (or pseudonymity) from him.

## 3.1.2   Enhancements

The basic scheme proposed by Chaum (described in Sect. 3.1.1) has been modified in a number of ways as researchers and implementers have studied the effects on *anonymity* (i.e., resistance to sender identification), *latency* (i.e., how long it takes a message to go from sender to receiver), and *bandwidth* (i.e., how much dummy ("cover") traffic is needed to prevent message tracing). As discussed in (Serjantov et al. 2003), and more recently in (BenGuirat et al. 2020), the following variations have all been examined.

– Topologies

- *Cascade*: Every message goes through a set of mixes (a cascade) in a predetermined order, with each mix sending all its output messages to the next mix in the cascade. Note that for large user populations multiple cascades may be run in parallel.
- *Free route*: A message may go through any path from sender to receiver (the path may be chosen by the sender or by the first mix). Note that the path length may be variable.

- *Stratified*: There is a fixed number of layers and each mix, at any given time, is assigned to one specific layer. Note that the first layer only receives incoming messages from senders and the final layer only sends outgoing messages to receivers; each mix in an internal layer is connected to every mix in the previous and subsequent layers.

– Mix Type

  - *Simple (with fixed parameters n, t)*

    *Threshold*: When the mix collects $n$ messages, it fires (delivering all $n$).
    *Timed*: The mix fires (delivering all the messages it currently holds) every $t$ seconds.
    *Threshold or timed*: The mix fires (delivering all the messages it currently holds) every $t$ seconds or when it has collected $n$ messages (whichever comes first).
    *Threshold and timed*: The mix fires (delivering all the messages it currently holds) every $t$ seconds, but only when it holds at least $n$ messages.

  - *Constant pool (with fixed parameters n, t, f)*

    *Threshold*: The mix fires when it has collected $n + f$ messages. The mix chooses $f$ of these messages, uniformly at random, to retain (this is the "pool") and outputs the remaining $n$ messages. It then waits until it has again collected $n + f$ messages.
    *Threshold and timed*: The mix fires every $t$ seconds. A pool of $f$ messages, chosen uniformly at random, is retained and the rest are output. Note that if $f$ or fewer messages are held in the mix at the specified firing time, the mix does not fire.

  - *Dynamic pool (with fixed parameters n, t, f, m, frac)*

    *Threshold and timed*: The mix fires every $t$ seconds, provided that it holds at least $n + f$ messages. However, instead of outputting $n$ messages (as in a "threshold-and-timed constant pool mix"), it sends the greater of 1 and $\lfloor m \times frac \rfloor$ messages (where *frac* is a specified fraction, such as one half or one third), and retains the rest in the pool, where $m + f$ is the number of messages in the mix ($m \geq n$).
    *Cottrell*: This is the special case of a "threshold-and-timed dynamic pool mix" where $n = 1$. Note that this is the mix type that has been used in the Mixmaster remailer system (see Sect. 3.2 below).

– Routing

  - *Source routing*: The sender of the message chooses the mixes for the entire route to the receiver.
  - *Hop-by-hop*: The sender of the message chooses the first mix, the first mix chooses the second mix, and so on, until the message reaches the receiver.

- *Rendezvous*: The receiver chooses a route from a chosen mix node $mix_i$ to himself and publishes this; the sender then chooses a route from herself to the node $mix_i$.
- *Multi-party*: The sender chooses one of a small number of first-layer mixes (see the *stratified* topology above) and sends the message to this mix. Then, for each subsequent hop, a collection of *routing entities* engages in a multi-party computation protocol (see Chap. 7, Sect. 7.2) to produce the verifiably-secure randomness that is used to select the next mix in the route (Shirazi et al. 2017).

Mix networks are still being studied in various settings as their security and usability properties continue to be explored.

### 3.1.3   Strengths

Chaum has proposed a fairly simple and elegant PET that is quite effective in meeting its design goals.

A *passive adversary* who simply watches the traffic on many communications links will not be able to trace a message as it passes through a correctly-operating cascade. Thus, senders retain their anonymity in the face of such a threat.

Furthermore, under appropriate constraints/assumptions (see Sect. 3.1.1), if even a single mix node in a cascade is operating correctly (i.e., is uncompromised) then an attacker will be unable to successfully trace a message from the original sender to the ultimate receiver. If Alice can choose a random set of mixes to form her own cascade, and if she changes this set for each message that she sends, then the probability that she only chooses compromised nodes for all her cascades quickly approaches zero. This is the intuition behind the claim that a mix network is also secure (in the sense of keeping the sender anonymous from the receiver) against an *active adversary* who has compromised many mixes (although note that anonymity can be reduced in networks that have a maximum route length; see (Serjantov and Danezis 2002)). This claim of security against compromised nodes is made even stronger when we take into account the fact that every mix in the network knows only its immediate predecessor and its immediate successor in the message transmission: no node (including the first one in the cascade) knows that Alice is the originator, and no node (including the last one in the cascade) knows that Bob is the intended recipient. Thus, even a mix that is compromised cannot reveal much useful information to the attacker.

A recent interesting development in this area is the *Loopix Anonymity System* (Piotrowska et al. 2017) which proposes a low-latency mix-based architecture with good resistance to both passive and active adversaries. *Loopix* is the network component of the *Nym* privacy infrastructure (https://nymtech.net/).

## 3.1.4  Disadvantages, Limitations, and Weaknesses

By far, the primary practical disadvantage to the original mix network in a real-world environment is the unpredictable delay inherent in message delivery. Every node in the cascade must wait until it has received exactly $n$ input messages before it can process them and send the batch to the next stops in their journey. If there are many active users in the network, accumulating $n$ messages at any given node may happen very quickly. However, if there are very few active users (or if there is only one!), the wait time at each node may be unacceptably long: a message may take hours or days (or longer) to arrive at its destination. Chaum suggests that such a situation may be mitigated by having all participants continuously send randomly-addressed dummy messages whenever they are not sending real messages. Alternatively, participants may send messages (real ones and dummies) only to a subset of other participants, rather than to all participants; another possibility is that dummy messages are created by a mix node itself (rather than participants) if it finds that it has been waiting for some specified period of time and still has not received $n$ input messages. All such solutions involving dummy traffic may help with delay, but will clearly consume very high levels of network bandwidth; this will certainly be undesirable in many settings.

As noted in Sect. 3.1.2, several variations have been proposed over the years to design *low-latency* mix networks, but unfortunately these often come at the price of reduced security. In particular, concerns have been raised regarding a different kind of *active adversary* than the one mentioned in Sect. 3.1.3. The previous section introduced an active adversary that can compromise some mix nodes. Here, we consider an adversary that can manipulate messages in the mix network in such a way as to facilitate careful timing analysis or allow tracing of legitimate messages. In particular, the attacker may inject bursts of traffic that contain unique timing patterns into the targeted flow; this may make it possible to identify this group of messages at a subsequent point elsewhere in the network (Shmatikov and Wang 2006). Conversely, the attacker may be able to drop or corrupt legitimate packets (at the application layer or at the TCP layer), and the resulting gaps in the traffic flow or the number of forced re-transmission requests may be observable (allowing tracing). A variation on injecting bursts is to create artificial bursts by delaying legitimate packets in a stream for a period of time and then releasing them all at once; again, the overall target flow may be identified using such a technique (Shmatikov and Wang 2006).

A class of attacks against many types of threshold mix networks is for the attacker to submit all-but-1 of a threshold number of messages to a given mix node (perhaps at the end of the cascade); when the (legitimate) final message arrives to trigger firing in the mix, the batch is processed and sent out. Since all-but-1 of these output messages are sent to the attacker, the destination of the remaining message can easily be observed (Cottrell 1994). In more sophisticated attacks (so-called "sleeper" attacks), the attacker may submit a small number of messages (even a single message) to a chosen mix node to determine which of a pair of nodes has received/

processed/output a batch of messages, allowing inference about the messages of other senders in the network (Syverson 2011a).

Research work continues on the variety of mix networks that have been proposed in order to understand, at a detailed level, the privacy guarantees that each can provide.

## 3.2   Anonymous Remailer

An *anonymous remailer* is a server that allows Alice to send an e-mail to Bob without Bob learning who the sender is. The server removes Alice's address from the e-mail and replaces it with a different address (a random string, or its own address) before forwarding the e-mail to Bob. Note that at the network layer, every IP packet contains both a source address and a destination address; furthermore, at the application layer, all standards-based e-mail messages contain defined fields for the source and transmitting entities as well as the destination entity. An anonymous remailer therefore needs to replace Alice's information at both layers if it is to provide effective anonymity.

Anonymous remailers have existed since 1988 (see footnote 94 of (duPont 2001)), but came to prominence in 1993, when the first well-known remailer (*anon. penet.fi*) was created in Finland. This remailer garnered such attention that over the next 3 years, dozens of similar services were launched all over the world. Since that time, there have been at least three successive generations of anonymous remailers with different features and capabilities.

### 3.2.1   The Basic Scheme

In 1993, Johan Helsingius (who was known as "Julf" and was reachable through the e-mail address julf@penet.fi) set up the world's first well-known anonymous remailer in his home city of Helsinki, Finland. He has stated that services such as his "have made it possible for people to discuss very sensitive matters, such as domestic violence, school bullying or human rights issues anonymously and confidentially on the Internet" (Helsingius 1996).

While it was in operation, the service was the target of many accusations. In one notable instance, the English newspaper *Observer* claimed that the remailer had been used for transmitting objectionable illegal images. A formal investigation by the Finnish police, with the involvement of police sergeant Kaj Malmberg from the Helsinki Police Crime Squad, a specialist in the investigation of computer crimes, found that the *Observer's* allegation was groundless. They found no cases where such images were transmitted from Finland and, in fact, found that a year prior to the investigation, Helsingius had restricted the operations of his remailer so that it could not transmit images.

It seemed that, indeed, Helsingius was operating his service for the benefit of society. Over the course of 3 years, his anonymous remailer became the most popular remailer in the world, with over half a million users worldwide.

The technology behind Helsingius' remailer was extremely simple:

- A user (Alice, with address *alice@domain.com*) sends an e-mail to *anon.penet.fi* with an embedded address of the intended recipient;
- The server removes the "From:" information in the e-mail, replacing it with a random-looking address in the server's domain (such as *anon43567@anon. penet.fi*);
- The server adds the mapping "*alice@domain.com* ←→ *anon43567@anon. penet.fi*"to a list stored on the server's hard drive;
- The server forwards the e-mail to the intended recipient.
- In the future, any e-mails sent with a "To:" address of *anon43567@anon.penet. fi* will have the "To:" address replaced with *alice@domain.com* (once the internal list has been consulted) and will be forwarded to Alice. Thus, Alice remains anonymous to the original intended recipient, but can receive replies from this person.

After 3 years of operation, Julf decided to shut down his remailer. Because of the existence of the internal list of sender addresses (which allows e-mail replies to be forwarded to the original senders), it is possible to break anonymity by accessing this list (for example, by breaking into the hard drive of the server, by bribing someone who runs or maintains the server, or simply by asking a court to order that the anonymity must be broken). With *anon.penet.fi*, some traffic about Scientology passed through the server and the Church of Scientology claimed copyright infringement and sued Helsingius (duPont 2001). The court ordered that the list must be made available. Helsingius resisted as long and as much as he could, but was eventually forced to reveal the real e-mail address of a specific sender implicated in this suit (purportedly an alumni account at Caltech, according to (Greenberg 2012, p. 134)).

Because he (and the public) felt he could no longer guarantee the identity confidentiality of his users, Helsingius ceased operation of his anonymous remailer and destroyed all his records (including the list). In a press release issued on August 30, 1996, he made the following statement:

> I will close down the remailer for the time being because the legal issues governing the whole Internet in Finland are yet undefined. The legal protection of the users needs to be clarified. At the moment the privacy of Internet messages is judicially unclear. (Helsingius 1996)

The remailer *anon.penet.fi* was never reopened. However, this PET is historically quite significant because it popularized the field of anonymous remailers and set the foundation for several generations of this technology that followed it.

## 3.2.2   Enhancements

The original anonymous remailers, such as the *anon.penet.fi* server, later came to be referred to as "Type 0" remailers because they were followed by subsequent generations of remailers known as "Type I", "Type II", and "Type III".

**Type I remailers** (circa 1995–1996), commonly called *cypherpunk remailers*, were created to rectify what was seen as the primary deficiency of the Type 0 remailers: the internal list mapping user addresses to random "anonymous" addresses. Cypherpunk remailers dispensed with this list, meaning that they were not susceptible to server break-in, bribery, or court order. On the other hand, this also meant that e-mail replies were no longer possible, which made the service much less useful in practice (although it still had value for posting anonymous messages to a public bulletin board, for example). Interestingly, the designers of these Type I systems also recognized and mitigated another potential weakness of their Type 0 predecessors: if someone was able to monitor both the input and the output of a Type 0 server, it would be trivial to associate an incoming e-mail with its outgoing counterpart, thereby learning the true identity of the sender. The Type I systems use encryption to reduce this risk. Alice sends an encrypted e-mail to a cypherpunk remailer, and the remailer decrypts this message, replaces the "From:" address, and forwards the plaintext to the embedded recipient address.

Type I remailers also implement a chaining option, whereby it is possible to chain two or three remailers (using encryption at each stage), ensuring that each remailer is unable to determine who is sending a message to whom.

**Type II remailers** (circa 2002), commonly called *mixmaster remailers*, are an implementation of Chaum's basic mix network (see Sect. 3.1.1 above). In particular, message splitting or padding is used to ensure that message blocks are all of equal size, and message reordering is used to further hide the correspondence between blocks of incoming and outgoing messages at a single node. Chaining (multiple remailers between the initial sender and ultimate receiver) is always used so that anonymity is maintained even if a subset of remailers is compromised. Messages are one-way only, unless the sender includes an *untraceable return address* (see Sect. 3.1.1 above) in the body of the original e-mail.

**Type III remailers** (circa 2007), commonly called *mixminion remailers*, add more advanced features to the mixmaster remailers that came before them (Danezis et al. 2003). For example, *mixminion remailers* include the following:

– Single-Use Reply Blocks (SURBs) are introduced to make replies indistinguishable from, and as secure as, forward messages;
– Key rotation (i.e., updating of keys) is implemented to prevent replay of messages;
– Synchronized redundant directory servers are integrated into the network so that remailers and keys can be found more reliably; and
– Dummy traffic is disseminated internally in the mix network (i.e., not sent or received by users) to thwart attackers who observe some or all network connections among the mix nodes.

Note that mix-based remailers (both *mixmaster* and *mixminion*), typically locate the nodes of their network in different legal and political jurisdictions so that attacks based on court orders and police action become prohibitively difficult (due to frictions between the multiplicity of laws, statutes, legal systems, and organizations involved). Furthermore, since many different servers and server operators – from several different countries – play a part in the operation of the network, the probability that any single attacker will be able to subvert the entire chain of remailers is extremely low.

### 3.2.3   Strengths

The first (Type 0) remailer systems were very simple designs. Since then, the complexity has increased substantially in order to protect against increasingly sophisticated potential attacks. However, the mix networks on which the current systems are based are still relatively elegant and easy to understand. Because of this, much academic analysis has been devoted to these systems and their privacy properties are well established. In particular, it is generally agreed that the anonymity provided by *mixminion remailers* appears to be sufficiently strong for most purposes.

### 3.2.4   Disadvantages, Limitations, and Weaknesses

Despite the significant academic work in this area, as well as the considerable number of free services available (see, for example, https://www.hongkiat.com/blog/anonymous-email-providers/), anonymous remailers are not currently widely deployed or commonly used. One possible reason for this is unreliability. Many of the free services are owned and operated by individuals working alone who maintain the systems in their spare time; consequently, the remailers are not as stable as they otherwise might be, and occasionally become unavailable (for varying periods of time) without warning. Remailer sites have also been blocked by authorities in some countries because of content that has been posted through them.

Another possible reason is that such networks can be targets of intense scrutiny by government entities (who are watching for illegal and nefarious uses of anonymous messaging systems) and law-abiding citizens may be wary of mistakenly being implicated in such activities.

However, the primary reason for the relatively low uptake of anonymous remailers may have less to do with reliability or "guilt-by-association", and more to do with straightforward practical issues. Mix-based remailers (which offer much stronger anonymity guarantees than the early Type 0 and Type 1 remailers) necessarily introduce delay (i.e., latency) into the message delivery process. While this may have been quite tolerable in the very early days of e-mail (when even an ordinary message might take anywhere from minutes to hours to reach a recipient and, in fact, might not ever arrive!), users today typically expect all forms of communication to take a few seconds or less. Near-instantaneous message delivery is almost universally demanded, and while some users may be willing to "pay" a little in delivery time in order to "buy" anonymity, they are usually not willing to "pay" very much. Although it is true that mix-based remailers can be designed to have various desired levels of latency, it has generally been found that lower-latency mix networks are more susceptible to anonymity attacks than their higher-latency counterparts. Therefore, it is not clear that the current low adoption of anonymous remailers will improve any time soon.

## 3.3  Onion Routing and Tor

As mentioned in Sect. 3.1, the ground-breaking work by Chaum on mix networks was intended for an e-mail environment. This is clear because only a store-and-forward messaging architecture can tolerate the delays incurred by having each node wait until it has received $n$ messages before processing and outputting the batch. In Chaum's design, a collection of mix nodes can be configured to provide strong anonymity properties for an e-mail sender.

However, what if the messaging environment is *not* a store-and-forward architecture? What if Alice wants her message to get to Bob as quickly as possible, without a potential batching delay at every node? Can anything be done to give her anonymity in such a setting? In the mid- to late-1990s, David Goldschlag, Michael Reed, and Paul Syverson proposed a scheme for anonymous messaging that borrowed from Chaum's design but was specifically targeted to real-time (or as close to real-time as possible) communications. They called their scheme *onion routing*.

Onion routing (analysis of the scheme itself as well as analysis of *Tor*, the widely-deployed implementation of the scheme) is one of the most active research topics in PETs. Like mix networks, there are scores of academic papers on this topic: using the same simple metric as with mix networks, in 2020 the website freehaven.net/anonbib had 80 papers with "Tor" in the title and another 25 or so with "onion" in the title. Again, this does not count the papers (including some of the original papers) about onion routing that do not have these specific words in the title. In addition, there is a host of articles in the popular press and elsewhere about this technology. In this section, we will describe the basic onion routing scheme as well as some of the enhancements that have been proposed over the past two decades.

### 3.3.1  The Basic Scheme

Between 1996 and 1999, Goldschlag, Reed, and Syverson published over half a dozen papers (with various permutations of the authors' names) introducing their new privacy enhancing technology, *onion routing*: Goldschlag et al. (1996, 1997, 1999), Reed et al. (1996, 1997, 1998) and Syverson et al. (1997).

Although they also use the concept of layered encryption proposed by Chaum for mix networks (i.e., a message is encrypted several times, once for each of the nodes it will pass through on the route to the ultimate receiver, and every node will perform a decryption operation that "peels away" one layer of the encrypted "onion"), onion routing networks differ from mix networks and early anonymous remailers in that onion routing is specifically designed to handle real-time bidirectional communication. Replies are accommodated in mix networks and Type 0 remailers, but simply enabling the possibility of a response to a previously-sent message is very different from establishing a long-term bidirectional conversation between two parties. Furthermore, having real-time (or near-real-time) performance means that an onion routing network can potentially be used for many types of data beyond e-mail (such as virtual private network (VPN) services, web browsing traffic, remote login interactions, and electronic cash).

The focus on bidirectional communications led to some design choices that were very different from mix networks. For example,

– A route (a connection) is set up between a sender and receiver, and this route persists for an indefinite period of time (so that back-and-forth conversational messages between these two participants can occur for the whole duration of their conversation). Setting up a cryptographic route provides route authentication: the route creator not only selects the nodes in the route, but is cryptographically guaranteed that traffic in both directions passes through exactly those nodes.
– Once a route has been established, all the cryptography uses symmetric encryption/decryption algorithms since these are generally much faster than the asymmetric (public key) algorithms that Chaum proposed for mix networks.
– Batching and reordering of messages at each node is not done. Instead, every node accepts a new input message from a sender and delivers the output message as soon as it has been processed. This helps to ensure acceptable performance for the bidirectional communications.

### 3.3.1.1   Architecture

Like mix networks, onion routing networks consist of a collection of nodes (referred to as *onion routers*). These onion routers have long-standing (essentially permanent) socket connections between them. When Alice wishes to establish an anonymous communication session with Bob, this will be defined at connection setup (i.e., a subset of onion routers will be chosen at random) and this anonymous connection will be multiplexed over the long-standing socket connections for as long as the session persists. Every message sent between Alice and Bob is encrypted many times (once for each node in the anonymous connection), and each node "peels off" one layer of encryption before forwarding the result to the next node. As with mix networks, every node knows only its immediate predecessor node and its immediate successor node; no node knows the original sender and the ultimate receiver of any message.

### 3.3.1.2  Operation

The original design of onion routing was presented in (Goldschlag et al. 1996). A second generation was described in (Reed et al. 1998), and a third generation was released as *Tor* (see below). In these different versions, some aspects evolved over time and some details or components exist in one but not another. (A good summary of the main distinctions between the generations can be found in (Syverson 2011b).) Conceptually, however, the onion routing network can be viewed as consisting of an *application proxy*, an *onion proxy*, an *entry funnel*, a collection of *onion routers*, and an *exit funnel*.

- When an initiating application on Alice's device (e.g., e-mail client, VPN client, web browser, *et cetera*) wants to begin a communication session with the associated receiving application on Bob's device, it will make a socket connection to the *application proxy* requesting a connection to Bob's device. This proxy modifies the connection request (and subsequent message data) to a generic application-independent format that can be accepted by, and sent through, the onion routing network. The *application proxy* then connects to the *onion proxy* (instead of directly to Bob's device as it would do if there was no onion routing network).
- The *onion proxy* specifies a route through the network by constructing a data structure called an *onion* and passes the onion to the *entry funnel*. An *onion* has layers of encryption (one for each node in the connection, using that node's public key); at every layer, the next node in the route is specified and a symmetric key (or seed data for generating a symmetric key) is provided. Thus, when onion router $OR_i$ receives this onion and decrypts the outer layer using its own private key, it acquires a symmetric key, $key_i$ (which it will subsequently use for processing messages once this connection has been established), learns that the next onion router is $OR_j$, and passes the remaining onion to it. $OR_j$ decrypts the outer layer using its private key, acquires symmetric key $key_j$ for subsequent message processing, learns that the next node is $OR_k$, and passes the remaining onion to it. This continues until the entire route is established.
- The *entry funnel* has a long-standing connection to a given *onion router*; this router is the one for whom the outermost layer of the *onion* is intended.
- The last *onion router* in the anonymous connection will forward data to an *exit funnel*, whose task is to transmit data between the onion routing network and the intended recipient, Bob. Analogously to the *entry funnel*, the *exit funnel* is associated with an *onion proxy* and an *application proxy* on the output side; this *application proxy* modifies the connection request (and subsequent message data) back to the application-specific format and connects directly to the receiving application on Bob's device.
- Once the anonymous connection has been established between the initiating application on Alice's device and the receiving application on Bob's device, actual message data can be sent back and forth. The *onion proxy* at Alice's end receives a message from the application and repeatedly symmetrically encrypts

it (using all the keys $key_i$ that were sent in the original onion that established the connection), adding a layer of encryption (in the correct order) for each *onion router* in the route. As the data moves through the connection, each *onion router* $OR_i$ removes one layer of encryption (using the symmetric key $key_i$ that it was given for this connection) so that the message arrives at Bob's end as plaintext.

- An *application proxy* and an *onion proxy* are needed both at Alice's end and at Bob's end of the connection because messages will be sent both from Alice to Bob and from Bob to Alice. The onion proxy at Alice's end knows all the symmetric keys $key_i$ (it sent them in the original onion), but the onion proxy at Bob's end does not know all these $key_i$ values: if it did, clearly it could trace messages through the network and break Alice's anonymity! So how can messages be sent from Bob to Alice? The answer is that messages travelling in this reverse direction go through a reverse process: each $OR_i$ in the connection <u>adds</u> a layer of encryption (rather than <u>removing</u> a layer as it does in the forward direction) using its key $key_i$. Then, Alice's onion proxy removes all these layers itself (since it knows all these keys) and passes the plaintext to the application proxy. (Note that in the actual design and implementation of onion routing, for additional security the authors supply two symmetric keys – one for each direction – in the original onion that establishes the connection. Thus, for communication of messages in the forward direction, $OR_i$ will receive data from $OR_{i-1}$, remove the outer layer by decrypting using $key_{iForward}$, and send the remaining portion to $OR_{i+1}$. For communication of messages in the reverse direction, $OR_i$ will receive data from $OR_{i+1}$, add an outer layer by encrypting using $key_{iReverse}$, and send the resulting value to $OR_{i-1}$.) *Very simple, and very clever!*

An example onion routing network is shown in Fig. 3.2.

### 3.3.1.3   Considerations

The <u>threat model for the onion routing network</u> is as follows. It is assumed that the network is subject to both passive and active attacks, and that traffic may be monitored and modified by both external attackers and internal attackers (including compromised onion routers). Multiple attackers can cooperate and share information and inferences, and attackers can move around to monitor different parts of the network at different times, but it is assumed that attackers are not able to observe the entire network at any given time (i.e., there is no global active or passive attacker). Assuming that the encryption algorithms used in the network are sufficiently strong to resist cryptanalysis, the techniques available to attackers are

- *Marker attacks* (where a compromised onion router uses distinguishable markers (that indicate where data cells begin) that can be observed elsewhere in the network),
- *Timing attacks* (where the attacker observes or causes a timing signature in the data cells of a single message in one portion of the network that can be subsequently measured in another portion of the network), and

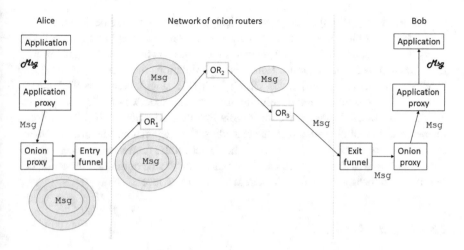

**Fig. 3.2   Onion Routing Network.** Alice's application proxy transforms her message to a generic format, her onion proxy adds layers of encryption, and each onion router $OR_i$ removes a single layer using its symmetric key $key_i$. Bob's application proxy transforms the received plaintext message to its application-specific format for delivery to Bob's application

– *Volume attacks* (where the observation of the number of cells of a single message at one compromised onion router can be correlated with corresponding cell totals observed at other compromised onion routers).

Despite these possible attacks, the overall goal of the network is to prevent traffic analysis (tracing messages along an anonymous connection in order to discover who is communicating with whom).

Onion routing was <u>designed to achieve close to real-time communication</u>. Note that although the *onion* is encrypted in layers using the public key of each *onion router* chosen for the anonymous connection, one of the primary tasks of the *onion* is to give a random symmetric key $key_i$ to each onion router $OR_i$. Thus, once the anonymous connection has been established, all data sent over this connection is encrypted in layers using symmetric encryption algorithms. This means that the delay incurred through the use of public key cryptography happens only at connection setup time, and the bidirectional communication between Alice and Bob can be as close to real-time as possible (since symmetric encryption/decryption is much faster than asymmetric encryption/decryption).

To <u>minimize the risk of traffic analysis</u>, splitting and padding is used so that all information (onions, message data, and network control material) is sent through the onion routing network in uniform-sized cells. Furthermore, it is important to note that onion routing defines a route at the application layer of the communications protocol stack, not at the IP layer. In particular, although the series of *onion routers* in an anonymous connection is fixed for the lifetime of that connection, the actual path that data travels between individual *onion routers* is determined by the underlying IP network (and may therefore change from moment to moment).

In order to <u>enhance usability and applicability</u>, the *proxies* are designed to be as generic as possible. In particular, the goal is that onion routing can be used with applications that are proxy-aware, as well as with several non-proxy-aware applications, without requiring modifications to the applications themselves. By 1999, the supported protocols included HTTP, FTP, SMTP, rlogin, telnet, NNTP, finger, whois, and raw sockets, and development work was underway to support Socks5, DNS, NFS, IRC, HTTPS, SSH, and Virtual Private Networks (VPNs). In addition, the network is designed such that one can adjust the placement of the different *proxies* in order to vary which elements of the system must be trusted by users and in what way. Proxies that reside in the same place can also be combined for efficiency purposes (so that they are only distinct at a conceptual level).

### 3.3.1.4   Tor

The technology proposed in the onion routing papers published between 1996 and 1999 was available briefly as an open wide-area network, but the only long-running public deployment was proof-of-concept code that implemented five onion routers on a single Sun Ultra 2 2170 machine. In 2004, Roger Dingledine, Nick Matthewson, and Paul Syverson published a paper (2004) presenting a modified and extended implementation that they called *Tor* (an acronym for "The Onion Routing", and the subsequent non-profit organization incorporated in 2006 was named *Tor Project* for "The Onion Routing Project"). *Tor*, which was deployed in October 2002 under a free and open software license, was a third-generation onion routing system (see the discussion in (Syverson 2011b, Section 4)) and it incorporated selected elements from the previous two designs, along with additional improvements described in (Syverson 2011b). Its features included the following:

- *Perfect forward secrecy* – keys used for the layered encryption of traffic are ephemeral and are deleted immediately when the anonymous connection is taken down;
- *Use of the standard SOCKS proxy interface* – a separate *application proxy* for each application was no longer needed;
- *No mixing, link padding (cover traffic), or traffic shaping* – providing efficiency without any provable anonymity degradation;
- *Multiplexing of many TCP streams over a single circuit* – providing both improved efficiency and improved anonymity;
- *Leaky-pipe circuits* – allowing traffic to exit the circuit prior to the end, potentially mitigating traffic shape and volume attacks;
- *Congestion control* – allowing nodes at the edge of the network to detect congestion or flooding, and to send less traffic until the congestion has subsided;
- *Directory servers* – allowing certain trusted nodes to hold (digitally signed) network state information which can be downloaded periodically by all other nodes;
- *Variable exit policies* – allowing any node to advertise a policy describing the hosts and ports to which it will connect so that each operator can decide what types of traffic will be permitted to exit from his/her node;

- *End-to-end integrity checking* – preventing compromised nodes from facilitating certain attacks by modifying the contents of data cells as they pass by; and
- *Rendezvous points and hidden services* – allowing clients to negotiate a way to connect with hidden servers at any time, allowing robustness if nodes in a path go down or change keys.

*Tor* has continued to evolve since 2004 and actively addresses issues and integrates new features as needed and appropriate. It is generally acknowledged to be the most widely-used tool for anonymity online with well over 2 million directly-connecting users around the world in mid-2020 (see [https://metrics.torproject.org/userstats-relay-country.html]; see also (Jansen and Johnson 2016) for more accurate measurements). Historically, the number of active users has tended to spike in a country whenever citizen oppression of some form occurs in that country, and it is well-known that individuals sometimes depend on this technology with their very lives. Applications such as *Tor Browser* (see [https://www.torproject.org/]) have made *Tor* readily accessible to many users (particularly those without a strong technical or software background).

### 3.3.2 Enhancements

There have been many enhancements to onion routing over the years to improve performance, security, or usability. A few of the most important changes are listed in this section.

The most significant enhancement to the original onion routing proposal was the development and deployment of *Tor* late in 2002, with the Usenix Security paper describing its design appearing in 2004 (Dingledine et al. 2004). This third generation onion router included many improvements (as outlined in the previous section) and put this technology into the hands of anyone that wanted to use it.

Hidden services, although they existed (in a rudimentary form) in the original onion routing implementation, were made significantly more reliable and usable with the introduction of *Tor* in 2002. Anonymous ("hidden") servers intentionally mask their IP addresses through *Tor* circuits and then provide services such as websites, marketplaces, or chatrooms. These services have a domain name of *.onion* (instead of *.com*, *.org*, *.gov*, *.ca*, and so on) and cannot be accessed outside of *Tor*: they are invisible to ordinary web browsers and search engines. Unlike typical *Tor* use where the client is anonymous but the server is known, hidden services provide bidirectional anonymity where both parties remain anonymous and never communicate directly with one another (Victors 2015). While it is true that hidden services are sometimes used for illegal activities on the *dark web*, they are also used for many legitimate purposes, such as censorship-free blogging in repressive regimes, whistleblowing, and creating chat rooms that are not vulnerable to social network analysis (Dingledine 2011 (e-mail to tor-talk)). In recent years, many of the biggest sites on the Internet have made themselves available through these hidden services (now more commonly known as *onion services*); one prominent example is Facebook, but the millions of sites that use Cloudfare's security and performance offerings will have the *Cloudfare onion service* enabled by default (https://blog. cloudflare.com/cloudflare-onion-service/). Journalism sites (such as *New York Times*), government sites (such as the US *Central Intelligence Agency* (https://www. cia.gov/stories/story/cias-latest-layer-an-onion-site/)), and many others now have onion service versions of their public-facing websites to allow users to connect privately (using *Tor browser*, for example).

The notion of "guard nodes" was introduced in 2006 (Øverlier and Syverson 2006) (see also (Wails 2020)) as a refinement of the "helper nodes" proposed in (Wright et al. 2003)). Initially, a *Tor* user client would select 3 nodes (called "relays") at random to create an anonymous connection to the intended receiver: an initial (or entry) relay; a middle relay; and an exit relay. However, it was found that this increased the risk that an attacker who had compromised several nodes in the network would have his/her nodes chosen by the user at some point, leading to loss of anonymity (particularly in the case where the compromised nodes are the first and last in the user's connection). Guard nodes are a specific subset of all the nodes in the network (and a node can only become a guard node if it satisfies a specified set of criteria); each user must choose a guard node as the first node in its connection (it can randomly choose the middle and exit nodes), and thereafter will use that same guard node (or one of a very small fixed set of guard nodes) for a specified amount of time. Various parameters for guard nodes have been examined over the years (how a node can become a guard node; how a user can choose a guard node; how many guard nodes the user can have in his/her set; how long a user should keep using a specific guard node; etc.) and extensive experimentation has been done to find the values that minimize the risk of anonymity loss to the user.

As mentioned in Sect. 3.3.1, *Tor Browser* was introduced in 2008. This made *Tor* available to large numbers of users who did not have either the time or the technical expertise to install, configure, and manage stand-alone client software for accessing the *Tor* network.

### 3.3.3  Strengths

Similarly to mix networks, with onion routing networks Goldschlag, Reed, and Syverson have proposed a fairly simple and elegant PET that is effective in meeting its design goals. Benefitting from 15 to 20 years of intense analysis, this appears to be a tool that provides good anonymity assurances in online environments, with strong resistance to both passive and active realistic attackers. (See, for example, (Feigenbaum et al. 2012) which provides a characterization of onion routing's anonymity protections in standard cryptographic terms (the *universal composability* framework).) Furthermore, the availability of *Tor* (and particularly the availability of *Tor Browser*) has made this PET accessible to virtually anyone, as evidenced by the very high usage statistics around the world.

A significant strength of this technology is that onion routing has wide applicability: it can be used to protect a user's IP address in any TCP-based protocol. It can therefore provide anonymity services to web searches, secure shell connections, instant messaging communications, and many other application-level interactions.

### 3.3.4 Disadvantages, Limitations, and Weaknesses

For much of its existence, the primary limitation of *Tor* was widely acknowledged to be its sluggish performance. It was not as "real-time" as onion networks were originally conceived to be, and the delay in establishing anonymous connections and in transmitting data from sender to receiver was quite noticeable to users. There are several reasons for this, including the fact that cryptographic operations are inherently computationally intensive, links in the network have varying bandwidth capacities (even in the absence of traffic), and connections are made up of nodes that are hosted in random locations around the globe (so, for example, a connection between Alice and a website located geographically close to her might cross an ocean several times or circumnavigate the globe more than once). In general, these performance problems discouraged the use of this PET: many people only used *Tor* when they felt that they really needed anonymity for a specific reason, rather than using it by default for all their Internet activity. Finding ways to improve performance without sacrificing anonymity has been, and continues to be, a very active research area within the PETs community. Example efforts in this area include the following.

- *Entry guard selection*: As mentioned in Sect. 3.3.2, a number of experiments and simulations have been done to find appropriate parameters for the selection and long-term use of entry guards. A nice introduction to this research area can be found in (Elahi et al. 2012).
- *Path selection algorithm*: A number of researchers have looked at how the route for an anonymous connection can be chosen by the *Tor* user client. For example, is it possible to select entry, middle, and exit relays that are not too distant from the client (thus avoiding unnecessary ocean crossings!) to improve the speed of connection construction without unduly increasing the risk of anonymity loss? Various proposals have been examined in several papers; the recent paper by Rochet et al. (2020) provides a good overview.
- *Load balancing*: Performance in an onion routing network requires good load balancing in order to avoid delays caused by either congestion or relay outages due to too much traffic. However, security in these networks also requires good load balancing: it is important to ensure that an attacker (a compromised node) is not able to process a disproportionately large amount of the network traffic. But load balancing in *Tor* is more difficult than, say, load balancing in a corporate LAN because *Tor* relays are run by volunteers who may not correctly report (or may not report at all) their actual relay bandwidths, which is the information that

*Tor* clients use to make route selection decisions. Understanding the best algorithms and practices in this area is also an active research topic; see, for example, (Johnson et al. 2017) for a thorough analysis of several approaches, as well as (Jansen et al. 2018) and (Traudt et al. 2020) for recent specific proposals.

As a result of this extensive work to improve performance, today *Tor* is far less sluggish than it was in its early years. In fact, websites blocking *Tor* or sending *Tor* users to CAPTCHAs are typically a bigger stumbling block to wider *Tor* adoption than performance at the present time.

Other limitations or weaknesses of *Tor*, or of onion routing in general, typically arise from academic research into potential threats or vulnerabilities related to low-latency anonymity networks. Some examples of this are as follows.

- *Routing attacks*: Sun et al. (2015) have examined the kinds of attacks that can be directed against *Tor* users if the attacker is able to compromise Autonomous Systems (ASes) in the Internet routing network. This threat was first discussed in the context of anonymity networks generally in (Feamster and Dingledine 2004), and specifically for *Tor* in (Edman and Syverson 2009). Sun et al., show that AS-level adversaries can increase the chance of observing user traffic in at least one direction at both ends of the communication, can arrange to lie on the Border Gateway Protocol (BGP) paths for increasing numbers of users over time, and can manipulate Internet routing to discover users using specific guard nodes and to do traffic analysis. In a subsequent paper, the authors propose some counter-measures to mitigate the risks of these attacks (Sun et al. 2017), but designing anonymity systems that properly take into account the dynamics of Internet routing is a continuing research topic; see, for example, (Wails et al. 2018) and (Wan et al. 2019).
- *Sybil attacks*: In a Sybil attack, an attacker obtains many virtual identities in order to gain unfairly large influence in a network. This can occur in many types of environments and can take many different forms; in *Tor*, it means a single attacker using many identities to control a large number of relays in order to attempt to deanonymize users. Sybil attacks are difficult to recognize and prevent in most settings, but are especially hard in *Tor*, which is a volunteer-run distributed anonymity network. Winter et al. (2016) developed a tool that they called *sybilhunter* to detect Sybil relays in *Tor*. Using this tool to examine 9 years of archived *Tor* network data, they discovered many insights into real-world Sybil attacks and provided useful techniques for uncovering these attacks, thereby improving security for all users. Research in this challenging area continues.
- *Website fingerprinting attacks*: Website fingerprinting allows a local passive adversary, who monitors a web-browsing client's encrypted (i.e., *Tor*) channel, to determine the client's web activity. A local adversary is one that can observe the network close to the client, such as an Internet Service Provider (ISP), a wiretapper, or a packet sniffer. In a website fingerprinting attack, such an adversary may be able to achieve accurate page classification to learn the client's browsing

behaviour. Wang and Goldberg (2016) showed that, although much previous research in this area was performed under laboratory conditions (leading to doubt that the results would be applicable to real-world settings), they could substantially improve existing attacks to make them operate effectively on packet sequences collected "in the wild". Thus, research continues into techniques to understand and defend against website fingerprinting attacks in *Tor*, both for ordinary websites (see, for example, (Wang and Goldberg 2017)) and for hidden services (see, for example, (Panchenko et al. 2017)).

– *Performance enhancing mechanisms attacks*: Performance enhancing mechanisms that have been proposed for use in *Tor* (including circuit scheduling, congestion control, and bandwidth allocation mechanisms) can give rise to attacks that rely on network measurements as a side channel. An example discussed in some detail in Geddes et al. (2013) is so-called *induced throttling attacks* that exploit such mechanisms to artificially throttle a circuit, resulting in (sometimes substantially) reduced anonymity for clients.

– *Attacks targeting a specific user or a small set of specific users*: Jaggard and Syverson (2017) (see also (Syverson 2017)) have argued that most *Tor* design decisions have focused on protecting against adversaries who are equally interested in any user of the network, but that adversaries who selectively target specific users are more significant threats to those who most rely on *Tor*'s protection. Furthermore, they have shown that the difference in goals and strategy of targeting adversaries (compared to the traditional adversary model) can lead to "attacks on *Tor* users at least as devastating and relevant as any *Tor* attacks set out in previous research". Ongoing research aims to understand how best to incorporate defenses against this new attacker model into *Tor*.

As with the research on performance improvement discussed above, research to improve the security of onion networks (i.e., to reduce any risk to user anonymity) continues at an active pace throughout the PETs community.

## 3.4  Summary

This chapter has looked at three example privacy enhancing technologies whose goal is to limit **exposure** by hiding the identity of the user: *mix networks*, *anonymous remailers*, and *onion routing networks*. At some level these are similar technologies: *onion routing* is a low-latency *mix-type network*, and Type II and Type III *remailers* are enhancements of the original *mix network* proposal. However, there are important differences in the services supported (e-mail versus web browsing, for example) and in how the services are provided (a *mix network* versus a Type 0 or Type I mail-forwarding *remailer*, for example).

A mix node hides the correspondence between its input items and its output items, and a mix network constructs a cascade of mix nodes between the sender and the receiver. Mix networks introduced the concept of layers of encryption (which are successively added or removed as a message traverses the network). Variations over the years have explored different topologies, mix types, and routing strategies to improve anonymity, latency, and bandwidth consumption.

Anonymous remailers began as simple mail-forwarding services that removed the original sender information and replaced it with the name of the service. Over time they evolved to Type I (cypherpunk), Type II (mixmaster), and Type III (mixminion) remailers to add features and improve privacy; however, long latency in delivery times continues to be a concern with this technology.

Onion routing was designed to achieve as close to real-time communication as possible. To do this, it constructs a fixed connection between Alice and Bob that persists for the length of their communication session. Once this connection is in place, fast symmetric cryptographic algorithms are used to minimize all processing delay (while still providing strong privacy properties). Extensive effort has been made over the years to improve resistance to a variety of attacks, as well as to improve efficiency. *Tor* is an implementation of onion routing that has been used by many people around the world to protect their Internet communication and activities.

In all three of the PETs described in this chapter, the focus is on providing anonymity: all parties should be prevented from learning the *identity* of the sender. On the other hand, the *action* of the sender (the *fact* that a message was sent and, in particular, the actual *content* of the message) is visible to both the intended recipient and to third-party observers of the network. The *action* is not hidden from observers at the receiving end because, in these PETs, the message is delivered to the recipient in plaintext. If Alice wishes to hide her *action* from third-party observers close to Bob's end of the communication, she may choose to start by encrypting the message for Bob (if she knows Bob's public key), but this step is not an intrinsic part of any of these PETs.

In the following chapter, we will look at PETs whose goal is to limit **exposure** by instead hiding the *action* of the user, even if the *identity* of the user is known to all. In this category, we will discuss *transport layer security* (SSL/TLS), *network layer security* (one specific mode of IPsec), and *private information retrieval* (PIR).

**Questions for Personal Reflection and/or Group Discussion**

1. As discussed in Sect. 3.1.2, a large number of variations on the basic *mix network* have been studied. Choose any of the listed variations and find the paper that proposed and analyzed this specific variation. How does this variation compare with the original *mix network* in terms of *anonymity*, *latency*, and *bandwidth*?
2. Download and use *Tor Browser* for a full day. How was your experience? Comment on *Tor Browser's* usability, performance, features, and limitations compared with the browser that you typically use. Was there anything that you were unable to do or search for with *Tor Browser* that is easy with your regular browser? Was there something about *Tor Browser* that you found especially interesting/useful/enjoyable?

# References

I. Ben Guirat, D. Gosain, C. Diaz, Mixim: A general purpose simulator for mixnet, in *Privacy Enhancing Technologies Symposium, HotPETs Session*, (2020)

D. Chaum, Untraceable electronic mail, return addresses, and digital pseudonyms. Commun. ACM **24**(2) (1981, Feb)

L. Cottrell, Mixmaster and remailer attacks, *essay* (1994)

G. Danezis, R. Dingledine, N. Matthewson, Mixminion: Design of a type III anonymous remailer protocol, in *Symposium on Security and Privacy*, (2003), pp. 2–15

W. Diffie, M.E. Hellman, New directions in cryptography. IEEE Trans. Inf. Theory **IT-22**(6), 644–654 (1976, Nov)

R. Dingledine, What is tor used for?, *e-mail to tor-talk chat group* (2011, Nov 3)

R. Dingledine, N. Matthewson, P.F. Syverson, Tor: The second-generation onion router, in *Usenix Security Symposium*, (2004), p. 17

G.F. du Pont, The time has come for limited liability for operators of true anonymity remailers in cyberspace: An examination of the possibilities and perils. J. Technol. Law Policy **6**, 175–218 (2001)

M. Edman, P. Syverson, AS-awareness in Tor path selection, in *Proceedings of the 16th ACM Conference on Computer and Communications Security*, (Chicago, Illinois, USA, 2009, Nov), pp. 380–389

T. Elahi, K. Bauer, M. AlSabah, R. Dingledine, I. Goldberg, Changing of the guards: A framework for understanding and improving entry guard selection in tor, in *Proceedings of the ACM Workshop on Privacy in the Electronic Society*, (2012, Oct), pp. 43–54

N. Feamster, R. Dingledine, Location diversity in anonymity networks, in *Proceedings of the ACM Workshop on Privacy in the Electronic Society*, (Washington, DC, USA, 2004, Oct 28), pp. 66–76

J. Feigenbaum, A. Johnson, P. Syverson, Probabilistic analysis of onion routing in a black-box model. ACM Trans. Inf. Syst. Secur. (TISSEC). **15**(3), article 14, 28pp (2012, Nov)

J. Geddes, R. Jansen, N. Hopper, How low can you go: Balancing performance with anonymity in tor, in *Privacy Enhancing Technologies Symposium*, (2013, July 10–12), pp. 164–184

D.M. Goldschlag, M.G. Reed, P.F. Syverson, Hiding routing information, in *Information Hiding*, ed. by R. Anderson, (Springer, LNCS 1174, New York, 1996), pp. 137–150

D.M. Goldschlag, M.G. Reed, P.F. Syverson, Privacy on the internet, in *Internet Society INET'97*, (Kuala Lumpur, Indonesia, 1997, June)

D.M. Goldschlag, M.G. Reed, P.F. Syverson, Onion routing. Commun. ACM **42**(2), 39–41 (1999, Feb)

A. Greenberg, *This Machine Kills Secrets: How Wikileakers, Cypherpunks, and Hacktivists Aim to Free the World's Information* (Dutton, 2012)

J. Helsingius, Press release 30.8.1996, 1996

A. Jaggard, P.F. Syverson, Onions in the crosshairs: When the man really *is* out to get you, in *Proceedings of the Workshop on Privacy in the Electronic Society*, (2017, Oct 30), pp. 141–151

R. Jansen, A. Johnson, Safely measuring tor, in *Proceedings of the ACM Conference on Computer and Communications Security*, (Vienna, Austria, 2016, Oct 24–28), pp. 1553–1567

R. Jansen, M. Traudt, J. Geddes, C. Wacek, M. Sherr, P. Syverson, KIST: Kernel-informed socket transport for tor. ACM Trans. Privacy Secur. article no. 3, 37pp (2018, Dec)

A. Johnson, R. Jansen, N. Hopper, A. Segal, P.F. Syverson, PeerFlow: Secure load balancing in tor. Proc. Privacy Enhancing Technol. **2**, 1–21 (2017)

R. Merkle, Secure communications over insecure channels. Commun. ACM **21**(4), 294–299 (1978, Apr)

L. Øverlier, P.F. Syverson, Locating hidden servers, in *IEEE Symposium on Security and Privacy*, (2006), pp. 100–114

A. Panchenko, A. Mitseva, M. Henze, F. Lanze, K. Wehrle, T. Engel, Analysis of fingerprinting techniques for tor hidden services, in *Proceedings of the Workshop on Privacy in the Electronic Society*, (2017, Oct 30), pp. 165–175

A. Piotrowska, J. Hayes, T. Elahi, S. Meiser, G. Danezis, The loopix anonymity system, in *Proceedings of the 26th USENIX Security Symposium*, (Vancouver, BC, Canada, 2017, Aug 16–18), pp. 1199–1216. (See also *arXiv.com, 1703.00536*, 16pp., 1 March 2017)

M.G. Reed, P.F. Syverson, D.M. Goldschlag, Proxies for anonymous routing, in *Proceedings 12th Annual Computer Security Applications Conference*, (San Diego, CA, USA, 1996, Dec 9–13), pp. 95–104

M.G. Reed, P.F. Syverson, D.M. Goldschlag, Protocols using anonymous connections: Mobile applications, in *Security Protocols 5th International Workshop*, (Paris, France, 1997, Apr 7–9), pp. 13–23

M.G. Reed, P.F. Syverson, D.M. Goldschlag, Anonymous connections and onion routing. IEEE J. Select. Areas Commun. **16**(4), 482–494 (1998, May)

R.L. Rivest, A. Shamir, L. Adleman, A method for obtaining digital signatures and public-key cryptosystems. Commun. ACM **21**(2), 120–126 (1978, Feb)

F. Rochet, R. Wails, A. Johnson, P. Mittal, O. Pereira, CLAPS: Client-location-aware path selection in tor, in *ACM Conference on Computer and Communications Security*, (2020, Nov 9–13), pp. 17–34

A. Serjantov, G. Danezis, Towards an information theoretic metric for anonymity, in *Proceedings of the Second International Workshop on Privacy Enhancing Technologies,* (Springer, LNCS 2482, San Francisco, USA, 2002, Apr 14–15), pp. 41–53

A. Serjantov, R. Dingledine, P.F. Syverson, From a trickle to a flood: Active attacks on several mix types, in *2002 International Workshop on Information Hiding*, (Springer LNCS 2578, 2003), pp. 36–52

F. Shirazi, E. Andreeva, M. Kohlweiss, C. Diaz, Multiparty routing: Secure routing for mixnets, *ePrint archive*, 1708.03387v2, (2017, Nov 9)

V. Shmatikov, M.-H. Wang, Timing analysis in low-latency mix networks: Attacks and defenses, in *Proceedings of ESORICS*, (2006), pp. 18–33

Y. Sun, A. Edmundson, L. Vanbever, O. Li, J. Rexford, M. Chiang, P. Mittal, RAPTOR: Routing attacks on privacy in tor, in *Usenix Security Symposium*, (2015, Aug 12–14), pp. 271–286

Y. Sun, A. Edmundson, N. Feamster, M. Chiang, P. Mittal, Counter-RAPTOR: Safeguarding tor against active routing attacks, in *IEEE Symposium on Security and Privacy*, (2017, May 22–24), 16p

P.F. Syverson, Sleeping dogs lie on a bed of onions but wake when mixed, in *Privacy Enhancing Technologies Symposium, HotPETs Session*, (2011a)

P.F. Syverson, A peel of onion, in *Proceedings of the 27th Annual Computer Security Applications Conference*, (Orlando, Florida, USA, 2011b, Dec 5–9), pp. 123–137

P.F. Syverson, presentation to *Privacy Enhancing Technologies Symposium, HotPETs session*, on the paper "Oft Target: Tor adversary models that don't miss the mark", (2017, July 21)

P.F. Syverson, D.M. Goldschlag, M.G. Reed, Anonymous connections and onion routing, in *Proceedings IEEE Symposium on Security and Privacy*, (1997, May 4–7), pp. 44–54

M. Traudt, R. Jansen, A. Johnson, FlashFlow: A secure speed test for tor. arXiv.com, 2004.09583, 20 (2020, Apr 20)

J. Victors, The onion name system: Tor-powered distributed DNS for tor hidden services, Master's thesis, Utah State University, All Graduate Theses and Dissertations 4484, 2015

R. Wails, presentation to *Privacy Enhancing Technologies Symposium, HotPETs session*, on the paper "CLAPS: Client-Location-Aware Path Selection in Tor" (by Florentin Rochet, Ryan Wails, Aaron Johnson, Prateek Mittal, and Olivier Pereira), (2020, July 23)

R. Wails, Y. Sun, A. Johnson, M. Chiang, P. Mittal, Tempest: Temporal dynamics in anonymity systems. Proc. Privacy Enhancing Technol. **2018**(3), 22–42 (2018, June)

G. Wan, A. Johnson, R. Wails, S. Wagh, P. Mittal, Guard placement attacks on path selection algorithms for tor. Proc. Privacy Enhancing Technol. **2019**(4), 272–291 (2019, Oct)

T. Wang, I. Goldberg, On realistically attacking tor with website fingerprinting. Proc. Privacy Enhancing Technol. **4**, 21–36 (2016)

T. Wang, I. Goldberg, Walkie-talkie: An efficient defense against passive website fingerprinting attacks, in *Usenix Security Symposium*, (2017, Aug 16–18), pp. 1375–1390

P. Winter, R. Ensafi, K. Loesing, N. Feamster, Identifying and characterizing sybils in the tor network, in *Usenix Security Symposium*, (2016, Aug, 10–12), pp. 1169–1185

M. Wright, M. Adler, B.N. Levine, C. Shields, Defending anonymous communication against passive logging attacks, in *IEEE Symposium on Security and Privacy*, (2003, May), pp. 28–41

# Chapter 4
# Limiting Exposure by Hiding the Action

**Abstract** This chapter considers the second leaf in the privacy tree, examining PETs that limit exposure by hiding the user's actions. As examples of this category, the following PETs are described: transport layer security; network layer security (IPsec in transport mode); and private information retrieval. As with the previous chapter, for each of these examples, the original scheme is given, enhancements made over the years are presented, and strengths and limitations of the technology are discussed.

**Keywords** Transport layer security · SSL/TLS · Network layer security · IPsec · Transport mode · Private information retrieval · Database privacy · IT-PIR · C-PIR

In this chapter, we consider another way to limit *exposure* of a user. Again, the goal is to de-couple or disassociate the user's *identity* and the user's *actions* from the perspective of external third-party observers of the network, and perhaps also from the perspective of the intended target or recipient of the actions. In Chap. 3, this de-coupling was accomplished by hiding the *identity* of the user, even though the *actions* were visible to everyone (for example, the transmitted message was in the clear at the receiver's end of the connection). Here, the de-coupling is accomplished by hiding the *actions* themselves, whereas the *identity* is visible. (Note that, in both cases, the user can choose to take additional steps to hide the portion that remains visible (i.e., the *actions* or the *identity*), but this is truly an additional step that is not part of the functionality of the PET itself. In Chap. 5, we will look at PETs that are designed to hide both the *identity* and the *actions* from observers.)

The example PETs discussed in this chapter are *transport layer security* (the *SSL/TLS* protocol), *network layer security* (the *IPsec* protocol, in a specific configuration known as *transport mode*), and *private information retrieval* (*PIR*).

© The Editor(s) (if applicable) and The Author(s), under exclusive license
to Springer Nature Switzerland AG 2021
C. Adams, *Introduction to Privacy Enhancing Technologies*,
https://doi.org/10.1007/978-3-030-81043-6_4

## 4.1 Transport Layer Security (SSL/TLS)

*Netscape Communications Corporation* (originally *Mosaic Communications Corporation*) designed and developed the *Secure Sockets Layer* (SSL) protocol, version 1.0, in 1994 for use with the *Netscape Navigator* browser (the dominant web browser at the time, with more than 90% of the market share). This original version was never published because some serious security flaws were found in the protocol; however, the subsequent version, SSL 2.0, was released in 1995. Public scrutiny quickly revealed security weaknesses in this version, and the company hired security consultant Paul Kocher to help them completely redesign the protocol. SSL 3.0 was released in 1996 and formed the basis for all subsequent work on this protocol.

In order to increase and intensify public analysis, SSL was submitted to the *Internet Engineering Task Force* (IETF) with the goal of standardizing the protocol so that it could be used by any web browser and any web server. The IETF *Network Working Group* made some minor modifications to the protocol (nothing significant, but enough to preclude interoperability with SSL 3.0) and changed the name to *Transport Layer Security* (TLS). In January 1999, the TLS 1.0 protocol specification was published by IETF as RFC 2246 (1999). Work has continued on this specification, with TLS 1.1 published in 2006 (RFC4346 2006), TLS 1.2 published in 2008 (RFC5246 2008), and TLS 1.3 published in 2018 (RFC8446 2018).

The SSL/TLS protocol was not designed specifically as a PET. Its goal was to protect communications between a web browser and a website to which it is connected so that eavesdropping, message tampering, and message forgery are prevented. Thus, it aimed to provide end-point authentication and communications confidentiality over the Internet. Its specific (if unstated) goal was to facilitate the nascent e-commerce market by giving users confidence that they were indeed at the website they were expecting (through cryptographic authentication of the web server) and that their credit card and other sensitive information would not be compromised during a purchasing transaction (through cryptographic confidentiality and integrity mechanisms). However, given the functionality provided by this protocol, we note that it works well as a PET to protect *exposure* by hiding the *actions* of the user.

### 4.1.1 The Basic Scheme

Since SSL 1.0 was never published and SSL 2.0 was so quickly replaced, we will treat SSL 3.0 as the "basic" scheme; this is the version that most security researchers are familiar with and the one that brought the concept of a "secure connection to a web server" to the general public. SSL 3.0 was never officially made available as a written specification by Netscape or any other group, and so it was published by IETF in 2011 as a historical document in RFC 6101 (2011) to allow easy referencing to the protocol; the description in this section is largely taken from that source.

The Secure Sockets Layer protocol consists of two layers: a *record protocol* on the bottom layer that is used to encapsulate various *higher-level protocols* in the top layer. This two-layered protocol sits on top of (i.e., is transmitted by) some reliable transport protocol (e.g., the Transmission Control Protocol, TCP), which itself sits on top of a networking protocol (such as IP), a data-link protocol, and physical layer communications software and hardware. Furthermore, SSL sits underneath (i.e., transmits) some application protocol – in fact, SSL is designed to be application protocol independent so that any application-level protocol can be put on top of the SSL protocol without modification.

The *record protocol* receives data from one of the higher-level protocols in non-empty blocks of arbitrary size. It first fragments this data into *SSLPlaintext* records of $2^{14}$ bytes or less. Each record contains a *protocol version* ("3.0" in this case), a *content type* (indicating which higher-level protocol the data came from), an integer specifying the *length* of the data, and the *data* itself. The record is then compressed (using the compression algorithm defined in the current session state) into an *SSLCompressed* record. This record is now protected (using the encryption and MAC (message authentication code) algorithms defined in the current CipherSpec) to an *SSLCiphertext* record. Finally, the *SSLCiphertext* record is handed to the underlying transport protocol for transmission to the intended destination. (Note that transmissions always include a sequence number so that missing, altered, or extra messages are detectable.)

Four *higher-level protocols* have been defined for the top layer of the SSL protocol; they are given as follows.

– *Handshake* protocol: This establishes the secure connection between the client and the server. It enables server authentication and (optionally) client authentication. It also allows negotiation of the cryptographic algorithms (the "Cipher Suite") and agreement on the cryptographic keys and parameters that will be used for the selected algorithms during the session (the "CipherSpec"). The connection thus provides confidentiality, integrity, and authenticity for the client-server communications.
– *Change Cipher Spec* protocol: This is a single message, protected under the current CipherSpec. It is sent by both the client and the server to notify the receiving party that subsequent messages will be protected under the just-negotiated CipherSpec. This message therefore changes the algorithm parameters and keys to new values that have recently been negotiated.
– *Alert* protocol: This is a status message consisting of 2 bytes. The first byte is an *alert level* ("warning" or "fatal") and the second byte is an *alert description* (such as "bad_record_mac", "handshake_failure", "illegal_parameter", "no_certificate", "certificate_revoked", and so on). Alert messages with a level of "fatal" result in the immediate termination of the connection.
– *Application Data* protocol: Application data messages are passed to the *record protocol* to be fragmented, compressed, and encrypted according to the current connection state and CipherSpec. The content of these messages (i.e., the actual application data itself) is treated as transparent data to the record layer: it is not

examined or understood in any way by the *record protocol*. Thus, SSL may readily be used under any application-layer protocol (e.g., FTP, SMTP, etc.); however, it is most commonly used under HTTP (to create the *HTTP-over-SSL* protocol, typically known as "HTTPS").

Clearly, the strength and flexibility of SSL comes from its *Handshake* protocol. RFC 6101 describes this protocol at a high level as follows (Section 5.5 of (RFC6101 2011) reproduced here for completeness):

> *The cryptographic parameters of the session state are produced by the SSL handshake protocol, which operates on top of the SSL record layer. When an SSL client and server first start communicating, they agree on a protocol version, select cryptographic algorithms, optionally authenticate each other, and use public key encryption techniques to generate shared secrets. These processes are performed in the handshake protocol, which can be summarized as follows: the client sends a* client hello *message to which the server must respond with a* server hello *message, or else a fatal error will occur and the connection will fail. The* client hello *and* server hello *are used to establish security enhancement capabilities between client and server. The* client hello *and* server hello *establish the following attributes: Protocol Version, Session ID, Cipher Suite, and Compression Method. Additionally, two random values are generated and exchanged: ClientHello.random and ServerHello.random.*
>
> *Following the hello messages, the server will send its certificate, if it is to be authenticated. Additionally, a* server key exchange *message may be sent, if it is required (e.g., if their server has no certificate, or if its certificate is for signing only). If the server is authenticated, it may request a certificate from the client, if that is appropriate to the cipher suite selected. Now the server will send the* server hello done *message, indicating that the hello-message phase of the handshake is complete. The server will then wait for a client response. If the server has sent a* certificate request *message, the client must send either the* certificate *message or a* no_certificate *alert. The* client key exchange *message is now sent, and the content of that message will depend on the public key algorithm selected between the* client hello *and the* server hello*. If the client has sent a certificate with signing ability, a digitally-signed* certificate verify *message is sent to explicitly verify the certificate.*
>
> *At this point, a* change cipher spec *message is sent by the client, and the client copies the pending CipherSpec into the current CipherSpec. The client then immediately sends the* finished *message under the new algorithms, keys, and secrets. In response, the server will send its own* change cipher spec *message, transfer the pending to the current CipherSpec, and send its* finished *message under the new CipherSpec. At this point, the handshake is complete and the client and server may begin to exchange application layer data.*

The Handshake protocol thus creates a secure channel (a "secure pipe") through which application-level data can flow in both directions between the endpoints (the client and the server). An essential component of this security is the agreement on cryptographic keys that will be used to encrypt/decrypt and MAC/verify the individual messages sent. Multiple options are available within the SSL 3.0 specification for how to achieve this key agreement. For example, the client can generate a 48-byte random value called a *premaster secret*, encrypt this with the server's RSA public key, and send it to the server (who can decrypt with its private key to obtain the value). As another example, the client and server can perform a Diffie-Hellman key agreement computation to jointly derive the *premaster secret* value.

Once both sides know the *premaster secret*, a specified procedure (involving the *premaster secret*, some constant values, the *ClientHello.random*, the *ServerHello. random*, and two cryptographic hash functions MD5 and SHA-1) is used to turn the *premaster secret* into a 48-byte *master secret*. Following this, a similar specified procedure is used to turn the *master secret* into a long string called a *key block*. This *key block* is then partitioned (in this order) into a MAC key for the client, a MAC key for the server, an encryption key for the client, an encryption key for the server, an *initialization vector* (IV) for the client, and an IV for the server. The partitioning is done in such a way that these keys and IVs are the specific sizes required for the MAC and encryption algorithms in the just-negotiated CipherSpec. Once this processing is complete, the *Change Cipher Spec* messages are exchanged and these algorithms, keys, and IVs are used to protect all subsequent traffic.

### 4.1.2    Enhancements

As mentioned in Sect. 4.1, there is very little technical difference between SSL 3.0 and TLS 1.0. For TLS 1.1, two changes were made to add protection against an attack on the way cipher block chaining (CBC) was used in the CipherSpec encryption and MAC algorithms: an explicit IV was specified (rather than an implicit IV); and the way that padding errors were handled was altered.

For TLS 1.2, the strong recommendations of the cryptographic community against the use of the MD5 hash algorithm (because of the speed with which collisions had been found in recent papers) were taken into account. In particular, all uses of MD5 or the MD5/SHA-1 combination were replaced with SHA-256 or with SHA-1 alone. Along with this, CipherSuites for the *Advanced Encryption Standard* (AES) algorithm were added, as well as support for *authenticated encryption* ciphers. The cryptographic algorithms available for use in TLS were thus significantly stronger with this version.

With TLS 1.3, a number of security-relevant improvements were made, such as

- Removing support for specific elliptic curves that were found to be weak,
- Replacing the broken RC4 stream cipher with the stronger ChaCha20 stream cipher,
- Adding stronger elliptic-curve-based key exchange algorithms,
- Adding stronger elliptic-curve-based digital signature algorithms,
- Mandating *perfect forward secrecy* (through the use of ephemeral Diffie-Hellman values during key agreement), and
- Encrypting all *Handshake* messages after the *ServerHello*.

Along with the above security-relevant improvements, at least one privacy-relevant feature has also been explored: protection of the *Server Name Indication* (SNI) information sent in the Client Hello message. In some network configurations, a server will host multiple "virtual" servers at a single underlying network address. If a client desires to use TLS to connect securely to one of these virtual servers, it must be able to tell the host server the name of the virtual server it wishes to contact. The SNI extension was created in 2003 to enable this in TLS 1.0 (RFC3546 2003). However, it was subsequently recognized that this information creates a privacy risk (allowing any observer to know which specific server a client wants to reach) and furthermore enables censorship in some places (see, for example, (Chai et al. 2019)).

This situation led to a proposal in TLS 1.3 for ESNI (Encrypted SNI), which hides the SNI information from observers. Further analysis revealed that ESNI is insufficient (because other types of information in the `Client Hello` message can also be sensitive) and so the IETF TLS Working Group is currently examining a more extensive scheme called *Encrypted Client Hello* (ECH) which aims to protect as much information as possible in this message. Work continues on finding an exact specification for ECH that is interoperable with existing deployed Internet infrastructure. Aside from ESNI/ECH, a general examination of the privacy offered by TLS 1.3 can be found in (Arfaoui et al. 2019).

(In separate but related work, the initial request from the client to a Domain Name Server (DNS) resolver to obtain the IP address that corresponds to the desired host server name must also be protected (otherwise observers will still learn where the client wants to connect). DNS queries and responses may themselves be protected using TLS (DNS-over-TLS (DoT) (RFC7858 2016)), or they may be protected using HTTPS (DNS-over-HTTPS (DoH) (RFC8484 2018)). Implementations of one or both of these mechanisms can be found in many current browsers and DNS resolver services, although some recent analysis has shown that these protections are still not enough (Siby et al. 2020).)

Other changes for TLS 1.3 included deprecating some little-used or obsolete features, and modifying how OCSP responses are sent within *Handshake* messages.

### 4.1.3  Strengths

SSL/TLS is undoubtedly the most widely used security protocol in the world. It is installed in every make and model of web browser (across all computing platforms, including all mobile platforms) and is supported by virtually every existing web server. It is therefore used countless times every day to establish a secure connection between a client and a server, typically for e-commerce purchasing transactions but, more generally, whenever any sensitive information needs to travel over a network between two end points. (For example, in the *Tor* network (see Chap. 3, Sect. 3.3), the connection between each pair of nodes is TLS protected, and *Tor* circuit-building and data exchange take place over those TLS connections.) The analysis and corresponding modifications over the years have resulted in a high degree of confidence in the current specification, TLS 1.3.

As a PET, this protocol can be used to limit *exposure* by hiding the *actions* of a user. Note that the *identities* of both the client and the server are visible to anyone observing the network. These are not explicitly included in the client or server *Hello* messages of the *Handshake* protocol, but will definitely appear in the sender and receiver addressing information of the supporting communication protocols (such as TCP and IP). Consequently, observers of the network will know who is talking with whom (or, at least, which device is talking with which device) even if TLS is used. However, the content of the messages (search requests, web page downloads, and any other transmitted information) will be hidden from all parties except the intended communicants because of the encryption applied by TLS. Thus, no third-party will be able to associate an *identity* with a specific *action* when a TLS connection has been set up.

### 4.1.4   Disadvantages, Limitations, and Weaknesses

The SSL/TLS protocol allows for mutual authentication (that is, authentication of both the client and the server), but it is worth noting that this capability is rarely used in practice. All web servers that support this protocol have a public key certificate (typically referred to as an "SSL certificate") that is used for authentication in the *Handshake* protocol. However, corresponding certificate-based authentication of the client requires that clients (i.e., end users) have a public key certificate for authentication purposes, which essentially necessitates a world-wide *Public Key Infrastructure* (PKI) for ordinary Internet users. Such a PKI does not exist (and may never exist, for a variety of technical and non-technical reasons). Thus, in common practice, unilateral authentication is performed in the *Handshake* protocol: only the server is authenticated, so that the user can be certain that the connection has been made to the intended website. Once the secure channel has been established, the communicating applications can be used to authenticate the end-user, if required: the user can be asked to provide a username/password pair (or 2-factor authentication data, or whatever other authenticating information may be needed) over the protected channel through the application messages themselves. Note that it is important for applications to know whether user authentication will be done within the SSL/TLS protocol (during the *Handshake*) or whether it must be done at the application level after the channel is established, but this is not relevant when the protocol is used as a PET (since the identity is not hidden in any case).

It must also be emphasized that SSL/TLS only constructs a protected channel between the client and the server (e.g., between a web browser and a website). The data transmitted across this channel enjoys a high level of confidentiality, integrity, and authenticity. However, as soon as it leaves the channel (at either end), it is unprotected plaintext data. This is why, in an e-commerce environment, no attacker tries to eavesdrop on the SSL/TLS channel to learn the user's credit card number and home address; rather, the attacker will try to break into the server's database and acquire hundreds or thousands of credit card numbers and addresses at once (if these have not been adequately protected by the server). This understanding is highly relevant to the use of this protocol as a PET: if the intended recipient might store the *action* information in an insecure way, then there is a significant risk that the user's *exposure* privacy will be lost if an attacker can gain access to the recipient's database.

Finally, we note that SSL 1.0, 2.0, and 3.0, and TLS 1.0 and 1.1 have all been officially deprecated for various security reasons (use of broken cryptographic algorithms, vulnerability to man-in-the-middle attacks, and so on). This leaves only TLS 1.2 and 1.3 as supported protocols; however, TLS 1.3 is the universally recommended protocol for all environments due to a number of security enhancements over TLS 1.2 (as mentioned in Sect. 4.1.2).

## 4.2   Network Layer Security (IPsec in Transport Mode)

For the next PET, we turn from (just above) the transport layer to the network layer. Following two decades of previous work in this area by US government departments (the *Advanced Research Projects Agency* (ARPA), the *National Security Agency* (NSA), the *National Institute of Standards and Technology* (NIST), and the *Naval Research Laboratory* (NRL)), corporations (including *Motorola*, *AT&T Bell Labs*, and *Trusted Information Systems* (TIS)), and academic institutions (including *Columbia University*), the IP Security Working Group was formed in the IETF to standardize these efforts as an open collection of security extensions called *IPsec*. In 1995, an initial set of three specifications was published:

- An overall architecture document, entitled *Security Architecture for the Internet Protocol* (RFC1825 1995);
- A document specifying how to do authentication within this architecture, entitled *IP Authentication Header* (RFC1826 1995); and
- A document specifying how to do encryption within this architecture, entitled *IP Encapsulating Security Payload (ESP)* (RFC1827 1995).

Work intensified and expanded greatly over the following 3 years until a suite of 12 specifications was published simultaneously by this Working Group in November 1998.

- Three of these specifications ((RFC2401 1998), (RFC2402 1998), and (RFC2406 1998)) replaced (and obsoleted) the original three above and came to be known collectively as *IPsec-v2*.
- Four other specifications ((RFC2407 1998), (RFC2408 1998), (RFC2409 1998), and (RFC2412 1998)) defined how key management can be accomplished within an *IPsec* environment and came to be known collectively as the *Internet Key Exchange* specifications, or *IKEv1*.
- Another four specifications ((RFC2403 1998), (RFC2404 1998), (RFC2405 1998), and (RFC2410 1998)) described particular cryptographic algorithms and the use of these algorithms within *IPsec*.

– Finally, one document ((RFC2411 1998)) was published as an informational "roadmap" document, explaining what all the other specifications were and how they fit together.

Since 1998, the specification suite has continued to be revised and to grow, reflecting "lessons learned" from significant worldwide implementation and operational experience. The base security and key exchange processes are now reflected in updated specifications collectively known as *IPsec-v3* and *IKEv2*. There are also many new documents specifying profiles for certain environments, configurations for atypical use cases, and a variety of beneficial additions and extensions to the base protocols. The original "roadmap" document has also been extended to incorporate all of these changes (see (RFC6071 2011)).

The goal of *IPsec* is to encrypt and/or authenticate <u>all</u> Internet traffic at the IP level (so that all distributed applications can be secured in a completely transparent way). Thus, security can be provided at the network layer without users or applications needing to worry about the details of cryptographic algorithms and keys. *IPsec* was explicitly designed to extend both *IP version 4 (IPv4)* and *IP version 6 (IPv6)* with solid security mechanisms for users who desire them. Good introductions to *IPsec* can be found in Frankel (2001), Doraswamy and Harkins (2003), and Kozierok (2005, chapter 29).

As with SSL/TLS (see Sect. 4.1 above), *IPsec* can function as a PET that limits **exposure** by hiding the *actions* of the user when this protocol is used in so-called *transport mode* (see Sect. 4.2.1).

### 4.2.1  The Basic Scheme

Given the comprehensive suite of specifications that was published by IETF at the end of 1998, and the fact that these specifications obsoleted the original three and fueled extensive deployment around the world, we will treat *IPsec-v2* and *IKEv1* as the "basic scheme" (rather than *IPsec-v1*).

The architecture document (RFC2401 1998) describes the mechanisms, procedures, and components that are needed to provide security services at the IP layer. It discusses their interrelationship and all the general processing required for incoming messages and for outgoing messages. As summarized in the "roadmap" document (RFC6071 2011), four specific components are defined in the architecture:

– SA (Security Association): a one-way (inbound or outbound) agreement between two communicating peers that specifies the *IPsec* protections to be provided to their communications. This includes the type of protection to be applied, the cryptographic algorithms to use, the keys to employ, and the types of traffic to be protected.
– SPI (Security Parameters Index): a value that, together with the destination address and security protocol (AH or ESP; see below), uniquely identifies a single SA.

- SAD (Security Association Database): each peer's SA repository. This database holds all the information that is needed to facilitate SA processing.
- SPD (Security Policy Database): a database that holds a description of the security protections to be applied to different types and classes of traffic. (Three general classes of traffic are defined in the specification: traffic that is to be discarded; traffic that is allowed without *IPsec* protection; and traffic that requires *IPsec* protection.)

*IPsec* allows the user (or the system administrator) to control the granularity at which a security protection is offered. For example, an encrypted channel can be created to carry all traffic between two security gateways (intermediate systems implementing *IPsec*, such as routers or firewalls), or an encrypted channel can be created for the TCP connection between each pair of hosts communicating across these security gateways.

The *Authentication Header* (AH) document (RFC2402 1998) specifies how integrity protection, data-origin authentication, access control, and replay protection can be provided for IP packets. Cryptographic computation is done using a *hash-based message authentication code* (HMAC) with either MD5 or SHA-1 as the underlying hash function. Data-origin authentication and access control are provided because HMAC uses a secret key that is known only to the communicating entities (no one who does not know this key will be able to construct a valid MAC, meaning that falsely-injected messages will be rejected by the receiver). Furthermore, the MAC is computed over the message, the message length, and a sequence number; this provides both integrity protection and replay protection. AH was specified as mandatory-to-implement in *IPsec-v2*, and so it is fully supported by all compliant implementations.

The *Encapsulating Security Payload* (ESP) document (RFC2406 1998) also specifies how integrity protection, data-origin authentication, access control, and replay and/or traffic analysis protection can be provided for IP packets. However, it also specifies how confidentiality can be provided through encryption. Thus, ESP is the security protocol to use (rather than AH) when the content of the messages needs to be hidden from network observers. Multiple encryption algorithms are possible for ESP (as long as they are supported by both communicants), but one explicitly defined algorithm for *IPsec-v2* is the *Data Encryption Standard* (DES) in *cipher block chaining* (CBC) mode.

The AH and ESP protocols may be applied alone, or in combination with each other (using multiple Security Associations), to provide a desired set of security services in IPv4 and IPv6. Each security protocol supports two modes of use: *transport mode* and *tunnel mode*. In *transport mode*, protection is primarily provided for upper-layer protocols, whereas in *tunnel mode*, protection is applied to full IP packets. We will discuss *tunnel mode* in Chap. 5, but *transport mode* is relevant to the use of *IPsec* as a PET in this current chapter. With *transport mode*, data from the upper protocols (for example, TCP or UDP (User Datagram Protocol) immediately above but, ultimately, application-layer data such as e-mail messages, web traffic, or client-server interactions) is packaged as *payload data* in an IP packet. AH or ESP is applied to this payload data (ensuring integrity, confidentiality, and so on, as desired), header information is added (specifying source and destination addresses), and the packet is transmitted to the next hop on the route to its intended receiver. Clearly, if the ESP protocol is applied for confidentiality purposes, then the user's *action* data, such as his/her web search request, will be hidden from network observers, even though the user's *identity* information (the source IP address in the packet header) will be visible to everyone.

Security services in *IPsec* use shared secret cryptographic keys (for authentication/integrity and for encryption). *IPsec* relies on a separate set of mechanisms for putting these keys in place. One possible (and allowed) mechanism is manual distribution of keys, but this is not very practical in many real-world environments. An automated public-key-based mechanism has also been defined for *IPsec* called the *Internet Key Exchange* (IKE). IKE is used for three distinct, but highly interrelated, purposes: peer authentication; negotiation, modification, and deletion of Security Associations (SAs); and negotiation of authenticated keying material for use within those SAs.

*IKEv1* is defined by a set of four specifications.

- The *OAKLEY Key Determination Protocol* (RFC2412 1998) is an informational document describing a key establishment protocol that two parties can use to agree on secure and secret keying material. It defines a number of different key exchange mechanisms, and the security properties provided by each (such as perfect forward secrecy for keys, identity protection, and entity authentication). It gives theory and background information to explain design decisions and security features of the various options.
- The *Internet Security Association and Key Management Protocol* (ISAKMP) (RFC2408 1998) defines procedures and packet formats to establish (negotiate, modify, and delete) SAs. ISAKMP is a general framework – it can be used to establish SAs for security protocols at all layers of the network stack and can work with many different key exchange protocols (all with different security properties).
- The *Internet IP Security Domain of Interpretation for ISAKMP* (DOI) (RFC2407 1998) defines an *IPsec* DOI for ISAKMP, which means that when *IPsec* uses ISAKMP to negotiate SAs, the AH and ESP protocols will use identical namespaces for algorithms, identical interpretations for various attributes and parameters, and identical key exchange protocol identifiers.
- The *Internet Key Exchange* (IKE) (RFC2409 1998) specifies a particular key exchange protocol that can be used to negotiate authenticated keying material for *IPsec* SAs. It implements a subset of the OAKLEY protocol and uses the ISAKMP framework (with the *IPsec* DOI) to obtain authenticated keying material for the AH and ESP security protocols.

Together, the *IPsec-v2* specifications and the *IKEv1* specifications define how the 1998 generation of *IPsec* is to be implemented and operated. Years of experimentation and experience then led to the next (and current) generation of this technology in 2005.

## *4.2.2   Enhancements*

In December 2005, a new set of *IPsec* specifications was published by IETF; these collectively defined *IPsec-v3* and *IKEv2*. The revised Architecture document (RFC4301 2005) incorporates "lessons learned" from years of implementation experience, specifically clarifying and expanding details that were found to be under-specified or ambiguous in *IPsec-v2*. It also provides much more detail around *IPsec* processing and the use of, and interactions among, the different *IPsec* databases (it additionally defines a new database called PAD (Peer Authorization Database) to assist with the peer authentication process). The revised AH document (RFC4302 2005) does not significantly change the protocol, but *IPsec-v3* specifies that AH is now optional-to-implement (it was mandatory-to-implement in v2). The revised ESP document (RFC4303 2005) adds some algorithms that necessitated changes to packet format and processing, and makes "NULL authentication" (which was mandatory-to-implement in v2) optional-to-implement in v3. Although *IPsec-v2* can still be found in operational use in some environments, *IPsec-v3* officially obsoletes *IPsec-v2* because these two versions are not interoperable.

IKEv2 also officially obsoletes *IKEv1* (because the two versions are not interoperable), but again *IKEv1* can still be found in some operational use. The revised IKE document (RFC4306 2005) clarifies details that were under-specified or ambiguous in *IKEv1*; it modifies key exchanges to make them simpler, faster, and more reliable (by removing some options and mandating a response for every request); and it uses the *IPsec* ESP protocol to protect IKE messages (rather than a method unique to IKE). It also incorporates all the relevant content of OAKLEY, ISAKMP, and DOI, so that this single IKE specification defines all of *IKEv2*. In October 2006 an *IKEv2 Clarifications and Implementation Guidelines* informational document was published by IETF (RFC4718 2006) to clarify sections that were prone to ambiguous interpretations in an effort to promote the development of interoperable implementations. A revised IKEv2 specification was published in September 2010 (RFC5996 2010) incorporating these clarifications and resolving a number of other implementation issues. Finally, some general clean-up to wording and references was done to make the document suitable for progression to official Internet Standard status; this was published as RFC 7296 (also known as STD 79) in October 2014 (RFC7296 2014), (STD79 2014).

As mentioned in Sect. 4.2 above, a number of documents have been published by the IETF describing a variety of profiles, configurations, additions, and extensions to the base *IPsec-v2* and *IPsec-v3* protocols. The documents related to *IPsec-v2* were produced by the *IP Security Working Group*, but when that group concluded (with the publication of the *IPsec-v3* specifications at the end of 2005), all further *IPsec*-related developments were handled by *IPsec Maintenance and Extensions (IPsecME)*, an IETF Working Group created in mid-2008 "to maintain the *IPsec* standard and to facilitate discussion of clarifications, improvements, and extensions to *IPsec*, mostly to ESP and IKEv2" [https://datatracker.ietf.org/wg/ipsecme/about/].

### 4.2.3   Strengths

Perhaps the greatest strength of *IPsec* is that it is transparent to applications (since it is below TCP/UDP in the communications protocol stack), so there is no need to change any software on user or server systems. It can therefore be used to secure remote logins, client/server interactions, e-mail messages, file transfer exchanges, web access, or any other network traffic without any application-level effort. It can also be used to secure the traffic that enables reliable operation of the network itself (for example, routing updates, redirect messages, and communications from new routers announcing their presence) so that such critical information cannot be forged or replayed by malicious users.

A consequence of the above strength is that *IPsec* is also transparent to end users, which is another significant advantage. Within an organization, there is no need to train users on security mechanisms, issue keying material to users, or revoke keying material when users leave the company. This is a huge benefit (in time and cost savings) for managers at all levels and for IT staff.

Another potential benefit is that an organization may choose to implement *IPsec* only on a firewall or router, thus providing strong security for all traffic that crosses a defined network perimeter, while ensuring that traffic within the subnetwork (which may be more trusted) does not incur the overhead of security-related processing. With such a configuration, *IPsec* is often used to create a *virtual private network* (VPN) that allows employees to access their company network securely from any external location.

The above security and usability benefits apply directly to the use of *IPsec* as a PET: the **exposure** of users is reduced by hiding their *actions* from all external network observers, and this happens without requiring any effort from the users themselves.

### 4.2.4   Disadvantages, Limitations, and Weaknesses

As with SSL/TLS (see Sect. 4.1.4 above), users and organizations must be aware that *IPsec* creates a secure channel between two endpoints in order to protect the traffic that is exchanged between them. Once application data exits this channel, it is unprotected plaintext. Therefore, if the data is not properly secured by the receiving application, all privacy protection that was guaranteed over the communications channel will be lost in the environment of the receiver's computer.

Furthermore, it is important to recognize that the transparency of *IPsec* to applications and end users can also be a risk: users will typically have no idea when *IPsec* is "turned on" (i.e., operating) in a network and when it is "turned off". This can lead to situations where a user assumes that *IPsec* is silently protecting his/her **exposure** privacy, when in fact it is not functioning at all (or begins only at the firewall, so that other users within the local network can readily observe the user's *actions*).

Consequently, despite the increased inconvenience, it may be better for overall privacy to have end users themselves explicitly and deliberately choose to use, or not use, a specific PET at any given time. If *IPsec* happens to also be operating at that moment, this will simply be an additional layer of protection for the user's privacy.

## 4.3  Private Information Retrieval (PIR)

Unlike SSL/TLS and *IPsec*, which are general *communications security* protocols that happen to be usable as privacy enhancing technologies, *private information retrieval* (PIR) is a technology that was specifically designed as a PET. (In this sense, it is somewhat like *mix networks* and *onion routing*.) In this chapter, we are discussing PETs that limit **exposure** by hiding the *actions* of the user, even if the identity of the user is visible to all observers. SSL/TLS and *IPsec* achieve this, but we have noted that the user's *actions* are hidden only from third-party network observers, not from the intended recipient of the *actions*. On the other hand, by using some cryptographic magic, the designers of PIR have found a way to allow the *actions* to be hidden *even from the intended recipient* (in other words, the recipient can receive and respond correctly to an *action* without learning what the action is!). We will discuss how such surprising functionality can be achieved in Sect. 4.3.1 below, but let us first motivate why such a thing might be useful in the real world.

Consider a user that wishes to access a database (whether this is a private database on a server in the user's own organization or, more likely, a publicly-accessible database somewhere on the web or in the cloud). The user would like to send a query to retrieve a specific record from the database, but does not fully trust the database administrator. Therefore, the user would like to obtain the desired information without the administrator learning what the information is. Perhaps Alice would like to know the value of a particular stock in the stock market database but does not want to reveal to the administrator the stock she is interested in buying/selling. Perhaps Alice would like to search the patent database for issued patents similar to her new idea but doesn't want to reveal her idea to anyone (in case it actually is patentable). In a military scenario, perhaps Alice (who works in the special operations department of the defense ministry) would like to retrieve a high-resolution map of region $X$ without dropping any hints that there may be a special operation in region $X$ in the near future.

In all these cases, there is a risk that an observer of Alice's query may learn some information that could compromise Alice's intended subsequent activities. Hiding Alice's *action* from network observers can be done using SSL/TLS or *IPsec* (or similar technologies), but this is insufficient: the query also needs to be hidden from the DB administrator who is able to observe both her query and the information that is sent as a response to her. Can the *action* be hidden from this administrator as well?

In 1995, Benny Chor, Oded Goldreich, Eyal Kushilevitz, and Madhu Sudan presented PIR as a proposed solution to this problem (1995) (the full journal paper was subsequently published in (1998)). Since that time, a number of researchers have proposed variations, extensions, and improvements to the original scheme.

## 4.3.1   The Basic Scheme

The *PIR problem* was originally framed by Chor et al., as follows. Assume that the database is a string $x$ of length $n$ bits. The user has some index $\mu$ and is interested in obtaining from the database the value of the bit $x_\mu$ without the database administrator (or anyone else) learning $\mu$.

The obvious solution to this problem is also the simplest: the user asks for the *whole database* (i.e., the entire string $x$) and then learns the bit $x_\mu$ in his/her local environment (which is not accessible or visible to the database administrator). This clearly works, and in fact provides *information-theoretic* privacy for the desired bit $x_\mu$, but of course has a communication complexity of the full $n$ bits. In realistic settings where the size of the database may be very large (or where the user may not be entitled to download the entire database content), this solution is highly impractical and/or unworkable.

There are two possible directions to improve on the obvious scheme. One is to protect the query and the response in some way from all observers (typically using cryptographic means) so that, for example, the database administrator can only learn the index $\mu$ if he has sufficient computing power (e.g., to solve some underlying difficult mathematical problem). This gives *computational privacy* for $x_\mu$: a database administrator with unlimited time and computing power would be able to learn $\mu$, but this index will be hidden from any *computationally-bounded* administrator. A proposal in this direction was given by Kushilevitz and Ostrovsky in 1997 (1997).

The other direction for improvement (the one chosen by Chor et al.) is to assume that there are multiple, non-cooperating servers (and associated administrators), each with its own copy of the full database. The user sends a (different, specially formulated) query to each of these servers, obtains the corresponding responses, and combines these responses in such a way that $x_\mu$ is revealed. The index $\mu$ is *information-theoretically* hidden from each individual database administrator. The goal, of course, is to ensure that the total communication cost for this solution is less than $n$ bits (the obvious solution above).

Chor et al., show that it might be possible to do better than asking for the entire database by describing a simple 2-server construction (which was based on an earlier paper by Pudlák and Rödl (1993)). Let there be $n$ indices $1, \ldots, n$. The user uniformly selects a set of indices $S \subseteq \{1, \ldots, n\}$ (i.e., each of the original $n$ indices is selected with probability ½) and defines set $S'$ to be $S \oplus \mu$ (so that if $S$ contains $\mu$ then $S'$ does not contain $\mu$, and if $S$ does not contain $\mu$ then $S'$ does contain $\mu$). The user then sends $S$ to *server*$_1$ and $S'$ to *server*$_2$. Each server replies with a single bit which is the exclusive-or of the database bits with indices in the query it received (i.e., *server*$_1$ replies with $\oplus_{j \in S} x_j$ and *server*$_2$ replies with $\oplus_{j \in S'} x_j$). The user exclusive-ors the two answers it receives, thereby learning $x_\mu$, but neither server learns anything whatsoever about $\mu$.

This 2-database solution *information-theoretically* hides μ from each server and only requires each server to send a single bit to the user (rather than the entire database of $n$ bits), and so it seems promising. However, it is clearly not an improvement over the original obvious solution because even though the responses are of minimum size, now the user must send approximately $n$ bits to the servers!

Chor, Goldreich, Kushilevitz, and Sudan took this 2-database solution and modified it in various ways, using *d-dimensional cubes* and *covering codes*, using *polynomial interpolation* and *function evaluation*, and using $k$ non-cooperating databases (where $k \geq 2$). For example, one of their constructions takes the following approach.

Assume that $n$ (the length of the database string $x$) is equal to $\omega^d$. Then $x$ can be viewed as a $d$-dimensional cube, and every index $j$ in the original string $x$ (i.e., $j \in \{1, \ldots, n\}$) will be represented as a $d$-tuple $(j_1, \ldots, j_d)$ where each of the $j_i$ is one of $\omega$ values. (To illustrate this more concretely, consider a string $x$ that is 64 bits in length. We can view $x$ as a 4 x 4 x 4 cube (since $4^3 = 64$) and an index $j$ in the string representation of $x$ will be a 3-tuple $(j_1, j_2, j_3)$ in the cube representation of $x$ where each length, width, and height component will be one of 4 possible values (encoded as a bit string of length $\omega$ with a single "1" and the rest "0").) The index for the bit that the user wants to privately retrieve is μ, which is represented by the $d$-tuple $(\mu_1, \ldots, \mu_d)$.

Let $k$ be the number of servers in the construction, and choose $k = 2^d$. Furthermore, name the servers in a natural way using $d$-bit strings (i.e., $server_{00\ldots0}, \ldots, server_{11\ldots1}$). (For our example, there would be $2^3 = 8$ servers, named $server_{000}, server_{001}, server_{010}, server_{011}, \ldots, server_{111}$.)

The user chooses uniformly and independently $d$ random sets, $S_1, \ldots S_d$, one for each component of a tuple. (For our example, the user chooses a random set of lengths, a random set of widths, and a random set of heights.) The user then constructs the corresponding sets $S'_i = S_i \oplus \mu_i$, for $i = 1, \ldots, d$ (as in the simple 2-server construction above). The sets are sent to the servers in accordance with the server names. (For our example, $(S_1, S_2, S_3)$ would be sent to $server_{000}$; $(S_1, S_2, S'_3)$ would be sent to $server_{001}$; $(S_1, S'_2, S_3)$ would be sent to $server_{010}$; $(S_1, S'_2, S'_3)$ would be sent to $server_{011}$; and so on.)

Upon receiving its $d$ sets, each server replies with the exclusive-or of the bits in the cube that correspond to the tuples formed by the sets received. That is, it sends the exclusive-or of all the bits $x_{j1,j2,\ldots,jd}$ where $j_1$ is in the $S_1$ (or $S'_1$) that it received, $j_2$ is in the $S_2$ (or $S'_2$) that it received, and so on.

The user exclusive-ors the bits that it receives from the $k$ servers ($2^d$ bits in total) to retrieve the desired bit $x_\mu$.

As a simple example, let the randomly-chosen sets be $S_1 = (1,0,0,0)$, $S_2 = (0,1,0,0)$, and $S_3 = (0,0,1,0)$ (that is, there is a single randomly-chosen point $(1, 2, 3)$), and let the user's desired index $\mu$ be $(4, 4, 4)$. Then $S'_1 = (1,0,0,1)$, $S'_2 = (0,1,0,1)$, and $S'_3 = (0,0,1,1)$.

The sends $(,,)$ to $S_1 S_2 S_3 server_{000}$, $(,,)$ to $S_1 S_2 S'_3 server_{001}$, ..., and $(,,)$ to $S'_1 S'_2 S'_3 server_{111}$.

The servers return the following bits to the :
$server_{000}$ returns the bit $x_{1,2,3}$
$server_{001}$ returns the bit $x_{1,2,3} \oplus x_{1,2,4}$
$server_{010}$ returns the bit $x_{1,2,3} \oplus x_{1,4,3}$
$server_{011}$ returns the bit $x_{1,2,3} \oplus x_{1,2,4} \oplus x_{1,4,3} \oplus x_{1,4,4}$
$server_{100}$ returns the bit $x_{1,2,3} \oplus x_{4,2,3}$
$server_{101}$ returns the bit $x_{1,2,3} \oplus x_{1,2,4} \oplus x_{4,2,3} \oplus x_{4,2,4}$
$server_{110}$ returns the bit $x_{1,2,3} \oplus x_{1,4,3} \oplus x_{4,2,3} \oplus x_{4,4,3}$
$server_{111}$ returns the bit $x_{1,2,3} \oplus x_{1,2,4} \oplus x_{1,4,3} \oplus x_{1,4,4} \oplus x_{4,2,3} \oplus x_{4,2,4} \oplus x_{4,4,3} \oplus x_{4,4,4}$

The exclusive-ors these eight responses and recovers , which is the desired bit $x_{4,4,4}$.

The communication involved in this construction consists of the user sending a sequence of $d$ sets (each of length $\omega$ bits) to each server, and receiving back a single bit from each server. Thus, the user sends $k \cdot d \cdot \omega$ bits and receives $k$ bits, for a total communication of $k \cdot (d \cdot \omega + 1)$ bits. Given that $k = 2^d$ and $n = \omega^d$, this is $2^d \cdot (d \cdot n^{1/d} + 1)$ bits. (For the simple 2-server construction above, $d = 1$ and this gives a communication complexity of $(2n + 2) = 130$ bits, as we saw. For the running example that we have been using, $d = 3$ and we have an 8-server construction with communication complexity of $2^3 \cdot (3 \cdot n^{1/3} + 1) = 104$ bits. Clearly, for large values of $n$, the complexity of $O(n^{1/d})$ instead of $O(n)$ will result in substantial savings for any $d>1$.) This construction was then improved using a concept from coding theory called *covering codes*: the communication complexity is essentially maintained, but the number of servers is reduced. For instance, in our running example, the authors showed that with very little additional communication, $server_{000}$ can emulate (i.e., give valid responses for) $server_{001}$, $server_{010}$, and $server_{100}$. Furthermore, $server_{111}$ can emulate $server_{011}$, $server_{101}$, and $server_{110}$. Thus, the 8-server construction becomes a 2-server construction with a communication complexity that remains $O(n^{1/3})$. *Very nice!*

The authors then went even further and improved their work in two important ways. First, they modified their constructions to allow the data to be partitioned into blocks of length $\lambda$, thus accommodating more realistic databases that hold *records* for retrieval, rather than individual bits. Second, they recognized that *completely non-cooperating servers* was an unreasonable constraint in the real world, and modified their constructions to allow coalitions of up to $t \leq (k-1)$ servers while still guaranteeing *information-theoretic* privacy for the index $\mu$.

The overall results of Chor, Goldreich, Kushilevitz, and Sudan can be summarized as follows:

– A 2-database scheme with communication complexity of $O(n^{1/3})$;
– A $k$-database scheme (for constant $k > 2$) with communication complexity of $O(n^{1/k})$;
– A $(1/3 \log n + 1)$-database scheme with polylogarithmic (in $n$) communication complexity.

Although some of the concepts in PIR built on ideas proposed in earlier papers addressing the so-called *instance hiding problem* (see the second paragraph of (Gasarch 2004)), the impressive paper by Chor et al., began the field of *private information retrieval* and led to much (equally impressive) follow-up work by several other researchers.

### 4.3.2  Enhancements

As mentioned at the beginning of Sect. 4.3.1, there are two primary approaches to achieve *private information retrieval*: single-server *computational privacy* techniques (C-PIR); and multi-server *information-theoretic privacy* techniques (IT-PIR). The C-PIR schemes proposed over the years have achieved different communication complexities depending on the different techniques used and the underlying hard problem considered (e.g., *quadratic residuosity*, *phi-hiding*, and *semantic security of specific homomorphic encryption algorithms*; see various summaries for relevant results (Gasarch 2004; Beimel and Ko 2017; Wikipedia 2021)), but the best current result is $O(\log^{3-o(1)} n + d)$, where $d$ is the bit-length of the retrieved data block (Gentry and Ramzan 2005). For special cases (in particular, when the data to be retrieved is much larger than the number of items in the database, such as a database of $10^5$ movies where each movie is significantly more than $10^9$ bytes in length), Kiayias et al., have focused on communication rate, which is the ratio of the total number of communication bits required in a non-private retrieval to the total number of communication bits required in a private retrieval, and have achieved a rate of $1 - o(1)$ (i.e., a rate of 1 as $n \to \infty$, which is an optimal result) (Kiayias et al. 2015).

The IT-PIR schemes proposed over the years generally assume $k$ non-cooperating servers, each holding a full copy of the database. Communication complexity results gradually improved to $O(n^{1/(2k-1)})$ (Ishai and Kushilevitz 1999) (see also (Beimel et al. 2005)) until Beimel et al., achieved $n^{O((\log \log k) / (k \log k))}$, which is the best current result for every $k \geq 3$ (Beimel et al. 2002).

Rather than looking at only C-PIR or only IT-PIR, there can be value in considering a carefully-constructed combination of the two techniques. Casey Devet and Ian Goldberg (2014) have shown that a hybrid PIR protocol that combines a C-PIR protocol with an IT-PIR protocol can achieve many positive features of both approaches while mitigating some of the negative aspects. In particular, a hybrid protocol can retain (at least) partial privacy of user query information even when the security assumptions of one of the component protocols is broken, and can achieve a total communication cost that is as good as, or better than, either of the component protocols. The construction given in (Devet and Goldberg 2014) is most effective when the number of records in the database is large compared to the size of each record, but the authors note that this is a situation that arises naturally in many network scenarios.

Researchers have also explored a number of variations and extensions for PIR. A few prominent examples are as follows.

- Along with communication rate, some authors have examined the amount of user computation and server computation required by the protocol and have sought ways to reduce this (particularly in the single-server C-PIR setting). Helger Lipmaa (2010), in particular, has shown a scheme that requires $(1 + o(1))n/\log n$ online public key operations, which is the first C-PIR protocol to achieve online computation that is sublinear in $n$.

- Work has been done on multi-server IT-PIR protocols that can still function correctly if some of the servers are non-responsive (*robust* PIR) or if some of the servers (through error or malice) send incorrect responses (*Byzantine robust* PIR). An IT-PIR scheme with $\lambda$ servers is $k$-out-of-$\lambda$ robust if Alice can learn her desired bit even when only $k$ servers respond. Furthermore, it is called "$v$-Byzantine robust" if Alice can learn her desired bit even when up to $v$ servers send incorrect responses. Finally, it is called "$t$-private" if her query remains hidden even when up to $t$ servers collude. Given a $\lambda$-server system where only $k$ of the servers respond, up to $v$ of these $k$ servers respond incorrectly, and up to $t$ of the $\lambda$ servers can collude, Devet, Goldberg, and Nadia Heninger (2012a, b) have proposed a "$t$-private $v$-Byzantine robust $k$-out-of-$\lambda$ PIR" construction. Based on the asymptotic limit of the error-correcting decoding algorithm they use in their scheme, the theoretical maximum value of the parameter $v$ is ($k - t - 2$); the authors show that their construction is able to provide IT-PIR up to this bound.

- PIR is concerned with keeping the user's index $\mu$ hidden from the server (i.e., protecting Alice from the database administrator). However, there are settings in which we may also want the database to be protected from Alice (specifically, although Alice can learn her desired bit $x_\mu$, we may want to prevent her from learning any other content in the database). This concept was introduced by Gertner et al. (2000); it is known as *symmetrically private information retrieval* (SPIR) and has been studied in both the *information theoretic* (Gertner et al. 2000) and *computational* (Mishra and Sarkar 2000) settings.

Work continues in this interesting research area.

### 4.3.3   Strengths

One of the great strengths of PIR is the fact that options are available for implementation: a given deployment can choose single-server *computational* privacy, multi-server *information theoretic* privacy, or a combination of the two; furthermore, parameters can be chosen to account for different computational capabilities of the user and server, different communication complexities, different attacker models (Byzantine failures, colluding servers, and so on), and symmetric or non-symmetric PIR requirements. Thus, the PIR system can be fine-tuned to suit the specific needs of a particular real-world environment.

The other great strength of PIR is its strong privacy guarantees, particularly in the IT-PIR setting (where no server learns anything whatsoever about the index that the user desires because there is literally insufficient information to compute $\mu$). This is very attractive compared to many other PETs where the privacy claims rest only on the assumed hardness of some specific mathematical problems.

### 4.3.4   Disadvantages, Limitations, and Weaknesses

Although PIR can provide strong privacy guarantees for a user's query, it is clear that it does suffer from some obvious disadvantages. In particular, in the *information theoretic* setting, the entire database must be replicated $k$ times and there is a requirement that at least some of the servers do not cooperate or collude in any way (which may be difficult to enforce in practice). In the *computational* setting, privacy rests on computational assumptions which may turn out not to be true in a specific real-world deployment for a variety of reasons. Furthermore, in both settings, the computation and communication costs are necessarily higher than the costs for retrieving $x_\mu$ without privacy protection, and some users or transaction scenarios may be unwilling to accept these costs.

Finally, recall that PIR protects the content of the query (that is, which index is requested), but does not protect the identity of the user and does not protect any metadata about the query, such as when the query is made, how often this user makes a query, and so on. It is important to recognize that, in some circumstances, query metadata can provide clues or hints (or may at least allow inferences) about what is requested. Consequently, there may exist real-world situations in which the strong theoretical privacy guarantees provided by PIR do not entirely hold for a specific user.

## 4.4  Summary

The previous chapter looked at some example PETs that limit **exposure** by hiding the user's *identity*; this chapter has considered some example PETs (SSL/TLS, *IPsec* in *transport mode*, and PIR) that instead limit **exposure** by hiding the user's *action* from external observers of the network (and, in the case of PIR, even from the intended recipient of the *action*). Both of these general approaches protect the user's privacy by breaking the observable link between *identity* and *action*.

SSL/TLS is the most widely used security protocol in the world, protecting communications between web browsers and websites countless times per day. However, this protocol constructs a secure channel *between* the browser and website; data is unprotected by SSL/TLS prior to entering the channel and after exiting the channel. Thus, care must be taken to store (e.g., in the website database) any sensitive transmitted data securely using separate cryptographic mechanisms if confidentiality and integrity properties are still desired after transmission has been completed.

*IPsec* provides security at the network layer (the IP layer) of the communications protocol stack. Over the years, it has evolved through three generations (*IPsec*, *IPsec-v2*, and *IPsec-v3*), with two associated generations of key exchange architecture (IKEv1 and IKEv2); each of these five generations has been described in its own suite of multiple IETF specifications. *IPsec* provides transparent data protection across the network (applications and end users do not need to know or do anything special in order to use *IPsec*) but, like SSL/TLS, transmitted data is unprotected once it has exited this secure channel. Furthermore, the transparency feature can be a privacy risk in some ways, since users will typically have no idea when *IPsec* is turned "on" or turned "off" in their network.

*Private information retrieval* (PIR) allows a user to retrieve a record from a database without the database (or the database administrator) learning which record was requested. There are two main types of PIR (although hybrid constructions have also been proposed): IT-PIR replicates the entire database at $k$ servers, but guarantees that the user's query is information-theoretically secure; C-PIR requires just a single database, but gives security only if all attackers are computationally-bounded. In either type, it is important to remember that PIR protects the query itself, but not any query metadata (note that the metadata may unintentionally give clues about the data requested that can reduce the privacy offered by PIR).

The third approach for limiting **exposure** is to simultaneously hide both the *identity* and the *action* of a user so that observers see neither of these. We will look at two PETs that achieve this in Chap. 5.

**Questions for Personal Reflection and/or Group Discussion**

1. *Private information retrieval* (PIR) schemes can be implemented as *information theoretically secure* (IT-PIR), *computationally secure* (C-PIR), or a combination. How do these alternatives compare with each other? Discuss their strengths and weaknesses in terms of security, usability, and underlying implementation assumptions.
2. Section 4.3.4 suggests that query metadata can sometimes reduce, or even nullify, the privacy guarantee provided by PIR. Give two example situations in which query metadata could degrade the privacy of a user. What can be done to prevent this problem? What are the disadvantages or limitations of your proposed solution?

# References

G. Arfaoui, X. Bultel, P.-A. Fouque, A. Nedelcu, C. Onete, The privacy of the TLS 1.3 protocol. Proc.. Privacy Enhancing Technol.. **2019**(4), 190–210 (2019, Oct)

A. Beimel, Y. Ishai, E. Kushilevitz, J.-F. Raymond, Breaking the $O(n^{1/(2k-1)})$ barrier for information-theoretic private information retrieval, in *Proceedings of the 43rd Annual Symposium on Foundations of Computer Science*, (2002), pp. 261–270

A. Beimel, Y. Ishai, E. Kushilevitz, General constructions for information-theoretic private information retrieval. J. Comput. Syst. Sci. **71**(2), 213–247 (2005, Aug)

A. Beimel, G. Ko, Private information retrieval, in *Slides for Applied Cryptography Course at Carnegie Mellon University*, (ca. 2017)

Z. Chai, A. Ghafari, A. Houmansadr, On the importance of Encrypted-SNI (ESNI) to censorship circumvention, in *9th USENIX Workshop on Free and Open Communications on the Internet*, (Santa Clara, CA, USA, 2019, Aug 13), 8pp

B. Chor, O. Goldreich, E. Kushilevitz, M. Sudan, Private information retrieval, in *Proceedings of the 36th Annual Symposium on Foundations of Computer Science*, (1995, Oct 23–25), pp. 41–50

B. Chor, O. Goldreich, E. Kushilevitz, M. Sudan, Private information retrieval. J. ACM **45**(6), 965–982 (1998, Nov)

C. Devet, I. Goldberg, N. Heninger, Optimally robust private information retrieval, *Cryptology ePrint Archive* (2012a, June 22). *(Extended version of the following paper)*

C. Devet, I. Goldberg, N. Heninger, Optimally robust private information retrieval, in *21st Usenix Security Symposium*, (2012b, Aug 8–10), pp. 269–283

C. Devet, I. Goldberg, The best of both worlds: Combining information-theoretic and computational PIR for communication efficiency, in *14th Privacy Enhancing Technologies Symposium*, (2014, July)

N. Doraswamy, D. Harkins, *IPsec: The New Security Standard for the Internet, Intranets, and Virtual Private Networks, 2nd Edition* (Prentice Hall, 2003)

S. Frankel, *Demystifying the IPsec Puzzle* (Artech House, 2001)

W. Gasarch, A survey on private information retrieval, in *The Computational Complexity Column*, ed. by Lance Fortnow, (ca. 2004)

C. Gentry, Z. Ramzan, Single-database private information retrieval with constant communication rate, in *International Colloquium on Automata, Languages and Programming*, (Springer LNCS 3580, 2005), pp. 803–815

Y. Gertner, Y. Ishai, E. Kushilevitz, T. Malkin, Protecting data privacy in private information retrieval schemes. J. Comput. Syst. Sci. **60**(3), 592–629 (2000, June)

Y. Ishai, E. Kushilevitz, Improved upper bounds on information-theoretic private information retrieval, in *Proceedings of the 31st ACM Symposium on Theory of Computing*, (1999, May), pp. 79–88

A. Kiayias, N. Leonardos, H. Lipmaa, K. Pavlyk, Q. Tang, Optimal rate private information retrieval from homomorphic encryption. Proc. Privacy Enhancing Technol.. **2**, 222–243 (2015)

C.M. Kozierok, *The TCP/IP Guide: A Comprehensive, Illustrated Internet Protocols Reference* (No Starch Press, 2005)

E. Kushilevitz, R. Ostrovsky, Replication is not needed: Single database, computationally-private information retrieval, in *Proceedings of the 38th Annual Symposium on Foundations of Computer Science*, (1997), pp. 364–373

H. Lipmaa, First CPIR protocol with data-dependent computation, in *12th International Conference on Information, Security and Cryptology*, (2010, Dec 2–4), pp. 193–210

S. Kumar Mishra, P. Sarkar, Symmetrically private information retrieval, in *Progress in Cryptology: Indocrypt 2000*, (2000, Dec 10–13), pp. 225–236

P. Pudlák, V. Rödl, Modified ranks of tensors and the size of circuits, in *Proceedings of the 25th Annual ACM Symposium on Theory of Computing*, (1993, May 16–18), pp. 523–531

S. Siby, M. Juarez, C. Diaz, N. Vallina-Rodriguez, C. Troncoso, Encrypted DNS → privacy? A traffic analysis perspective, in *Network and Distributed System Security Symposium*, (San Diego, CA, USA, 2020, Feb 23–26), 18pp

Wikipedia, *Private Information Retrieval* (2021, Jan 13)

## IETF Specifications[1]

RFC 1825: R. Atkinson, Security Architecture for the Internet Protocol, in *Internet Engineering Task Force (IETF) Request for Comments RFC 1825*, (1995, Aug)

RFC 1826: R. Atkinson, IP Authentication Header, in *Internet Engineering Task Force (IETF) Request for Comments RFC 1826*, (1995, Aug)

RFC 1827: R. Atkinson, IP Encapsulating Security Payload, in *Internet Engineering Task Force (IETF) Request for Comments RFC 1827*, (1995, Aug)

RFC 2246: T. Dierks, C. Allen, The TLS Protocol Version 1.0, in *Internet Engineering Task Force (IETF) Request for Comments RFC 2246*, (1999, Jan)

RFC 2401: S. Kent, R. Atkinson, Security Architecture for the Internet Protocol, in *Internet Engineering Task Force (IETF) Request for Comments RFC 2401*, (1998, Nov)

RFC 2402: S. Kent, R. Atkinson, IP Authentication Header, in *Internet Engineering Task Force (IETF) Request for Comments RFC 2402*, (1998, Nov)

RFC 2403: C. Madson, R. Glenn, The Use of HMAC-MD5-96 within ESP and AH, in *Internet Engineering Task Force (IETF) Request for Comments RFC 2403*, (1998, Nov)

RFC 2404: C. Madson, R. Glenn, The Use of HMAC-SHA-1-96 within ESP and AH, in *Internet Engineering Task Force (IETF) Request for Comments RFC 2404*, (1998, Nov)

RFC 2405: C. Madson, N. Doraswamy, The ESP DES-CBC Cipher Algorithm with Explicit IV, in *Internet Engineering Task Force (IETF) Request for Comments RFC 2405*, (1998, Nov)

RFC 2406: S. Kent, R. Atkinson, IP Encapsulating Security Payload, in *Internet Engineering Task Force (IETF) Request for Comments RFC 2406*, (1998, Nov)

RFC 2407: D. Piper, The Internet IP Security Domain of Interpretation for ISAKMP, in *Internet Engineering Task Force (IETF) Request for Comments RFC 2407*, (1998, Nov)

RFC 2408: D. Maughan, M. Schertler, M. Schneider, J. Turner, Internet Security Association and Key Management Protocol (ISAKMP), in *Internet Engineering Task Force (IETF) Request for Comments RFC 2408*, (1998, Nov)

RFC 2409: D. Harkins, D. Carrel, The Internet Key Exchange (IKE), in *Internet Engineering Task Force (IETF) Request for Comments RFC 2409*, (1998, Nov)

RFC 2410: R. Glenn, S. Kent, The NULL Encryption Algorithm and Its Use with IPsec, in *Internet Engineering Task Force (IETF) Request for Comments RFC 2410*, (1998, Nov)

RFC 2411: R. Thayer, N. Doraswamy, R. Glenn, IP Security Document Roadmap, in *Internet Engineering Task Force (IETF) Request for Comments RFC 2411*, (1998, Nov)

RFC 2412: H. Orman, The OAKLEY Key Determination Protocol, in *Internet Engineering Task Force (IETF) Request for Comments RFC 2412*, (1998, Nov)

RFC 3546: S. Blake-Wilson, M. Nystrom, D. Hopwood, J. Mikkelsen, T. Wright, Transport Layer Security (TLS) Extensions, in *Internet Engineering Task Force (IETF) Request for Comments RFC 3546*, (2003, June)

---

[1] *The following references are IETF specifications (Request for Comments (RFC) or Standard (STD)). Note that these are not listed alphabetically by first author because IETF specifications are invariably referred to in the literature by their number (such as "RFC 1321" or "STD 79"), rather than by author. Thus, these have been listed below in sequential numerical order for the RFCs, followed by STD.*

RFC 4301: S. Kent, K. Seo, Security Architecture for the Internet Protocol, in *Internet Engineering Task Force (IETF) Request for Comments RFC 4301*, (2005, Dec)

RFC 4302: S. Kent, IP Authentication Header, in *Internet Engineering Task Force (IETF) Request for Comments RFC 4302*, (2005, Dec)

RFC 4303: S. Kent, IP Encapsulating Security Payload, in *Internet Engineering Task Force (IETF) Request for Comments RFC 4303*, (2005, Dec)

RFC 4306: C. Kaufman, Internet Key Exchange (IKEv2) Protocol, in *Internet Engineering Task Force (IETF) Request for Comments RFC 4306*, (2005, Dec)

RFC 4346: T. Dierks, E. Rescorla, The Transport Layer Security (TLS) Protocol Version 1.1, in *Internet Engineering Task Force (IETF) Request for Comments RFC 4346*, (2006, Apr)

RFC 4718: P. Eronen, P. Hoffman, IKEv2 Clarifications and Implementation Guidelines, in *Internet Engineering Task Force (IETF) Request for Comments RFC 4718*, (2006, Oct)

RFC 5246: T. Dierks, E. Rescorla, The Transport Layer Security (TLS) Protocol Version 1.2, in *Internet Engineering Task Force (IETF) Request for Comments RFC 5246*, (2008, Aug)

RFC 5996: C. Kaufman, P. Hoffman, Y. Nir, P. Eronen, Internet Key Exchange Protocol Version 2 (IKEv2), in *Internet Engineering Task Force (IETF) Request for Comments RFC 5996*, (2010, Sep)

RFC 6071: S. Frankel, S. Krishnan, IP Security (IPsec) and Internet Key Exchange (IKE) Document Roadmap, in *Internet Engineering Task Force (IETF) Request for Comments RFC 6071*, (2011, Feb)

RFC 6101: A. Freier, P. Karlton, P. Kocher, The Secure Sockets Layer (SSL) Protocol Version 3.0, in *Internet Engineering Task Force (IETF) Request for Comments RFC 6101*, (2011, Aug)

RFC 7296: C. Kaufman, P. Hoffman, Y. Nir, P. Eronen, T. Kivinen, Internet Key Exchange Protocol Version 2 (IKEv2), in *Internet Engineering Task Force (IETF) Request for Comments RFC 7296*, (2014, Oct)

RFC 7858: Z. Hu, L. Zhu, J. Heidemann, A. Mankin, D. Wessels, P. Hoffman, Specification for DNS over Transport Layer Security (TLS), in *Internet Engineering Task Force (IETF) Request for Comments RFC 7858*, (2016, May)

RFC 8446: E. Rescorla, The Transport Layer Security (TLS) Protocol Version 1.3, in *Internet Engineering Task Force (IETF) Request for Comments RFC 8446*, (2018, Aug)

RFC 8484: P. Hoffman, P. McManus, DNS Queries over HTTPS (DoH), in *Internet Engineering Task Force (IETF) Request for Comments RFC 8484*, (2018, Oct)

STD 79: C. Kaufman, P. Hoffman, Y. Nir, P. Eronen, T. Kivinen, Internet Key Exchange Protocol Version 2 (IKEv2), in *Internet Engineering Task Force (IETF) Internet Standard STD 79*, (2014, Oct)

# Chapter 5
# Limiting Exposure by Hiding the Identity-Action Pair

**Abstract** This chapter looks at the final category for limiting exposure: PETs that hide both the identity and the actions of the user. The example technologies in this leaf are network layer security (IPsec in tunnel mode) and off-the-record messaging. The chapter discusses the original scheme, some enhancements made over the years, and strengths and limitations of each technology.

**Keywords** Network layer security · IPsec · Tunnel mode · Off-the-record messaging · Instant messaging (IM) communications · Deniability · Perfect forward secrecy

In this chapter, we consider the third approach for limiting *exposure*: hiding the *identity-action* pair. Ultimately, the goal in limiting *exposure* is to prevent observers (third-party observers of the network, but sometimes also the intended recipient of the interaction) from being able to learn the linkage between Alice's *identity* and an *action* that Alice performs. We have seen that this can be achieved by hiding only her *identity* (the observer sees the *action*, but does not know who is performing this *action*). Alternatively, this can be achieved by hiding only her *action* (the observer sees that Alice is involved in an exchange, but does not know what *action* she is performing). However, a user may wish to simultaneously hide both the *identity* and the *action*, without having to use two different PETs.

The number of PETs that address this third approach is relatively small, but there are some. Here we will look at two particular examples: the *IPsec* protocol (in a specific configuration known as *tunnel mode*), and the *Off-the-Record* (OTR) Messaging protocol.

© The Editor(s) (if applicable) and The Author(s), under exclusive license to Springer Nature Switzerland AG 2021
C. Adams, *Introduction to Privacy Enhancing Technologies*,
https://doi.org/10.1007/978-3-030-81043-6_5

## 5.1    Network Layer Security (IPsec in Tunnel Mode)

The *IPsec* protocol was presented in some detail in Chap. 4, and so the reader is referred to that chapter for the overall description. But Chap. 4 was about PETs that hide the user's *actions* (not the user's *identity*), and *IPsec* in *transport mode* can be used to accomplish this. Here, we are interested in PETs that hide both the *action* and the *identity*. *IPsec* has another configuration, *tunnel mode*, which is well-suited to provide this functionality.

### *5.1.1    The Basic Scheme*

As discussed in the previous chapter, when *IPsec* is operated in *transport mode* as a PET, only the payload of the IP packet is encrypted; the IP header is not encrypted or modified in any way. This is why the *identity* of the communicants is visible to everyone (i.e., the source and destination IP address fields in the header portion are in the clear) even though the *action* (the content of the payload) is hidden. See Fig. 5.1.

In *tunnel mode*, the entire IP packet (payload and header) is protected. Because the original source and destination addresses are now unreadable ciphertext, this packet is encapsulated into the payload portion of a new IP packet, and the new packet is given its own header portion. The new "outer" header will of course have fields for source and destination addresses, but these can contain different values from the corresponding fields in the original ("inner") header. See Fig. 5.2. (Some additional helpful diagrams for both *tunnel mode* and *transport mode* can be found here: http://www.firewall.cx/networking-topics/protocols/870-ipsec-modes.html.)

The way that *tunnel mode* is typically used is as follows. Say Alice in Company$_A$ wants to communicate with Bob in Company$_B$. The application at Alice's end (e-mail, file transfer, web access, etc.) prepares its outgoing message as usual. At the network layer, this message is packaged into IP packets with Alice's IP address in the sender field and Bob's IP address in the destination field, and the packets are transmitted across the local network in Company$_A$ until they reach Company$_A$'s external firewall, *Firewall$_A$*. This is where *IPsec* begins. Each packet from Alice is integrity protected, encrypted, and put into the payload of another packet whose

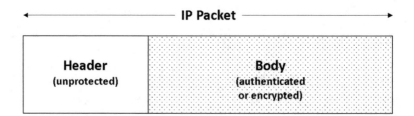

**Fig. 5.1**  Protection of an IP packet in IPsec transport mode

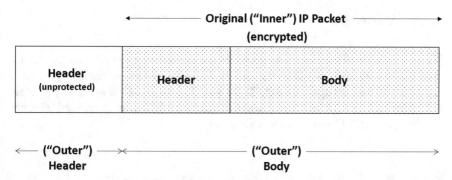

**Fig. 5.2**  Protection of an IP packet in IPsec tunnel mode

header has the IP address of *Firewall$_A$* in the source field and the IP address of *Firewall$_B$* in the destination field (*Firewall$_B$* is the external firewall of Company$_B$). These packets are then sent across the Internet to *Firewall$_B$* at Company$_B$. This is where *IPsec* ends. At *Firewall$_B$*, the payload is decrypted, verified and (if valid) sent through the local network of Company$_B$ to Bob's IP address (which is now readable because the header of this "inner" packet has been converted back to plaintext).

*Tunnel mode* clearly hides both the identities of the communicants and the contents of their communicated data. In the arrangement just described, third-party observers on the Internet see only that *Firewall$_A$* is talking with *Firewall$_B$*, but cannot know that Alice and Bob are involved and cannot know what they are saying to each other.

More generally, *tunnel mode* is how *IPsec* is used as a *virtual private network* (VPN) connecting any two endpoints. Common use-cases include network-to-network communications (e.g., between gateways to allow traffic to be protected from the edge of one subnetwork to the edge of another subnetwork, as in the scenario above), host-to-network communications (e.g., to enable remote user access to a corporate LAN), and host-to-host communications (e.g., to facilitate private chat interactions between users).

Note that the *IPsec-v2 Architecture* document (RFC2401 1998) specifies that both network-to-network and host-to-network communications MUST use the *tunnel mode* configuration, whereas host-to-host communications MAY use *tunnel mode* or *transport mode*. Therefore, *tunnel mode* is much more commonly used for IP packet protection across the Internet than *transport mode*.

## 5.1.2   Enhancements

The general enhancements to *IPsec* over the years have been outlined in Sect. 4.2.2 (*IPsec-v3, IKEv2*, and a number of additional related IETF documents). There were no enhancements specifically to the *tunnel mode* configuration of *IPsec*.

### 5.1.3   Strengths

The strengths for *IPsec* that are given in Sect. 4.2.3 also apply here: transparency to applications; transparency to users; and implementation options for organizations. Again, these benefits apply directly to the use of *IPsec* in *tunnel mode* as a PET to hide both the *identity* and the *action* – the **exposure** of users is reduced without requiring any effort from the users themselves.

### 5.1.4   Disadvantages, Limitations, and Weaknesses

Similarly, the limitations of *IPsec* that are given in Sect. 4.2.4 also apply here: the receiving application must properly protect the data that exits the *IPsec* channel; and users will not normally know when *IPsec* is operating and when it is not.

This second limitation is a bit more subtle when *IPsec* is used in *tunnel mode*, however. Although the *tunnel mode* configuration can theoretically be installed anywhere, it is important to note that in corporate environments it is typically installed only at the perimeter of a network or subnetwork (on a router or firewall). Thus, in many deployments, *tunnel mode* will begin at Company$_A$'s external firewall and end at Company$_B$'s external firewall. The crucial implication of this (with respect to privacy and the use of *IPsec* as a PET) is that the hiding of Alice's *identity* and *action* occurs <u>only</u> between the two firewalls (i.e., only on the open Internet connecting Company$_A$ and Company$_B$). In particular, other users on the local network in Company$_A$ and other users on the local network in Company$_B$ will know for certain that Alice is communicating with Bob (if *IPsec* in *transport mode* is used within the local networks), and may actually know the full content of their interaction (if *IPsec* is not used at all inside the external firewalls, which is the usual deployment choice). Therefore, Alice will have to deliberately set up a *tunnel mode* host-to-host VPN connection directly with Bob, or use a different PET altogether, if she wants to limit her **exposure** with respect to co-workers as well as strangers.

## 5.2   Off-the-Record (OTR) Messaging

*Off-the-Record* (OTR) Messaging is a protocol that allows two users to have a private conversation in an *instant messaging* (IM) environment. OTR was proposed by Nikita Borisov, Ian Goldberg, and Eric Brewer in 2004 (2004) as an improvement over other message protection technologies such as *Pretty Good Privacy* (PGP) (see (Zimmermann 1995; RFC2440 1998)) and *Secure/Multipurpose Internet Mail Extensions* (S/MIME) (RFC2633 1999).

OTR is a PET that limits **exposure** by hiding both the *identities* and the *actions* of its users. Like many other technologies (including *IPsec* in this chapter and SSL/

TLS in the previous chapter), the *action* is hidden through the use of encryption. However, unlike those technologies, the *identity* is protected through the use of *deniability* (see Sect. 5.2.1 below). This interesting twist is one of two features (the other being *perfect forward secrecy*; see Sect. 5.2.1 below) that sets OTR apart from prior messaging schemes such as PGP and S/MIME.

Since its initial publication, the OTR protocol has been built into a number of IM clients and is available as a plugin for several more (although note that these days most people no longer use classic *instant messaging* for their communications).

## 5.2.1   The Basic Scheme

OTR was originally presented in October 2004, and a reference implementation of the protocol (referred to as version 0.8.0) was published a month later. This first version is the basis for the description given in this section. There have been a number of subsequent versions since then; these will be discussed in Sect. 5.2.2 below.

The motivating scenario included in (Borisov et al. 2004) is the following. Suppose that Alice and Bob have exchanged messages for some time using a secure e-mail protocol such as PGP or S/MIME. For each message that Alice sends, she digitally signs it using her private signature key and encrypts the result using Bob's public encryption key; Bob does a similar process with his messages (i.e., signs using his private signature key and encrypts the result using Alice's public encryption key). The intended recipient of a message (Bob or Alice) is the only one that can read it, and this recipient is confident that only the other party could have sent it. These exchanges can continue for days, weeks, months, or longer and everything seems perfectly fine. If an eavesdropper (Eve) records all these messages, there is little cause for concern because the eavesdropper cannot read any of the data.

One day, however, Eve is able to acquire Bob's private decryption key (through legitimate means, such as a subpoena, or illegitimate means, such as remotely inserting malware into Bob's computer). Eve is now able to decrypt and read all the past messages to Bob that she has recorded. Furthermore, she has convincing evidence (in the form of cryptographically-strong digital signatures) that Alice is the one who sent each of these messages. *In this undesirable situation, we see that Alice's privacy depends entirely on Bob's private key being unobtainable by third parties, which Alice of course has no control over.* This is very different from an in-person face-to-face conversation: Alice can verify that no one else is around to hear what is spoken and, after the fact, Bob's "claim" – ultimately, Bob's memory – is the only (unreliable) evidence available to anyone about what Alice actually said.

The OTR protocol was designed to bring the privacy of face-to-face conversations to online communications. Although it is important to ensure that only Bob can read the messages sent to him and to make sure that Bob can confirm that Alice was the author, the goal of OTR is to guarantee that no one else is able to do either of these. In particular, at any later time, no party (including Alice and Bob themselves) should be able to read or verify the authenticity of a message sent to Bob, even if a copy of the message was recorded and Bob's private key was somehow compromised.

OTR uses the following cryptographic primitives: (1) the *Diffie-Hellman* (D-H) *key exchange protocol* (with public parameters $p$, a prime number of sufficient size, and $g$, a generator of a subgroup of $Z_p^*$ of large prime order); (2) the *message authentication code* HMAC; (3) the *encryption algorithm* AES (operated in counter mode); and (4) the *hash function* SHA-1. Assume that Alice has a signature verification public key $V_{Alice}$ that is known to Bob, and that Bob has a signature verification public key $V_{Bob}$ that is known to Alice. (These may be exchanged in an in-person meeting, or may be enclosed in public key certificates whose authenticity and integrity can be verified using the public key of a trusted *Certification Authority* (CA), or may be mutually shared using any other reliable mechanism.) Alice has a corresponding signature private key $K_{Alice}$ and Bob has a corresponding signature private key $K_{Bob}$. The OTR protocol can be summarized in four steps.

- **Step 1: Authenticated Diffie-Hellman computation and symmetric key derivation**

  - Alice randomly chooses a value $x_1$ and sends to Bob $g^{x_1}$ mod $p$ and $\text{sig}_{KAlice}(g^{x_1} \bmod p)$
  - Bob randomly chooses a value $y_1$ and sends to Alice $g^{y_1}$ mod $p$ and $\text{sig}_{KBob}(g^{y_1} \bmod p)$
  - Both Alice and Bob compute $S_1 = g^{x_1 y_1} \bmod p$, $EK_1 = H(S_1)$, and $MK_1 = H(EK_1)$, where $S_1$ is the D-H shared secret, $EK_1$ is an encryption key to be used with AES, and $MK_1$ is a MAC key to be used with HMAC

- **Step 2: Message protection ($i = 1$ after Step 1 and increments with every re-key operation)**

  - Alice (Bob) sends to Bob (Alice) $\text{enc}_{EKi}(M)$ and $\text{mac}_{MKi}(\text{enc}_{EKi}(M))$, where $M$ is the message to be transmitted

- **Step 3: Re-keying (done after $n$ messages have been transmitted protected with $EK_i$ and $MK_i$)**

  - Alice randomly chooses a value $x_{i+1}$ and sends to Bob $g^{x_{i+1}}$ mod $p$ and $\text{mac}_{MK_i}(g^{x_{i+1}} \bmod p)$
  - Bob randomly chooses a value $y_{i+1}$ and sends to Alice $g^{y_{i+1}}$ mod $p$ and $\text{mac}_{MK_i}(g^{y_{i+1}} \bmod p)$
  - Both Alice and Bob compute $S_{i+1} = g^{x_{i+1} y_{i+1}} \bmod p$, $EK_{i+1} = H(S_{i+1})$, and $MK_{i+1} = H(EK_{i+1})$
  - At this point, both Alice and Bob securely erase $S_i$, $x_i$, $y_i$, and $EK_i$

- **Step 4: Publicize old $MK$**

  - Append $MK_i$ to the first message protected with $EK_{i+1}$ and $MK_{i+1}$

In **Step 1** above, if Bob is certain that $V_{Alice}$ is the correct and valid signature verification public key for Alice, then he will be certain that the Diffie-Hellman public value $g^{x_1}$ mod $p$ came from her. Therefore, he will be certain that she is the only other party who can compute $S_1$, $EK_1$, and $MK_1$. Therefore, when he receives a message protected with $EK_1$ and $MK_1$ in **Step 2**, he will be certain that (a) only he and Alice can read this message and (b) Alice must have sent the message (since he knows that he did not send it, and Alice is the only other person with these two keys). Thus, the OTR protocol provides *confidentiality* and *authentication*.

In **Step 3**, once re-keying has been accomplished (i.e., $EK_{i+1}$ and $MK_{i+1}$ have been established) and $S_i$, $x_i$, $y_i$, and $EK_i$ have been securely erased from both Alice's device and Bob's device, then all previous messages encrypted using $EK_i$ become unreadable to anyone, anywhere (including Bob and Alice), regardless of whether these messages have been recorded and stored by Eve. Thus, the OTR protocol provides *perfect forward secrecy*: compromise of any keying material on any machine will not reveal previously-transmitted messages.

Finally, because of the use of MACs on messages rather than digital signatures, although Bob is certain that the current incoming message was sent by Alice, he cannot convince any other party of this (Alice can simply claim that Bob created the message himself since he also knows the MAC key). In **Step 4**, this property is extended further. Once $MK_i$ has been published, any party anywhere can create a forged transcript of messages (purportedly from Alice) that are entirely as convincing as the real transcript that she sent. Thus, the OTR protocol provides *deniability*: for any given past message, no one can rule out any particular person as a potential sender of that message; consequently, there is no convincing evidence that it was in fact sent by Alice.

The OTR protocol proposed in (Borisov et al. 2004) is quite simple and elegant, employs standard and well-understood cryptographic primitives, and is fairly easy to use (perhaps the only potential difficulty is the secure initial sharing of signature verification public keys between Alice and Bob in order to perform **Step 1** above). It quickly attracted a community of interested users who for years had active participation and discussion on the *otr-users* (https://lists.cypherpunks.ca/mailman/listinfo/otr-users) and *otr-dev* (https://lists.cypherpunks.ca/mailman/listinfo/otr-dev) mailing lists.

### 5.2.2  Enhancements

One year after the original protocol was presented, Mario Di Raimondo, Rosario Gennaro, and Hugo Krawczyk published a careful security analysis of OTR (2005). The authors found a number of security shortcomings and then proposed alternative designs and improvements to strengthen the protocol. In particular, they showed the following.

– The *authenticated key exchange* in the original protocol is vulnerable to an "identity misbinding" attack in which Eve interjects in the key exchange between Alice and Bob. At the end of **Step 1**, although Eve does not learn the secret value

$S_1$ generated by the D-H protocol, Alice believes she is talking with Bob, while Bob believes he is talking with Eve (that is, Bob believes that all messages he sends and receives are between himself and Eve). This can clearly have privacy implications for their protected communications!

- The "identity misbinding" vulnerability above can be mitigated by including the identity of the intended receiver in the signed portion. However, although this prevents the misbinding vulnerability, the protocol loses some of the *deniability* property that it was intended to achieve.
- If an attacker is ever able to learn the ephemeral value $x_1$ used by Alice in **Step 1**, the attacker will be able to impersonate Alice to any other party in the system for as long as the signature verification public key of Alice is not revoked.
- If an attacker can learn any MAC key $MK_{i-1}$, then the attacker can run the next $i^{th}$ message D-H key exchange with Alice, pretending to be Bob (since the attacker knows the key that will be used for authentication). Similarly, the attacker can run the $i^{th}$ message D-H key exchange with Bob, pretending to be Alice. This now becomes an effective man-in-the-middle (MITM) attack and all subsequent messages exchanged by Alice and Bob will be visible to, and modifiable by, the attacker.

As a result of this security analysis, OTR *version 2* was released in 2005. This version replaced the original *authenticated key exchange* protocol with a slightly-modified implementation of the SIGMA protocol suggested by Di Raimondo, et al. (instead of sending her public D-H value in the clear, Alice sends it encrypted using a randomly-chosen symmetric key so that it is concealed from passive observers, and only sends this key to Bob after he has sent his public D-H value to Alice). This modified SIGMA protocol entails some extra computation (for example, two MAC keys and one encryption key are generated for each participant, and additional MAC and encryption processing is required (see the description in (Alexander and Goldberg 2007) for the detailed protocol). However, the computation is not prohibitive and the new protocol is effective in preventing the "identity misbinding" attack.

When the popular IM client *GTK + AOL Instant Messenger* ("gaim") changed to "pidgin" in 2007 (as a result of a trademark dispute with AOL), the OTR plugin for gaim was modified to become a plugin for pidgin. The OTR designers took this opportunity to make two major changes to the OTR protocol. The full description of OTR *version 2* with these two additional features was published in 2007 (see https://otr.cypherpunks.ca/Protocol-v2-3.1.0.html).

- First, message fragmentation was added in order to accommodate the many IM protocols that have a maximum allowable size for any transmitted message (usually 1–2 KB). Since some OTR messages were larger than this, automatic fragmentation and reassembly was introduced to avoid the "Message too large" errors that many users were receiving.
- Second, the step of initially sharing and verifying public keys (mentioned as a potential usability issue at the end of Sect. 5.2.1) was greatly simplified. Instead of having users compare public key "fingerprints" (i.e., the hash values of the participants' public keys), a version of the *Socialist Millionaires Problem* (SMP) was implemented as the default mechanism ("fingerprint" comparison was left as

an option for advanced users). SMP, in which two millionaires wish to know whether they are equally rich, was introduced by Jakobsson and Yung (1996) as a variant of Yao's *Millionaires Problem* (1982), in which two millionaires wish to know who is richer (without revealing any other information about their wealth). OTR used an efficient solution to SMP (Boudot et al. 2001) in order to determine whether two participants know the same secret value. This secret value can be something simple such as a low-entropy password that the two users have previously shared. If, for example, Alice confirms using SMP that the other participant knows a particular secret, she can be confident that it must be Bob (with whom she shared this secret some time ago in an offline meeting) and key exchange can proceed with the modified SIGMA protocol mentioned above. The details of the OTR SMP technique are given in (Alexander and Goldberg 2007).

OTR *version* 3 was published in 2012 (https://otr.cypherpunks.ca/Protocol-v3-4.0.0.html). This version introduced message labels ("tags") in order to handle situations where a user is logged in multiple times (avoiding the risk that an OTR client attempts to establish an OTR session indefinitely if there are interleaving messages from each of the sessions). In terms of security features, the only major change was to derive an additional symmetric key during the SIGMA protocol *authenticated key exchange*. This additional key can then be used by the participants for secure communication over a completely different channel (such as file transfer or voice chat).

It is interesting to note that in 2013, the company *Open Whisper Systems* introduced a protocol called *TextSecure v*1 for their *TextSecure* app. This protocol was based entirely on OTR Messaging *version* 3 (Wiedemann 2014). *TextSecure v*2 was introduced in 2014 and this version incorporated some concepts from the *Silent Circle Instant Messaging Protocol* (SCIMP). Later that year, other minor modifications were made to create *TextSecure v*3 which, in 2016, was renamed to the *Signal protocol* (and the *TextSecure* app was renamed to *Signal*). The *Signal protocol* is claimed to be used in several closed-source applications, including *WhatsApp* (which is thought to encrypt the conversations of more than a billion people worldwide), *Facebook Messenger* (for its *Secret Conversations*), and *Skype* (for its *Private Conversations*). A number of researchers (*Ruhr University Bochum* (Germany), *University of Oxford* (UK), *Queensland University of Technology* (Australia), and *McMaster University* (Canada)) have done a formal security analysis of the *Signal protocol* and have found it to be cryptographically sound.

OTR *version* 4 was published in 2018 (Bini and Celi 2018), with a production-ready C library implementation available at https://github.com/otrv4/libotr-ng. This version can handle both online and offline conversations and claims to provide stronger *deniability* than all previous secure messaging protocols in use, including OTR *version* 3 and the *Signal protocol*. It also provides stronger *confidentiality* properties: backwards secrecy; forward secrecy; and post-compromise security (where the compromise of both long-lived and short-lived key material does not compromise the *confidentiality* of past or future messages). Finally, it also uses up-to-date cryptographic primitives, such as Edwards curves for the elliptic curve cryptography (Hamburg 2015) and XSalsa20 for the stream cipher (Bernstein 2011). To support the claim of a "production-ready" implementation, the library takes into account numerous security measures such as ensuring that generated ECC keys are not the identity element, using constant time cryptographic operations, and checking for initialized memory, memory leaks, double-freeing, and race conditions in multi-threads.

### 5.2.3  Strengths

As discussed in Sect. 5.2.1 above, the OTR protocol provides *confidentiality*, *authentication*, *perfect forward secrecy*, and *deniability*. It therefore replicates the privacy of a face-to-face conversation much more closely than secure e-mail protocols such as PGP and S/MIME.

OTR is also widely available. It has been built into a large number of *instant messaging* clients (including Adium (OS X), Kopete (Unix-like), ChatSecure (iOS), and IM+ (Android)) and is available as a plugin for many more (including Pidgin, Miranda, WeeChat, xchat, and Psi/Psi+); see [https://otr.cypherpunks.ca/software.php] for a known list.

The protocol also continues to be revised and extended, for example to provide additional features and to update the cryptographic primitives used, so that it remains relevant and useful for any communities that wish to use it.

### 5.2.4  Disadvantages, Limitations, and Weaknesses

Given the design of the protocol, OTR does not support multi-user group chat. This is a direction that has been discussed for several years (see, for example, (Goldberg et al. 2009)), and it is possible that it will be added in the future, but this feature is not currently available. Furthermore, there is no (current or planned) support for encrypted audio or video; OTR is for IM text communications only.

It is important to remember that OTR was originally created exclusively for real-time conversations. If either party in a conversation decides to save messages (and the corresponding decryption keys for those messages), this not only violates the design goals of OTR, but it also puts the privacy of the other party at risk (if an attacker is able to somehow acquire those messages and keys from wherever they are stored). Therefore, if two communicants wish to have a persistent (or relatively long-term) record of their conversation – or portions of their conversation – for any reason, OTR should not be their chosen PET. (Note that OTR *version* 4 does support offline conversations (see also (Firoozjaei et al. 2017) for related work), but the authors concede that the *deniability* property is somewhat diminished when offline mode is used.)

## 5.3 Summary

This chapter completes the set of three chapters that discuss PETs which limit *exposure* by hiding the *identity-action* linkage. Chap. 3 examined PETs that do this by hiding the *identity* (while leaving the *action* visible), and Chap. 4 examined PETs that do this by hiding the *action* (while leaving the *identity* visible). Here we looked at two specific PETs (*IPsec* in *tunnel mode* and OTR Messaging) that accomplish this by simultaneously hiding both the *identity* and the *action*.

When *IPsec* is operated in *tunnel mode* (as opposed to *transport mode*), it is possible to use it as a PET to hide both the *identities* and the *actions* of the two parties in a communication. Specifically, every full IP packet (i.e., header and body) is integrity-protected, encrypted, and put into the body of an outer IP packet with its own (different) header information. Thus, observers on the network cannot see the true sender and receiver of the packet, and cannot see the packet content. As with *IPsec* in *transport mode*, and as with SSL/TLS, sensitive data must be protected with some other cryptographic mechanism once it exits the secure channel. Furthermore, users may not always know when *IPsec* is operating in a network and so they must not simply assume that their data is constantly being privacy protected.

*Off-the-Record* (OTR) Messaging was designed to allow private conversations in *instant messaging* (IM) environments. It hides the user's *action* (i.e., the message content) with encryption but, in contrast to other popular PETs, protects the *identity* through *deniability*, rather than through typical cryptographic means. Improvements over the years (in both security and efficiency) have resulted in the adoption of OTR (or similar protocols based on OTR) in a large number of messaging and social media client applications.

In the following three chapters, we will discuss PETs that limit *disclosure* by hiding the *identity-attribute* linkage. We begin with those that hide the *identity* (while leaving the *attributes* visible); our example PETs will be *k*-anonymity and *credential systems*.

**Questions for Personal Reflection and/or Group Discussion**

1. The *Off-the-Record* (OTR) protocol hides *identity* by providing *plausible deniability*. What are the advantages and disadvantages of this approach, compared with the anonymity techniques that are used in other PETs? Is it possible that some details in the message content, or something in the message metadata (such as the time it was sent), could strongly implicate a specific sender and reduce *plausible deniability*, or does the protocol mitigate this concern? Discuss.
2. An essential component in the privacy properties of OTR is the assumption that keys and keying material have been securely erased from the devices of both communicants. As discussed in Sect. 5.2.4, if either party retains decryption keys, the privacy of the other party is at risk. How realistic is the assumption of *secure deletion*? Discuss the technical feasibility of securely deleting data on various types of mobile devices. Even when *secure deletion* is technically possible on a given device, does each party simply have to trust that the other party has securely deleted old keys, or is there a way to ensure this?

# References

C. Alexander, I. Goldberg, Improved user authentication in off-the-record messaging, in *Workshop on Privacy in the Electronic Society*, (2007, Oct 29), pp. 41–47

D.J. Bernstein, Extending the Salsa20 nonce (2011, Feb 4)

O. Bini, S. Celi, No evidence of communication: Off-the-record protocol version 4, in *Privacy Enhancing Technologies Symposium, HotPETs session*, (2018, July 27)

N. Borisov, I. Goldberg, E. Brewer, Off-the-record communication, or, why not to use PGP, in *Workshop on Privacy in the Electronic Society*, (2004), pp. 77–84

F. Boudot, B. Schoenmakers, J. Traoré, A fair and efficient solution to the socialist millionaires' problem. Discrete Appl. Math. **111**(1–2), 77–85 (2001, July 15)

M. Daghmehchi Firoozjaei, S.M. Lee, H. Kim, $O^2TR$: Offline Off-the-Record (OTR) messaging, in *18th World Conference on Information Security Applications (WISA)*, (2017, Aug 24–26)

M. Di Raimondo, R. Gennaro, H. Krawczyk, Secure off-the-record messaging, in *Workshop on Privacy in the Electronic Society*, (2005, Nov 7), pp. 81–89

I. Goldberg, B. Ustaoğlu, M. D. Van Gundy, H. Chen, Multi-party off-the-record messaging, in *ACM Conference on Computer and Communications Security*, (2009, Dec 9–13)

M. Hamburg, Ed448-Goldilocks, a new elliptic curve, ePrint archive 2015/625 (2015, June 30)

M. Jakobsson, M. Jung, Proving without knowing: On oblivious, agnostic and blindfolded provers, in *Advances in Cryptology: Proceedings of Crypto '96*, (Springer LNCS 1109, 1996), pp. 186–200

RFC 2401: S. Kent, R. Atkinson, Security architecture for the internet protocol, in *Internet Engineering Task Force (IETF) Request for Comments RFC 2401*, (1998, Nov)

RFC 2440: J. Callas, L. Donnerhacke, H. Finney, R. Thayer, OpenPGP message format, in *Internet Engineering Task Force (IETF) Request for Comments RFC 2440*, (1998, Nov)

RFC 2633: B. Ramsdell, S/MIME version 3 message specification, in *Internet Engineering Task Force (IETF) Request for Comments RFC 2633*, (1999, June)

B. Wiedemann, *WhisperSystems/TextSecure Protocol* (GitHub, Inc., 2014, Mar 2)

A.C. Yao, Protocols for secure computations, in *Proceedings of the 23rd IEEE Symposium on Foundations of Computer Science*, (1982), pp. 160–164

P. Zimmermann, *The Official PGP User's Guide* (MIT Press, 1995)

# Chapter 6
# Limiting Disclosure by Hiding the Identity

**Abstract** This chapter begins the examination of techniques that are designed to limit disclosure (rather than exposure). In particular, it focuses on technologies that limit disclosure by hiding the identity of the user. The chapter describes the following example PETs in this category: *k*-anonymity and credential systems. The basic scheme, enhancements, strengths, and limitations are presented for each of these PETs.

**Keywords** Database privacy · *k*-anonymity · Quasi-identifier · Generalization · Suppression · Data utility · *ℓ*-diversity · *t*-closeness · Credential system · Pedersen commitment · Blind signature · Zero-knowledge proof-of-knowledge (ZKPoK) · Non-transferability · Unlinkability

With this chapter and the following two chapters, we change our focus from limiting *exposure* to limiting *disclosure*. That is, instead of looking at PETs designed to prevent the *actions* of users from being seen by unintended observers, we look at PETs designed to prevent the *attributes* of users from being seen by unintended observers. Note that limiting exposure and limiting disclosure are reminiscent of the notions of *communications privacy* and *data privacy* (which, particularly in legal circles, are sometimes referred to as protection of *data in motion* and *data at rest*). While in the broadest sense these can be identical concepts, in practice *communications privacy* is often assumed to just mean hiding the content of a communicated message (e.g., through encryption), whereas limiting exposure explicitly also includes hiding the fact that Alice sent a message and can be accomplished by simply hiding her identity as much as by hiding the message and all its metadata. Likewise, *data privacy* is often assumed to concentrate on just hiding data itself (e.g., through encryption or access control), whereas limiting disclosure aims to hide the linkage between Alice and her data which, again, might involve hiding only Alice's identity.

Another pair of privacy-related notions is relevant to this discussion: *technical means for providing privacy* and *technical means for measuring privacy* (i.e., *privacy metrics*). Often the former are associated with *communications privacy* and the

© The Editor(s) (if applicable) and The Author(s), under exclusive license to Springer Nature Switzerland AG 2021

C. Adams, *Introduction to Privacy Enhancing Technologies*,
https://doi.org/10.1007/978-3-030-81043-6_6

latter with *data privacy* but, in fact, both providing and measuring privacy have been explored in both domains. Thus, limiting exposure explicitly encompasses not just technologies for providing *communications privacy* such as *mix networks* and *onion routing*, but also entropy-based definitions of anonymous communication (see, for example, (Serjantov and Danezis 2002; Díaz et al. 2002)), possibilistic and probabilistic metrics of anonymity (see, for example, (Syverson and Stubblebine 1999)), considerations of how network usage, configuration dynamics, and adversary-accrued information affect the measurement of anonymity, and so on. In the same way, limiting disclosure deliberately encompasses not just means for the measurement of *data privacy* (such as those described for *k-Anonymity* in this chapter and for *ε-differential privacy* in Chap. 7), but also technologies to provide *data privacy* (such as *Credential Systems* in this chapter and *APEX* in Chap. 8).

Exposure and disclosure are therefore intended to incorporate and embrace the broadest interpretations of these other privacy-related notions.

In the context of limiting disclosure, often the *attributes* of users (such as home address, salary, credit card number, political affiliation, health record, and so on) are stored in a database of some kind and so the PETs provide protections related to the reading, writing, or manipulation of specific records in the database. However, sometimes these *attributes* are used within the framework of user *actions* to accomplish some task; in such cases, the emphasis of these three chapters is on techniques to limit disclosure related to the *attribute values* themselves, rather than on techniques to prevent observers from seeing the particular *actions* performed (as in the previous two chapters).

Similarly to exposure, limiting disclosure can be achieved by breaking the *identity-attribute* linkage (from the point of view of unintended observers) through hiding the *identity*, hiding the *attributes*, or hiding both simultaneously. In this chapter, we look at the first of these options: limiting disclosure by hiding the *identity*, even though the *attributes* involved in the task at hand may be visible to everyone. Two example PETs that exemplify this approach are *k-Anonymity* and *Credential Systems*.

## 6.1  *k*-Anonymity

There is a significant, and growing, interest in making health data from research institutions and healthcare organizations publicly available for the purposes of further research. Along with the opportunity for subsequent research, there are many other compelling reasons why making such data publicly available may be attractive, including validating existing research results, eliminating the cost and inconvenience of re-collecting the data in the future, and facilitating instruction and education. Because of this, some entities (including institutes of health research, academic journals, and funding agencies) require researchers to make their data available when publishing research results or, at the very least, to provide an explicit data sharing plan when submitting applications for research funding. (Further discussion and examples can be found in the Introduction section of (ElEmam and Dankar 2008).)

Although the benefits of publicly sharing health data are recognized, the privacy risks are also quite clear. Health data can be highly sensitive, and in the wrong hands it can have adverse effects on a person's employment/employability, insurance/ insurability, and personal/social relationships (among many other potential negative consequences). Thus, privacy researchers have considered the question, *"How can a database be publicly released without compromising individual privacy?"*

The simple approach to anonymizing a database of records is to remove *unique identifiers*, such as *Name* and *Social Insurance Number* (SIN) or *Social Security Number* (SSN). However, this is insufficient because researchers have found that other attributes (which are not themselves unique identifiers) can sometimes be grouped together to re-identify a specific individual. Such attributes are known as *quasi-identifiers*. The first and highly-cited illustration of this was published by privacy researcher Latanya Sweeney, who showed in 2000 that approximately 87% of the US population can be uniquely identified by just the combination of their {5-digit *zip code*, *gender*, and *date of birth*}; furthermore, roughly 53% can be uniquely identified by the combination of {*place*, *gender*, and *date of birth*} (where *"place"* is simply the city, town, or municipality in which the person currently resides) (Sweeney 2000). This now-famous study has caused researchers to avoid using these values together in database records that they wish to anonymize, but it is not always obvious which other attributes – and which combinations of attributes – can allow re-identification in a given data set. Thus, the risk of privacy breaches in data sets that have been "anonymized" simply by the removal of *unique identifiers* can be quite high. Researchers have therefore concluded that in order to have a privacy guarantee, actual privacy levels for a given data set must be established and proved mathematically.

Another approach to protecting privacy in publicly-released databases is called *output perturbation*, in which whenever a database query is submitted, the response is formulated and random "noise" is added to the result before the value is returned to the requester. For example, a query for Alice's salary might return the value "$67,000" or "$61,900" even though her actual salary is $63,250. This technique clearly helps to protect the privacy of Alice's information, but obviously the responses provide inaccurate information, which can make the data unhelpful or misleading in many real situations. It would be preferable to give accurate answers while still protecting user privacy.

In 1998, Pierangela Samarati and Latanya Sweeney proposed the concept of *k-anonymity* (1998), (Samarati 2001); see also (Sweeney 2002a, b) for additional detailed descriptions. This technique is intended to achieve the following goal: given a database of information, a release of data has the *k-anonymity* property if the information for each person in the release cannot be distinguished from at least *k-1* other individuals whose information also appears in the release. Thus, each person in the released data resides in an *anonymity set* (Pfitzmann and Hansen 2010) of size *k* and cannot be identified more narrowly than as a member of this set of *k* individuals. This appears to mitigate the deficiencies of the previous two approaches: the data released is guaranteed to be accurate; and any record in a *k-anonymized* data set has a maximum probability $p = 1/k$ of being re-identified.

### 6.1.1   The Basic Scheme

#### 6.1.1.1   Definitions and Goals

The 1998 paper by Samarati and Sweeney introduced the notion of *k-anonymity* for publicly-released data sets. For a data set, *D*, in which *unique identifiers* (such as *names*, *addresses*, and *phone numbers*) have been removed, the authors note that other distinctive data in *D*, which they term *quasi-identifiers*, "often combine uniquely and can be linked to publicly available information to re-identify individuals." Examples of such *quasi-identifiers* include *ZIP code*, *date of birth*, *ethnicity*, *sex*, and *marital status*; these can be matched against population registers that are available to the public (either for free, or for a nominal fee), such as local census data, voter lists, city directories, and information from motor vehicle agencies, tax assessors, and real estate agencies. Since population registers typically contain identities of individuals along with basic demographic information, individuals in *D* can be re-identified with minimal effort. The authors give a concrete illustration of this by taking a table of de-identified ("anonymous") medical data and linking it to a voter list (that they purchased for $20) to explicitly identify a particular individual and learn her medical condition.

   If *quasi-identifiers* are attributes that can be exploited for linking with other information sources, *k-anonymity* characterizes the degree of protection of data with respect to such linking inferences. In particular, the authors define the *k-anonymity requirement* as follows: "Each release of data must be such that every combination of values of *quasi-identifiers* can be indistinctly matched to at least *k* individuals." (More precisely, note that there may be some combinations that result in no matches, such as "all men between 150 and 160 years of age". But all combinations that match any record in the database (think of these as "successful combinations") will be guaranteed to match at least *k* records.) As a simple example, consider a publicly-released data set as shown in Table 6.1.

   The above data set has 3-*anonymity* with respect to the *quasi-identifiers postal code*, *age*, and *sex*: any successful combination of those quasi-identifiers matches 3 records in the data set and so it is not possible to link these quasi-identifiers with other information sources to re-identify an individual and learn the disease for which he/she is being treated.

#### 6.1.1.2   Techniques

Once *unique identifiers* have been removed from a data set, *D*, there are two techniques that can be used to give *D* the *k-anonymity* property. Samarati and Sweeney note that both these techniques, **generalization** and **suppression**, had been used

**Table 6.1**  Example of a publicly-released medical data set

| Name | Postal code | Age | Sex | Disease |
|------|-------------|-----|-----|---------|
| * | SW1 | 20–29 | M | Respiratory |
| * | SW1 | 20–29 | M | Cardiovascular |
| * | SW1 | 20–29 | M | Cancer |
| * | NW5 | 40–49 | F | Liver |
| * | NW5 | 40–49 | F | Tuberculosis |
| * | NW5 | 40–49 | F | Heart |
| * | E11 | 30–39 | * | Diabetes |
| * | E11 | 30–39 | * | Cancer |
| * | E11 | 30–39 | * | Viral infection |

prior to their work (in (Hundepool and Willenborg 1996) and (Sweeney 1997)), but without any formal foundation or abstraction. They therefore provide a formal foundation for the anonymity problem (with respect to linkage to external information sources) and for the use of *generalization* and *suppression* in its solution.

*Generalization* is the replacement of a specific attribute value with a broader category. In a classical relational database system, a "domain" describes the set of values that an attribute can assume. For example, the "domain" for the attribute *age* might be *integers* (or perhaps *integers from 0 to 120*). To achieve *k-anonymity*, the "domain" for *age* is replaced with a more general, less specific "domain" that can still be used to describe the age of an individual (such as 10-year age ranges). So, for example, an *age* value of "19" may be replaced by the range "10–19", and an *age* value of "23" may be replaced by the range "20–29". In this way, if *age* is a *quasi-identifier* that may be linked to external information sources to help identify a particular individual, *generalization* (i.e., the use of a broader "domain" for *age*) can be used to ensure that no fewer than *k* data records will be associated with the new "domain" value. Successively broader "domains" can be defined and used until *k-anonymity* for that *quasi-identifier* has been achieved.

*Suppression* is the removal of attribute values altogether. Thus, a specific attribute value is replaced with "*" (or "-", or "NULL"). *Suppression* is of course used for *unique identifiers* (such as *name*), but it can be used for *quasi-identifiers* as well. For example, in Table 6.1 above, the *Sex* attribute in the final three rows has been suppressed (in this case, one can presume that it is because the three individuals in postal code "E11" do not have the same sex and so suppression is the only way to achieve 3-*anonymity* for these records).

*Generalization* and *suppression* can be used individually, but are typically most effective when used together (some attribute values are generalized; others are suppressed). The goal is to achieve *k-anonymity* while ensuring that the released data set remains as useful as possible. For example, if every attribute value was suppressed, or if every attribute was generalized to its broadest possible domain, the released data set *D* would guarantee perfect privacy for all the individuals, but the data itself would clearly be of little utility to anyone.

### 6.1.1.3 Algorithm

Given a data set, multiple generalizations are possible for the *quasi-identifiers* that it contains. It can be the case that several of these generalizations achieve *k-anonymity*; however, these generalizations may not be equally satisfactory. For example, with Table 6.1 above, one could choose in postal code SW1 to generalize all the *Age* values to 0–119. The table modified in this way would still exhibit *k-anonymity*, but researchers studying cardiovascular disease would be able to learn nothing about the age group in which this disease occurred among the participants in this region. Clearly, the original Table 6.1 would be more useful to such researchers, even though it provides the same level of privacy as the modified version.

This realization about the *utility* of a data set led Samarati and Sweeney to the notion of *minimal generalization*: a data set generalization $D_j$ satisfying *k-anonymity* is *minimal* if and only if there does not exist another generalization $D_z$ satisfying *k-anonymity* which is dominated by $D_j$ in the *domain generalization hierarchy* (i.e., a $D_z$ which uses a less general domain for any of the contained *quasi-identifiers*). All *k-anonymous* generalizations of a given original data set will provide an equivalent level of privacy, and all will contain correct data, but the *minimal generalization* will be most useful to users of the released data set.

Similarly, Samarati and Sweeney define *minimal required suppression* as exactly the amount of suppression needed to achieve *k-anonymity*. For any given generalization of an original data set that does not achieve *k-anonymity*, its *minimal suppression* removes <u>all and only</u> the tuples that appear with fewer than *k* occurrences. As mentioned above, in Table 6.1, for postal code E11, there were originally more than 0 and fewer than 3 males (similarly for females); suppression was used on <u>only</u> the *Sex* attribute in <u>only</u> the E11 postal code to achieve 3-*anonymity* in the released data set. This is the *minimal required suppression*; any additional suppression (such as other *Sex* values, or some *Age* or *Postal Code* values) would be unnecessary for 3-*anonymity* and would make the released data set less useful.

The question therefore arises: to achieve *k-anonymity*, is it preferable to *generalize* (given that this leads to less precision in the released data), or to *suppress* (given that this leads to less completeness in the released data)? Samarati and Sweeney suggest that if an *acceptable suppression threshold* (i.e., a maximum number of suppressed tuples that is considered acceptable for the released data) has been specified, then – within that threshold – *suppression* is better than *generalization*. That is, they feel that it is better to suppress more tuples than to perform more generalization. This is because *suppression* affects single tuples, whereas *generalization* changes all the values associated with an attribute (because the attribute domain itself has been generalized) and so it affects all the tuples in the data set.

Recall that the overall goal of this PET is to achieve *k-anonymity* while releasing accurate data. However, judicious use of *generalization* and *suppression* allows the data owner to additionally retain as much utility in the released data set as possible. To this end, Samarati and Sweeney define *k-minimal generalization*: given a data set *D*, a generalization $D_j$ is *k-minimal* if and only if

1. $D_j$ satisfies *k-anonymity*,
2. $D_j$ does not enforce more *suppression* than allowed (i.e., more than the specified threshold),
3. There does not exist a *generalization* of $D$ that is less general than $D_j$ and satisfies 1 and 2, and
4. There does not exist a *generalization* of $D$ that is as general as $D_j$ and satisfies 1 and 2 with less *suppression*.

A *k-minimal generalization* is therefore ideal in terms of achieving *k-anonymity*, *correctness*, and maximum *utility* in the released data set. However, the authors note that there may be more than one *k-minimal generalization* for a given data set, *suppression* threshold, and *k-anonymity* constraint. Which of these is "best" will depend on the subjective preferences of the data recipient (for example, a particular use of the data may dictate that generalizing (or suppressing) attribute "A" is better than generalizing (or suppressing) attribute "B"). Thus, a potential data recipient may specify a *preference policy* for choosing a *k-minimal generalization*. Such a *preference policy* may specify, for example, that "a *k-minimal* $D_j$ with the narrowest *generalizations* of these particular attributes is preferred", or "a *k-minimal* $D_j$ with the fewest *suppressions* of these particular attributes is preferred", or "a *k-minimal* $D_j$ with the greatest number of distinct tuples is preferred".

Samarati and Sweeney designed and implemented an algorithm that finds a *preferred k-minimal generalization* for a data set, given a specific *threshold of suppression* and a specific *preference policy*. Some clever logic is used so that the algorithm does not need to follow every imaginable *generalization strategy* and compute every possible *generalization* in order to find a set of *k-minimal generalizations* from which the preferred one can be selected. They ran their algorithm on a real data set containing the medical records of 265 patients and were able to efficiently produce a releasable *k-minimal* data set.

## 6.1.2  Enhancements

The concept of *k-anonymity*, and the use of *generalization* and *suppression* techniques to achieve it, has not changed in any substantial way since the original 1998 paper. However, two extensions to *k-anonymity* have been introduced: *ℓ-diversity* and *t-closeness*.

### 6.1.2.1  ℓ-diversity

In 2007, Machanavajjhala, Kifer, Gehrke, and Venkitasubramaniam proposed the notion of *ℓ-diversity* (where "*ℓ*" is a script font of the letter "ell") (2007). They note two potential privacy vulnerabilities for a *k-anonymized* data set that contains a set of *quasi-identifiers* and some associated sensitive information (as in Table 6.1

above, where *Disease* is the sensitive attribute). First, if all the values (or if the vast majority of the values) of the sensitive attribute are the same within the set of *k* records having identical *quasi-identifiers*, then the value of the sensitive attribute for any individual in that set will be known with virtual certainty. As a simple example, if the *Disease* in the first three rows of Table 6.1 is *Cancer*, then anyone in the data set who lives in the SW1 postal code, or who is between 20 and 29 years of age, will have his disease known by everyone. In such a situation, *k-anonymity* alone cannot protect these individuals from having their sensitive information revealed to the world. The authors refer to this as a *homogeneity attack* and note that it was described in the literature prior to their work (e.g., in (Øhrn and Ohno-Machado 1999)).

Second, even if the sensitive attribute has a few different values within a set of records (i.e., the values are not homogeneous or near-homogeneous), it may be possible for an external observer to use additional background knowledge to learn sensitive information. The authors give an example of a 4-*anonymized* data set in which one record corresponds to a 21-year-old Japanese female named Umeko. In the set of 4 indistinguishable records (with respect to the *quasi-identifiers*) that include Umeko, two have a sensitive attribute of *Heart Disease* and two have a sensitive attribute of *Viral Infection*. These attribute values are clearly not homogeneous or near-homogeneous: there is exactly a 50% probability for each health condition. However, it is well-known that Japanese have an extremely low incidence of *heart disease*, and so an external observer who knows that Umeko's record is in the data set can conclude with near certainty that Umeko has a *viral infection*. Again, *k-anonymity* alone cannot prevent the privacy loss that results from this *background knowledge attack*.

To protect against these two vulnerabilities, the authors propose extending *k-anonymity* with *ℓ-diversity*. Let a block of records which are indistinguishable with respect to *quasi-identifiers* be called an *equivalence class*. An equivalence class is *ℓ-diverse* if it contains *ℓ* "well-represented" values for the sensitive attribute; furthermore, a data set is *ℓ-diverse* if every *equivalence class* contained in the data set is *ℓ-diverse*. The notion of "well-represented" can be realized in several different ways, such as

- *distinct ℓ-diversity*: each *equivalence class E* in the data set contains at least *ℓ* distinct values for the sensitive attribute,
- *entropy ℓ-diversity*: each *equivalence class E* in the data set has $Entropy(E) \geq \log(\ell)$ (for *equivalence class E*, let *p* be the fraction of records in *E* that have the sensitive value *s*, and define $Entropy(E)$ to be $-\Sigma p \log(p)$ where the sum is taken over the domain of the sensitive attribute), and
- *recursive (c-ℓ)-diversity*: for each *equivalence class E* in the data set, the frequency of the most common sensitive value is less than a constant *c* times the sum of the frequencies of all the other sensitive values, and this remains true recursively for each successive subset if the most frequent value is removed (in practice, this definition ensures that common values do not appear too frequently, and less-common values do not appear too infrequently).

Machanavajjhala et al., were able to show (through theoretical analysis, imple-mentation, and experimentation) that *ℓ-diversity* and *k-anonymity* are sufficiently similar in structure that *k-anonymity* algorithms can readily be modified to also achieve *ℓ-diversity*. Furthermore, such modified algorithms have similar (sometimes even faster) running times and comparable *utility*, compared with the original *k-anonymity* algorithms. The authors therefore conclude that *ℓ-diversity* is practical, efficient, and useful, while providing stronger privacy guarantees (in the sense of protecting against both *homogeneity attacks* and *background knowledge attacks*) than *k-anonymity* alone.

### 6.1.2.2   *t*-closeness

As an alternative to *ℓ-diversity*, Li, Li, and Venkatasubramanian proposed the notion of *t-closeness* in 2007 (2007). For *ℓ-diversity*, the goal is to ensure that *each equiva-lence class E* in the data set contains *ℓ* "well-represented" values of the sensitive attribute. However, as pointed out by Li et al., if attribute values are distinct but are semantically very similar, an observer may still be able to learn sensitive informa-tion. For example, if the diseases in the first three rows of Table 6.1 are *gastric ulcer*, *gastritis*, and *stomach cancer*, an observer who knows that 23-year-old David is in the released data set will be able to conclude with certainty that David has stomach-related problems.

Furthermore, given that the entire data set is public, an observer can easily deter-mine the distribution of any desired sensitive attribute over the data set. If the distri-bution of that attribute within a specific *equivalence class* is substantially different, the observer has learned important information about the individuals within that class. For example, suppose that 99% of a given population tests <u>negative</u> for a par-ticular health condition. An *equivalence class* in which the <u>positive</u> test rate is 75% clearly has greater privacy implications for its individuals than another class in which the <u>negative</u> rate is essentially equal to the population rate.

The proposed solution to these concerns, *t-closeness*, suggests that the distribu-tion of sensitive values in each *equivalence class E* (taking into account sematic similarity) should be close to the distribution of this attribute in the entire data set. In particular,

- An *equivalence class* is said to have *t-closeness* if the distance between the dis-tribution of a sensitive attribute in this class and the distribution of the attribute in the whole data set is no more than a threshold *t*. A data set is said to have *t-closeness* if all *equivalence classes* have *t-closeness*.

The difficulty with this definition, of course, is how to measure the "closeness" of two distributions. Li et al., investigated a number of alternatives and selected a metric called "Earth Mover's Distance" (EMD) (Rubner et al. 2000) which has several properties that make it particularly useful in the context of *t-closeness*. They implemented an EMD-based algorithm for *t-closeness* and compared it (using $t = 0.20$ and $t = 0.15$) with *k-anonymity*, *entropy ℓ-diversity*, and *recursive* (*c-ℓ*)-*diversity*. They found that, although it does not have the highest efficiency or utility, their *t-closeness* algorithm (particularly with $t = 0.20$) is only slightly slower than the fastest algorithm (*entropy ℓ-diversity*) and has only minimal degradation in data quality compared to the highest-utility algorithm (*k-anonymity* alone). The authors conclude that *t-closeness*, when used in conjunction with *k-anonymity*, provides meaningful privacy that overcomes the limitations of *ℓ-diversity*.

---

**In Case You Were Wondering...**
As discussed by Li et al. (2007), if new attribute information about some individuals is revealed in a released data set, an observer may be able to infer the characteristics of a particular individual, or a particular set of individuals, more accurately than would be possible without the release. This is clearly a loss of privacy, because the observer may learn sensitive information about certain individuals (even if their identities are not discovered). The techniques of *ℓ-diversity* and *t-closeness* have been proposed to limit this privacy loss (which occurs because of the disclosure of *attribute* information in the released data set). Therefore, these two techniques should ideally be discussed in the following chapter ("*Limiting Disclosure by Hiding the Attributes*"). However, they have been included in the present section because they were created to be extensions of *k-anonymity* and have been deliberately designed to improve the effectiveness of this *identity*-hiding PET.

---

## 6.1.3   Strengths

The *k-anonymity* technique proposed by Samarati and Sweeney is conceptually simple and achieves the intended goals of *accuracy* and good *utility* in the released data set while providing a mathematically-rigorous guaranteed *privacy level* (i.e., a maximum probability $1/k$ of re-identification for individuals in the data set). This PET thus hides the *identity* of individuals by putting each record into an *anonymity set* of size $k$. An external observer is therefore unable to link an individual to a specific record in the released data set.

Another strength of *k-anonymity* is that it is a general technique which can be used for more than just protecting the privacy of individuals in released data sets. One example of this is its use in a service for checking whether a user's password may be known to attackers. An online site called "*Pwned Passwords*" contains a list of more than 570 million real passwords that have been leaked in various data breaches [https://haveibeenpwned.com/Passwords]. Alice would like to know if her password is in this list, but she doesn't want to download the entire list from the website, and she certainly doesn't want to send her password to the site to have it checked there (this will reveal her password to the site owner, as well as to anyone else who may see her query). Even sending a *cryptographic hash* of her password will reveal too much information to any observers of her query. In 2018, *Cloudflare* [https://www.cloudflare.com/] engineer Junade Ali proposed ((Brodkin 2018); see also (Ali 2018) and (Li et al. 2019)) that Alice could send only the first 5 characters of the hash of her password to the site; the site would then return to her the hashes of all the passwords in the list whose first 5 characters equal what she sent. Alice can then compare (on her own machine) those hashes with the full hash of her own password to see if there is a match. *No match* means that her password is not in the site's list of known passwords (the ideal situation); a *positive match* means that her password is in the list and should be changed (although the site owner does not see Alice's local match result and so learns only that Alice's password might be in a *k-anonymous* set of passwords, where $381 \leq k \leq 584$ (Ali 2018)). This password-checking technique has been used by some password managers (such as *1Password* (Watchtower 2020)) and browser extensions (such as for *Google Chrome* (Branscombe 2018)).

### 6.1.4  Disadvantages, Limitations, and Weaknesses

Although *k-anonymity* is a powerful tool, like all technology it is not perfect. The *homogeneity attack* and *background knowledge attack* have been discussed above, and so it is clear that *k-anonymity* must be extended with other techniques (such as *ℓ-diversity* and *t-closeness*) to mitigate these vulnerabilities. In addition, one must be careful to ensure that the sensitive values included in the released data set do not inadvertently reveal information that was suppressed in the *quasi-identifiers*. For example, certain health conditions are unique to males or to females; their presence in the *Disease* column would therefore negate any intended benefit of suppressing a *Sex* attribute. More generally, one must also be careful that the *generalizations* and *suppressions* selected do not inadvertently skew the data to give unrepresentative or misleading results to those that will use the data set. Angiuli and Waldo (2016) have shown how to improve *generalization* and *suppression* to achieve *k-anonymity* while better preserving the original statistical properties of the data set.

As mentioned in Sect. 6.1.3 above, *k-anonymity* mathematically guarantees a maximum re-identification probability of $1/k$. However, El Emam and Dankar (2008) examined two re-identification scenarios that *k-anonymity* protects against (*re-identify a specific individual*, and *re-identify an arbitrary individual*) and found that the actual probability of re-identification with *k-anonymity* is much lower than $1/k$ for the second scenario, meaning that using the standard *k-anonymity* algorithm leads to excessive (and unnecessary) information loss in the data set for that scenario. They analyzed three different modifications to *k-anonymity* and identified one that ensures the actual risk is close to the desired threshold risk, which means that information loss can be reduced considerably in the released data set. They give guidelines for deciding when to use the original versus their modified *k-anonymity* algorithm.

Aggarwal (2005) has discussed "the curse of dimensionality" with respect to *k-anonymity*. In particular, when a data set contains a large number of attributes that may be considered *quasi-identifiers*, it becomes difficult to anonymize the data without an unacceptably high amount of information loss. This is because an exponential number of combinations of these attributes can be used to make inferences about individuals. Consequently, Aggarwal concludes that when a data set has a large number of attributes that may be used in inference attacks, the data set owner is left with the choice of either completely suppressing most of the data, or losing the desired level of anonymity. Surprisingly, he shows that in many cases with large numbers of *quasi-identifiers* (so-called "high dimensionality" cases – in some experiments, as few as 15–20 such attributes), the level of information loss required to achieve even 2-*anonymity* may be intolerable from a data mining point of view.

Furthermore, various researchers have shown that finding the best *k-anonymous* data set is actually quite difficult (regardless of considerations about information loss). Let the set of possible values for attributes in a data set be called the *alphabet* of the data set. Meyerson and Williams (2004) proved that suppressing a minimum number of values in a data set and achieving a privacy level $k \geq 3$ ("*minimum-cost 3-anonymity*") is *NP-hard* (in the general case when the alphabet is of large size). Building on this, Aggarwal et al. (2005), proved that *minimum-cost 3-anonymity* is *NP-hard* for an alphabet of size 3, and Bonizzoni et al. (2009), proved that *minimum-cost 3-anonymity* is *NP-hard* even for an alphabet of size 2 (i.e., binary attributes). It is known that *minimum-cost 2-anonymity* can be achieved in polynomial time, but clearly 2-*anonymity* does not provide very much privacy for individuals. Some researchers have been able to find heuristic or approximation algorithms that appear to work reasonably well in practice on real data sets (examples include Meyerson and Williams (2004), Bayardo and Agrawal (2005), and Kenig and Tassa (2012)), but the complexity and data loss results that have been found for *k-anonymity* will very often preclude its use for production-level data protection.

## 6.2  Credential Systems

In Sect. 6.1, the scenario is that a data owner has a database of information and wishes to extract a data set that can be released publicly. This data set is to be anonymized in such a way that users of the data set will find the contained information (particularly the *quasi-identifiers* and sensitive attribute values) useful, but individuals within the data set will not be able to be identified. The *k-anonymity* technique is a PET that has been designed to meet these requirements.

In this section we consider another scenario that does not involve a database or a publicly-released data set. In particular, suppose that Alice wishes to engage in an online transaction with a website or another person (to keep things generic, we will refer to the intended recipient of Alice's transaction messages as "Bob"). In order to initiate, process, or conclude the transaction, Bob needs to know whether Alice has a particular *attribute* or *set of attributes*. For example,

- If Bob is a government website, he may want to know whether Alice is a *citizen*;
- If Bob is a gateway to a company internal network, he may require that Alice is an *employee*;
- If Bob is a store or service provider, he may ask if Alice is on the *preferred client list* (e.g., a "*gold card member*");
- If Bob sells alcohol or other restricted products, he may insist that Alice is of *legal age*.

The question to be addressed in this section is whether such an online transaction can be conducted anonymously. That is, can Alice convince Bob that she validly has the specified *attributes* without revealing who she is? The goal is, as much as possible, to replicate in the online world what can already be done in the physical world. To purchase a restricted product in a physical store, it is sufficient for Alice to prove that her age is above a certain value; she does not technically need to reveal her identity (although very often in practice she will prove her age by showing a driver's license, which coincidentally divulges her name, address, photograph, and license number). To purchase items in other physical stores, Alice may only need to show a *loyalty card* or *coupon* to receive a discount; it is unnecessary for her to reveal her name if she chooses to pay with cash.

In 2000, Stefan Brands published a detailed treatise on a technology he called *Digital Credentials* (2000) (see also (2002) for a somewhat shorter summary). The core technology was described in a patent filed in 1993 (and issued in 1997) (Brands 1997) that borrowed heavily from seminal and extensive work on many different aspects of electronic privacy (including the concept of *credentials* as statements about an individual issued by one organization and shown to other organizations) by David Chaum throughout the period 1982–1992; see references 19–38 in (Brands 2002).

Brands' *Digital Credentials* extend and generalize Chaum's original *credentials* in a number of interesting ways. Perhaps most significantly, they allow a user to disclose a *property of an attribute*, rather than the *attribute* itself, in a transaction with a verifier (see Chap. 8 for a discussion of this). For example, Alice can prove that her citizenship is not American, or that she is European, without revealing her actual citizenship; similarly, Alice can prove that she is over 18, or over 21 (i.e., that she is legally allowed to purchase an item in the liquor store), without revealing her actual age. Another extension is that a *Digital Credential* can contain sensitive information that can be recovered by a central party only if the credential is used more than a predetermined number of times (prior to that point, the sensitive information is completely hidden in all transactions). As a generalization, Brands notes that *Digital Credentials* can be used to implement not only anonymous versions of gift certificates, coupons, railway tickets, and so on, but also diplomas, work permits, birth certificates, and other objects that traditionally identify their subject. Furthermore, if desired and appropriate, a *Digital Credential* can serve as an *identity certificate*: an *identifier* is simply treated as any other *attribute* that can be encoded in the *Digital Credential* and Alice can choose to disclose this *identifier* (or merely a *property* about it) whenever this is requested in a transaction with a verifier.

*Credential systems* (including *Digital Credentials* and a number of alternative technologies such as *Anonymous Credentials*) are not just an active area of research, but have also been deployed in the products of several major companies, including Microsoft (*UProve* (Microsoft 2012)) and IBM (*Identity Mixer* (*idemix*) (Neven 2011), (Camenisch et al. 2015)). This is therefore another of the PETs that has successfully made the transition from academic papers to the real world.

## 6.2.1  The Basic Scheme

### 6.2.1.1  Goal and Approach

The *Digital Credentials* technology that Brands proposed has *privacy-respecting authorization* as its primary goal. In particular, the idea is that a requester should be able to give a verifier only what is actually needed in order for the verifier to make an access decision (no more data, and no less data). The example in the previous section mentioned that in order to show a proof of age, often an entity (Alice) will show a driver's license. Alice's license is an official government-issued document that does include a birthdate, and so it clearly proves her *age*, but at the same time it reveals additional information to the verifier (her *name*, her *home address*, her *license number*, and so on). In most cases, this is more information than the verifier needs to see. In fact, in many situations, the verifier does not even need to see her *age*; all that is actually needed is a proof that her age is not below some threshold (e.g., 18 years or 21 years). If the verifier acquires any more information than this, it reduces Alice's level of privacy because additional (unnecessary) information may permit linkages to be found between this transaction and other transactions, or between this transaction and independent databases (census data, voter lists, and so on).

The name and (especially) the photo on the driver's license bind this document to the physical person presenting it, and so the contained birthdate can be trusted by the verifier to belong to this person. Brands needed a way to bind a *Digital Credential* to the person presenting it *without* revealing identifying information. He decided to adopt a slight variant of the methodology used for *public key certificates* in a *Public Key Infrastructure* (PKI).

> In a traditional PKI, Alice has a public key which is signed by a *Certification Authority* (CA) to form a *certificate*, and she has the corresponding private key (which she alone knows). The *certificate* also contains an *identifier* for Alice, along with some other relevant information such as an *expiry date*; the CA's digital signature on this *certificate* binds the public key to this *identifier* and warrants that whoever knows the private key corresponding to this public key is the legitimate owner of this public key, and therefore of the identifier bound to it.

(continued)

In an interaction, Alice proves to the other party (Bob) that she knows the private key. (She could do this by revealing the private key, but then the public key would have no subsequent value. Therefore, she instead typically proves her knowledge of the private key through a *challenge-response protocol* with Bob.) Once Bob becomes convinced that Alice knows the private key, he then believes that Alice is the owner of the public key in the *certificate*, and therefore of the *identifier* in the *certificate*. This authenticates Alice to Bob.

Brands' proposal still uses a CA to digitally sign a *certificate*, and still uses Alice's knowledge of the private key to prove her ownership of the *certificate* contents. What is different is how Alice proves knowledge of the private key. There is still a type of *challenge-response protocol*, but now the *challenge* is Bob telling Alice how to modify her public key (using a random value jointly computed by both Alice and Bob). This modified public key – which has never been seen before and which will not be seen in the future because it is constructed using this random one-time value – has a corresponding private key. As her *response*, Alice reveals this new private key to Bob. Brands was able to prove that
this new private key divulges nothing about the original private key to Bob, and Alice can only compute this new private key if she actually knows the original private key.

Therefore, showing Bob this new private key convinces him that Alice knows the original private key, and thus he is convinced that she is the owner of the *certificate* contents.

### 6.2.1.2 Construction

The <u>construction</u> of a *Digital Credential* merges, and builds on, two earlier technologies: *Pedersen commitment* and *blind signature*. Very briefly, these can be described as follows.

*Pedersen commitment*: Suppose Alice and Bob would like to do an online version of the coin-tossing game (Alice picks "heads" or "tails"; Bob tosses the coin and announces the side that is showing; Alice has either won or lost). To do this fairly, there must be a way to *bind* Alice to her initial choice (so that she cannot change it after the toss in order to win) and *hide* that choice from Bob until the coin has been tossed (so that he cannot secretly keep tossing the coin until Alice has lost). The *Pedersen commitment* from 1991 (Pedersen 1991) is a cryptographic technique to *bind* a value to Alice and *hide* this value from Bob (until it is later revealed). It works in the following way.

(continued)

Bob chooses primes $p$ and $q$, and a generator $g$ of the $q$-order subgroup of $Z_p^*$. Bob also chooses a value $b \in Z_q$ and computes $h = g^b \bmod p$. He makes $p$, $q$, $g$, and $h$ public, and keeps $b$ secret.

Alice commits to a value $x \in Z_q$ by choosing a random value $r \in Z_q$ and computing the commitment $com = g^x h^r \bmod p$. She sends $com$ to Bob.

Whenever appropriate, Alice can reveal $x$ and $r$ to Bob; he can check whether $g^x h^r \bmod p$ is equal to the *commitment com* that he received earlier from Alice. If so, he is convinced that this is the true value $x$ to which Alice originally committed.

Note that a minor variation of the above scheme turns it into a *commitment* that is instead *computationally hiding* and *unconditionally binding*, for environments where this might be preferable. Note, too, that the *Pedersen commitment* can easily be generalized to be a *commitment* on more than one value (for example, a *commitment* on three values would be $com = g_1^{x_1} g_2^{x_2} g_3^{x_3} h^r \bmod p$).

This scheme is *unconditionally hiding*: Bob cannot learn anything at all about Alice's committed value $x$ unless she reveals it to him, regardless of how much time and computing power he has. It is also *computationally binding*: Alice cannot find a different pair $(x', r')$ such that $g^x h^r \bmod p = com$ unless she has the computational ability to compute discrete logarithms modulo $p$.

---

*Blind signature*: The concept of a *blind signature* was proposed in 1982 by David Chaum (1983) who envisioned its use in *voting systems* and *untraceable payment systems*, among other applications. It is an ordinary *digital signature*, with two important differences. First, there are two parties: a user, Alice, who would like to get her message signed; and a signer, Sam, who possesses the private signing key and is therefore the only one that can compute the signature. Second, Alice does not want Sam to learn anything about the message. To achieve the latter property, the message is modified ("blinded") by Alice prior to giving it to Sam; this "blinding" is done in such a way that the resulting signature can be verified by anyone against the original, unmodified message.

Shafi Goldwasser and Mihir Bellare have presented a simple example of how the *RSA digital signature* algorithm could be used to achieve *blind signatures* (2008).

Alice has a message $m$ that she wants Sam to sign, but she doesn't want Sam to learn $m$. She chooses a random number $r$ and computes $m' = mr^e \bmod n$. (The value $r$ unconditionally hides the message $m$.) Alice gives $m'$ to Sam.

Sam signs the value $m'$ by computing a conventional *RSA signature operation*: $s' = (m')^d \bmod n$. Sam gives $s'$ to Alice.

Alice computes $s'(r^{-1}) \bmod n = (m')^d(r^{-1}) = (mr^e)^d(r^{-1}) = (m^d)(r^{ed})(r^{-1}) = (m^d)(r)(r^{-1}) = m^d \bmod n = s$.

(continued)

Alice thus obtains a valid message-signature pair $(m, s)$ that can be verified by anyone using Sam's public key $(e, n)$ in the familiar *RSA signature verification operation*: "Is $s^e \bmod n = m$?" Note, however, that Sam has never seen – and cannot compute – $m$ or $s$.

With *Digital Credentials*, Brands proposed that the value in the *commitment* would be an *attribute* of a user (e.g., Alice's *name*, or her *birthdate*, or her *Social Insurance Number*, or her *gold card membership*). In fact, there would be multiple (say $m$) *attributes* encoded into the same *commitment*. Let these be denoted $x_1$, $x_2, \ldots, x_m$. Then Alice's *commitment* would have the form

$$h = \left(g_1{}^{x_1} \cdot g_2{}^{x_2} \cdot \ldots \cdot g_m{}^{x_m} \cdot h_0\right)^{\alpha} \; (this\ whole\ computation\ is\ reduced\ modulo\ p)$$

where $g_1, \ldots g_m$ and $h_0$ are part of the CA's public key, $p$ is a prime number of sufficient size for security (e.g., 2048 bits or more), and $\alpha$ is a random number chosen by Alice and known only to her. Thus, Alice's private key is this value $\alpha$, along with her $m$ *attribute values* (although she may reveal some or all of these *attribute values* to various verifiers over time; see "Transaction" below), and her corresponding public key is the *commitment* (i.e., the single integer) $h$, as computed above.

*Constructing a Digital Credential: the issuing protocol*. Suppose that Alice has a number of *attributes* that are intrinsically hers (such as *name*, *birthdate*, and *home address*) and a number of attributes that have been legitimately assigned to her (such as *Social Security Number*, *gold card membership* at a particular business, and *job position* at her workplace). Alice would like to encode $m$ of these *attributes* into a *Digital Credential*. She adopts whatever convention/policy has been defined in her environment for encoding different types of *attributes* (for example, perhaps *name* is a character string interpreted as an integer, *birthdate* is in DDMMYYYY format interpreted as a single integer, *home address* is an arbitrary-length character string that is cryptographically hashed and then interpreted as an integer, and so on) and computes the commitment $h$ as specified above on these $m$ *attribute values* $x_1, x_2, \ldots, x_m$. She then contacts a CA to prove (typically in an offline interaction) that she indeed has these *attribute values*. Following this, she and the CA conduct the issuing protocol which results in the CA creating a *blind signature* for $h$.

Let $G_q$ be a group of prime order $q$, and let $g_0$ be a randomly-chosen base (i.e., a generator) of $G_q$. The CA chooses $m + 1$ numbers at random, $y_1, \ldots, y_m$ and $x_0$, and computes $g_i = g_0{}^{y_i}$ for $i = 1 \ldots m$ and $h_0 = g_0{}^{x_0}$. The public key of the CA is the set of integers $\{g_0, g_1, \ldots, g_m, h_0\}$ and its corresponding private key is the set of integers $\{y_1, \ldots, y_m, x_0\}$.

(continued)

Alice has attribute values $\{x_1, \ldots, x_m\}$ and she creates the *commitment* on those values $h = (g_1{}^{x_1} \cdot g_2{}^{x_2} \cdot \ldots \cdot g_m{}^{x_m} \cdot h_0)^\alpha$ using a randomly-chosen value $\alpha$ (note that for simplicity we will omit the "mod $p$" term from these expressions although it is to be understood that all computation is done modulo $p$ unless otherwise indicated). The public key of Alice is the *commitment* $h$ and its corresponding private key is the set of values $\{x_1, \ldots, x_m, \alpha\}$.

The **Digital Credential issuing protocol** is as follows.

Step 1: The CA generates a random number $w_0$ and sends $a_0 = g_0{}^{w_0}$ to Alice.

Step 2: Alice generates random numbers $\beta$, $\gamma$ and computes $c_0{}' = H(h, g_0{}^\beta(g_1{}^{x_1} \cdot g_2{}^{x_2} \cdot \ldots \cdot g_m{}^{x_m} \cdot h_0)^\gamma a_0)$, where $H()$ is a publicly-known strong one-way hash function. Alice *blinds* the value $c_0{}'$ using her random number $\beta$ by computing $c_0 = c_0{}' - \beta \bmod q$; she then sends the *blinded* value $c_0$ to the CA.

Step 3: The CA computes $r_0 = (w_0 - c_0) / (x_0 + x_1 y_1 + \ldots + x_m y_m) \bmod q$ and sends $r_0$ to Alice.

Alice accepts if and only if $g_0{}^{c_0}(g_1{}^{x_1} \cdot g_2{}^{x_2} \cdot \ldots \cdot g_m{}^{x_m} \cdot h_0)^{r_0}$ is equal to the $a_0$ that she received from the CA in Step 1. If this verification holds, then Alice *blinds* the value $r_0$ by computing $r_0{}' = (r_0 + \gamma)/\alpha \bmod q$.

At the conclusion of this protocol, the CA has seen only the values $a_0$, $c_0$, and $r_0$, but Alice has obtained $\{h, (c_0{}', r_0{}')\}$, a {*public key, CA digital signature*} set (in essence, a *public key certificate*) that is unrecognizable to the CA, but that can be verified by anyone using the CA's public key; this is her *Digital Credential*. Note, however, that the public key of Alice in this construction is unlike an *RSA public key* or a *DSA public key* in a conventional PKI; this public key holds all $m$ of Alice's attribute values (*name*, *job position*, etc.), even though it is only a single integer of size $|p|$.

### 6.2.1.3   Transaction

Alice now has a public key $h$ and a CA signature on this public key $(c_0{}', r_0{}')$. Any verifier, knowing the CA's public key (in particular, the CA's public value $g_0$), can use the following *verification equation* to check that the public key was validly signed by the CA, and so be convinced that $h$ is a legitimate *commitment* on a set of *attribute values*.

$$\text{Verification equation} : c_0{}' = H\left(h, g_0{}^{c_0{}'} h^{r_0{}'}\right)$$

(Note that it may seem counter-intuitive to have the integer $c_0{}'$ on both the left side and the right side of the above equation, but careful algebraic manipulation will confirm that if $h$, $c_0$' and $r_0$' are valid, then the hash of $h$ concatenated with $g_0{}^{c_0'}h^{r_0'}$ will indeed be equal to $c_0$'.)

Similarly to the proposal for <u>construction</u> above, Alice's <u>use</u> of a *Digital Credential* in an online transaction with Bob also builds on an earlier technology: *zero-knowledge proof of knowledge*. Briefly, this can be described as follows.

---

*Zero-knowledge proof of knowledge*: Suppose that Alice would like to convince Bob that she knows a particular value, but she does not want him to learn anything at all about what the value is. A *zero-knowledge proof of knowledge* (often referred to simply as a *zero-knowledge proof*; see (Goldreich et al. 1986) and (Goldwasser et al. 1989) for the original discussion of this topic) is a cryptographic protocol or technique that allows Alice to prove her knowledge, but to prove it in "zero-knowledge" (i.e., to prove it in such a way that Bob learns nothing except the fact that she actually knows what she is claiming to know). As an example, say $y = g^x \bmod p$ where $p$ is a prime and $g$ is a generator of the $q$-order subgroup of $Z_p{}^*$. Bob knows $y$, $g$, $q$, and $p$, but is unable to compute discrete logarithms modulo $p$ and so does not know the value $x$. Alice wants to convince Bob that she knows $x$ without revealing anything about $x$ to him. This can be accomplished as follows (see (Chaum et al. 1988) for additional details).

Alice chooses a random value $r \in Z_q$ and computes $t = g^r \bmod p$. She sends $t$ to Bob.

Bob chooses a random value $c \in Z_q$. He sends $c$ to Alice.

Alice computes $s = cx + r \bmod q$ and sends $s$ to Bob.

Bob checks to see whether $g^s \bmod p$ is equal to $ty^c \bmod p$. If so, he is convinced that Alice must know $x$ (otherwise, she could not have correctly computed the value $s$), but he learns nothing whatever about $x$.

As a second example, say that Alice has sent a *Pedersen commitment* $com = g^x h^r \bmod p$ to Bob. She can prove that she knows the value $x$ in her commitment without revealing $x$ to Bob. This can be accomplished as a slight extension to the above protocol.

Alice chooses two random values $r_1$, $r_2 \in Z_q$ and computes $t = g^{r_1}h^{r_2} \bmod p$. She sends $t$ to Bob.

Bob chooses a random value $c \in Z_q$. He sends $c$ to Alice.

Alice computes $s_1 = cx + r_1 \bmod q$ and $s_2 = cr + r_2 \bmod q$. She sends $(s_1, s_2)$ to Bob.

Bob computes $t(com^c) \bmod p$. (The value $t(com^c) = (g^{r_1}h^{r_2} \bmod p) \cdot (g^x h^r \bmod p)^c = (g^{r_1}h^{r_2} \bmod p) \cdot (g^{cx}h^{cr} \bmod p) = g^{(cx + r_1 \bmod q)}h^{(cr + r_2 \bmod q)} \bmod p$. Note that exponents of like terms combine in the usual algebraic fashion, but because $g$ is a generator of the $q$-order subgroup of $Z_p{}^*$, all expressions in the exponents are reduced modulo $q$ while all expressions in the bases are reduced modulo $p$.)

---

(continued)

Bob then computes $g^{s_1}h^{s_2} \bmod p$ using the $s_1$ and $s_2$ he received from Alice. If $g^{s_1}h^{s_2} \bmod p$ is equal to $t(com^c) \bmod p$, Bob is convinced that Alice must know $x$ (otherwise, she could not have correctly computed $s_1$ and $s_2$), but he learns nothing whatever about $x$.

With a *Digital Credential*, Alice has her public key $h$ (which is a *commitment* on a number of *attribute values*) and she wishes to prove to Bob that she knows its corresponding private key (thereby convincing him that she is the legitimate owner of this public key, and therefore of the *attribute values* it contains). Along with this, she may choose to reveal one or more specific *attribute values* to Bob (for example, her *age* so that she can purchase alcohol, or her *gold card membership* so that she can obtain a discount on a desired item or service). The structure of the *Digital Credential* and the form of the showing protocol allow Alice to do both of these simultaneously. However, for clarity we will begin with proving knowledge of the private key and then describe how to concurrently reveal specific *attribute values*.

*Transacting with a Digital Credential: the showing protocol.* As was done in (Brands 2002), we will begin with a simpler form of the public key in order to aid understanding of the logic involved in the showing protocol. We will then discuss the showing protocol for the actual public key format that was constructed in the issuing protocol above.

Let Alice's public key take the form $h = (g_1^{x_1} \cdot g_2^{x_2} \cdot \ldots \cdot g_m^{x_m} \cdot h_0^{\alpha})$. Note that, in this form, the random value $\alpha$ is inside the parenthesis rather than outside; therefore, it is an exponent only for the term $h_0$ and does not serve as a multiplier for all the $x_i$ exponents. The **Digital Credential showing protocol** is conducted between Alice and Bob as follows.

Step 1: Alice generates $m + 1$ random numbers $w_1, \ldots, w_m, w_{m+1}$ and computes a random value in the form of a public key: $a = (g_1^{w_1} \cdot g_2^{w_2} \cdot \ldots \cdot g_m^{w_m} \cdot h_0^{w_{m+1}})$. She sends $h$, the CA's signature on $h$, and this random value $a$ to Bob.

Step 2: Bob verifies the CA's signature on $h$ using the *verification equation* (see the first paragraph under the heading "Transaction" above for the *verification equation*). If it is valid, he generates a random number $c$ and sends this to Alice.

Step 3: Alice computes
$r_1 = cx_1 + w_1 \bmod q$,
$r_2 = cx_2 + w_2 \bmod q$,

...

$r_m = cx_m + w_m \bmod q$,
$r_{m+1} = c\alpha + w_{m+1} \bmod q$.
She then sends $r_1, \ldots, r_m, r_{m+1}$ to Bob.

Bob computes $h^c a$ and checks whether the result is equal to $(g_1^{r_1} \cdot g_2^{r_2} \cdot \ldots$ $\cdot g_m^{r_m} \cdot h_0^{r_{m+1}})$. If so, Alice has demonstrated that she knows the private key (i.e., $r_1, \ldots, r_m, r_{m+1}$) for the modified public key $h^c a$ (that is, the key $h$ modified by both a random value from Bob ($c$) and a random value from Alice ($a$), so that neither side can cheat). Since she knows this new private key for the modified public key $h^c a$, she must know the private key for the original public key $h$ and, consequently, must be the legitimate owner of $h$ and the *attribute values* it contains.

We now consider the case in which Alice wants to reveal a specific attribute value to Bob. Assume that she wants to prove that $x_2 = 17$. The showing protocol described above is modified only slightly: no random number $w_2$ is generated; the computed random value $a$ does not contain $g_2^{w_2}$; and no value $r_2$ is sent to Bob (the actual value of 17 is sent instead).

The ***showing protocol* for revealing $x_2$** is conducted as follows.

Step 1: Alice generates $m$ random numbers $w_1, w_3, \ldots, w_m, w_{m+1}$ and computes a random value in the form of a public key: $a = (g_1^{w_1} \cdot g_3^{w_3} \cdot \ldots \cdot g_m^{w_m} \cdot h_0^{w_{m+1}})$. She sends $h$, the CA's signature on $h$, and this random value $a$ to Bob.

Step 2: Bob verifies the CA's signature on $h$ using the *verification equation*. If it is valid, he generates a random number $c$ and sends this to Alice.

Step 3: Alice computes
$r_1 = cx_1 + w_1 \bmod q$,
$r_3 = cx_3 + w_3 \bmod q$,
$\ldots$
$r_m = cx_m + w_m \bmod q$,
$r_{m+1} = c\alpha + w_{m+1} \bmod q$.
She then sends $r_1, 17, r_3, \ldots, r_m, r_{m+1}$ to Bob.

Bob computes $h^c a$ and checks whether the result is equal to $(g_1^{r_1} \cdot g_2^{17c} \cdot g_3^{r_3} \cdot \ldots \cdot g_m^{r_m} \cdot h_0^{r_{m+1}})$. If so, not only has Alice demonstrated that she knows the private key for the modified public key $h^c a$, but she has also revealed the specific private value $x_2$. Thus, she has proved to Bob that she is the legitimate owner of $h$ and that she has *attribute value $x_2 = 17$*.

As mentioned earlier, the previous discussion has used a simpler form of the public key. In the issuing protocol, Alice's public key actually takes the form $h = (g_1^{x_1} \cdot g_2^{x_2} \cdot \ldots \cdot g_m^{x_m} \cdot h_0)^\alpha$. Thus, the ***showing protocol* for revealing $x_2$** (above) must be modified to take this new form into account. However, upon careful examination it should be clear that conceptually it is achieving the identical functionality. Again, let us assume that Alice wants to prove ownership of $h$ and reveal $x_2 = 17$ to Bob.

Alice's public key $h = (g_1{}^{x_1} \cdot g_2{}^{x_2} \cdot \ldots \cdot g_m{}^{x_m} \cdot h_0)^{\alpha}$ can be re-written in the following way: $h = (g_1{}^{\alpha x_1} \cdot g_2{}^{\alpha x_2} \cdot \ldots \cdot g_m{}^{\alpha x_m} \cdot h_0{}^{\alpha}) = (g_1{}^{z_1} \cdot g_2{}^{z_2} \cdot \ldots \cdot g_m{}^{z_m} \cdot h_0{}^{z_0})$, where $z_1 = \alpha x_1, \ldots z_m = \alpha x_m$ and $z_0 = \alpha$. This final form looks very much like the simplified form above, except that the $z_i$ ($i = 1, \ldots, m$) are not her actual *attribute values*, but are the values multiplied by the random number $\alpha$. Therefore, Alice cannot simply reveal $x_2$ (as was done in the previous version of the ***showing protocol* for revealing $x_2$**) because $\alpha$ is not known by Bob and so Bob would have no way of confirming whether the value Alice revealed is correct. Furthermore, Alice cannot reveal both $z_2$ and $\alpha$, because although this would show the true value of $x_2$, it would also make it possible for Bob to learn all the other $x_i$ values. Rather, the approach taken is for Alice to prove that $z_2 = 17z_0$ and $z_0 \neq 0$ (thus proving that $x_2 = 17$).

The **modified *showing protocol* for revealing $x_2$** is conducted as follows.

<u>Step 1</u>: Alice generates $m$ random numbers $w, w_1, w_3, \ldots, w_m$ and computes a random value in this way: $a = h^{-w}(g_1{}^{w_1} \cdot g_3{}^{w_3} \cdot \ldots \cdot g_m{}^{w_m})$. She sends $h$, the CA's signature on $h$, and this random value $a$ to Bob.

<u>Step 2</u>: Bob verifies the CA's signature on $h$ using the *verification equation*. If it is valid, he generates a random number $c$ and sends this to Alice.

<u>Step 3</u>: Alice computes

$c' = c/\alpha + w \bmod q$,

$r_1 = cx_1 + w_1 \bmod q$,

$r_3 = cx_3 + w_3 \bmod q$,

$\ldots$

$r_m = cx_m + w_m \bmod q$.

She then sends $c'$, $r_1$, $17$, $r_3$, $\ldots$, $r_m$ to Bob.

Bob computes $h^{c'}a$. (Note that $h^{c'}a = h^{(c/\alpha + w)}a = (h^{(c/\alpha)}h^w)(h^{-w}(g_1{}^{w_1} \cdot g_3{}^{w_3} \cdot \ldots \cdot g_m{}^{w_m})) = (g_1{}^{cx_1} \cdot g_2{}^{cx_2} \cdot g_3{}^{cx_3} \cdot \ldots \cdot g_m{}^{cx_m} \cdot h_0{}^c)(g_1{}^{w_1} \cdot g_3{}^{w_3} \cdot \ldots \cdot g_m{}^{w_m}) = (g_1{}^{cx_1 + w_1} \cdot g_2{}^{cx_2} \cdot g_3{}^{cx_3 + w_3} \cdot \ldots \cdot g_m{}^{cx_m + w_m} \cdot h_0{}^c)$.) Bob then checks whether $h^{c'}a$ is equal to $(g_1{}^{r_1} \cdot g_2{}^{17c} \cdot g_3{}^{r_3} \cdot \ldots \cdot g_m{}^{r_m} \cdot h_0{}^c)$. If so, it is clear that $z_0$ cannot be zero (because $h^{c'}a$ obviously contains an $h_0$ term) and that $z_2$ is equal to $17z_0$ (i.e., the exponent on $g_2$ is 17 times the exponent on $h_0$), and so Alice has proved to Bob that she is the legitimate owner of $h$ and that she has *attribute value $x_2 = 17$*.

Thus, the issuing protocol and the showing protocol together allow Alice to obtain a *Digital Credential* that holds her *attribute values*, and convincingly reveal any chosen *attribute values* in this *Digital Credential* to a verifier.

### 6.2.1.4  Privacy-Respecting Authorization

The above protocols allow Alice to prove ownership of specific *attribute values* (e.g., *birthdate, citizenship, employee* status, *gold card membership*, and so on). The fact that she validly owns these values has been confirmed by an authority (during

Alice's offline interaction with the CA immediately prior to conducting the issuing protocol), and the authority has attested to this ownership by digitally signing a public key for Alice that contains these values. Thus, when Alice proves in a showing protocol that her *birthdate* is, for example, 26/04/2000, the verifier can believe that this is her true *birthdate* and service her transaction request accordingly.

It is important to recognize that this communication with the verifier is privacy-respecting. The verifier, Bob, learns Alice's *age* without also learning her *name*, her *address*, and her *license number*, as he would in a traditional setting by examining her driver's license. Indeed, because of the *blinding factor* in the public key (the random number α) and the random values used in both the issuing protocol and the showing protocol, Brands was able to prove that *Digital Credentials* guarantee privacy in the strongest possible sense: *even if all verifiers and CAs conspire in an active attack, jointly establish secret information in a preparatory phase, and have unlimited computing power, they cannot learn more than what can be inferred from the attribute information that Digital Credential owners voluntarily disclose* (Brands 2002).

The *information-theoretic security* of all *Digital Credential* information that is not intentionally revealed in the transaction is a very powerful property. It is analogous to Alice taking her physical driver's licence and crossing out – with an opaque black marker – everything on the card except her *birthdate* (and possibly also her *photo* in order to convince the verifier that the card belongs to her). However, it is much more flexible than this analogy because Alice has the ability to do the equivalent of "erasing the black marks": she can prove only her *birthdate* and her *gold card membership* to one verifier, and only her *employee* status to another, if she chooses.

## 6.2.2 Enhancements

Since the publication of the full *Digital Credentials* proposal in 2000, a number of researchers have explored enhancements and variations of this technology. As with every technology, there has been interest in improving time or space efficiency, reducing implementation complexity, and so on. However, two properties in particular have been the focus of several proposals: *non-transferability* and *unlinkability*. (Note that one paper has also explored a construction for privacy-preserving *delegation* in the context of *Digital Credentials* (Knox and Adams 2011).)

*Non-Transferability*. Suppose Alice has a *Digital Credential* containing an *attribute value* that allows her to read an online newspaper or magazine (perhaps it is some kind of *subscription token*). Clearly, Alice knows the private key for this *credential* (i.e., all *m attribute values* as well as the random value α) so that she can use this *credential* in showing protocols. However, if Alice tells Betty this private key, then Betty will also be able to use this *credential* in showing protocols; in particular, Betty will be able to read the newspaper or magazine without having to purchase her own *subscription token*. In fact, Alice could share her private key with 1000 friends and then they could all read for free. This is called *credential transfer* and this situation is sometimes referred to as the *lending problem* (Alice can easily lend her *credential* to others for their use without any CAs or verifiers being aware of this). Thus, CAs and verifiers desire *non-transferability* in *credential systems* so that lending among users can be prevented.

Brands was aware of the *lending problem* and suggested that the CA could include a particular *attribute* (or set of *attributes*) in the *Digital Credential* that Alice may be unwilling to share. He proposed *attributes* such as her credit card data, a digital coin or other electronic token of value, or an external private key of Alice that can be used to sign e-mail or to authenticate access to a bank account (Brands 2002); see also a similar proposal in (Syverson et al. 1997). Others have suggested that the *attribute* could be a key that enables decryption of externally-held encrypted sensitive information of Alice (Camenisch and Lysyanskaya 2001), or that it could be *biometrics* of Alice (such as her *fingerprint*, *retinal scan*, or a combination of *eye colour*, *height*, and other personal characteristics) that would allow her to be identified (Brands 2000). Still others have suggested that lending could be made to automatically restrict *credential* usage, such as forcing *attribute values* to be revealed in a specific order (Chen et al. 2008) or limiting the number of times a *credential* can be involved in a transaction (Camenisch et al. 2006), (Blanton 2008). Note that all of these proposals may discourage lending, but do not actually prevent it (especially between very close friends, or among criminals in a gang). Another suggestion is the use of *tamper-resistant smart card technology* (see (More 2003), (Impagliazzo and More 2003)) as a means to prevent credential lending.

The work of Adams (Adams 2011) and Bissessar et al. (2014) instead proposes that the *attribute* should be a *Pedersen commitment* on a *biometric* (such as a *fingerprint* or *retinal scan*). During a showing protocol, a fresh *biometric* is taken, a *commitment* is computed (within the *biometric reader device*) on this *biometric*, and this new device-computed *commitment* is given to the verifier. Then, a *zero-knowledge protocol* is used to prove to the verifier that this new *commitment* and the *commitment* encoded in the *credential* are actually *commitments* on the same hidden value (i.e., the same *biometric*), without revealing any information about the value. Thus, the verifier is convinced that the individual currently using the *credential* is the same as the individual to whom this *credential* was originally issued (i.e., there was no lending). This proposal is reasonably efficient and has the advantage (over the previous proposals) that it actually <u>prevents</u> lending (for a *computationally-bounded user*), rather than simply <u>discouraging</u> lending, without the need for expensive smart card hardware.

*Unlinkability*. Suppose Alice has a *Digital Credential* $\{h, (c_0', r_0')\}$. She uses this *credential* in a showing protocol to prove ownership of some *attribute value* $x_i$. When she subsequently uses this *credential* in another showing protocol to prove ownership of another *attribute value* $x_j$ (either with the same verifier or with another verifier), it will be clear that the same individual has been involved in both transactions (assuming that the *lending problem* (above) has been prevented) because the same public key and CA signature have been submitted. Observers can thus *link* her individual transactions; Alice would ideally like to have the property of *unlinkability* for her *credentials* in order to prevent this.

Brands recognizes that *unlinkability* is a desirable property and acknowledges that his *Digital Credentials* are *linkable*. To mitigate this, he proposes two techniques (both can be used within the same environment). First, he designed an efficient batch issuing protocol that can simultaneously create many unlinkable *credentials* for Alice (that is, many *Digital Credentials* with the same *attributes* encoded within them, but each with its own public key); she can then choose to use any or all of these variations only once. Second, he designed a privacy-preserving *refresh protocol* in which the CA "blindly" creates a fresh unlinkable *credential* with the same *attribute values* as the submitted "spent" *credential* (a similar idea was earlier proposed in (Syverson et al. 1997)).

An entirely different approach to *unlinkability* was proposed by Jan Camenisch and Anna Lysyanskaya in 2001 (2001). In their system, which they called *Anonymous Credentials*, a user $U$ has a master secret $x$ and an organization $O$ has a set of public values $\{n, a, b, d, g, h\}$, where $n$ is an *RSA modulus* (the product of two safe primes) and $a$, $b$, $d$, $g$, and $h$ are *quadratic residues* modulo $n$. The proposal can be described at a very high level in the following way (note that all computation below is done modulo $n$).

A user $U$ and an organization $O$ participate in the creation of a *name-tag* pair $(N, T)$ that they each store in their own local database. The name $N$ is the concatenation of a random string from the user and a random string from the organization: $N = \{r_U \,\|\, r_O\}$. The tag $T$ is computed by the user from the user's master secret $x$, values $a$ and $b$ from the organization's public values, and a random value $s$ contributed to by both the user and the organization: $T = a^x b^s$. (The user engages in a protocol to prove to the organization that $T$ was correctly formed without revealing either $x$ or $s$ to the organization.) The pair $(N, T)$ is referred to as a *pseudonym*; the organization knows the user by this *pseudonym* and, depending on the requirements of the environment, may not learn the user's true identity.

Once the *pseudonym* has been established, the organization can create a *credential* for the user: the organization chooses a random prime $e$ and computes $c = (Td)^{1/e}$. The *credential* is the pair $(c, e)$; this *credential* is given to the user (who checks that $c^e = Td$). Both the user and the organization append the *credential* to the corresponding *pseudonym* in their local database. The creation and storage of a *pseudonym-credential* pair for this user and organization is analogous (in functionality) to the issuing protocol in Brands' *Digital Credentials* scheme.

The user is now able to interact with a verifier to execute the analogue of the showing protocol in *Digital Credentials*. The huge difference in *Anonymous Credentials* (compared with *Digital Credentials*) is that the user does not reveal the actual *credential* to the verifier. Rather, the user engages in a *zero-knowledge proof* to prove knowledge of a correctly-formed tag $T$ and a *credential* $(c, e)$ on that tag. This is done by the user sending to the verifier statistically secure *commitments* to both the tag and the *credential*, and proving relationships between these *commitments* using the organization's public values $a$, $b$, $g$, and $h$. The user furthermore proves that the user's master secret $x$ is the same in both the original issued tag and the just-computed *commitment* on that tag (without revealing $x$, of course). The verifier is convinced that the user actually has a valid *credential* with the specified organization, without ever seeing the *credential* (or the *pseudonym* by which this user is known to that organization). This is why *Anonymous Credentials* are intrinsically multi-show; they can be used an unlimited number of times with any number of verifiers because they are never revealed in any showing transaction.

Note that the *credential* in this system is just a generic concept without any specific defined meaning ("User Alice has a *credential* with Organization Y"). However, Camenisch and Lysyanskaya note that an *expiration date* and other *attributes* of the *credential* (or of the user) can be encoded into the exponent $e$ (which will then no longer be a completely random prime) at the organization's discretion. This can be done by dividing the interval of values allowed for $e$ into subintervals. Then, if a verifier requires Alice to prove a specific *attribute* of her *credential* (e.g., *gold card membership*), she can prove that $e$ is an integer that lies in the appropriate subinterval rather than proving simply that $e$ is an integer of the originally stipulated bit length.

Since *zero-knowledge proofs* can involve significant computational overhead and implementation complexity, *Anonymous Credentials* may not be ideally suited to all situations and environments. (Although *Coconut* anonymous credentials (Sonnino et al. 2019) are a notable exception, providing many desirable credential properties with very high efficiency. Along with the *Loopix* mix network (Piotrowska et al. 2017) mentioned in Chap. 3, *Coconut* is a component in the *Nym* privacy infrastructure (https://nymtech.net/).) In (Fan and Adams 2018), Fan and Adams propose the use of *malleable signatures* to provide *unlinkability* for *Digital Credentials*. (Note that a digital signature scheme is *malleable* if, for a given message and its signature, it is possible to efficiently modify the signature to be a valid signature on a related message without using the private signing key (Chase et al. 2014).) The basic idea is as follows.

> In Brands' original proposal, the *blinding* process happens once (i.e., between Alice and the CA during the issuing protocol, so that the CA cannot later trace Alice's movements as she uses her *credential* and signature). However, once Alice has her issued *credential* and signature, she will use these with all verifiers. Her transactions can therefore be *linked* across different verifiers; furthermore, collusion among verifiers is possible so that each of them can learn more about Alice. The proposal by Fan and Adams is to have the *blinding* process happen in the showing protocol with every transaction. In this way, different verifiers will not know that they have interacted with the same entity (i.e., Alice) and so *linking* of her transactions and collusion among verifiers are both prevented. (Note that it remains true that the CA cannot trace Alice's movements because Alice is using a randomized *credential* every time).
>
> In order to have the *blinding* process in the showing protocol, it is necessary for Alice to not only randomize the *credential*, but to correspondingly randomize the CA's digital signature so that this "new" *credential* can be verified. In other words, Alice requires a "new" CA digital signature – *unlinkable* to the original signature – that can verify the "new" *credential* using the CA's public key, but of course without requiring the CA's private key to create the "new" signature.

The proposal instantiates the above idea by using the *malleability* of the *RSA digital signature scheme*. This provides a very efficient way to transform Brands' original construction from *single-show credentials* into *unlinkable multi-show credentials* without sacrificing any of their inherent security or privacy properties. At a very high level (omitting some details in order to give a brief description), Alice creates her public key $h = (g_1{}^{x_1} \cdot g_2{}^{x_2} \cdot \ldots \cdot g_{m-1}{}^{x_{m-1}} \cdot g_m{}^{ID} \cdot h_0{}^{\alpha})$ containing $m-1$ of her *attributes* along with the *ID* of the issuing CA, and she also creates a random value $w = (g_1{}^{w_1} \cdot g_3{}^{w_3} \cdot \ldots \cdot g_m{}^{w_m} \cdot h_0{}^{w_{m+1}})$. In the issuing protocol, the CA signs $h$ and $w$ with its RSA key to create $sig_h = h^d \bmod n$ and $sig_w = w^d \bmod n$; the CA then gives these values to Alice.

The *showing protocol* **for revealing** $x_2$ **using a** *malleable signature* **and a** *multi-show credential* is conducted as follows (compare with the *showing protocol* **for revealing** $x_2$ in Sect. 6.2.1 above). Suppose that Alice has $h$, $w$, $sig_h$, and $sig_w$ (as defined in the previous paragraph), and she wishes to prove to Bob that $x_2 = 17$.

Step 1: Bob generates a random value $b$ and sends this to Alice.

Step 2: Alice generates a random value $a$. Alice then creates a fresh *showing key* and corresponding *showing signature* for this transaction only: $h_{show} = h^a w^b$ and $sig_{show} = (sig_h)^a (sig_w)^b$.

Step 3: Alice computes

$$r_1 = ax_1 + bw_1,$$
$$r_2 = g_2^{bw_2}$$
$$r_3 = ax_3 + bw_3,$$
$$\ldots$$
$$r_{m-1} = ax_{m-1} + bw_{m-1}$$
$$r_m = g_m^{bw_m},$$
$$r_{m+1} = a\alpha + bw_{m+1}.$$

She then sends $h_{show}$, $sig_{show}$, $x_2 = 17$, $ID$, and $\{r_1, \ldots, r_{m+1}\}$ to Bob.

Bob checks whether $(g_1^{r_1} \cdot r_2 g_2^{17a} \cdot g_3^{r_3} \cdot \ldots \cdot g_{m-1}^{r_{m-1}} \cdot r_m g_m^{IDa} \cdot h_0^{r_{m+1}})$ is equal to $h_{show}$. Bob additionally checks whether $(sig_{show})^e \bmod n$ is equal to $h_{show}$, where $(e, n)$ is the RSA signature verification key of the CA with *identifier=ID*. If both of these are correct, Alice has proved to Bob that she is the legitimate owner of $h_{show}$ and that she has *attribute value* $x_2 = 17$.

Note that in this *multi-show credential* construction, any subsequent showing protocol interaction (with Bob, or with any other verifier) will use different random numbers $a$, $b$. Thus, a new $h_{show}$ and $sig_{show}$ will be created for each interaction; these will be unlinkable to any $h_{show}$ and $sig_{show}$ used previously.

## 6.2.3 Strengths

One very important strength of many *credential systems* is their conceptual simplicity: the image of crossing out fields on an official document with black marker before handing the document to a verifier is easy to understand and immediately conveys the idea that privacy is being enhanced.

Perhaps the greatest strength of many *credential systems*, however, is their mathematical proof of *information-theoretic security* for all *attribute* information that is not intentionally revealed in various showing protocols. This is a powerful privacy feature that few (if any) PETs proposed prior to *credential systems* were able to claim (most other early PETs based their privacy on assumptions about the limited computational resources of attackers or the non-collusion of various entities).

Last, but certainly not least, another important strength of many *credential system* proposals is their general and comprehensive architecture. For example, in (Brands 2000), Brands has described numerous related techniques and protocols for this PET, including how to anonymously update a *Digital Credential*, how to show a *Digital Credential* in zero-knowledge, how to design a two-move issuing protocol, how to combine *attributes* from different *credentials* and even from different issuers, how to cope with broken connections and self-revocation, how to protect the CA's private key, and so on.

### 6.2.4  Disadvantages, Limitations, and Weaknesses

Despite the conceptual simplicity of *Digital Credentials*, it is clear that the actual credential and associated issuing/showing protocols are not trivial. According to some sources (see, for example, [https://cryptography.fandom.com/wiki/Digital_credential]), Brands' *Digital Credentials* can be as much as 1–2 orders of magnitude more computationally efficient than comparable *credential system* alternatives. However, this does not guarantee that all performance concerns have been eliminated. As is often the case with public key cryptographic techniques, the integers involved can be huge (2048 bits in length, or more); this has time implications (because of the numerous exponentiation operations required) and space implications (for storage and transmission of various values) in any implementation. Furthermore, the defined protocols and data structures in *Digital Credentials* are somewhat complex and easy to get wrong. As Brands has stated (Brands 2002), there are many security subtleties and dependencies, and "seemingly innocent changes (e.g., for optimization purposes) may have far-reaching security implications."

Another complexity in any *credential system* is to negotiate specific agreements for all items that must be understood by users, CAs, and verifiers throughout an environment. This includes an agreed encoding format for every kind of *attribute value* that may be stored in a *credential* (as mentioned in Sect. 6.2.1), as well as an agreed identifier for every type of *attribute* that may be requested (so that, for example, the user can understand that the verifier is asking for a proof of *gold card membership* rather than a proof of *employee* status). It also includes an agreed ordering for attribute values inside a *credential* (so that when a verifier asks for *gold card membership*, both the user and the verifier know that this *attribute value* is in exponent $x_3$ of the user's *Digital Credential* public key $h$, for example).

Although several techniques have been proposed for achieving *non-transferability* and *unlinkability* in *credential systems*, it is clear that most of these techniques have limitations. They may be complex to implement or computationally inefficient, or they may simply make lending or linking *harder* (rather than *impossible*, which of course would be the ideal situation).

Another limitation in *credential systems* generally is the set of requirements for the user device. Clearly the user's local device must be sufficiently powerful to do the computations needed in the issuing and showing protocols. Although this was a bigger concern at the time of Brands' original paper (in 2000, before the ubiquitous availability of high-performance smart phones and tablets), it is still the case that some users may not have such devices or may be worried about battery drain or phone plan data-usage constraints. Furthermore, in all cases, the local device must store sensitive values (in particular, the user's private key) and so it is subject to the usual fears regarding malware, physical theft, and so on. Given that many phones are locked using very simple PINs or finger swipes (or are not locked at all!), the risk that an attacker may acquire a user's phone and then successfully use the contained *credential* to obtain goods and services is reasonably high.

Finally, a concern common to all *credential systems* is that revealing attributes increases the risk that the user will be identified. As more and more attributes are revealed (even to different verifiers since it is always possible that these verifiers may collude), it becomes increasingly possible for observers to narrow down the size of the *anonymity set* until a single individual is pinpointed. It is important to note that *information-theoretic security* guarantees cannot protect against this: for example, if any $m$-1 of the $x_i$ values in a *Digital Credential* are known, the $m^{th}$ $x_i$ value may <u>mathematically</u> be *information-theoretically secure*, but <u>in practice</u> an observer who sees those $m$-1 attribute values may be able to deduce who the individual is and thereby infer the $m^{th}$ value with high probability (for example, by consulting additional external data sources). Furthermore, any revealed *attributes* that are unique to Alice (e.g., her *passport number*) will of course allow her to be identified regardless of the protections put in place in the issuing/showing protocols themselves. Thus, it is always recommended that users should be very careful about the *attributes* they reveal over time and perhaps modify their *credential* or their behaviour in some way when the risk of identification is thought to be too high.

## 6.3   Summary

This chapter has discussed PETs that limit **disclosure** by hiding the *identity* of the user while allowing other *attributes* of the user to be visible in the transaction (perhaps to just the intended recipient, or perhaps to any external observer). The example PETs described are *k-Anonymity* and *Credential Systems*.

With *k-Anonymity*, the goal is to create a public data set of records (for example, health records) and to ensure that any specific individual's record cannot be distinguished from $k$-1 other individuals' records for the *attribute values* under consideration. Thus, the individual's *identity* is effectively hidden within an *anonymity set* of size $k$. Attention must be paid to not just *unique identifiers* in the data, but also to *quasi-identifiers* (which can often be combined with external data to re-identify individuals). The techniques of *generalization, suppression, ℓ-diversity*, and *t-close-ness* are used to achieve *k-anonymity*; computational costs can be prohibitive, but sometimes good heuristic algorithms can be found.

*Credential Systems* enable online transactions in which ownership of *attribute values* can be proven with an extremely high level of certainty, even though the user's *identity* is never revealed to the verifying entity. Thus, the anonymous user convincingly has the specific *attribute values* required for the transaction. Building on previous work in *commitments, blind signatures*, and *zero-knowledge proofs of knowledge*, these systems make use of an issuing protocol for credential creation, and a showing protocol for proving ownership of selected *attribute values*. Mechanisms for providing *non-transferability* and *unlinkability* have also been explored for various types of *credential systems*. Powerful and flexible credential schemes have been designed and deployed, but there is still room for improvement in a number of areas related to efficiency and practical implementation.

A second option to break the *identity-attribute* linkage is to hide the *attribute values* while allowing the *identity* to be visible. In the following chapter we will examine three PETs that take this approach to limiting **disclosure**.

**Questions for Personal Reflection and/or Group Discussion**

1. Section 6.1.4 notes that achieving *minimum-cost k-anonymity* is *NP-hard*, even for $k = 3$ (although heuristic algorithms have shown promise). In real situations, though, most people with an interest in privacy would want to be in a significantly larger anonymity set, such as $k = 100$ or $k = 1000$. How can this be reconciled? What can be done to meet the demand for a large $k$ while satisfying the need for the data set to be useful?

2. *Digital credentials* rely on a user device that is both powerful enough to perform the necessary computations, and secure enough to be trusted to hold secret data (such as attributes and private keys). Given that many users choose relatively simple PINs or finger swipes to unlock their phones, what other measures can be taken to preserve the intended security and privacy properties of *credential systems*? How can the classic "security/privacy versus usability" trade-off be addressed in these systems?

3. With *credential systems*, it was noted in Sect. 6.2.4 that revealing too many *attributes* can compromise the privacy of the *attributes* that have not yet been shown. What can be done about this? How can the user's implementation determine that a "threshold" is being approached and warn the user not to reveal further information?

# References

C. Adams, Achieving non-transferability in credential systems using hidden biometrics. Secur. Commun. Netw. **4**(2), 195–206 (2011, Feb)

C. Aggarwal, On *k*-anonymity and the curse of dimensionality, in *Proceedings of the 31st Conference on Very Large Databases*, (Trondheim, Norway, 2005, Aug), pp. 901–909

G. Aggarwal, T. Feder, K. Kenthapadi, R. Motwani, R. Panigrahy, D. Thomas, A. Zhu, Anonymizing tables, in *Proceedings of the International Conference on Database Theory*, (Springer LNCS 3363, 2005, Jan 5–7), pp. 246–258

J. Ali, Validating Leaked Passwords with *k*-Anonymity. Cloudfare blog (2018)

O. Angiuli, J. Waldo, Statistical tradeoffs between generalization and suppression in the de-identification of large-scale data sets, in *IEEE 40th Annual Computer Software and Applications Conference*, (2016), pp. 589–593

R.J. Bayardo, R. Agrawal, Data privacy through optimal *k*-anonymization, in *Proceedings of the 21st International Conference on Data Engineering*, (2005, Apr), pp. 217–228

D. Bissessar, C. Adams, D. Liu, Using biometric key commitments to prevent unauthorized lending of cryptographic credentials, in *Proceedings of the 12th Annual Conference on Privacy, Security and Trust (PST 2014)*, (Toronto, Canada, 2014, July 23–24)

M. Blanton, Online subscriptions with anonymous access, in *Proceedings of the ACM Symposium on Information, Computer and Communications Security (ASIA CCS)*, (Tokyo, Japan, 2008, Mar 18–20), pp. 217–227

P. Bonizzoni, G. Della Vidova, R. Dondi, The k-anonymity problem is hard, in *International Symposium on Fundamentals of Computation Theory*, (Springer LNCS 5699, 2009, Sep 2–4), pp. 26–37

S. Brands, Privacy-protected transfer of electronic information, U.S. Patent (filed August 1993), patent number 5,604,805, issued February 1997

S. Brands, *Rethinking Public Key Infrastructures and Digital Certificates: Building in Privacy* (The MIT Press, 2000)

S. Brands, A technical overview of digital credentials, *Credentica paper*, (2002, Feb 20)

M. Branscombe, PassProtect tells you if your password has been pwned, *ZDNet*, (2018, May 25)

J. Brodkin, Find out if your password has been pwned – Without sending it to a server, *Ars Technica*, (2018, Feb 23)

J. Camenisch, A. Lysyanskaya, An efficient system for non-transferable anonymous credentials with optional anonymity revocation, in *Advances in Cryptology: Proceedings of Eurocrypt 2001*, (Springer LNCS 2045, 2001), pp. 93–118

J. Camenisch, S. Hohenberger, M. Kohlweiss, A. Lysyanskaya, M. Meyerovich, How to win the clone wars: Efficient periodic n-times anonymous authentication, in *Proceedings of the 13th ACM Conference on Computer and Communications Security*, (Alexandria, Virginia, USA, 2006, Oct), pp. 201–210

J. Camenisch, M. Dubovitskaya, P. Kalambet, A. Lehmann, G. Neven, F.-S. Preiss, T. Usatiy, IBM identity mixer: Authentication without identification, *Idemix Presentation, IBM Research – Zurich*, (2015, Nov 12)

M. Chase, M. Kohlweiss, A. Lysyanskaya, S. Meiklejohn, Malleable signatures: New definitions and delegatable anonymous credentials, in *IEEE 27th Computer Security Foundations Symposium*, (Vienna, 2014), pp. 199–213

D. Chaum, Blind signatures for untraceable payments, in *Advances in Cryptology: Proceedings of Crypto '82*, (1983), pp. 199–203

D. Chaum, J.-H. Evertse, J. van de Graaf, An improved protocol for demonstrating possession of discrete logarithms and some generalizations, in *Advances in Cryptology: Proceedings of Eurocrypt '87*, (Springer LNCS 304, 1988), pp. 127–141

L. Chen, A.N. Escalante, B.H. Löhr, M. Manulis, A.-R. Sadeghi, A privacy-protecting multi-coupon scheme with stronger protection against splitting, in *Proceedings of the 11th International*

*Conference on Financial Cryptography and Data Security (FC 2007)*, (Springer LNCS 4886, 2008), pp. 29–44

C. Díaz, S. Seys, J. Claessens, B. Preneel, Towards measuring anonymity, in *Proceedings of the Second International Workshop on Privacy Enhancing Technologies*, (Springer, LNCS 2482, San Francisco, USA, 2002 Apr 14–15), pp. 54–68

K. El Emam, F. Kamal Dankar, Protecting privacy using k-anonymity. J. Am. Med. Inform. Assoc. **15**(5), 627–637 (2008, Sep-Oct)

J. Fan, C. Adams, Using malleable signatures to allow multi-show capability in digital credentials. Int. J. Sensor Netw. Data Commun. **7**(4), 6 (2018)

O. Goldreich, S. Micali, A. Wigderson, Proofs that yield nothing but their validity and a methodology of cryptographic protocol design, in *Proceedings of the 27th Annual IEEE Symposium on Foundations of Computer Science*, (1986, Oct 27–29), pp. 174–187

S. Goldwasser, M. Bellare, Lecture notes on cryptography, in *Lecture Notes for a Week-Long Course on Cryptography Taught at MIT Over Ten Summers*, (2008, July)

S. Goldwasser, S. Micali, C. Rackoff, The knowledge complexity of interactive proof systems. Soc. Indust. Appl. Math. (SIAM) J. Comput. **18**(1), 186–208 (1989, Feb)

A. Hundepool, L. Willenborg, μ- and τ-Argus: Software for statistical disclosure control, in *Third International Seminar on Statistical Confidentiality*, (Bled, 1996)

R. Impagliazzo, S. Miner More, Anonymous credentials with biometrically-enforced non-transferability, in *Proceedings of the Workshop on Privacy in the Electronic Society*, (Washington, DC, USA, 2003, Oct 30), pp. 60–71

B. Kenig, T. Tassa, A practical approximation algorithm for optimal k-anonymity. Data Min. Knowl. Disc. **25**, 134–168 (2012)

D.A. Knox, C. Adams, Digital credentials with privacy-preserving delegation. Secur. Commun. Netw. **4**(8), 825–838 (2011, Aug)

N. Li, T. Li, S. Venkatasubramanian, t-Closeness: Privacy beyond k-anonymity and l-diversity, in *Center for Education and Research Information Assurance and Security (CERIAS) Tech Report 2007–78*, (Purdue University, 2007)

L. Li, B. Pal, J. Ali, N. Sullivan, R. Chatterjee, T. Ristenpart, Protocols for checking compromised credentials, arXiv.org, arXiv:1905.13737v3 (2019, Sep 4)

A. Machanavajjhala, D. Kifer, J. Gehrke, M. Venkitasubramaniam, l-diversity: privacy beyond k-anonymity. ACM Trans. Knowl. Discov. Data, **1**(1), article 3, 52pp (2007, Mar)

A. Meyerson, R. Williams, On the complexity of optimal k-anonymity, in *Symposium on Principles of Database Systems*, (2004, June 14–16), pp. 223–228

Microsoft, U-Prove, in *Research Project Description*, (2012, Feb 25)

S. Kendall More, Secure group communication: Self-healing key distribution and nontransferable anonymous credentials, PhD thesis, University of California, San Diego, 2003

G. Neven, IBM identity mixer (idemix), in *Presentation Given at NIST Meeting on Privacy Enhancing Technology*, (Gaithersburg, MD, USA, 2011 Dec 8–9)

A. Øhrn, L. Ohno-Machado, Using boolean reasoning to anonymize databases. Artif. Intell. Med. **15**(3), 235–254 (1999)

A. Pfitzmann, M. Hansen, A terminology for talking about privacy by data minimization: Anonymity, unlinkability, undetectability, unobservability, pseudonymity, and identity management, in *Anonymity Terminology Document, Version v0.34* (2010, Aug 10)

A. Piotrowska, J. Hayes, T. Elahi, S. Meiser, G. Danezis, The loopix anonymity system, in *Proceedings of the 26th USENIX Security Symposium*, (Vancouver, BC, Canada, 2017, Aug 16–18), pp. 1199–1216. (See also *arXiv.com, 1703.00536*, 16pp., 1 March 2017)

T. Pryds Pedersen, Non-interactive and information-theoretic secure verifiable secret sharing, in *Advances in Cryptology: Proceedings of Crypto '91*, (1992), pp. 129–140

Y. Rubner, C. Tomasi, L.J. Guibas, The earth mover's distance as a metric for image retrieval. Int. J. Comput. Vis. **40**(2), 99–121 (2000, Nov)

P. Samarati, Protecting respondents identities in microdata release. IEEE Trans. Knowl. Data Eng. **13**(6), 1010–1027 (2001, Nov-Dec)

P. Samarati, L. Sweeney, Protecting privacy when disclosing information: k-anonymity and its enforcement through generalisation and suppression, in *SRI International*, (1998)

A. Serjantov, G. Danezis, Towards an information theoretic metric for anonymity, in *Proceedings of the Second International Workshop on Privacy Enhancing Technologies,* (Springer, LNCS 2482, San Francisco, USA, 2002, Apr 14–15), pp. 41–53

A. Sonnino, M. Al-Bassam, S. Bano, S. Meiklejohn, G. Danezis, Coconut: Threshold issuance selective disclosure credentials with applications to distributed ledgers, in *Network and Distributed System Security (NDSS) Symposium*, (San Diego, CA, USA, 2019, Feb 24–27), 15pp

L. Sweeney, Guaranteeing anonymity when sharing medical data, the Datafly system, in *Proceedings of the Fall Symposium of the American Medical Informatics Association*, (1997), pp. 51–55

L. Sweeney, Simple demographics often identify people uniquely, in *Carnegie Mellon University, Data Privacy Working Paper 3*, (Pittsburgh, 2000)

L. Sweeney, *K*-anonymity: A model for protecting privacy. Int. J. Uncertain. Fuzziness Knowlege-Based Syst. **10**(5), 557–570 (2002a)

L. Sweeney, Achieving *k*-anonymity privacy protection using generalization and suppression. Int. J. Uncertain. Fuzziness Knowlege-Based Syst. **10**(5), 571–588 (2002b)

P.F. Syverson, S.G. Stubblebine, Group principals and the formalization of anonymity, in *Proceedings of the First World Congress on Formal Methods in the Development of Computing Systems (FM '99), Volume 1*, (Springer, LNCS 1708, Toulouse, France, 1999, Sep 20–24), pp. 814–833

P.F. Syverson, S.G. Stubblebine, D M. Goldschlag, Unlinkable serial transactions, in *Proceedings of the First International Conference on Financial Cryptography*, (Springer, LNCS 1318, Anguilla, British West Indies, 1997, Feb 24–28), pp. 39–55

Watchtower, About Watchtower Privacy in 1Password. *1Password Support* (2020, Oct 8)

# Chapter 7
# Limiting Disclosure by Hiding the Attribute

**Abstract** Continuing with the goal of limiting disclosure, this chapter examines technologies that hide the attribute information of the user. The following example PETs in this category are described: ciphertext-policy attribute-based encryption; multi-party computation; and $\varepsilon$-differential privacy. For each presented PET, the basic scheme, enhancements, strengths, and limitations are described.

**Keywords** Attribute-based encryption (ABE) · Key-policy attribute-based encryption (KP-ABE) · Ciphertext-policy attribute-based encryption (CP-ABE) · Access structure · Multi-party computation · Garbled circuit · Adversary model · $\varepsilon$-Differential privacy · ($\varepsilon$, $\delta$)-differential privacy · Database privacy · Privacy-utility trade-off

In this chapter, we will look at mechanisms to limit ***disclosure***, not by hiding the *identities* of the entities involved, but rather by hiding the *attributes* of these entities. Thus, external observers may be able to easily learn whose data may be in a database, or who is participating in a given transaction, but will not know the actual *attribute values* of those identified users. This is useful for situations in which the *identity* of a person is not confidential information (in fact, it might be known by everyone), but the data associated with that person is considered to be highly sensitive.

Two PETs exemplifying this category of ***disclosure*** limitation that have gained widespread attention are *Multi-Party Computation* (MPC) and *ε-Differential Privacy*. We begin, however, with a family of database protection approaches that includes both simple data encryption and *Ciphertext Policy Attribute-Based Encryption* (CP-ABE).

© The Editor(s) (if applicable) and The Author(s), under exclusive license to Springer Nature Switzerland AG 2021
C. Adams, *Introduction to Privacy Enhancing Technologies*,
https://doi.org/10.1007/978-3-030-81043-6_7

## 7.1 Database Protection Approaches

If the goal is only to hide a user's data (i.e., fields or records) in a database, a number of mechanisms to achieve this have been widely available for many decades. In particular, the data may be *encrypted* using conventional and well-understood *cryptographic algorithms* (such as AES), or the database may have *access controls* in place to restrict who is able to read/write/modify the data. With *encryption*, the data will be readable only by those to whom the appropriate *decryption key* has explicitly been given. With *access control*, the data will be accessible only by those to whom the appropriate *permissions* have been granted. For either mechanism, an observer may be able to learn which record in the database belongs to Alice, but will not be able to learn any of Alice's data.

Note that if Alice's data in the database is (or includes) her personal *attributes*, then these two mechanisms effectively become *privacy enhancing technologies*. However, *encryption* and *access control* are generic tools that were designed to protect any kind of data, not just personal *attributes*. Thus, they are more properly viewed as general *security mechanisms* than as PETs. On the other hand, an encryption technique known as *Ciphertext Policy Attribute-Based Encryption* (CP-ABE) – which, at some level, may be seen as a combination of *encryption* and *access control* – meets the definition of the category of PETs considered in this chapter. We describe the original 2007 proposal by Bethencourt, Sahai, and Waters in the following section.

### 7.1.1 The Basic Scheme

In 2007, John Bethencourt, Amit Sahai, and Brent Waters proposed an encryption technique that they called *Ciphertext Policy Attribute-Based Encryption* (CP-ABE) (2007). This technique built on the work of Sahai and Waters (2005) and Goyal, Pandey, Sahai, and Waters (2006), but achieved an important modification to make it particularly useful as a *privacy enhancing technology*.

The concept of *attribute-based encryption* (ABE) was first alluded to by Yao, Fazio, Dodis, and Lysyanskaya in 2004 (2004), but was explicitly named and instantiated with an efficient construction in (Sahai and Waters 2005). ABE was proposed as a generalization of *identity-based encryption* (IBE), where a user's *identity* can serve as the public key for that user, eliminating the need for a public key certificate (Shamir 1985). In ABE, the user's *identity* is not a simple string (such as "*alice@ gmail.com*"), but instead is a collection of *attributes* of the user (such as "*Computer Science Faculty*", "*Theory Group*", and "*Hiring Committee*"); a document can be encrypted for this collection of *attributes*, and any user with an "identity" that contains all these *attributes* will be able to decrypt the document. In fact, Sahai and Waters designed an error-tolerant version of IBE (which they called *Fuzzy-IBE*) that was able to bring flexibility to their resulting ABE construction: if a document was encrypted for a set of *attributes* $w$, then a user whose "identity" was a set of *attributes* $w'$ would be able to decrypt if and only if $w$ and $w'$ are *close to each other* (as judged by a "set overlap" distance metric). This allows a system administrator to be less rigid about the number of *attributes* required to access a document, for environments in which this might be desirable.

Note that in this construction of ABE, the collection of *attributes* is the <u>public key</u> for the encryption process and any given ciphertext is associated with ("labeled with") the public key used to encrypt it. (The corresponding <u>private key</u> is a set of points of a randomly-chosen polynomial – one point for each *attribute* in the public key – and polynomial interpolation is used to reconstruct a value that is required in the decryption process; this is why a private key for a sufficiently similar collection of *attributes* will be able to decrypt.) Goyal, et al., extended and generalized this construction to a scheme that they called *Key Policy Attribute-Based Encryption* (KP-ABE) (Goyal et al. 2006): here, the ciphertext is still "labeled with" a <u>public key</u> that is a collection of *attributes*, but the corresponding <u>private key</u> is now an *access structure* that controls which ciphertexts the user can decrypt. Thus, the <u>private key</u> effectively encodes an *access control policy* (such as "$(x$ AND $y)$ OR $((any\text{-}2\text{-}of\{a, b, c\})$ AND $z))$", where $a, b, c, x, y, z$ are specific *attributes*), and the user will be able to decrypt only ciphertexts whose associated *attributes* satisfy that particular *policy* (for example, ciphertexts labeled with the *attribute* collection "$(x, y)$", or ciphertexts labeled with the *attribute* collection "$(a, c, z)$").

KP-ABE works well as an encryption scheme and is useful for a number of applications (including *sharing of audit log information* and *broadcast encryption*, as discussed in (Goyal et al. 2006)). However, it clearly cannot be used as a PET to limit **disclosure** by hiding the *attributes* of the user because a collection of *attributes* is precisely the public key that is explicitly associated with a ciphertext, and so this information is known to everyone. If Alice is able to decrypt a ciphertext with the label "$(a, c, z)$", for example, then even though Alice's private key (i.e., her particular *access structure*) may remain secret, it will be obvious to all that she indeed has the attributes $a, c,$ and $z$.

The work of Bethencourt, Sahai, and Waters, CP-ABE, reverses the design of KP-ABE. In particular, ciphertexts are associated with a <u>public key</u> that describes an *access control policy*, and a user's <u>private key</u> is explicitly linked to a collection of the user's *attributes*. If the *attributes* in the <u>private key</u> satisfy the specified *policy* for a ciphertext, decryption will be possible for that user. Because the *attributes* are affiliated with the user's <u>private key</u> rather than a <u>public key</u>, CP-ABE can be used as a PET that limits **disclosure** by hiding the *attributes* of the user: if Alice is able to decrypt a given ciphertext, then she must have *attributes* that satisfy the associated *access structure* label, but it will not be known which specific *attributes* she has. For instance, in the example given above, if the public *access structure* is "$(x$ AND $y)$ OR $((any\text{-}2\text{-}of\{a, b, c\})$ AND $z))$", an observer will not know whether Alice has attributes $(x, y)$, or attributes $(a, b, z)$, or attributes $(a, c, z)$, or attributes $(b, c, z)$. In fact, she might even have attributes $(a, b, c, z)$ or attributes $(a, b, c, x, y, z)$.

Note that, unlike generic *encryption* and *access control* mechanisms that can protect any kind of data and are therefore not specifically PETs, CP-ABE is a PET. Although what is encrypted by CP-ABE can also be any kind of data, the fact that personal *attributes* are linked to the <u>private key</u> means that this technology is used to enhance a user's privacy during the *decryption operation* itself.

At a very high level (omitting a number of details for the sake of a simpler exposition), the CP-ABE scheme works as follows.

**The Ciphertext Policy Attribute-Based Encryption (CP-ABE) Scheme**
Consider an *access structure* represented as a tree, $T$. Each non-leaf node $X$ has a specific number of children, $num_X$, and a threshold value $k_X$, where $1 \leq k_X \leq num_X$. When $k_X = 1$, this represents an OR gate in the tree; when $k_X = num_X$, this represents an AND gate in the tree; otherwise, the gate specifies "any $k_X$ out of $num_X$". Each leaf node $L$ in $T$ is an *attribute* (with an implicit $k_L$ value of 1). Finally, an *ordering* is defined for $T$: the children of every node $X$ are numbered from 1 to $num_X$.

To illustrate, the *access structure* shown in Fig. 7.1 with leaf nodes $\{x, y, a, b, c, z\}$ would correspond to the example policy given previously: "($x$ AND $y$) OR (($any$-$2$-$of$ $\{a, b, c\}$) AND $z$))". This is because the leftmost "(2 of 2)" says "there are 2 branches and both are needed" (which corresponds to an "AND" of $Att_1$ and $Att_2$ (i.e., "($x$ AND $y$)")), the topmost "(1 of 2)" says "there are 2 branches and only 1 is needed" (which corresponds to an "OR" of its children), and so on.

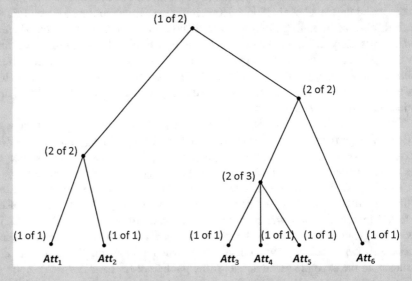

**Fig. 7.1** Access structure

(continued)

**Encryption**

If Bob wishes to encrypt a message $M$, he will choose a random polynomial $q_X()$ of degree $d_X = k_X - 1$ for each node $X$ in the tree.

The polynomial for the root node of the tree, $q_R()$, will be created as follows: Bob chooses a random value $s$ and sets $q_R(0) = s$; he then chooses at random $d_R$ other points of $q_R()$ to define it completely.

For each of the $num_R$ children of the root node, the polynomial $q_i()$ of the $i^{th}$ child will be created such that $q_i(0) = q_R(i)$, and $d_i$ other points of $q_i()$ will be chosen randomly to define it completely.

This process continues until the polynomials for all the nodes of $T$ have been created. Note that for a leaf node $L$ that is the $i^{th}$ child of its parent node $X$, its "polynomial" is of degree 0 (since $k_L = 1$): specifically, its value is an *attribute* and Bob must create an "adjustment factor" to turn this value into the required value $q_X(i)$.

With the *access structure* and the random polynomials defined as above, it can be seen that for every node $X$ in $T$, $k_X$ of its children will produce $k_X$ different points of the polynomial $q_X()$ for $X$ – these are all the respective $q_i(0)$ $(= q_X(i))$ values of the children. Since $q_X()$ was chosen to have degree $k_X - 1$, polynomial interpolation can be used to learn the actual polynomial $q_X()$ for $X$, at which point $q_X(0)$ can be evaluated.

Bob encrypts $M$ by computing $C = Mz^s$, where $z$ is one of the public parameters of the System Authority, and publishes $\{C, T, A\}$, where $A$ is the set of "adjustment factors" (one for each *attribute value* at a leaf of $T$).

**Decryption**

For Alice to decrypt, she first combines her *attribute values* with the adjustment factors published by Bob; this allows her to learn $k_X$ points for each parent $X$ of leaf nodes, and thus use interpolation to discover its polynomial $q_X()$ and compute its $q_X(0)$ value. She can then repeat the process for the next layer up in the tree since all the $q_X(0)$ values she collected for the first set of parents will be points for their respective parent nodes in the next layer. Once she has traversed the tree from the leaves to the root, she will be able to recover the original random value $q_R(0) = s$.

Alice can now decrypt by raising the public parameter $z$ to the power $s$ and dividing the result into $C$ to recover the plaintext message $M$.

Note that if Alice is missing any of the required *attribute values*, she will be missing at least one point for a parent $X$ of leaf nodes and will thus be unable to interpolate to discover that parent's polynomial $q_X()$ and compute $q_X(0)$. This will continue up the tree and she will ultimately not compute the correct $s$ and therefore will not obtain the plaintext $M$.

As mentioned above, the full scheme by Bethencourt, Sahai, and Waters contains significant additional detail. In particular, the System Authority has a *Master Key* which is used to generate private keys for users (i.e., Alice's private key is <u>derived from</u> her *attribute values*, but is <u>more</u> than simply her *attribute values* so that she is unable to create the key herself). This prevents someone from simply trying different *attribute values* with a given ciphertext $\{C, T, A\}$ until a sensible decryption is obtained. Furthermore, the System Authority randomizes every private key that it generates (with unique random numbers known only to itself) in order to prevent collusion between users (in which a user with only *attribute X* and another user with only *attribute Y* collude in order to decrypt a ciphertext that requires ($X$ AND $Y$) in its *access structure*). The full scheme also makes clever use of *bilinear pairing-based cryptography* over *elliptic curve groups* for many of its algorithmic computations.

## 7.1.2   Enhancements

Although *attribute-based encryption* has seen considerable interest since its introduction (for example, in April 2020 the *International Association for Cryptologic Research* (IACR) bestowed its "Test of Time" award to the Sahai and Waters paper that introduced ABE (2005); see (BusinessWire 2020)), there has not thus far been an explosion of enhancement proposals for CP-ABE. However, three enhancements in particular seem significant and may yet be starting points for much future work.

- In 2008, Brent Waters published his work on security proofs for CP-ABE (2008). Specifically, rather than proving security in the *generic group model* (as was done in the original paper (Bethencourt et al. 2007)) – an artificial model which assumes that the attacker must access an oracle to do any group operation – he was able to prove the security of various CP-ABE constructions under much weaker assumptions. In one particular construction, security is proved in the *standard model* under only the *decisional Bilinear Diffie-Hellman* assumption. Achieving a security proof under this more solid and widely-accepted model unfortunately required some trade-off in performance, but undoubtedly there will be future research to find ways to maintain the security proof while improving overall efficiency.
- A. Balu and K. Kuppusamy (2010) have examined a largely-unaddressed aspect of privacy in CP-ABE systems. Given that a ciphertext is labeled with an *access structure*, this means that the structure itself (i.e., the tree $T$) is public information. Although $T$ does not identify any *attributes*, it clearly does reveal some information about what is required to decrypt the ciphertext. At the very least, the number of leaf nodes in the tree provides an estimate of the total number of *attributes* that may be involved in the decryption process. But it can reveal more: for example, in the access structure shown above, since the root node is an OR gate and its first child is an AND gate, an observer can immediately see that although there are 6 leaf nodes, only 2 *attributes* will be sufficient for decryption. Balu and Kuppusamy designed a CP-ABE scheme in which $T$ is hidden – even a legitimate decryptor Alice cannot learn anything about the *access structure* associated with

a ciphertext beyond the fact that she can decrypt the data using the set of *attributes* that she currently owns.

- In recent work (2019), Yujiao Song, Hao Wang, Xiaochao Wei, and Lei Wu proposed a technique to reduce trust in the private key generator of a CP-ABE Scheme (2019). Typical CP-ABE designs assume a System Authority with a *Master Key* that creates keys for all users in the environment. Thus, the System Authority knows both the *attributes* and the *private key* of every user, which can be a security and privacy risk (especially in some environments, such as industrial design and manufacturing, where confidentiality of data is a primary concern). Song, et al., propose having two non-colluding entities: an *attribute auditing center* (AAC) and a *key generation center* (KGC). The user proves ownership of his/her *attributes* to the AAC and obtains a <u>blind token</u>, which only certifies valid *attribute* ownership but reveals nothing about the actual *attributes* themselves. The user then presents this <u>blind token</u> to the KGC, who verifies the token and issues a <u>blind key</u>, from which the user can extract the final private key. Thus, the KGC never learns the user's *attributes*, and the AAC never learns the user's key.

Additional enhancements on different aspects of CP-ABE technology are expected as time moves on.

## 7.1.3   Strengths

As discussed by Bethencourt, Sahai, and Waters (2007), access control for data typically requires a trusted server to store the data and mediate access control (i.e., verify whether a requesting user has the required credentials or attributes). However, if the server is compromised, the protection of the data is clearly at risk. Distributed storage exacerbates the risk since if the data is stored at several locations, the probability that every location remains uncompromised decreases dramatically with time.

CP-ABE works similarly to other access control schemes that are built on *attributes* or *roles*, such as RBAC (*Role-Based Access Control*), but its combination of *encryption* and *access control* removes the need for a trusted *reference monitor* to examine user *attributes* in real time. Furthermore, CP-ABE is well-suited to distributed storage environments because the data is encrypted and so is not vulnerable to a compromise at any of the storage locations.

The CP-ABE scheme of Bethencourt, Sahai, and Waters is also reasonably efficient. In the performance measurements of their implementation with various parameter sizes, they reported that for 50 *attributes* and 100 leaf nodes in the *access structure*, they were able to achieve less than 3 seconds for encryption, less than 2 seconds for private key generation, and less than 0.1 seconds for the decryption operation itself. Although 3 seconds may seem long for encryption of a single block of plaintext (512 bits in their implementation), note that in an actual deployment, the "plaintext message M" in CP-ABE may be, for example, an AES-256 key, which is then used to encrypt/decrypt the actual (much larger) document at significantly higher speeds.

### 7.1.4   Disadvantages, Limitations, and Weaknesses

Perhaps the biggest disadvantage to most CP-ABE schemes is the same problem that plagues many of the identity-based schemes from which it derives: there is a System Authority that generates a private key for every user; this authority can therefore decrypt all ciphertext in the environment. Such a trust assumption may be acceptable in specific small, closed, settings, but it would be unworkable in many others. As mentioned in Sect. 7.1.2, there has been some initial work on relaxing this assumption, but that work requires two non-colluding entities, which may be equally unworkable in many realistic deployments.

Another concern is that an observer who sees several ciphertexts (i.e., several *access structures*) that Alice is able to decrypt may be able to infer some information about her *attributes* (for example, how many *attributes* she has, or which *attributes* she does not have (if the tree includes NOT terms)). Again, some initial investigation has begun in this area (see Sect. 7.1.2), but that work currently limits *access structures* to AND gates and OR gates (no *k*-out-of-*num* gates are possible) and requires all *attribute values* to be split into multiple shares for secret-sharing purposes.

In all current CP-ABE schemes, performance is not yet sufficient for high-throughput environments (multiple seconds for encryption and for private key generation). However, this is not unique to CP-ABE; performance improvement is an active area of research across all facets of cryptographic algorithm and protocol implementation.

Finally, it is worth noting that creating a good set of *attributes* for an environment, and a suitable *access structure* for a given document to be protected, is not a trivial exercise. Again, this is not unique to CP-ABE (this work is required for any comprehensive access control system), but it can be a complex and difficult aspect of the deployment process, even though it is rarely mentioned in academic research papers.

## 7.2   Multi-Party Computation

*Multi-party computation* (MPC) is another PET that has begun to see increased deployment in real-world environments for interesting and useful applications. Although MPC has existed as a concept since the mid-1980s and saw theoretical feasibility advances for its first two decades, it was not until its third decade that efficiency improvements were sufficient to garner the attention of potential users of this technology. In the last few years, performance speed-ups of several orders of magnitude have been achieved, making MPC now fast enough to be used for a wide variety of problems in industry and government settings.

MPC (which is sometimes referred to as *secure multi-party computation* (SMPC) or as *secure function evaluation* (SFE), and which includes the special cases of *private set intersection* (PSI) and *threshold cryptography*) addresses the general problem of a number of distinct (yet connected) parties that wish to jointly compute some function. Typically, each party has some data that will be used as input to the computation, but it considers this data to be confidential and does not want to share it with any of the other parties. Furthermore, an external entity – as well as some subset of the participating parties – may be malicious and try to subvert the protocol execution and/or learn the confidential data of other parties.

Despite the adversarial and confidentiality constraints of the environment, the goal of any MPC protocol is to achieve _privacy_ (the only information that any entity can learn about the input of other parties is what can be explicitly derived from the output of the function computation) and _correctness_ (each party is guaranteed that the output it receives is correct). This is generally referred to as a _secure MPC_ protocol. Additional desirable security properties include (Lindell 2020) the following:

- _Independence of Inputs_ (parties that have been compromised in some way (i.e., corrupted parties) must choose their inputs independently of the inputs of other honest parties);
- _Guaranteed Output Delivery_ (corrupted parties must not be able to prevent any honest party from receiving its output); and
- _Fairness_ (corrupted parties must not receive their outputs unless all honest parties also receive their outputs).

MPC is a PET that limits **disclosure** by hiding the _attributes_ of the users. In particular, there is no attempt to hide the _identities_ of the parties involved in the joint computation of the function; these _identities_ can be known by everyone (including other parties in the computation, any malicious adversaries, and all casual observers of the protocol exchanges). On the other hand, the protocol is designed to guard the confidentiality of each party's input data. This data may be a _personal attribute_ of the party (such as his or her DNA information) or may be a non-personal but still highly sensitive _attribute_ of the party (such as a commercial company's customer list). Thus, the parties involved, the fact that they are using an MPC protocol, and the end result of the function evaluation are all open and known to everyone; however, each user's _attributes_ remain hidden throughout.

A brief introduction to _multi-party computation_ was published in 2020 by Yehuda Lindell (2020) and a much more detailed and comprehensive overview of the field was published by David Evans, Vladimir Kolesnikov, and Mike Rosulek in 2018 (2018); these are both good sources for additional information on this topic. The following section will present the original proposals for MPC from Yao (1986) and from Goldreich, Micali, and Wigderson (1987).

### 7.2.1  The Basic Scheme

In 1986, Andrew Yao introduced the concept of MPC with the proposal of a two-party protocol (2PC) to compute _any polynomially-computable function_, where each party uses private information known only to itself (1986). This work built on the 1979 _mental poker_ protocol by Adi Shamir, Ronald Rivest, and Leonard

Adleman (1979), as well as Yao's own 1982 proposal (1982) of a solution to the *millionaire's problem* – a specific two-input function with a Boolean predicate. Yao's 1986 approach, although the paper itself did not use this term, was described in his oral conference presentation as a "scrambled circuit" (see p. 194 of (Goldreich 2003)), and subsequent literature on *scrambled circuits* (later called *garbled circuits*) points to his paper as the origin of this technique.

Yao's proposal can be briefly described as follows. Any *polynomially-computable function* can be described (e.g., in a hardware implementation) as a Boolean circuit composed of a collection of AND gates and OR gates. Each gate has exactly two inputs and a single output (although it is possible that this output will fan-out to become an input for several subsequent gates). The overall circuit thus has a set of input values and produces a set of output values. In the two-party case, some of these circuit inputs will come from Alice and the rest will come from Bob. The goal is to allow both Alice and Bob to evaluate the circuit (i.e., to obtain the circuit outputs) even though Alice never learns Bob's input values and Bob never learns Alice's input values. The *garbled circuit* allows this to be achieved.

Consider a single AND gate (the process for a single OR gate will be similar, but using an "OR" truth table). This AND gate will take an input from Alice, $a$ (which will be either 0 or 1), and an input from Bob, $b$ (which will be either 0 or 1), and will produce an output ($a$ AND $b$) (again, either 0 or 1). The truth table for this gate is as shown in Table 7.1:

**Table 7.1** Truth Table for $a$ AND $b$

| $a$ | $b$ | $a$ AND $b$ |
|-----|-----|-------------|
| 0   | 0   | 0           |
| 0   | 1   | 0           |
| 1   | 0   | 0           |
| 1   | 1   | 1           |

Alice chooses two pairs of random values, $(u, v)$, $(w, x)$, and randomly assigns the label "0" to one member of each pair and the label "1" to the other member of each pair. Say, for example, Alice sets the labels as $u=0$, $v=1$, $w=1$, $x=0$. She then uses a *key derivation function* (KDF) that will generate a cryptographic key (e.g., an AES-256 key) from its input parameters, along with her four random values, to *garble* this gate by constructing a randomized version of the above truth table. In particular, let $KDF(u, x) = p$, $KDF(u, w) = q$, $KDF(v, x) = r$, and $KDF(v, w) = s$. Then her randomized truth table is as shown in Table 7.2.

**Table 7.2** Randomized truth table for $a$ AND $b$

| first garbled input | 2nd garbled input | garbled output |
|---------------------|-------------------|----------------|
| $u$                 | $x$               | $E_p(0 \| 0...0)$ |
| $u$                 | $w$               | $E_q(0 \| 0...0)$ |
| $v$                 | $x$               | $E_r(0 \| 0...0)$ |
| $v$                 | $w$               | $E_s(1 \| 0...0)$ |

Note that $E_y(z)$ is the AES-256 encryption of the string $z$ using the key $y$, and "0 || 0...0" represents a bit 0 concatenated with a redundancy string of $n$ zero bits (similarly for "1 || 0...0"). Alice sends those four ciphertexts (in a random order) to Bob, along with the random value that represents her actual input $a$ (that is, $u$ if $a=0$, or $v$ if $a=1$, in this example). Clearly Bob cannot learn Alice's true input value from $u$ or $v$ since these are random values that were randomly assigned to the labels "0" and "1".

Bob now needs to evaluate the *garbled gate*, but he does not have $w$ or $x$. Alice cannot give him both values, because this would allow Bob to decrypt <u>two</u> of the four ciphertexts (instead of just the single ciphertext he should decrypt). On the other hand, Bob cannot simply ask for the value that corresponds to his true input $b$, because he does not want Alice to learn $b$. The solution is for Alice and Bob to conduct a *1-out-of-2 oblivious transfer protocol* (in which Bob obtains the (single) value he needs, but Alice does not learn which value he acquired). Bob therefore has one of $(u, v)$ and one of $(w, x)$ and uses KDF to generate one of $p, q, r, s$. He uses this key to try decrypting each of the four ciphertexts from Alice; only one of these will decrypt correctly (i.e., with a valid redundancy string).

At this point, Bob knows the correct output of the gate (i.e., 0 or 1) although he was never given Alice's input value $a$. He can communicate this output value to Alice (so that she knows it even though she was never given Bob's input value $b$). [Note that a much more common instantiation of the *garbled gate* is as follows. Alice chooses a third pair of random values $(y, z)$ and randomly assigns label "0" to one of them (say $z$) and label "1" to the other ($y$). She then gives Bob the following four ciphertext values: $E_p(z \text{ || } 0...0)$, $E_q(z \text{ || } 0...0)$, $E_r(z \text{ || } 0...0)$, $E_s(y \text{ || } 0...0)$. The rest of the protocol remains the same. Bob learns that the gate output is, say, $z$. He communicates this value to Alice and she communicates her output labels ($y=1$, $z=0$) to Bob; in this way, they jointly learn the true output of the gate.]

A *garbled circuit* is simply a collection of such *garbled gates*, constructed so that the circuit computes the intended *polynomially-computable function*. Alice will send four ciphertexts and a random value representing her hidden input, for each of the gates, to Bob. For each gate, Bob will conduct an *oblivious transfer protocol* with Alice to obtain the proper random value representing his input for that gate. Bob is then able to evaluate the full circuit (one gate at a time, where the output of one gate is used as an input to another gate); when the evaluation is complete, he and Alice can jointly determine the function output.

The above *garbled circuit two-party computation* protocol is able to achieve <u>privacy</u> and <u>correctness</u> for any *polynomially-computable function*. This was a major advance in cryptographic protocol design and generated significant interest among the cryptographic community (especially those with an inclination toward theoretical computer science). But it accommodated only two parties, Alice and Bob.

In 1987, Oded Goldreich, Silvio Micali, and Avi Wigderson extended Yao's 2PC protocol to the multi-party case (1987). Their proposal is similar to Yao's *garbled circuit*, but has two major differences. First, for an individual *garbled gate*, there are *n* participants in the protocol (rather than 2), and Alice sets it up such that the *n*-1 other participants evaluate the gate and then all *n* participants jointly determine the gate output. The authors proposed the use of a *secret sharing scheme*, where Alice takes her input and splits it into *n* shares, one for each participant (herself, plus *n*-1 other parties). The specific *secret sharing scheme* used by Goldreich, et al., involved *permutations in* $S_5$ (the symmetric group on 5 elements), but the underlying principle is identical to many types of *secret sharing schemes*: Alice picks *n*-1 random values, and then computes (and keeps) an $n^{th}$ value such that the combination of the *n* values is equal to Alice's actual input value (e.g., $share_n = share_1 \oplus \ldots \oplus share_{n-1} \oplus input$, or $share_n = (share_1 \times \ldots \times share_{n-1})^{-1} \times input$); the *n*-1 random values are then distributed as shares to the *n*-1 other participants. Alice can then do an *oblivious transfer* protocol with each other participant to obliviously give each participant a share that corresponds to that participant's proper input value. Finally, each other participant evaluates the gate and obtains a share of the output value. Those *n*-1 output shares, along with Alice's output share, jointly determine the true gate output.

This can be seen as a generalization of Yao's proposal in which Alice has a single other participant Bob. Alice gives Bob a random value (a "share" of her input) and she alone knows the relationship between that random value and her true input value (i.e., the label, which effectively acts as the second "share" that she keeps). Through *oblivious transfer*, Bob receives a share representing his own proper input; he then evaluates the gate, obtaining a share of the gate output. This output share, combined with Alice's output "share" (i.e., her output labeling scheme), determines the true gate output.

The second difference with respect to Yao's scheme is that, because there are now multiple shares of each party's secret inputs, the individual gates in the *garbled circuit* need to be evaluated differently. As proposed by the authors, for each *garbled gate*

- The bits 0 and 1, along with all variables, are encoded as *5-permutations* (i.e., elements in $S_5$) so that the *gate* is generalized from Boolean values to elements in a finite field, and
- Every instruction (in the algorithm for computing with shares) consists of multiplying two *5-permutations*, where each *5-permutation* is a constant, or a variable, or the inverse (in $S_5$) of a variable.

The authors explicitly describe how to construct a *garbled* AND gate using shares with *n* participants, and remark that a *garbled* NOT gate is a trivial variation. With these two gates, it is clearly possible to build a *garbled circuit* that will implement any *polynomially-computable function*, and so the generalization from Yao's 2PC protocol to an MPC protocol is complete. Beyond this, however, because there are *n* parties instead of 2, a *secret sharing scheme* can be used that tolerates a certain number of *malicious* parties (that is, parties that deviate from the prescribed protocol in any possible way). Goldreich, et al., show that their proposed scheme provides _correctness_ and _privacy_ even when up to $(n/2-1)$ of the participants are _malicious_.

Note that the purpose of this 1987 work was to prove _feasibility_ (in effect, to demonstrate that secure _multi-party computation_ is possible); there was no consideration of _efficiency_ other than to show that the protocol can be accomplished in _polynomial time_.

## 7.2.2   Enhancements

Over the decades since MPC was introduced, there have been a significant number of important enhancements. These enhancements have fallen into two broad categories: theoretical and practical (see (Lindell 2020) for further discussion of all the enhancements summarized in this section).

**Theoretical**   Three different types of adversary model have been developed.

- _Passive_ (sometimes called _semi-honest_ or _honest-but-curious_) adversaries, who correctly follow the protocol specification but attempt in whatever way they can to learn information that should remain private. This category also includes _fail-stop_ adversaries, who may choose to halt the protocol execution before it is complete if it will give them some advantage in learning private information.
- _Malicious_ (sometimes called "active") adversaries, who can arbitrarily deviate from the protocol specification. If they do deviate, however, this is detectable by the honest participants.
- _Covert_ adversaries, who are similar to _malicious_ adversaries except that detection of their attack will happen with some specified probability that can be tuned to the application. Note that if the attack is not detected, the _covert_ adversary will successfully cheat (e.g., undetectably learn some private information).

Adversaries may also have various corruption strategies.

- _Static_ corruption, in which the number and identity of corrupted parties is fixed before the protocol begins.
- _Adaptive_ corruption, in which the adversary may decide who to corrupt, and when, during the execution of the protocol. These decisions may depend on the environment or context, which is why it is called an _adaptive_ corruption strategy.
- _Proactive_ corruption, in which not only may honest parties become corrupted, but corrupted parties may also become honest during the execution of the protocol. This is to model real-world systems that are discovered to be breached, but then are "cleaned" and allowed to continue operating during the protocol run.

There is also theoretical consideration of how the MPC protocol interacts with the larger system in which it runs.

- In *sequential composition*, the MPC protocol can run as a sub-protocol of another protocol, with an arbitrary number and type of other messages sent before and after the MPC protocol. However, the full MPC protocol must be run without any other messages being sent in parallel. The MPC protocol is said to exhibit *modular composition* if it is secure in this *sequential composition* setting.
- In *concurrent composition*, the MPC protocol can run concurrently with any number of other protocols. The MPC protocol is said to exhibit *universal composability* if it is secure in this *concurrent composition* setting.

Finally, the following important theoretical *feasibility* results have been proved when there are $n$ participants and $t$ is a bound on the number of parties that may be corrupted.

- For $t < n/3$ (i.e., less than a third of the parties can be corrupted), *secure MPC* with *fairness* and *guaranteed output delivery* can be achieved for any function. If we assume only a synchronous point-to-point network with authenticated channels, *computational security* is possible; if we additionally assume that the channels are private, *information-theoretic security* is possible.
- For $t < n/2$ (i.e., in the case of a guaranteed honest majority), *secure MPC* with *fairness* and *guaranteed output delivery* can be achieved with both *computational* and *information-theoretic security* for any function, if we assume that the parties also have access to a broadcast channel.
- For $t \geq n/2$ (i.e., an unlimited number of corrupted parties), *secure MPC* can be achieved, but without *fairness* or *guaranteed output delivery*.

***Practical***  Performance improvements in MPC began with reducing the overhead of cryptographic primitives, but this led to quite minor speed-ups in actual implementations. Researchers then focused on the use of special hardware instructions to decrease memory and communication costs. This was helpful but, again, resulted in modest gains in performance. Next, recognizing that manually constructing circuits is labour-intensive and difficult, effort was put into the design of special-purpose MPC compilers to translate code to circuits in an automated way. Compilers were built that minimized the number of expensive AND gates (in favour of considerably more XOR gates which can be computed almost for free), or that generated the smallest possible circuit, or that generated a circuit with the lowest depth, or that created circuits with other characteristics that were targeted to particular algorithms or environments; see (Hastings et al. 2019) for a survey of work in this area. Finally, massive parallelism (in multi-core CPUs with implementation optimizations such as pipelining (Kreuter et al. 2012), (Shelat and Shen 2013), or in standard desktop GPUs (Frederiksen and Nielsen 2013)) has been exploited, along with other protocol techniques such as the *cut-and-choose paradigm* (Lindell 2013), (Huang et al. 2013), to dramatically improve the throughput of MPC protocol environments.

Together, the above achievements have produced performance improvements of many orders of magnitude, and ultimately allowed MPC to be fast enough to be used for a wide variety of practical problems.

It is expected that further advances, both theoretical and practical, will continue to be reported in the coming years.

### 7.2.3   Strengths

The strengths of MPC are quite clear:

- It provides strong security and privacy guarantees under an assortment of attack models and implementation settings; and
- It has seen impressive improvements in efficiency in recent years.

Furthermore, MPC has successfully demonstrated its utility in a number of high-profile use cases, including an analysis of the gender wage gap among the Greater Boston area work force (Lapets et al. 2018), Google's computation of the conversion rate from advertisements to purchases (Ion et al. 2017), and privacy-preserving correlation of sensitive information between different government departments in Estonia (Sharemind 2015).

Another area that is getting increased attention is *threshold cryptography*, which allows cryptographic operations (such as *decryption* or *digital signing*) to be computed without the private key being stored in any single place. By putting key shares in many different environments, it is vastly more difficult for an adversary to acquire all (or a threshold number of) shares and obtain the key, but MPC can be used to compute the cryptographic operations in this setting. This is clearly of tremendous interest to companies looking for alternatives to legacy hardware for storing and protecting important cryptographic keys; see, for example, page 13 ("MPC for cryptographic key protection") of (Lindell 2020).

### 7.2.4   Disadvantages, Limitations, and Weaknesses

Notwithstanding all the remarkable strengths of MPC mentioned in Sect. 7.2.3, it is critically important to recognize that MPC secures the *process* of multi-party computation, but it does not secure the *inputs* to that process. In particular, adversarial parties may input any values that they wish, and there is no general way to prevent this. For example, if Alice and Bob want to run a *private set intersection* protocol to see what customers they have in common, a malicious Alice could input a list that contains none of her actual customers; if the protocol produces an intersection, Alice will learn some of Bob's customers without revealing any of her own customers to him. Therefore, if the security of an application depends on every party using *correct inputs*, additional mechanisms (external to MPC) will have to be used to ensure this; such mechanisms may be non-trivial, may not be guaranteed to work, and may incur significant costs.

Similarly, it is equally critically important to recognize that MPC secures the *process* of multi-party computation, but it does not secure the *outputs* of that process. The output result of the function being computed may inadvertently reveal some sensitive information that cannot be protected by MPC. For example, if Alice and Bob use a secure two-party protocol to compute the average of their salaries, clearly each party, knowing his/her own salary and the average, will immediately be able to compute the exact salary of the other (even though the 2PC protocol itself might hide the other party's input with *information-theoretic* security). As another simple example, if Bob is evaluating a *garbled* AND gate and his input is a "1", then the true gate output will immediately reveal Alice's hidden input even though the share she gave him was *information-theoretically* secure during the protocol: a gate output of "0" means that her input was "0", and a gate output of "1" means that her input was "1". Thus, in any given environment, it is important to decide what functions should and should not be computed using MPC, based on overall privacy concerns.

Lastly, as noted by Lindell in (Lindell 2020), it is important to remember that the feasibility results for MPC are proven under specific models and under cryptographic hardness and/or settings assumptions. As with all cryptographic algorithms and protocols, any violation of these assumptions in a real implementation risks nullifying the expected security guarantees.

## 7.3  ε-Differential Privacy

The final example PET in this chapter, like the PET given in Sect. 7.1, pertains to privacy protection in a database setting. Here, the focus is on a *statistical database*; that is, a database that holds *statistics* of a sample population, or that is used to answer *statistical queries* on that population. It has been shown (Dwork 2006) that such a setting is obliged to disclose information, and thus privacy will inevitably be degraded. However, the goal of *ε-differential privacy* is to ensure that this privacy loss is minimized: any given information disclosure will be, within a small chosen multiplicative factor, just as likely whether or not a specific individual participates in the database.

For example, consider a statistical database without *ε-differential privacy*. Bob submits a query asking for the average salary of all the *n* employees in the company where he works. This is a permitted query and so Bob obtains an answer. Clearly, this answer does not reveal any particular individual's salary. However, after the company hires Joseph, Bob submits this query again; combining the new answer with his previous answer, he can accurately compute Joseph's salary. When David is fired, Bob submits the query again and is able to determine what David's salary was. When Alice gets a promotion and a raise, Bob submits his query again to learn the exact amount of Alice's raise.

*ε-differential privacy* was designed to hide (as much as possible) the changes that occur in query responses as a result of changes in the database, so that observers learn as little as possible from these separate responses. The core idea is to add *noise* to the returned answer so that the variations resulting from modifications to the database are hidden by the noise (i.e., Bob cannot tell if a change in answer is a result of the difference in the database, or is simply the result of noise in the new answer).

The techniques of *ε-differential privacy* developed over a series of papers (Dinur and Nissim 2003), (Dwork and Nissim 2004), (Blum et al. 2005), and culminated in the 2006 paper by Cynthia Dwork, Frank McSherry, Kobbi Nissim, and Adam Smith (2006a). Overviews of this research area were given by Dwork in (Dwork 2006) and (Dwork 2008), and a nice introductory summary was presented by Avrim Blum in (Blum 2013).

### 7.3.1   The Basic Scheme

*ε-differential privacy* (an application of the closely related notion of *ε-indistinguishability*; see (Desfontaines and Pejó 2020)) was defined by Dwork, et al. (2006a, b) as follows. Consider two databases $X$ and $X'$ that differ in only one entry (i.e., one row in the first database, $x_i$, is changed to $x_i'$ in the second database, where "changed" means that the row content was modified from an actual value to a NULL value (i.e., the row was "removed"), or the content was modified from a NULL value to an actual value (i.e., the row was "added"), or the content was modified from one actual value to another actual value). Furthermore, consider some function $A$ that can be run on a database $X$ to produce an output $A(X)$, and let $\Pr(A(X) = v)$ be the probability that the output $A(X)$ is equal to a particular value $v$. Then $A$ is *ε-differentially private* if for all outputs $v$

$$\Pr\big(A(X) = v\big) \le e^{\varepsilon} \bullet \Pr\big(A(X') = v\big)$$

This is sometimes written in the following form to explicitly compensate for which probability is larger:

$$e^{-\varepsilon} \le \Big[ \Pr\big(A(X) = v\big) / \Pr\big(A(X') = v\big) \Big] \le e^{\varepsilon}$$

Using the notation "|y|" for the absolute value of $y$, the previous equation is sometimes written as

$$\ln\Big(\Pr\big(A(X) = v\big) / \Pr\big(A(X') = v\big)\Big) \le \varepsilon$$

Finally, given that $\varepsilon \approx \ln(1 + \varepsilon)$ when $\varepsilon$ is small, the latter equation becomes

$$\Pr\big(A(X) = v\big) / \Pr\big(A(X') = v\big) \in \big[1 \pm \varepsilon\big]$$

Thus, the probability that the function $A$ gives a certain answer when run on a database $X$ that includes Joseph, is within a multiplicative factor $\varepsilon$ of the probability that $A$ gives the same answer when run on a database $X'$ that does not include Joseph. Note that we may more broadly consider all measurable sets $V$ of possible outputs, and instead write (as in (Dwork 2008), for example)

$$\Pr\big(A(X)\in V\big)/\Pr\big(A(X')\in V\big)\in[1\pm\varepsilon]$$

This is a powerful notion of privacy because it guarantees a statistical property about the behaviour of the function $A$, independent of the computational power and auxiliary information available to an adversary (including knowledge of every other row in the database).

As mentioned above, $\varepsilon$-*differential privacy* is achieved by adding noise to the query response. However, the privacy guarantee is only achieved if care is taken regarding what type of noise is added. For example, adding a fixed/constant amount of noise does not work, because the requester may be able to determine the value of the noise and then remove it. (Since Bob is able to query for his own salary, he can simply request his own salary several times. If he sees that $3000 is always added to the answer, then he will be able to subtract $3000 from a response he gets to a query for Joseph's salary and learn the true value.) Similarly, if the added noise is random but is simplistically symmetric about the origin, then Bob may ask any given query many times, average the responses, and cancel out the noise.

It is also important to recognize that there is an inherent trade-off between *privacy* and *utility*. Ultimately, the query response must be *useful* to the requester (clearly, the requester is asking in order to learn something from the data!). At one extreme, if <u>no noise</u> is added to the response then the answer is perfectly useful but privacy is clearly compromised. (What would this situation mean for $\varepsilon$? Say that Joseph's salary is anything other than $v$. If the probability that the average salary equals $v$ in the database $X$ that includes Joseph is 1, then the probability that the average salary equals $v$ in the database $X'$ that does not include Joseph will be 0 (since no noise is added). Thus, $\varepsilon = \infty$.) At the other extreme, if <u>total noise</u> is added to the response (e.g., the returned answer $A(X)$ is a value that is uniformly drawn from the interval $[c_1, c_2]$), then the answer is perfectly private but the utility is zero. (What would this situation mean for $\varepsilon$? Say that there are $m$ equally-likely values $v_1, \ldots, v_m$ in the interval $[c_1, c_2]$. The probability that the average salary in $X$ is a specific value $v_i$ is exactly $1/m$, and the probability that the average salary in $X'$ is the same value $v_i$ is also $1/m$. Thus, $\varepsilon = 0$.)

Ultimately, what is required is a <u>*good*</u> trade-off between privacy and utility: we need to add enough noise to provide privacy to the records in the database, but not so much noise that the query responses become useless. How can this be done? The solution is to have a noise value that is randomly drawn from a *distribution* around the actual/correct value.

**One approach** Very often, when a *distribution* for noise is discussed, the first thought is a Gaussian (normal) distribution (e.g., in error control coding theory, communication channels are initially modeled as using additive white Gaussian noise (AWGN) to corrupt the transmitted code words). Let us consider that approach here. The average salary in the database $X$ with Joseph included is $b/n$ (the sum of all the salaries, divided by the number of people in the database). If we add noise with a Gaussian distribution, then the returned answers for "average salary" will have a Gaussian distribution centered at $b/n$ as shown in Fig. 7.2:

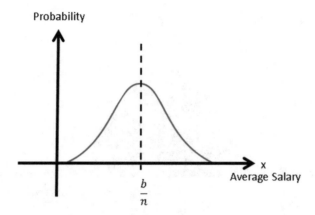

**Fig. 7.2** Gaussian distribution centered at $b/n$

Therefore, if the actual average salary in $X$ is \$50,000, then the probability that the function $A$ returns \$50,000 (i.e., the probability that $x = 50,000$ in the above graph) is $\Pr(noise_X = 0)$ and the probability that $x = 60,000$ is $\Pr(noise_X = 10,000)$, where $noise_X$ is the amount of noise (in dollars) added to the true answer when querying database $X$.

The average salary in $X'$ without Joseph is $(b-s)/(n-1)$, where $s$ is Joseph's salary. The returned answers for "average salary" will have a Gaussian distribution centered at $(b-s)/(n-1)$ due to the addition of $noise_{X'}$, the amount of noise (in dollars) added to the true answer when querying database $X'$. Therefore, there are two distributions, one centered at $b/n$ and one centered at $(b-s)/(n-1)$; see Fig. 7.3.

Let $\Delta$ be the difference between the two means (i.e., $\Delta = |\, (b/n) - (b-s)/(n-1)\, |$). Say $\Delta = 15,000$ and the average salary is higher without Joseph. Then the probability that the returned answer for "average salary" is \$60,000 for the database $X$ with Joseph (the probability that $x = 60,000$) is $\Pr(noise_X = 10,000)$ and the probability that $x = 60,000$ for database $X'$ without Joseph is $\Pr(noise_{X'} = -5000)$. The ratio of these two probabilities is $\Pr(noise_X = 10,000)/\Pr(noise_{X'} = -5000)$, which depends on the amount of noise added. As a simple example, the ratio $\Pr(noise_X = 10,000)/\Pr(noise_{X'}=-5000)$ is some value $r_1$ (not equal to 1), but the ratio $\Pr(noise_X=450,000)/\Pr(noise_{X'} = 435,000)$ is another value $r_2$ that is much closer to 1 than $r_1$ is: the two probabilities for an answer of \$500,000 are almost identical (both very low!), whereas the two probabilities for an answer of \$60,000 are farther apart; this is shown in Fig. 7.4.

We can see this numerically as follows. The formula for a Gaussian (normal) distribution (with *mean* $\mu$ and *variance* $\sigma^2$) is

$$\frac{e^{-\frac{1}{2}\frac{(x-\mu)^2}{\sigma^2}}}{\sigma\sqrt{2\pi}}$$

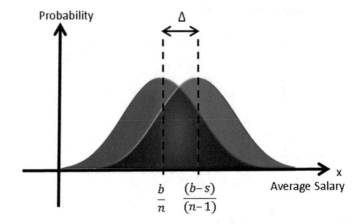

**Fig. 7.3** Two gaussian distributions, centered at $b/n$ and at $(b-s)/(n-1)$

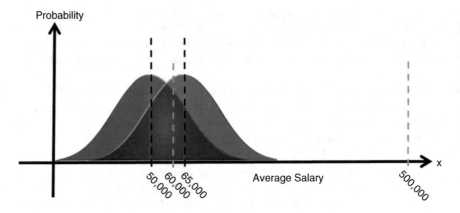

**Fig. 7.4** An average salary answer of \$60,000 and an average salary answer of \$500,000

and so the ratio of the two probabilities will be proportional to $exp(-(x-\mu_X)^2)/exp(-(x-\mu_{X'})^2)$, which is proportional to $exp(2\Delta x)$. This has $x$ in it: the ratio of the answer for $X$ and the answer for $X'$ depends on the actual answer $x$ that is returned – this ratio might be (quite) different if we asked again! This is counter-intuitive; we would expect the ratio to depend only on the question, not on the generated answer. Furthermore, we may want the ratio to be bounded by some value that we set beforehand.

So, in summary, the ratio of the probabilities is quite close to 1 if the returned answer is very far from the true answer, and is further from 1 if the returned answer is very close to the true answer. Clearly this is not ideal. It would be much better if the ratio remained the same for all possible returned answers so that the pair of queries (i.e., to the database with Joseph, and to the database without Joseph) does not return answers that leak information about how correct the answers are.

**A better approach** The proposal of Dwork, et al., is to use the Laplacian distribution for the generated noise. This distribution (with *mean* μ and *scale* λ) has a formula of

$$\frac{e^{\frac{x-\mu}{\lambda}}}{2\lambda}$$

with a corresponding Probability Density Function (PDF) graph as shown in Fig. 7.5.

(Note that the scale parameter λ determines the width of the function.) Thus, the ratio of the two probabilities (i.e., for databases with and without Joseph) is $e^{(\Delta/\lambda)}$ (observe that this does <u>not</u> have $x$ in it, and so it leaks no information about the correctness of the returned answer). For a desired ratio of $e\varepsilon$, we simply set $\lambda = \Delta/\varepsilon$ (for any chosen $\varepsilon$). Therefore, λ is the amount of noise to add to the answers, for a chosen privacy level $\varepsilon$.

As mentioned above, we do not want to add so much noise that the answer is useless. Recall that the average salary in the database $X$ is $b/n$, where $b$ is the sum of all the salaries and $n$ is the number of people in the database. Noise is added by modifying the sum of the salaries (not by modifying the number of people, since this is known to all observers). Therefore, we can specify that the sum in database $X'$ must be within $\pm\alpha b$ (to set a bound on the utility of the answers). In this case, λ needs to be $\alpha b$, which means that $(\Delta/\varepsilon) = \alpha b$, and so $\Delta = \varepsilon\alpha b$. But we know that $\Delta$

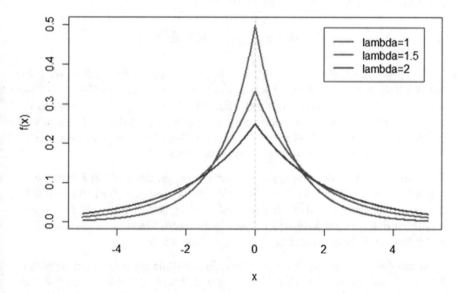

**Fig. 7.5** PDF of laplace distribution with mean 0

is proportional to $b$ and inversely proportional to $n$, so $\Delta$ is proportional to $b/n$. Therefore, $b/n \approx \varepsilon\alpha b$, and so $n \approx 1/\varepsilon\alpha$ (recall that $n$ is the size of the database).

This gives us a *privacy/utility/DB-size* (i.e., $\varepsilon/\alpha/n$) trade-off when designing the database: fixing any two of these parameters determines the third. However, since the *database size* is typically outside our control in a real-world situation – we are presented with a particular database of records to protect – we can choose any desired level of *privacy* and compute the resulting level of *utility* (or *vice versa*).

**Moving beyond Joseph**  In our example database and query function $A$ ("average salary"), it is clear that the change in the answer due to noise should not be greater than the true average salary $b/n$ (it would not make sense for a returned answer to be negative!), and so $\Delta$ (the change in the answer for $X'$ without Joseph) must be at most $b/n$ (so that the change due to Joseph leaving can always be "hidden" by the noise that is added). Therefore since $\lambda$ (the amount of noise added) is equal to $\Delta/\varepsilon$, we have that $\lambda = (b/n)(1/\varepsilon)$ for a privacy level of $\varepsilon$. The value $b/n$ represents the *sensitivity* of the function $A$ to Joseph's data (i.e., to the presence or absence of Joseph's actual salary).

However, for any given function $A$, if we want to protect everyone's privacy, we need to consider the *sensitivity* of $A$ to *each person's data*. In the example we have been using, the *sensitivity* will be the same for all people (i.e., $b/n$, since this our maximum allowed change in the answer if any person leaves). But it is not difficult to imagine a scenario in which the *sensitivity* is different for different people. For example, if the company has multiple job positions, and each position has a defined salary range, then removing Alice's salary may have a larger possible effect on the average than removing David's salary. Dwork, et al., therefore define the *Global Sensitivity* of $A$, $GS_A$:

$$GS_A = \max_{\text{databases X,X'}}\left(\left\|A(X)\text{-}A\left(X'\right)\right\|\right)$$

This gives the maximum change in answer with and without Alice, with and without Bob, with and without Charlie, and so on (for all the people in the database). Once $GS_A$ has been determined, then noise $\lambda = (GS_A)(1/\varepsilon)$ is added to the query responses in order to provide a privacy level of $\varepsilon$. This gives a database with $\varepsilon$-*differential privacy* no matter who leaves (and no matter who joins or how anyone's data is modified, as long as the change is within $GS_A$).

**Accommodating Additional Queries**  The discussion thus far has focused on a single query (e.g., "What is the average salary in the database?") and has defined a chosen privacy level $\varepsilon$ such that the probability of a specific answer to this query on a database that *includes* Joseph is within a multiplicative factor $\varepsilon$ of the probability of this same answer on a database that does *not include* Joseph.

In real database environments, however, there will be multiple queries, not one. The *composability property* of *differential privacy* ensures that if you have $k$ queries, you can decide how much privacy loss to give to each query. In effect (as explained by Dwork, et al.), you have a "privacy budget" and can "spend" it as you choose. *Composability* means that an $\varepsilon_1$-*differentially private* mechanism, followed by an $\varepsilon_2$-*differentially private* mechanism, will be $(\varepsilon_1 + \varepsilon_2)$-*differentially private*. As a simple example, given $\lambda = (GS_A)(1/\varepsilon)$, if we know that there will be $k$ queries, we can set the privacy level to be $\varepsilon/k$ for each of them. Then $\lambda_{new} = \lambda k$; after $k$ queries and responses, the privacy level will be $\varepsilon$ (as desired).

This value of $\lambda_{new}$ makes sense because the *maximum likelihood estimator* (MLE) of the mean for a *Laplacian distribution* from which $k$ samples are drawn is the median of the $k$ samples. Therefore, since our original noise distribution had a scale factor of $\lambda$ and allowed one query, if we are going to allow $k$ queries (i.e., get $k$ samples), then we need to make $\lambda$ bigger by a factor of $k$ (so that the MLE is an equally poor estimate of the mean). Recall that the mean of the distribution is the true answer, and so we want to ensure that the best estimate of the mean when we have $k$ samples essentially corresponds to the best estimate of the mean when we have only one sample. We can do this by making the distribution $k$ times wider.

[As an aside, note that the *maximum likelihood estimator* (MLE) is the statistic of interest here, not the *central limit theorem* (CLT), because the CLT is concerned with what happens as the number of samples approaches infinity, whereas the MLE applies for $k$ samples (regardless of $k$).]

## 7.3.2  Enhancements

The first enhancement of $\varepsilon$-*differential privacy* was proposed by Cynthia Dwork, Krishnaram Kenthapadi, Frank McSherry, Ilya Mironov, and Moni Naor in 2006 (the same year that $\varepsilon$-*differential privacy* was introduced) (2006b). Although $\varepsilon$-*differential privacy* is computed over all possible pairs of databases that differ in only one entry and over <u>all</u> possible outputs, it is recognized that in many real-world environments, outputs with extremely low probability are ignored (or perhaps their risk is weighted according to their probability). In (Dwork et al. 2006b), Dwork, et al., relax the definition of $\varepsilon$-*differential privacy* by allowing an additional small probability in which the upper bound $\varepsilon$ does not hold. This is intended to accommodate outputs for which the privacy loss is greater than $e\varepsilon$. This proposal of *approximate differential privacy*, generally denoted $(\varepsilon, \delta)$-*DP*, has been widely cited and used in the research literature.

A function $A$ is $(\varepsilon, \delta)$-*DP* if for any databases $X$ and $X'$ that differ only in one record, and for all measurable sets $V$ of possible outputs of $A$, $\Pr(A(X) \in V) \leq e\varepsilon \cdot \Pr(A(X') \in V) + \delta$.

Since 2006, there has been a tremendous amount of research in the field of *differential privacy*. The remarkable paper by Damien Desfontaines and Balázs Pejó (2020) reveals that *225 different notions* – all inspired by *differential privacy* – were defined between 2006 and 2020. Some of these are *extensions* or *generalizations* that build on DP and encompass the original $\varepsilon$-*differential privacy* as a special case. Others are *variants* or *modifications* that change the original definition to deliberately weaken or strengthen some aspect of it (typically to make it more applicable to specific environments or use cases). Sorting through this vast literature was a challenging task because, as the authors note in their paper, a number of the notions were defined independently multiple times, often with identical meaning but different names, or with identical names but different meanings.

Desfontaines and Pejó propose a taxonomy of *extensions* and *variants* of *differential privacy*, with the aim of simplifying the understanding of these different notions and the relationships between them. Their taxonomy consists of seven so-called *dimensions* of DP, where each *dimension* describes one way in which the original definition of *ε-differential privacy* can be changed. The seven *dimensions* can be viewed conceptually as *axes* or *basis vectors* in a multidimensional space, and each proposed *extension* or *variant* in the literature can then be seen as a unique point in that space. This way of categorizing the literature is beneficial not only because it helps to organize the plethora of definitions, but because it enables concrete ways to move forward with further research: definitions that vary along _different dimensions_ can be combined to form new, meaningful definitions; and definitions that vary along the _same dimension_, although they cannot be combined to form new meaningful definitions, can be usefully compared with each other.

The seven *dimensions* defined by Desfontaines and Pejó are as follows. (Note that the "attacker" mentioned in these dimensions is any entity that tries to learn some sensitive information about some input data by using the output of a query function $A$ on neighbour databases $X$ and $X'$.)

- *Quantification of Privacy Loss*. This *dimension* describes how privacy loss is quantified and measured across outputs. In particular, there may be value in averaging the loss over all the outputs, rather than designing only for the maximum (worst-case) loss.
- *Neighbourhood Definition*. This *dimension* considers which data is protected from the attacker. For example, rather than a *neighbour database* being one that differs only in a single record, it may be a database that differs only in one specific field of a record, or a database that differs in a specified group of records.
- *Variation of Privacy Loss*. This *dimension* considers whether privacy loss can be varied across the inputs. If so, this makes it possible to model simultaneous users that have different privacy requirements (for example, by associating a specific risk with each individual user).
- *Background Knowledge*. This *dimension* looks at how much background information the attacker is assumed to have. In realistic environments where the attacker does not have unlimited background knowledge, mechanisms that add less noise (or no noise) to outputs may be used to improve performance.
- *Formalism Change*. This *dimension* examines the formalism used to describe the attacker's knowledge gain. For example, rather than modeling the explicit information gain of the attacker, a hypothesis testing model can be used which attempts to limit the Type 1 and Type 2 errors of the hypothesis that a given output originates from database $X$ instead of $X'$. The use of different formalisms can allow the designer to explore other intuitive notions of privacy (such as privacy for any group of values in a dataset, rather than just for one particular user).

- *Relativization of Knowledge Gain.* This *dimension* examines alternate ways in which information can leak (including side-channel functions and knowledge about the structure of a social network). In particular, alternative models can make it possible to guarantee privacy for correlated data in the database.
- *Computational Power.* This *dimension* questions the computational power available to the attacker. If the attacker does not have unlimited power (that is, if a *computationally-bounded* attacker is assumed), then certain cryptographic techniques may be combined with *differential privacy* to improve time or space efficiency in an implementation.

The authors further describe three desirable *properties* of *differential privacy* from the literature; each proposed DP definition is then examined to see whether it satisfies any or all of these properties.

- *Composability.* This property was mentioned at the end of Sect. 7.3.1 above; it was defined by Dwork in (2006). Note that there are actually three flavours of this property. <u>*Parallel composition*</u> says that if $A_1$ is $\varepsilon_1$-*differentially private*, $A_2$ is $\varepsilon_2$-*differentially private*, and database $X$ is separated into two disjoint databases $X_1$ and $X_2$, then $A(X) = (A_1(X_1), A_2(X_2))$ is $max(\varepsilon_1, \varepsilon_2)$-*differentially private*. <u>*Sequential composition*</u> (which is the variant mentioned in 7.3.1) says that if $A_1$ is $\varepsilon_1$-*differentially private* and $A_2$ is $\varepsilon_2$-*differentially private*, then $A(X) = (A_1(X), A_2(X))$ is $(\varepsilon_1 + \varepsilon_2)$-*differentially private*. Finally, <u>*adaptive composition*</u> is equivalent to *sequential composition* except that it allows $A_2$ to depend on the value of $A_1(X)$ (in order to model the <u>information gain over time</u> of an attacker who interacts with a *differentially-private* query mechanism).
- *Convexity.* This property was defined by Daniel Kifer and Bing-Rong Lin in 2010 (2010): any privacy definition *DEF* satisfies the *convexity axiom* if, for any two mechanisms $A_1$ and $A_2$ satisfying *DEF*, the mechanism $A$ defined by $A(X) = A_1(X)$ with probability $p$ and $A(X) = A_2(X)$ with probability $1$-$p$ also satisfies *DEF*.
- *Post-Processing.* This is a second property defined by Kifer and Lin in 2010 (2010): any privacy definition *DEF* satisfies the *post-processing axiom* if, for any mechanism $A$ satisfying *DEF* and any probabilistic function $f$, the mechanism $f(A(X))$ also satisfies *DEF*.

Not surprisingly, Desfontaines and Pejó found that the 225 forms of *differential privacy* that they discovered in the literature are used in many different ways. Some are purely theoretical notions and serve only "as technical tools to get better results on *composition* or *privacy amplification*" or "to provide a deeper understanding of guarantees offered by DP and its alternatives". Others are highly practical and have been successfully used to apply *differential privacy* to a variety of real-world problems (such as location privacy, streaming services, random access memory (RAM) requests, private information retrieval, text and image operations, genomic data analysis, recommender systems, and training for machine learning applications). Some have launched flourishing sub-areas of research, while others have not (yet) seen much follow-up.

The Desfontaines and Pejó paper vividly demonstrates that the field of *differential privacy* has been extremely active since its inception, and it shows no signs of slowing down anytime soon. Like MPC (see Sect. 7.2.2 above), we can expect to see continued advances in DP, both on the theoretical front and on the practical front, for many years to come.

### 7.3.3  Strengths

*ε-differential privacy* is a very powerful PET that allows us to design a database query-response system in such a way that the probability that a specific response value is returned remains essentially unchanged (i.e., within a multiplicative factor $ε$, which can be chosen to be as small as desired) whether or not any specific person's data is included in the database. This is a very nice privacy guarantee! As Cynthia Dwork puts it (2008), *differential privacy* "ensures that (almost, and quantifiably) no risk is incurred by joining a statistical database." One example she gives pertains to a database of health information: if the database were to be consulted by an insurance provider before deciding whether or not to insure Alice, then the presence or absence of Alice's data in the database will not significantly affect her chance of receiving coverage.

Avrim Blum phrases it somewhat more colourfully (2013): *any event (anything an adversary might do to you) has nearly the same probability whether you join or don't join, lie or tell the truth.*

As mentioned in Sects. 7.3.1 and 7.3.2, this technology also has a nice *composability property* that allows the designer to achieve a desired privacy level even in environments where there are $k$ queries instead of one, and even when the queries are *adaptively chosen* (i.e., each new query is constructed based on the responses received from all previous queries).

Given its rigorous mathematical foundations and strong privacy guarantee, it is not surprising that *ε-differential privacy* has been used by a number of well-known organizations, including the US Census Bureau (Machanavajjhala et al. 2008), Google (Erlingsson et al. 2014), (Eland 2015), Apple (2016), Microsoft (Ding et al. 2017), LinkedIn (Rogers et al. 2020), and Uber (Johnson et al. 2018).

Finally, note that although *ε-differential privacy* is perhaps most naturally a technology for *interactive* query-response systems, work has also been done for the *non-interactive* setting (such as releasing a "sanitized database" that people can then examine as they wish, asking queries that the "sanitizers" did not anticipate before the release); see, for example, (Blum et al. 2013) for an extensive discussion.

### 7.3.4   Disadvantages, Limitations, and Weaknesses

In order to achieve *ε-differential privacy* for a database in the interactive setting, a designer will need to have an accurate picture of what types of queries will be asked, how many queries of each type will be received, and how many people might leave (or join), over the lifetime of the database. In many environments, acquiring this amount of knowledge prior to making the database available may be unrealistic.

Furthermore, although this technology provides a simple mathematical mechanism for making a trade-off between *privacy* and *utility*, it may be non-trivial in some environments to select the <u>best</u> level of *privacy* (*utility*) for the specific data and people involved in a given database application. Obviously, most users would desire both *maximum privacy* and *maximum utility*, and so diminishing one in favour of the other may not be an easy consensus to reach.

It has also been noted by some researchers (see, for example, Blum (2013)) that *ε-differential privacy* is a pessimistic/paranoid notion: by definition, it designs for a privacy level that deals with the *global sensitivity* of the query function (i.e., the worst-case change that could occur in the query response over all databases $X$ and $X'$ that differ in one row). Thus, it may be more restrictive than needed. For example, if this worst-case change would only happen extremely rarely then, the vast majority of the time, more noise is added to query responses than needed, which unnecessarily reduces the utility of almost all the answers. As discussed in Sect. 7.3.2, however, even though the original definition of *ε-differential privacy* has this limitation, many researchers have worked on *extensions* or *variants* of this definition to make it more suitable to other environments.

Additionally, it is important to note that determining the *global sensitivity $GS_A$* will be computationally intensive for any database of realistic size, and that $GS_A$ will need to be re-evaluated whenever the database changes (i.e., someone leaves or joins the company). Although this is a cost that occurs only at initial deployment and for each subsequent database change (i.e., it is not a per-query cost), computing $GS_A$ may be a significant effort that needs to be taken into consideration.

Finally, when using this technology, it is essential to remember that although $\varepsilon$ is a parameter and can be chosen to be as small as desired, <u>it is not zero</u>. Thus, privacy losses are inevitable and they can accumulate over time. Designers, and especially users who allow their data to be included in the database, need to be aware that a "privacy guarantee" is not the same as a "guarantee of absolute privacy"!

## 7.4   Summary

This chapter has presented three PETs that limit ***disclosure*** by hiding the *attributes* of the user: *Ciphertext Policy Attribute-Based Encryption*; *Multi-Party Computation*; and *ε-differential privacy*. These are all powerful PETs that are seeing increasing use in real applications.

In CP-ABE, Alice's *attributes* are part of her private key and allow her to decrypt data without anyone discovering the values of her *attributes*. Ciphertext is associated with an *access structure* that specifies what particular combination of attributes is required for decryption to be successful; a user with the correct attributes (in the specified combination) will thus be able to decrypt. Research continues in solving some of the trust, efficiency, and practical deployment issues associated with this technology.

In MPC, Alice and others can jointly perform some computation that requires inputs from each of them, but no party learns the private inputs of any other party. Using a technique called *garbled circuits*, privacy and correctness can be achieved for any *polynomially-computable function*. Over the years, extensive theoretical and practical advances have been made in many areas of MPC, so that it has now been successfully demonstrated in a number of high-profile use cases around the world.

Finally, in $\varepsilon$-DP, arbitrary users can perform query processing on a database to obtain desired statistics without learning whether Alice's data is included in the database or not. Noise is added to a query response in order to hide the presence or absence of an individual's data, but the noise must be drawn from an appropriate distribution in order to provide the desired privacy property. A *privacy level* parameter can be chosen and tuned to achieve privacy for all database participants and to accommodate a larger number of queries. Hundreds of extensions and variants of the original $\varepsilon$-DP notion have been defined over the years, demonstrating significant continued interest in this PET.

In the following chapter, we will look at the final branch of the privacy tree: technologies that limit **disclosure** by hiding both the *identity* and the *attributes* of the user.

**Questions for Personal Reflection and/or Group Discussion**

1. *Ciphertext policy attribute-based encryption* (CP-ABE) schemes typically require a System Authority that must be fully trusted because this entity generates a private key for every user (and can therefore decrypt all ciphertext in the environment). Name two specific environments in which such an entity would be acceptable. What can be done for other environments that wish to use CP-ABE but do not want an all-knowing System Authority?

2. Section 7.2.4 discusses the fact that MPC protocols secure the <u>process</u> of *multiparty computation*, but do nothing to secure the various <u>inputs</u>, or the <u>outputs</u>, of that process. Thus, it is possible to use MPC in a given setting and still compromise the privacy of one or more participants in the computation. What can be done to deal with this limitation? Propose and analyze three different measures that you would take with inputs and outputs in order to protect MPC users.

3. The following disadvantage is listed in Sect. 7.3.4:

    *In order to achieve $\varepsilon$-differential privacy for a database in the interactive setting, a designer will need to have an accurate picture of what types of queries will be asked, how many queries of each type will be received, and how many people might leave (or join), over the lifetime of the database. In many environments, acquiring this amount of knowledge prior to making the database available may be unrealistic.*

If you are in charge of database operations for a large company and you have been tasked with making the database *$\varepsilon$-differentially private*, how will you obtain this information? Will you put any assumptions, procedures, or restrictions in place so that you can achieve *$\varepsilon$-differential privacy*? What might be the implications of these decisions?

# References

Apple Newsroom, Apple previews iOS 10, the biggest iOS release ever. *press release* (2016, 13 June)

A. Balu and K. Kuppusamy, Ciphertext policy Attribute based Encryption with anonymous access policy. *Int. J. Peer-to-Peer Networks*, 1(1) October 2010. (See also *Quality, Reliability, Security and Robustness in Heterogeneous Networks (QShine 2013)*, K. Singh and A. K. Awasthi (eds), Lecture Notes of the Institute for Computer Sciences, Social Informatics and Telecommunications Engineering, Springer, vol. 115, pp. 696–705, 2013)

J. Bethencourt, A. Sahai, and B. Waters, Ciphertext-policy attribute-based encryption. *IEEE symposium on security and privacy*, Berkeley, CA, pp. 321–334 (2007)

A. Blum, A brief tour of differential privacy. Your guide: Avrim Blum. *StudyLib*, ca. (2013)

A. Blum, C. Dwork, F. McSherry, and K. Nissim, Practical privacy: The SuLQ framework. *Proceedings of the 24th ACM SIGMOD-SIGACT-SIGART symposium on principles of database systems*, pp. 128–138 (2005, 13–15 June)

A. Blum, K. Ligett, and A. Roth, A learning theory approach to noninteractive database privacy. *J. ACM* 60(2) Article 12: 1–25 (2013, April)

BusinessWire, NTT research distinguished scientist brent waters and UCLA Professor Amit Sahai Win IACR Test-of-Time Award. *News release* (2020, 9 April)

D. Desfontaines and B. Pejó, SoK: Differential privacies. *Proceedings on privacy enhancing technologies*, vol. 2, pp. 288–313, 2020. (The extended version of this paper is "SoK: Differential Privacies: A taxonomy of differential privacy variants and extensions", *arXiv.org*, arXiv:1906.01337v4, 58pp, 10 July 2020)

B. Ding, J. Kulkarni, and S. Yekhanin, Collecting telemetry data privately. *31$^{st}$ Conference on neural information processing systems*, Long Beach, CA, 10pp, (2017, December)

I. Dinur and K. Nissim, Revealing information while preserving privacy. *Proceedings of the 22nd ACM SIGMOD-SIGACT-SIGART symposium on principles of database systems*, pp. 202–210, (2003, June)

C. Dwork, Differential privacy. *Proceedings of the 33$^{rd}$ international colloquium on automata, languages and programming*, Springer LNCS 4052, Venice, Italy, pp. 1–12, (2006, 10–14 July)

C. Dwork, Differential privacy: A survey of results. *International conference on theory and applications of models and computation*, Springer LNCS 4978, pp. 1–19 (2008)

C. Dwork and K. Nissim, Privacy-preserving datamining on vertically partitioned databases. *Advances in cryptology: Proceedings of crypto*, pp. 528–544 (2004, 15–19 August)

C. Dwork, F. McSherry, K. Nissim, and A. Smith, Calibrating noise to sensitivity in private data analysis. *Proceedings of the 3$^{rd}$ theory of cryptography conference*, pp. 265–284 (2006a, 4–7 March)

C. Dwork, K. Kenthapadi, F. McSherry, I. Mironov, and M. Naor, Our data, ourselves: Privacy via distributed noise generation. *Advances in cryptology: Proceedings of eurocrypt*, Springer LNCS 4004, St. Petersburg, Russia, pp. 486–503, (2006b, 28 May – 1 June)

A. Eland, Tackling urban mobility with technology. *Google Europe blog* (2015, 18 November)

Ú. Erlingsson, V. Pihur, and A. Korolova, RAPPOR: randomized aggregatable privacy-preserving ordinal response. *Proceedings of the 21$^{st}$ ACM conference on computer and communications security*, pp. 1054–1067, (2014, November)

D. Evans, V. Kolesnikov and M. Rosulek, *A pragmatic introduction to secure multi-party computation*, NOW Publishers (2018, December )

O. Goldreich, Cryptography and cryptographic protocols. Distrib. Comput. **16**, 177–199 (2003)

O. Goldreich, S. Micali, and A. Wigderson, How to play ANY mental game, or, A completeness theorem for protocols with honest majority. *Proceedings of the 19$^{th}$ annual ACM symposium on theory of computing*, pp. 218–229 (1987, January)

V. Goyal, O. Pandey, A. Sahai, and B. Waters, Attribute Based Encryption for Fine-Grained Access Control of Encrypted Data. *Proceedings of the 13$^{th}$ ACM conference on computer and communications security*, pp. 89–98, (2006, October)

M. Hastings, B. Hemenway, D. Noble and S. Zdancewic, SoK: General purpose compilers for secure multi-party computation. *Proceedings of the IEEE symposium on security and privacy*, pp. 479–496 (2019, 19–23 May)

Y. Huang, J. Katz, and D. Evans, Efficient secure two-party computation using symmetric cut-and-choose. *Advances in cryptology: proceedings of crypto 2013*, Springer LNCS 8043, pp. 18–35, (2013, 18–22 August)

M. Ion, B. Kreuter, E. Nergiz, S. Patel, S. Saxena, K. Seth, D. Shanahan and M. Yung, Private intersection-sum protocol with applications to attributing aggregate Ad conversions. *Cryptology ePrint archive, 2017:738* (2017, 31 July)

N. Johnson, J. P. Near, J. M. Hellerstein, and D. Song, Chorus: Differential privacy via query rewriting. *arXiv.com, 1809.07750*, (2018, 23 September)

T. Kasper Frederiksen and J. Buus Nielsen, Fast and maliciously secure two-party computation using the GPU. *Applied cryptography and network security*, Springer LNCS 7954, pp. 339–356 (2013)

D. Kifer and B.-R. Lin, Towards an axiomatization of statistical privacy and utility. *Proceedings of the 29th ACM SIGMOD-SIGACT-SIGART symposium on principles of database systems*, pp. 147–158, (2010, June)

B. Kreuter, A. Shelat, and C.-H. Shen, Billion gate secure computation with malicious adversaries. *Proceedings of the 21st usenix security symposium*, Bellevue, WA, pp. 285–300, (2012, August)

A. Lapets, F. Jansen, K. Dak Albab, R. Issa, L. Qin, M. Varia and A. Bestavros, Accessible privacy preserving web-based data analysis for assessing and addressing economic inequalities. *Proceedings of the 1st ACM conference on computing and sustainable societies (COMPASS)*, Article no. 48, pp. 1–5, (2018, June)

Y. Lindell, Fast cut-and-choose based protocols for malicious and covert adversaries. *Advances in cryptology: Proceedings of Crypto 2013*, Springer LNCS 8043, pp. 1–17, (2013, 18–22 August)

Y. Lindell, Secure multiparty computation (MPC). *Cryptology ePrint Archive, 2020/300*, 7 March 2020 (last revised 30 January 2021)

A. Machanavajjhala, D. Kifer, J. M. Abowd, J. Gehrke, and L. Vilhuber, Privacy: Theory meets practice on the Map. *Proceedings of the 24th international conference on data engineering*, pp. 277–286, (2008, 7–12 April)

R. Rogers, S. Subramaniam, S. Peng, D. Durfee, S. Lee, S. Kumar Kancha, S. Sahay, and P. Ahammad, LinkedIn's Audience Engagements API: A Privacy Preserving Data Analytics System at Scale. arXiv.*org, 2002.05839*, 14 February 2020 (last revised 16 November 2020)

A. Sahai and B. Waters, Fuzzy identity based encryption. *Advances in cryptology – Proceedings of eurocrypt*, Springer LNCS 3494, pp. 457–473 (2005)

A. Shamir, Identity-based cryptosystems and signature schemes. *Advances in cryptology: Proceedings of crypto 84*, Springer LNCS 196, pp. 47–53 (1985)

A. Shamir, R. L. Rivest, and L. M. Adleman, Mental Poker. *Technical Report LCS/TR-125*, Massachusetts Institute of Technology (1979, April)

Sharemind, Track big data between government and education. *blog post* (2015, 26 October)

A. Shelat, and C.-H. Shen, Fast two-party secure computation with minimal assumptions. ACM Conference on computer and communications security, pp. 523–534, (2013, November)

Y. Song, H. Wang, X. Wei, and L. Wu, Efficient attribute-based encryption with privacy-preserving key generation and its application in industrial cloud. *Security and communication networks*, vol. 2019, Article ID 3249726, 9pp (2019, 23 May)

B. Waters, Ciphertext-policy attribute-based encryption: An expressive, efficient, and provably secure realization. *Cryptology ePrint archive, 2008/290*, 27 June 2008 (last revised 20 December 2010)

A. C. Yao, Protocols for secure computations. *Proceedings of the 23rd IEEE symposium on foundations of computer science*, pp. 160–164 (1982)

A. C.-C. Yao, How to generate and exchange secrets. *27th Annual symposium on foundations of computer science*, Toronto, Canada, pp. 162–167 (1986)

D. Yao, N. Fazio, Y. Dodis, and A. Lysyanskaya, Id-based encryption for complex hierarchies with applications to forward security and broadcast encryption. *Proceedings of the 11th ACM conference on computer and communications security*, pp. 354–363 (2004, October)

# Chapter 8
# Limiting Disclosure by Hiding the Identity-Attribute Pair

**Abstract** This chapter looks at the last leaf in the privacy tree: limiting disclosure by hiding both the identity and the attribute information. Example PETs described in this category are Hippocratic databases, P3P, APEX, and credential systems that prove properties of attributes. As with the previous five chapters, the basic scheme, enhancements, strengths, and limitations are discussed for each PET.

**Keywords** Hippocratic databases (HDB) · Privacy policy · Platform for privacy preferences project (P3P) · Privacy Bird · A P3P preference exchange language (APPEL) · Architecture for privacy enforcement using XML (APEX) · Credential systems · Boolean functions of attributes

The final branch in the privacy tree represents PETs that limit *disclosure* by hiding both the *identity* and the *attributes* of a user. Very often, these tend to be PETs that incorporate some kind of *privacy policy* specifying who is allowed to see what data, and what they can do with this data once they have it. (In the examples given in this chapter, *Hippocratic Databases* (HDB), *Platform for Privacy Preferences Project* (P3P), and *Architecture for Privacy Enforcement using XML* (APEX) are all centred on the explicit presence of such a policy.) However, there are PETs that hide *identities* and *attributes* in other ways; our fourth PET – another way of using the *Credential Systems* we introduced in Chapter Six – is an example of a non-policy-centered approach to *disclosure* protection.

## 8.1 Hippocratic Databases (HDB)

Inspired by the privacy principle embedded in the Hippocratic Oath that has guided physicians for centuries ("*And about whatever I may see or hear in treatment, or even without treatment, in the life of human beings – things that should not ever be blurted out outside – I will remain silent, holding such things to be unutterable*"

© The Editor(s) (if applicable) and The Author(s), under exclusive license to Springer Nature Switzerland AG 2021

C. Adams, *Introduction to Privacy Enhancing Technologies*,
https://doi.org/10.1007/978-3-030-81043-6_8

175

(VonStadon 1966)), Rakesh Agrawal, Jerry Kiernan, Ramakrishnan Srikant, and Yirong Xu proposed the idea of *Hippocratic Databases* (HDB) in 2002 (2002). In particular, Agrawal, et al., suggested that the database community could play a central role in the escalating discussions around personal privacy by "re-architecting our database systems to include responsibility for the privacy of data as a fundamental tenet." However, although this proposal is naturally focused on *database* privacy, the authors recognize that not all data lives in database systems, and they anticipate that *Hippocratic Databases* will provide guidance for incorporating similar goals in other types of data repositories.

HDB uses a *privacy policy*, data owner *privacy preferences*, and a set of automated tools to assess every database query before, during, and after it is run in order to ensure that *identities* and *attributes* are hidden from unintended observers.

### 8.1.1 The Basic Scheme

In their paper, Agrawal, Kiernan, Srikant, and Xu propose *Hippocratic Databases* (HDB) as a way to bring privacy to database systems (2002). They acknowledge the prior work in privacy protection for *statistical databases* (such as *query restriction* and *data perturbation* techniques), but note that the class of queries that *Hippocratic Databases* will have to deal with is much broader. Furthermore, the existing literature on general database security mechanisms (such as *access control, encryption,* and *multi-level secure relations*) did not adequately meet the complex privacy requirements they envisioned, including *consented sharing*, real-time *query modification*, and *data purging* to meet strict retention rules.

The authors begin by listing the "founding principles of a *Hippocratic Database*", which they created by aggregating and distilling privacy regulations and guidelines from several countries (including USA, Canada, Japan, and Australia; see (Bennett 1992), (Rotenberg 2000)), as well as the *OECD data protection principles*. Their ten principles describe "what it means for a database system to responsibly manage private information under its control." They are described as follows (Agrawal et al. 2002) (note that a person who submits his/her personal information to the database is referred to as the "donor" of personal information).

1. *Purpose Specification. For personal information stored in the database, the purposes for which the information has been collected shall be associated with that information.*
2. *Consent. The purposes associated with personal information shall have consent of the donor of the personal information.*
3. *Limited Collection. The personal information collected shall be limited to the minimum necessary for accomplishing the specified purposes.*
4. *Limited Use. The database shall run only those queries that are consistent with the purposes for which the information has been collected.*

5. *Limited Disclosure. The personal information stored in the database shall not be communicated outside the database for purposes other than those for which there is consent from the donor of the information.*
6. *Limited Retention. Personal information shall be retained only as long as necessary for the fulfillment of the purposes for which it has been collected.*
7. *Accuracy. Personal information stored in the database shall be accurate and up-to-date.*
8. *Safety. Personal information shall be protected by security safeguards against theft and other misappropriations.*
9. *Openness. A donor shall be able to access all information about the donor stored in the database.*
10. *Compliance. A donor shall be able to verify compliance with the above principles. Similarly, the database shall be able to address a challenge concerning compliance.*

With these ten principles as goals, Agrawal, et al., design a database architecture that has *purpose* as the central concept around which privacy protection is built. They begin by defining *privacy metadata*. For each *purpose* and for each piece of data collected for that *purpose*, three additional pieces of information are stored in the database tables – *external recipients* (entities to whom the data can be given); *retention period* (the length of time for which the data can be stored); and *authorized users* (the set of users/applications that can access this data).

The organization (i.e., the database owner) will have a *privacy policy* that specifies what data is collected from users, what it is used for, how long it is retained, who it is shared with, and so on. The *privacy metadata* is derived (using automated tools, if possible) from this privacy policy. In addition, before a user submits any personal information to the database, a *Privacy Constraint Validator* checks whether the privacy policy sufficiently matches the user's *privacy preferences*. If so, an *audit trail* of the user's acceptance of the privacy policy is maintained (in order to address any possible future challenges), the submitted data is checked by a *Data Accuracy Analyzer* for correctness, and the data is stored in the database tables with an additional attribute *purpose* that encodes the set of purposes associated with this data to which the user has agreed.

Queries submitted to the database must be tagged with a *purpose* for which the query is being made. Before the query is allowed to run, an *Attribute Access Control* process ensures that the query's *purpose* matches an allowed *purpose* for the data it is trying to access, and that the submitter of the query is one of that data's *authorized users*. As the query is run, a *Record Access Control* process will ensure that only records whose *purpose* attribute matches the query's *purpose* will be visible to the query. Finally, after the query is run but before the results are returned, a *Query Intrusion Detector* process analyzes whether the query's access pattern is different from the usual access pattern for queries with that *purpose* and from that requester (if not, the query is flagged as *suspicious* and the results are not returned). An *audit trail* of all queries is maintained for future examination, in case this is ever needed.

A *Data Retention Manager* process is run periodically to delete any data item that remains in the database after the specified *retention period* for the *purpose* under which it is stored. (If the data was submitted for several *purposes*, it is stored for the longest of the corresponding *retention periods*.)

A *Data Collection Analyzer* process does a general clean-up, periodically checking the entire database to see whether any data is being collected but not used, and whether any entities have unused (or unnecessary) authorizations to issue queries with a given *purpose*.

Finally, it is worth noting that, along with the *metadata* and processes outlined above, *Hippocratic Databases* additionally make use of traditional database security mechanisms such as *access control* and *data encryption*.

Agrawal, et al., describe the above concepts as a "strawman architecture" for a *Hippocratic Database*, an initial design that they expect will be refined and extended over time to make such databases a reality. In this vein, they list a number of technical challenges that still need to be addressed. Some of these are the following.

- On the subject of automated creation of *privacy metadata* from a privacy policy, the authors note that a *P3P Policy* (see Sect. 8.2) and its related draft for encoding a user's *privacy preferences* (APPEL), may be good starting points. However, it is not yet clear whether P3P's web shopping vocabulary is sufficiently rich to support all expected HDB environments (including, for example, finance, insurance, and healthcare).
- Techniques for reducing the cost of the various processes in the architecture must be found (database efficiency is a paramount consideration in many settings), but it is recognized that design choices made for efficiency will also impact both disk space and the complexity of adding new processes.
- To support the principle of *Limited Collection*, it might be desirable to have a process that takes any given query and performs real-time generation of a *minimal query* that accomplishes the intended task (i.e., it identifies data that would be collected but not used, and determines the granularity at which information is required, in order to reformulate the query to request only what is specifically needed). Clearly, this is a non-trivial task in general.
- Supporting *Limited Retention* in real business environments can be quite complex. For example, although deleting a record from a database might be simple, how can it also be deleted from logs and past checkpoints without affecting necessary recovery processes? More generally, how can accurate historical analysis and long-term statistical queries be supported if the relevant data has been removed?
- The principle of *Openness* can also lead to unexpected difficulties. For example, if Alice wishes to access information about her that was not provided by her (i.e., she is not the donor), it may not be trivial to do this if the actual donor has not listed Alice as an *authorized user*. Thus, the mechanisms created to protect privacy in the database may prohibit the very *Openness* they are intended to achieve.
- The principle of *Safety* has implications that also need to be taken into consideration. Database protection mechanisms can be effective at controlling unauthorized access to tables, but the media on which the database is stored

might be subject to other forms of attack (e.g., a malicious entity that has acquired *super-user* permissions may be able to freely access database files using low-level operating system calls). Encryption of the database files on disk may help to enforce the *Safety* principle, but this can have serious performance implications and may render searching and querying operations much more difficult, if not impossible.

A *Hippocratic Database* is a PET that limits **disclosure** by hiding both the *identity* and the *attributes* of a user. The *privacy metadata* associated with a user's personal information, which is derived from the organization's privacy policy, constrains exactly who can see this data and for what specific *purposes* they are allowed to see it. All other accesses are blocked by the database privacy protection mechanisms and so both *identity* and *attributes* are hidden from submitters of such queries.

## 8.1.2 Enhancements

There has been some additional work on *Hippocratic Databases* since the original 2002 proposal, but there has not yet been an extensive amount of research in this field. Some of the main advances are listed below.

- In 2004, Kristen LeFevre, Rakesh Agrawal, Vuk Ercegovak, Raghu Ramakrishnan, Yirong Xu, and David DeWitt proposed mechanisms that enable *cell-level* access control in databases (rather than *table-level* access control that restricts access only to certain rows or columns of a table) (2004). In their proposed system, a *policy meta-language* automatically translates a privacy policy (which may be expressed in any specification language) into the *privacy metadata* that is required in the database Tables. A *query interceptor* automatically infers the *purpose* and *recipient* of a query from context information stored in a meta-data table (so that no modification to existing database applications is required), and a *query modifier* alters the SQL query to reflect the rules regarding the inferred *purpose* and *recipient*. The *cell-level* access control mechanisms then process these modified SQL queries. In their performance experiments, the authors found that the performance overhead of database-level privacy enforcement is small; furthermore, the overhead is often more than offset by the efficiency gains that result from record filtering (at the query modification stage).

  LeFevre, et al., note that although their work was done in the context of *Hippocratic Databases*, it is not exclusive to that domain and has broader use for applications in content management, customer support, financial analysis, and e-commerce (in fact, any setting in which *cell-level* access control driven by a privacy policy would be of value).

- Also in 2004 (published at the same conference as the previous paper), Rakesh Agrawal, Roberto Bayardo, Christos Faloutsos, Jerry Kiernan, Ralf Rantzau, and Ramakrishnan Srikant (2004a) proposed an auditing framework for determining whether a database system is complying with its advertised data disclosure policy (i.e., to whom it will release personal data, and for what reasons). More precisely, the goal is to ascertain whether the database system executed a query at some prior time that invalidly accessed a specified piece of data. The auditing system should be non-disruptive (not over-burden normal query processing), efficient and correct (identify all relevant queries quickly), fine-grained (able to audit a single field of a specified record), and intuitive (convenient and easy for a user to specify data of interest). The authors show that their proposed framework meets all these requirements.

As with the previous paper, the work in this proposal is essential for implementing *Hippocratic Databases* (particularly in order to satisfy the principle of *Compliance*), but is broadly applicable to database systems that need to satisfy the principles of *Limited Disclosure* and *Compliance* in any government, business, or healthcare setting.

- In 2006, Yasin Laura-Silva and Walid Aref published a *Technical Report* at Purdue University entitled "Realizing Privacy-Preserving Features in Hippocratic Databases" (2006). In this report, the authors identify, study, and implement a number of privacy-preserving features that extend the 2004 work of LeFevre, et al. (above). In particular, they propose a mechanism to map the *purpose, recipient*, and *data type* specified in a privacy policy to explicit *privacy rules* in the database. They also apply the access constraints for the SQL "SELECT" command (described in prior work) to the commands "INSERT", "UPDATE", and "DELETE". They suggest a mechanism to support *Limited Retention* that is similar to opt-in/opt-out preferences and does not require deletion of data, so that necessary recovery processes remain unaffected. They design an approach to handle multiple versions of a privacy policy co-existing simultaneously within an organization (a situation encountered in the vast majority of real-world organizations). Finally, they make a step toward integrating *Hippocratic Database* research and *k-anonymity* research (see Sect. 6.1 of Chap. 6) by incorporating the concept of *data generalization* in a HDB: rather than a binary opt-in/opt-out choice for a piece of personal data, a user is able to specify a *level of generalization* for the data and agree to disclosure of only that level. (For example, rather than registering a *yes/no* for disclosure of a particular illness such as "cold", "flu", or "bronchitis", Alice may choose to allow disclosure of the level-2 generalization of this data ("respiratory infection"), or the level-3 generalization ("respiratory system problem"), or the level-4 generalization ("some disease"). This simultaneously addresses some aspects of the principles of *Consent, Limited Use, Limited Disclosure*, and *Safety*.)

Laura-Silva and Aref implemented the extensions mentioned above and conducted a performance study analyzing the overhead, scalability, and effect of record filtering due to these mechanisms. They found that the overhead is small and scales well to large databases. Furthermore, record filtering can have a significant impact on performance because, even when there is a greater cost associated with updating multiple database tables, this cost is compensated by the performance gains associated with operations that do not need to be executed because their privacy check fails. The work of the authors in this report helped to move forward the design of practical *Hippocratic Databases*.

* In 2008, Tyrone Grandison, Christopher Johnson, and Jerry Kiernan published the chapter "Hippocratic Databases: Current Capabilities and Future Trends" in the *Handbook on Database Security: Applications and Trends* (2008). They describe a set of technologies that existed (at the time of writing) for HDB. These are the following.

  - An *active enforcement system*: a system that limits access to, and disclosure of, personal information in accordance with fine-grained privacy policies, applicable laws, and individual opt-in/opt-out choices. The authors point to the work described in (Agrawal et al. 2003a, b) and (Agrawal et al. 2006) (see also (Dillard 2011)).
  - A *compliance auditing mechanism*: a tool that tracks past disclosures of information in order to support investigations of suspicious disclosures. The authors point to the work described in (Agrawal et al. 2004a, b).
  - A *Sovereign Information Integration (SII) architecture*: a design that allows secure information sharing among multiple autonomous databases without using a trusted third party. The authors cite the work described in (Agrawal et al. 2003b), (Agrawal and Terzi 2006), and (Agrawal et al. 2006).
  - An *Order-Preserving Encryption Scheme (OPES)*: an encryption scheme for numeric data that preserves the order of encrypted values so that range queries and MIN, MAX, and COUNT queries can be processed on the server without decrypting the data. The authors reference preliminary work in this area described in (Agrawal et al. 2004b).

  Grandison, et al., also discuss a number of technologies that in 2008 still needed to be created or developed in order for HDB to be suitable for real-world environments. These include good tools to support the principles of *Limited Collection*, *Limited Retention*, and *Openness* (as mentioned in Sect. 8.1.1 above), as well as improved *policy specification languages*, mechanisms that enforce disclosure policies *after* data has been legitimately extracted and transferred outside the database, and a *query intrusion detector* process with acceptable performance and false-positive/false-negative statistics. Most of these technologies are complex and would be difficult to do well.

## 8.1.3   Strengths

*Hippocratic Databases* is a comprehensive vision for personal data protection in a database setting. The inventors of this PET (primarily Rakesh Agrawal and his numerous students and colleagues) have thought carefully about the many tools, techniques, and mechanisms that would be needed to realize a database that has privacy as a fundamental tenet and lives up to the spirit of the *Hippocratic Oath*.

Furthermore, this ambitious research project has directly led to the creation of several such tools and mechanisms.

### 8.1.4   Disadvantages, Limitations, and Weaknesses

As stated in Grandison, et al. (2008), HDB "is not a fixed group of technologies, but rather an evolving set of capabilities that enable the responsible management of sensitive information." The technologies that have been proposed for *Hippocratic Databases* "are at various stages of development, but demonstrate the potential for future information systems to comply with the HDB vision."

The above statements still appear to be true today. HDB is perhaps most correctly seen as a *concept* (inspired by the privacy provision of the *Hippocratic Oath*) of how individual privacy can be protected in a database setting. At present, it is not possible to go to a store or to a website and purchase or download a *Hippocratic Database*: the HDB vision, although compelling, does not seem to have been implemented as a single piece of software. This may be one reason why it has not yet garnered the attention that it deserves. Additionally, though, HDB was overshadowed by the largely concurrent work in *ε-differential privacy* (see Sect. 7.3 of Chap. 7), which captured the interest of a significant number of theoreticians and implementers around the world.

## 8.2   Platform for Privacy Preferences Project (P3P)

The previous section on *Hippocratic Databases* looked at a policy-centered PET that provides privacy in a database setting. This section examines a policy-centered PET that provides privacy in the context of web browsing. The *Platform for Privacy Preferences Project* (P3P) is the result of a standardization effort within the *World Wide Web Consortium* (W3C) in the early 2000s. W3C is the international standards body that produced the specifications for URL, HTTP, HTML, XML, and many other fundamental technologies of the Web. P3P was produced by the *P3P Specification Working Group* as part of the *Privacy Activity* in the W3C *Technology & Society Domain*.

The specification "P3P 1.0" was published as a *W3C Recommendation* on April 16, 2002 (Cranor et al. 2002b). A subsequent specification, "P3P 1.1", that incorporated community feedback on limitations and shortcomings of version 1.0, as well as a handful of (backward-compatible (Cranor and Wenning 2018)) new features and extensions, was published as a *W3C Working Group Note* on November 13, 2006 (Cranor et al. 2006b). Despite some evidence of P3P use among the top one million websites at the beginning of 2018, both specifications were officially Retired ("Obsoleted") by the W3C on August 30, 2018, due to insufficient deployment and implementation support.

Even though it is now obsolete, P3P is historically significant as a PET because it was the first technology to integrate an organization's privacy policy into the browsing activity of a user in an automated way.

## 8.2.1   The Basic Scheme

The "P3P 1.0" specification was authored by Lorrie Cranor, Marc Langheinrich, Massimo Marchiori, Martin Presler-Marshall, and Joseph Reagle within the *P3P Specification Working Group* of W3C; it was published as a *W3C Recommendation* in 2002. The short description of "What is P3P?" is given on the W3C P3P website as follows (Cranor and Wenning 2018):

> The Platform for Privacy Preferences Project (P3P) enables Websites to express their privacy practices in a standard format that can be retrieved automatically and interpreted easily by user agents. P3P user agents will allow users to be informed of site practices (in both machine- and human-readable formats) and to automate decision-making based on these practices when appropriate. Thus users need not read the privacy policies at every site they visit.

Ultimately, the problem which P3P addresses is that websites typically advertise their privacy practices (as they are required to do by law in many jurisdictions) using complex, hard-to-understand legal language in a privacy policy that is accessible by clicking a link somewhere on the web page. The privacy policies not only are expressed in difficult language, but they are often quite long as well (several pages of dense text). Consequently, the vast majority of users do not read these policies at all, and the vast majority of users that do read the policies only give a cursory glance at the first few paragraphs. Thus, although the organizations have met their legal obligation to make their policies available to users, it is clear that most users are not aware of the practices that will take place regarding their data, and therefore have no effective basis for consenting or objecting, for choosing to opt-in or opt-out, or even for deciding to abandon a particular website and go to another website instead.

P3P seeks to resolve this problem by proposing three interrelated components:

- A standard template for privacy practices ("*P3P policy*") that is written in machine-readable (and human-readable) *eXtensible Markup Language* (XML);
- A standard format ("*user preferences*") for encoding the privacy preferences of a user; and
- A piece of software in the user's local environment ("*user agent*") that can compare the *P3P policy* and the *user preferences* and take appropriate action at the moment of browsing (including warning the user about a mismatch between the *policy* and the *preferences*).

The P3P 1.0 specification is the first of these three components. Using this specification, an organization can document its privacy practices in a standardized XML format that can be read and understood by software. The creation of this *P3P policy* can be done in conjunction with the creation of the privacy policy (written in legal language) that must be put on the website anyway, and so this is a relatively small additional piece of work for the organization. In particular, one of the explicit goals of the *P3P Specification Working Group* is that no special server software needs to be created, installed, or configured: the organization simply needs to construct its *P3P policy* and store it in a specified location on the website (so that the *user agent* is able to find it at browsing time).

The specification defines five technologies:

- A standard vocabulary for describing a set of *uses, recipients, data categories,* and other privacy disclosures;
- A standard *schema* for the data that a website may wish to collect;
- An XML format for expressing a privacy policy (i.e., a collection of privacy practices) in a machine-readable way;
- A means of associating a particular privacy policy with a website, or with a particular web page (or set of pages) on that website; and
- A protocol for transporting *P3P policies* over HTTP.

More specifically, the standard vocabulary in a *P3P policy* includes the following:

- Name and contact information for the website;
- The kind of data access provided to the user Alice, namely

  - *"nonident"*: the website does not collect identifiable data about Alice,
  - *"all"*: Alice can access all identified information about her that the website stores,
  - *"contact-and-other"*: Alice can access her identified online and physical contact information as well as other identified information about her that the website stores,
  - *"ident-contact"*: Alice can access her identified online and physical contact information,
  - *"other-ident"*: Alice can access other identified information related to her (such as her online account charges),
  - *"none"*: no access to identified data is given;

- Mechanisms for resolving privacy disputes (such as submitting a complaint to the organization's customer service department, contacting an independent organization, filing a legal complaint, or appealing to an explicitly-referenced applicable law);
- The kinds of data collected about an individual (such as address, phone number, credit card number, or click-stream data);
- How the collected data is used (i.e., the purpose for which each piece of data is collected) and whether individuals can opt-in or opt-out of any of these uses;
- Whether/when data may be shared with external parties, and whether individuals can opt-in or opt-out of this sharing; and
- Data retention practices for the various types of data collected.

The process outlined by the P3P 1.0 specification is fairly straightforward. In a traditional HTTP transaction scenario, when Alice clicks on a link, it causes a request message (typically an HTTP "GET page" message) to be sent to the server hosting that page, and the response (if it is not an error) is an HTTP "OK" message along with the HTML content of the requested page. With P3P 1.0, Alice's click on a link causes the request message to instead be an HTTP "GET host/w3c/p3p.xml" message. If the response to this message is an error, then the server does not support P3P and the exchange reverts to the original scenario (i.e., "GET page" followed by "OK" and the HTML content). Otherwise, the server responds with a *policy reference file*. As defined by the specification, a *policy reference file* makes statements about what *P3P policy* applies to any given URI within the website. Given this file, therefore, the *user agent* can determine which specific *P3P policy* to request (for the particular link that Alice has clicked); it then sends a request for that *P3P policy* and the policy is returned as a response.

Having acquired the relevant *P3P policy*, the *user agent* can now compare the *P3P policy* with the *user preferences*. If there is no mismatch, the "GET page" and "OK" sequence is executed: Alice sees her requested page and does not need to be aware that P3P-related background processing has preceded this display of her page. On the other hand, if there is a mismatch, the *user agent* can display a warning message to Alice, explaining (in simple terms) how the website's practices differ from her stated preferences. For example, the *user agent* may display a pop-up window that says something like "*Unless you **opt-out**, this site may share financial information or information about your purchases with other companies (i.e., companies other than those that help the site provide services to you.*" Armed with this information, Alice can decide whether she wishes to continue interacting with this website, abort the interaction with this website, or modify her *user preferences* so that she will not receive warnings about this type of mismatch in the future.

With P3P, Alice has a degree of control over her personal information (both her *identity* and her *attributes*), and this control is derived from the advertised privacy practices of the website whose link she has clicked. Specifically, she can decide not to interact with an organization that collects information that she does not wish to release, or that shares this information with third parties that are unknown to her, or that retains this information for longer than she desires, *et cetera*. This PET therefore gives Alice a simple way to limit ***disclosure*** of her personal data in any web browsing situation.

### 8.2.2 Enhancements

There were three primary efforts in P3P that occurred concurrently with, or just subsequent to, the work of the P3P 1.0 specification: P3P 1.1; *Privacy Bird*; and APPEL.

## P3P 1.1

As mentioned at the beginning of Sect. 8.2, a revised specification, P3P 1.1, was developed within the *P3P Specification Working Group* between 2002 and 2006. At the conclusion of this effort, the Working Group felt that the specification was "lacking the necessary support from implementers to carry on through the *Recommendation Process*" and decided to publish the specification as a *Working Group Note* after a successful Last Call (Cranor et al. 2006b). Thus, although P3P 1.1 did not achieve *W3C Recommendation* status, it is nevertheless a stable, implementable specification that addresses all the limitations, shortcomings, and errata of P3P 1.0 and includes a number of new features that are built using the P3P *extension mechanism* in order to ensure backward compatibility with P3P 1.0 deployments.

P3P 1.1 incorporates new definitions, optional elements, explanatory text, and guidelines that together make implementation simpler, particularly for implementers of *user agents*. On top of this, it contains two important additions:

– A new generic attribute is added to make it possible to use *P3P policies* in XML applications other than HTTP transactions (for example, binding *P3P policies* to XML elements that describe interfaces, such as in XForms (Boyer 2009) or *Web Services Description Language* (WSDL) (Chinnici et al. 2007)).
– New formatting, syntax, and guidelines are provided to support the creation and use of *compact policies*. *Compact policies* are optional and non-authoritative, but make more granular statements about data practices than is possible with the P3P 1.0 syntax and thus lead to performance optimization.

### The Privacy Bird User Agent

During the development of the specifications P3P 1.0 and P3P 1.1, work was also conducted on the creation of a *user agent* to read and process *P3P policies*. This effort, documented in a 2006 journal paper by Lorrie Faith Cranor, Praveen Guduru, and Manjula Arjula (2006a), culminated in a *user agent* known as *Privacy Bird*. The design of *Privacy Bird* was guided by four prototype *user agents* developed over a four-year period while the P3P specification was evolving: *W3C Prototype* in 1997; *Privacy Minder* in 1999; *P3P Browser Helper Object* ca. 2000; and *Usability Testing Prototype* in 2001. The first two prototypes were evaluated only informally; the third received more formal feedback from a focus group of users; and the fourth involved both a focus group and a laboratory study. Following this implementation and evaluation experience, *Privacy Bird* was released as a 1.1 beta version in February 2002, as a 1.2 beta version in February 2003, and as a 1.3 beta version ca. 2006. The first beta version gathered feedback from a survey of beta testers, and the second beta version was evaluated more formally in a laboratory study.

*Privacy Bird* is an add-on for the Internet Explorer (IE) 5.01, 5.5, and 6.0 browsers on Microsoft Windows 98/2000/ME/NT/XP operating systems. It is implemented as a browser helper object that loads when IE starts and runs in the same memory context as IE. The software is available as a free self-extracting executable download and as an open-source release from the http://privacybird.org website.

Once *Privacy Bird* has been installed, a bird icon with a song bubble appears in the title bar of the browser window (in the top right corner). The bird changes colour, and the content of the song bubble is modified, to indicate to the user whether the current website is P3P-enabled and (if so) whether its privacy policy matches the user's privacy preferences. The user can click on the bird icon to obtain additional information about the website's privacy policy (for example, an automatically-generated summary of the policy in relatively simple language) as well as the policies that apply to content embedded in the web page (such as images, sounds, frames, and other objects). The additional information that is displayed includes links to opt-in or opt-out instructions if the website provides a way for users to choose these. Finally, a configuration window can also be accessed that allows the user to select or customize privacy settings.

**The APPEL Specification for User Preferences**
A W3C specification authored by Lorrie Cranor, Marc Langheinrich, and Massimo Marchiori, entitled *A P3P Preference Exchange Language* (APPEL), defines an XML encoding for user preferences about privacy policies (Cranor et al. 2002a, b).

APPEL is a rule-based language, but it is recognized that writing APPEL rule files is fairly complex and difficult, even for experts, and so it is assumed that a P3P *user agent* may automatically create an APPEL file from the user choices made in the *user agent's* configuration window. Furthermore, the authors envision that an APPEL file could be produced by one *user agent* and imported/understood by another *user agent*.

A P3P *user agent* compares APPEL rules with a given *P3P policy* to determine whether or not a website's policy matches a user's preferences. The result of this comparison will be "request" (the resource at the specified website SHOULD be accessed), "limited" (the resource at the specified website SHOULD be accessed, but in a limited way – all but the absolutely necessary request headers should be suppressed), or "block" (the resource at the specified website SHOULD NOT be accessed). In the case of "limited" or "block", the *user agent* can present explanatory text to the user so that the user is aware of the problem and can make a decision regarding how to proceed.

The authors note in Appendix A of the specification that, although this first draft of APPEL met the requirements they had set, the resulting language is "complex and difficult to grasp fully" (Cranor et al. 2002a, b). An effort was made to simplify the specification by separating a set of extensions from the core language and by omitting a significant number of useful constructs, but they still found that "developing APPEL rule sets is difficult for nonexperts."

The work on APPEL was never completed: it was considered somewhat experimental and did not go through the extensive review process to progress to *W3C Recommendation* status. The April 15, 2002, *working draft* was published as a *W3C Note* and the Working Group effort on this topic was discontinued.

### 8.2.3   Strengths

The P3P architecture (*P3P policy*, *user preferences*, and *user agent*) promises tremendous benefit to the web browsing user. Alice no longer has to read long, complex privacy policies written in difficult legal language; the underlying software will do this automatically and will immediately warn her if there is a mismatch between a given policy and her privacy preferences. Furthermore, this automated checking of the policy happens *every time* Alice visits a website (without P3P, even if Alice spent the time and energy to thoroughly read a policy this morning, there is virtually no chance that she will read it again in such detail this afternoon to see if it has been modified by the organization). Finally, the automated checking is done for every object on a web page, including ads and invisible images (again, without P3P, Alice will miss much of this no matter how diligent she is).

The *P3P policy* itself is also quite beneficial. In particular, it does not allow any "fuzzy" language: many of its component sections require the company to specify one of multiple choices (and so the company must explicitly place itself in one "bucket" or another). Compliance with the specification (i.e., creating a valid *P3P policy*) means that disclosures must be included in every required component, and so a company cannot "forget" to mention some important privacy-violating practice in which they engage. The policy is also precisely scoped: it is clear what it applies to, when it might be revised/updated, and so on. Finally, even if a company ultimately decides not to produce a *P3P policy*, the mere exercise of reading through the specification to see what is required can force the company to think carefully about its privacy policy and to do a systematic assessment of its privacy practices, which can potentially lead to modification or improvement of its privacy behaviours.

### 8.2.4   Disadvantages, Limitations, and Weaknesses

P3P also has a number of shortcomings and disadvantages (many of which are listed on its website (Wenning 2018)). A few examples are the following.

– The syntax of the specification provides very limited ability for the company to give detailed explanations (e.g., specific circumstances under which some data may be collected and why this is necessary). Of course, in a natural-language privacy policy, explanatory text can be as detailed as required.
– The P3P specification requires that the created *P3P policy* must be consistent with the natural-language privacy policy for the website, but of course it is difficult to guarantee this in practice.
– The legal standing of a *P3P policy* is not clear. In some jurisdictions, regulators and courts may treat *P3P policies* and natural-language policies equivalently, but this is far from universal. Thus, it is possible that the *P3P policy* has no legal weight whatever, and so (coupled with the previous point that it may differ from the natural-language policy) having a *user agent* rely on the *P3P policy* for

deciding whether to allow a user to interact with a given website may be problematic.

– Client-side tools (such as *Privacy Bird*) are still quite limited. Users may not understand what the *user agent* is trying to tell them, and in any case the *user agent* cannot prevent the user from doing inappropriate things (such as going to a website even if it will violate their preferences). In addition to this, the functioning of the *user agent* is predicated on the user having a *user preferences* file. The work on APPEL demonstrated that this is not a simple task (in part because, as noted by Cranor et al. (2006a, b), "user privacy preferences are often complex and nuanced, users tend to have little experience articulating their privacy preferences, users are generally unfamiliar with much of the terminology used by privacy experts, users often do not understand the privacy-related consequences of their behaviour, and users have differing expectations about the type and extent of privacy policy information they would like to see").

– There is currently no standard technical mechanism to <u>enforce</u> a *P3P policy* (i.e., it is informative only; there is no way to ensure that the company will actually act in accordance with the practices it has advertised in its *P3P policy*). Thus, a full suite of non-automated processes (including formal audits, privacy seal programs (see, for example (Markert 2002)), and the legal infrastructure) is required to check a company's compliance with its posted privacy policy. (Note that this is required in the absence of P3P, but the creation of a *P3P policy* does nothing to reduce this effort.)

Finally, perhaps the biggest disadvantage/limitation of P3P is that this specification has now been obsoleted and so, unless this changes, there is currently little incentive for a company to support this PET.

## 8.3   Architecture for Privacy Enforcement Using XML (APEX)

The end of Sect. 8.2.4 above noted that one of the limitations of P3P is that there is no standard technical mechanism to enforce a P3P policy. The 2006 book chapter by Carlisle Adams and Katerine Barbieri (2006) proposed a step in this direction called *Architecture for Privacy Enforcement using XML* (APEX) that begins to add an enforcement piece to the web browsing privacy provided by P3P.

### 8.3.1   The Basic Scheme

As described in Sect. 8.2, a user's P3P experience begins with the click of a URL/URI: this initiates the multi-message exchange between the browser and the web server by which the browser obtains the *policy reference file* (to know which policy to ask for), the *P3P policy* (associated with the desired URL/URI so that the relevant policy can be compared with the *user preferences*), and finally the requested web page. It is important to recognize, however, that the mere existence of a *P3P policy* (or, indeed, any privacy policy) on a website gives no guarantee about the actual behaviour of the organization that owns or operates that website. The organization might engage in any kind of behaviour with the user's personal data "behind closed doors" (for example, it might give or sell this data to other companies, use the data for additional undisclosed purposes, retain the data for longer than the specified amount of time, and so on), and the user might never find out about this.

One protection that is typically suggested for reducing the risk of malicious organization behaviour is to have external third-party auditors periodically examine the internal actions of the company (in great detail) and compare those actions with the advertised privacy policy. The auditor (in the case of a privacy seal program) would issue a so-called *privacy seal* if the organization lived up to its privacy promises, and the *seal* would be displayed on the organization's website so that users could have some confidence that the organization was behaving in accordance with its public claims.

The idea of a privacy audit works well in theory, but suffers from a major problem in practice. For an auditor to confirm that an organization is complying with its privacy policy, the auditor will have to examine every single data flow and data storage point throughout the organization. For a large organization, this can be prohibitively complex and time consuming (not to mention expensive!). Thus, audit exercises are often incomplete (i.e., are limited to a specified subset of the organization's IT infrastructure) and, when they are complete, are performed quite infrequently.

*Architecture for Privacy Enforcement using XML* (APEX) (Adams and Barbieri 2006) seeks to address this audit limitation by imposing an explicit binding between an organization's *P3P policy* and its internal access control infrastructure. In particular, given that access to any data in an organization (including user personal data) is governed by access control policies, and given that access control policies can often be written entirely in XML (see, for example, the *eXtensible Access Control Markup Language* (XACML) specification (Rissanen 2017)), APEX proposes that *eXtensible Stylesheet Language Transformation* (XSLT) technology (Kay 2017) can be used to derive a *P3P policy* from an *XACML policy* in a fully automated way.

Briefly, the general XACML processing model can be described as follows.

At system initialization time, a *policy writer* creates an *access control policy* using the syntax and semantics from the XACML specification to produce an *XACML policy*. Later, when a user submits a request to access a stored data item, the request is intercepted by a *Policy Enforcement Point* (PEP) and is forwarded to a *Policy Decision Point* (PDP). The PDP will examine the following:

> User request;
> Attributes of the requesting user;
> Attributes of the requested object (the data item);
> Context of the request (for example, "Did the request originate from inside or outside the firewall?", "Was the request submitted during regular working hours or outside working hours?", and so on); and
> Relevant *XACML policy*.

Given all this information, the PDP will render a decision ("permit" or "deny") and send this decision to the PEP. The PEP's task is then to enforce this decision: if the decision is "permit", the PEP should return the data item to the user; if the decision is "deny", the PEP should prevent the user from obtaining the data item.

Similarly, XSLT can be summarized at a very high level as follows.

XSLT is a language for transforming XML documents into other XML documents. The transformation is achieved by a set of *template rules* that associate *patterns* (typically, nodes in the source document) with *sequence constructors* (which cause new nodes to be constructed in the output document). In general, the structure of an output document can be completely different from the structure of its input document, since nodes from the input document can be filtered and reordered, and arbitrary additional structure can be inserted. XSLT is often used to add styling information to an input document (hence the name *stylesheet language transformation*), but XSLT can be used for a wide range of transformation tasks, not just for formatting and visual presentation applications.

If XACML defines and constrains all data access and use across an organization, it follows that a *P3P policy* automatically derived from an *XACML policy* must necessarily reflect the organization's actual behaviour with the personal data that it holds (which is a subset of all the data stored by the organization). An XSLT *stylesheet* can be created by the organization to explicitly define how a given *XACML policy* is automatically transformed into its corresponding *P3P policy*.

Thus, the auditor's job is reduced to examining the relevant *XACML policies*, the XSLT *stylesheets* (to confirm that the *P3P policies* were actually derived from these access control policies), and the relatively small number of PDPs and PEPs in the infrastructure that fulfill the intentions of the *XACML policies*. This set of tasks is much more tractable than examining every possible information flow and storage location in a very large organization.

The auditor is thus able to confirm that the *XACML policies* are actually being used by the organization and that the organization's *P3P policies* are actually derived from these *XACML policies*. This means that the organization's public privacy promises faithfully reflect its internal practices, at least at the time of the audit. Naturally, it is possible that a malicious organization might change an internal *XACML policy* without changing its advertised *P3P policy* (i.e., not perform the XSLT transformation on the revised *XACML policy*). Without continuous external auditing (which is impractical for many reasons), the best way to protect against this is to have the external auditors do random "surprise" (unannounced) audits. If these are done frequently, and if there are substantial consequences for failing an audit, then even malicious organizations will be likely to maintain synchronization between their *XACML policies* and their *P3P policies*.

APEX, therefore, is a PET that adds a layer of enforcement to the P3P proposal, ensuring that an organization acts in accordance with the *P3P policy* it has advertised to its web-browsing users.

### 8.3.2  Enhancements

The APEX proposal addresses one aspect of enforcement in a P3P environment: ensuring that an organization's <u>actual</u> behaviour regarding data access and use (as regulated by its internal *access control policies*) matches its <u>claimed</u> behaviour (as advertised in its privacy policy). However, another possible concern is that a malicious organization might pretend to have gone through an audit when it has not. A *privacy seal* is an image/icon that is displayed on a website; it would be trivial for a malicious organization to copy this *privacy seal* from another company's website and paste it on their own site. People who visit this malicious organization's website would think that an audit has been performed and therefore that the organization complies with its stated privacy policy, but in reality the audit was never performed and the organization might be using the acquired data without constraints. Users can of course contact the auditor to find out whether (and when) an audit was completed on this organization, but no users will do this for every website they visit. Furthermore, even if a user suspects a problem and subsequently brings legal action against the organization, privacy has already been lost and cannot be recovered.

The 2020 paper by Carlisle Adams, Yu Dai, Catherine DesOrmeaux, Sean McAvoy, NamChi Nguyen, and Francisco Trindade (2020) proposes a mechanism to enforce privacy in the above scenario. The mechanism builds on a cryptographic technology known as *Identity-Based Encryption* (IBE) (proposed by Adi Shamir

(1985) and realized by Dan Boneh and Matt Franklin (2001)). In IBE, an arbitrary string is mapped to a public key that can be used for encryption purposes. Adi Shamir's original proposal was to use an individual's e-mail address as the string, but it was subsequently recognized that the string can be even a full-length policy, giving rise to the concept of *Policy-Based Encryption* (PBE). Thus, the proposal of Adams, et al., is to use the organization's *P3P policy* as the string that is mapped to a public key for that organization.

In IBE/PBE, users do not create their own key pairs. Rather, a trusted entity called a *Private Key Generator* (PKG) takes its own private key and a user's public key as inputs, and creates a private key for that user. In this P3P environment, the external auditor (specifically, the privacy seal company) can play the role of the *Private Key Generator*, creating for the organization a private key that corresponds to its public key (i.e., its *P3P policy*) only if the audit confirms that the organization fully complies with its *P3P policy*.

The architecture of this PBE-extended APEX proposal works as follows. The organization uses XSLT to derive its *P3P policy* from its relevant internal *XACML policies*, and it posts the *P3P policy* on its website. A user visits the site and the *user agent* automatically downloads the *policy reference file* and then the appropriate *P3P policy*; the *user agent* then compares the *P3P policy* with the *user preferences*. If there is no mismatch, the user's browser displays the requested web page. If personal information is required by the website (for example, in a fillable form requesting mailing address, credit card number, and so on), the *user agent* will encrypt this data using the public encryption key derived from the *P3P policy* (in the manner defined by IBE/PBE technology) and upload it to the website. If this organization has undergone a successful audit, it will have the corresponding private key and will be able to decrypt and obtain the user's data. On the other hand, if the audit was unsuccessful (or if the malicious organization did not have an audit, but simply copy-and-pasted another company's *privacy seal* image), then the organization will not have the corresponding private key and will be unable to do anything with the ciphertext that it receives from the *user agent*.

A diagram of this architecture is shown in Fig. 8.1.

This extended APEX adds privacy enforcement to P3P environments. Users can share their personal information with websites (when this is required in order to obtain the goods and services they desire), confident in the knowledge that the organization will behave internally in compliance with their advertised privacy policy. Furthermore, if the organization's behaviour is not consistent with the privacy policy for any reason, the user can rest assured that the information sent will be unintelligible and unusable to the organization.

Note that it is theoretically possible to incorporate negotiation/personalization into this extended APEX architecture. Imagine that the user agent on the browser negotiates with the website to come to a mutually-acceptable set of modifications to the original P3P policy. (For example, the *retention period* is reduced to 3 months (a compromise between the 6-month period specified in the original *P3P policy* and the 1-month period specified in the *user preferences*), and *data sharing* with external companies can only happen for parcel-tracking purposes during shipping and

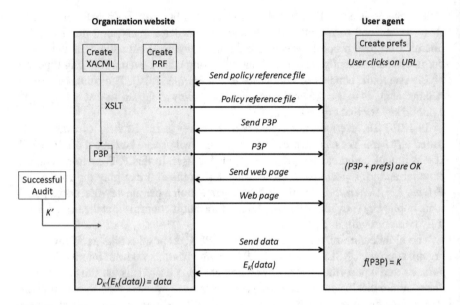

**Fig. 8.1** APEX Architecture and Processing

not for advertising purposes.) The result of this negotiation is effectively a new APPEL file for the user (call it APPEL') and a new P3P policy for the organization (call it P3P').

However, P3P' is for this user only, not for all users. This can be accomplished as follows. The user submits APPEL' to the organization, and the organization uses XSLT to transform APPEL' to XACML syntax (call it XACML-prefs). The organization also uses XSLT to transform its original *P3P policy* to XACML syntax (call it XACML-p3p). Then XACML-prefs and XACML-p3p are combined to form an XACML *policy set*, and XSLT is used to transform this *policy set* into a new *P3P policy* (call it P3P'). P3P' is stored in the organization's database indexed by some random number, and this random number is stored in a cookie sent to the user's browser. The user agent stores APPEL' with this URL in a file on the user's disk. Then, on a subsequent visit to this website, when the user clicks the URL, the user agent will send a request (for the *policy reference file* and the *P3P policy*) that includes the cookie. The website will obtain the random number from the cookie, retrieve P3P', and send this to the user agent. The user agent can then read the relevant APPEL' for this URL from its local file and compare P3P' and APPEL' to determine what the user should do next.

*The above process demonstrates a theoretical possibility, but it must be recognized that negotiation would be a rare event in practice. This is because the organization would not want to have a different P3P policy for every user who visits its website (not only would this require significant additional storage space, but the organization would need a successful audit against each new P3P' in order to obtain a private key corresponding to this new public key).*

### 8.3.3   Strengths

The primary strength of APEX (particularly its PBE-extended version) is that it adds privacy enforcement to a P3P environment. Furthermore, it does this while reducing (and much more narrowly targeting) the workload for external auditors, and protecting users from malicious organizations that do not comply with their advertised privacy policies (because personal data is not inadvertently released to them).

Although P3P is currently obsolete, the *General Data Protection Regulation* (GDPR) (Regulation 2016) on data protection and privacy in the European Union (EU) and the European Economic Area (EEA), which aims to give control to individuals over their personal data, has been effective in raising awareness of privacy internationally. This regulation contains provisions and requirements related to the processing of personal data of individuals who are located in the EEA, and applies to any organization that is processing such data inside the EEA (regardless of the location of the organization, or the citizenship or residence of the individuals). The GDPR (and similar regulation in other countries) could possibly revive interest in P3P and related technologies since organizations will need to be able to prove that user data is properly protected and that the principles of *Consent, Limited Use, Limited Disclosure*, and so on, are fully respected.

### 8.3.4   Disadvantages, Limitations, and Weaknesses

Aside from the fact that P3P is currently obsolete, perhaps the biggest limitation of APEX is that, because it is built on P3P, it relies on a good *user preferences* file. Again, experience with APPEL has shown that this may not be a simple problem to solve (see Sect. 8.2.4).

The PBE extension of APEX mitigates the concern with malicious organizations, but requires a significant amount of trust in the *Private Key Generator* (i.e., the privacy seal auditing company) because that company can theoretically decrypt all personal information submitted by the users. However, note that submitted information would normally be sent over an SSL/TLS connection to the organization's website (and so the auditor will not have access to this data). Furthermore, it is also possible to use *secret sharing* and *threshold cryptography* with several auditing companies so that no single auditor has the private key that corresponds to the organization's *P3P policy* (i.e., the organization's public key).

Finally, there may be environments in which *Policy-Based Encryption* is not efficient enough to protect the expected volume of data (such as websites with a high number of simultaneous browsing users that each have a significant amount of personal data to submit). However, for these environments, PBE could potentially be used only to encrypt a random AES key, and the AES key can then be used to encrypt (much more efficiently) each user's submitted personal information.

The PBE-extended APEX architecture is a PET that limits **disclosure** by hiding both the *identity* and the *attributes* of a user through a policy-based approach. Although its foundation is P3P, which is currently obsolete, GDPR (and similar regulation elsewhere in the world) may stimulate renewed interest in technologies that protect the data of web browsing users by forcing websites to be open and transparent about their privacy practices.

## 8.4   Credential Systems Showing Properties of Attributes

The previous PETs in this chapter are policy-centred technologies for protecting privacy in a database setting (*Hippocratic Databases*) or in a web browsing setting (P3P and APEX). The final PET, which we present next, is somewhat different: it is used for protecting privacy in *general online transactions* (i.e., not just web browsing or database access) and it does not use an explicit privacy policy in any way.

In Chapter Six, Section 6.2, Brands' *Digital Credentials* technology was described as a PET that can be used to limit **disclosure** by hiding the *identity* of the user. It accomplishes this by treating *identity* simply as one more *attribute* of the user Alice, and by giving Alice the power to reveal only a subset of her *attributes* (i.e., excluding *identity*) in any given transaction. However, it is also possible for this PET to hide the revealed *attributes* of the subject, both from external observers of a transaction and from the intended recipient in a transaction. What can it mean to "hide a revealed attribute"? *Digital Credentials* allow a user to reveal a *property of an attribute*, rather than the actual *attribute value*, in a transaction (so that, for example, Alice can prove that her age is within a specified range without disclosing her actual age). This capability gives *Digital Credentials* a power and flexibility that most other *credential systems* do not have and makes it appropriate to include Brands' technology as a PET in the current chapter.

### 8.4.1   The Basic Scheme

The *Digital Credentials* technology proposed by Stefan Brands (2000) (see Chapter Six) is able to do more than unconditionally hide some *attributes* and reveal others. Brands describes how it is possible to reveal *properties of attributes*, rather than explicit *attribute values*, in the showing protocol between a user Alice and a verifier Bob.

**Proving "NOT"**
As a simple example, recall the showing protocol in Section 6.2.1 in which $h = (g_1^{x_1} \cdot g_2^{x_2} \cdot \ldots \cdot g_m^{x_m} \cdot h_0^{\alpha})$ and Alice wants to prove that $x_2 = 17$ (the case for the form $h = (g_1^{x_1} \cdot g_2^{x_2} \cdot \ldots \cdot g_m^{x_m} \cdot h_0)^{\alpha}$ is slightly more complex, but is quite similar). Now let us assume that instead of proving that $x_2$ is 17, Alice wishes only to prove that $x_2$ is

_not_ 16 (without revealing its actual value). That is, Alice wishes to prove that the statement "NOT($x_2 = 16$)" is true. This can be accomplished using the protocol below.

---

The **showing protocol** for proving that $x_2 \neq 16$ can be conducted as follows. Let $\xi = 16 - x_2$. Then Alice needs to convince Bob that $\xi$ is nonzero. Given that $x_2 = 16 - \xi$, Alice's public key can be written as

$$h = \left( g_1^{x_1} \cdot g_2^{16-\xi} \cdot g_3^{x_3} \cdot \ldots \cdot g_m^{x_m} \cdot h_0^{\alpha} \right)$$

<u>Step 1</u>: Alice generates $m + 1$ random numbers $w_1, w_2, w_3, \ldots, w_m, w_{m+1}$ and computes a random value in the form of a public key: $a = \left( g_1^{w_1} \cdot g_2^{-\xi w_2} \cdot g_3^{w_3} \cdot \ldots \cdot g_m^{w_m} \cdot h_0^{w_{m+1}} \right)$. She sends $h$, the CA's signature on $h$, and this random value $a$ to Bob.

<u>Step 2</u>: Bob verifies the CA's signature on $h$ using the *verification equation* (see Chapter Six, section 6.2.1). If it is valid, he generates a random number $c$ and sends this to Alice.

<u>Step 3</u>: Alice computes

$$r_1 = cx_1 + w_1 \bmod q,$$
$$r_2 = \xi(w_2 + c) \bmod q = (16 - x_2) \cdot (w_2 + c) \bmod q,$$
$$r_3 = cx_3 + w_3 \bmod q,$$
$$\ldots$$
$$r_m = cx_m + w_m \bmod q,$$
$$r_{m+1} = c\alpha + w_{m+1} \bmod q.$$

She sends $r_1, r_2, r_3, \ldots, r_m, r_{m+1}$ to Bob.

---

Bob first confirms that $r_2 \neq 0$. If so, then he is convinced that $\xi$ must be nonzero (and therefore $x_2$ must not be 16). He computes $h^c a$ and checks whether the result is equal to $\left( g_1^{r_1} \cdot g_2^{16c - r_2} \cdot g_3^{r_3} \cdot \ldots \cdot g_m^{r_m} \cdot h_0^{r_{m+1}} \right)$. (Refer to the second example of *zero-knowledge proof of knowledge* in Section 6.2.1 for a hint as to why these will be equivalent if Alice has given valid/correct values to Bob.)

If these two values are equal, Alice has proved to Bob that she is the legitimate owner of $h$ and that her *attribute value* $x_2 \neq 16$. Bob learns nothing about the actual value of $x_2$ (other than the fact that it is not 16) and learns nothing about the other $x_i$ or $\alpha$.

Such a protocol might come in handy at a boarding gate when a security officer has a blacklist of names of people that are not allowed to board the plane. Alice could engage in the above exchange for every name on the blacklist to prove that she was not one of the blacklisted people, without revealing any information about her actual name.

## Proving "OR"

The above protocol demonstrates the proof of a "NOT" property ($x_2$ is not 16). Proving an "OR" property uses a "trick" that is nice because it is so conceptually simple. *Zero-knowledge proofs of knowledge* (see Section 6.1) only work if the challenge from Bob is unknown to Alice before the protocol begins. If she knows (even worse, if she can somehow choose) this challenge beforehand, she can construct responses that will look convincing to Bob even if she does not know the value (the secret) she is trying to convince him she knows. On the other hand, if the challenge is unknown to her prior to the start of the protocol, she will only be able to construct valid responses if she really knows the secret.

Suppose that Alice wishes to prove to Bob the statement "$(x_2 = 16)$ OR $(x_2 = 17)$". Bob will therefore learn that one of these clauses is correct, but will not learn the actual value of $x_2$. Assume, as in our example from Chapter Six, that $x_2 = 17$. Alice begins by choosing a value $c'$ as a "challenge" and constructing appropriate "responses" $(r'_1, r'_3, ...)$ that would convince a verifier that $x_2 = 16$. Alice then begins the protocol with Bob. When she receives the random challenge, $c$, from Bob, she computes $c'' = c - c'$. Even though she chose a specific value of $c'$ in order to create her fake "proof" for $x_2 = 16$, the fact that $c$ is a random value means that $c''$ is a random value that she could not have known beforehand. She therefore uses $c''$ as a challenge and constructs appropriate responses $(r''_1, r''_3, ...)$ that would convince a verifier that $x_2 = 17$.

Alice sends $(c', r'_1, r'_3, ..., c'', r''_1, r''_3, ...)$ to Bob. Bob confirms that $c' + c'' = c$ (his original challenge) and then checks both proofs. Bob is convinced that one of these proofs is valid and the other is fake, but he has no way of determining which is which. He therefore believes that "$(x_2 = 16)$ OR $(x_2 = 17)$" without learning the true value of $x_2$. Beautifully elegant!

## Proving "Range"

Brands describes a protocol (due to unpublished work by Berry Schoenmakers; see reference #342 cited in Chap. 3 of (Brands 2000)) for proving a range property of an attribute that uses the previous "OR" proof. Suppose that $h = g_1^{x_1} \cdot h_0^{\alpha}$ and Alice wishes to prove that $x_1 \in \{0, ..., 2^t - 1\}$. Alice constructs and gives to Bob $t$ additional commitments

$$h_0 = g_1^{b_0} \cdot h_0^{\alpha_0}, ..., h_{t-1} = g_1^{b_{t-1}} \cdot h_0^{\alpha_{t-1}}$$

The $b_i$ satisfy $\sum_{i=0}^{t-1} b_i 2^i = x_1$ (i.e., they are the bits in the binary expansion of $x_1$), and the $\alpha_i$ are chosen at random subject to the condition that $\alpha = \sum_{i=0}^{t-1} \alpha_i 2^i \bmod q$. For each $b_i$, Alice proves that "$(b_i = 0)$ OR $(b_i = 1)$" (using the "OR" proof technique described above), and Bob also checks that

$$\prod_{i=0}^{t-1} h_i^{2^i} = h$$

Alice can use this protocol to prove, for example, that $0 \le x_1 < 16$, without revealing the actual value of $x_1$. Brands notes that generalization to arbitrary intervals is accomplished by proving that $x_1$ is in the intersection of two appropriately shifted intervals, each of length a power of 2.

**Proving "NOT" along with "AND"**

Brands presents an example of a compound proof in Chap. 3, Example 3.4.7 of (2000). Suppose Alice has three *attributes* $x_1$, $x_2$, $x_3$ and wishes to prove that the following formula is true:

$$\text{NOT}\left(x_1 + 3x_2 + 5x_3 = 7\right) \text{ AND } \left(3x_1 + 10x_2 + 18x_3 = 23\right)$$

Using the same approach as the "NOT" example above, let $\xi = 7 - x_1 - 3x_2 - 5x_3$. Therefore, $x_1 = 7 - 3x_2 - 5x_3 - \xi$. Plugging this into the second clause and solving for $x_2$, we have

$$10x_2 = 23 - 3\left(7 - 3x_2 - 5x_3 - \xi\right) - 18x_3$$

$$\text{Thus,} 10x_2 = 23 - 21 + 9x_2 + 15x_3 + 3\xi - 18x_3$$

$$10x_2 = 2 + 9x_2 - 3x_3 + 3\xi$$

$$x_2 = 2 - 3x_3 + 3\xi$$

Now, plugging this expression for $x_2$ into the expression for $x_1$, we have

$$x_1 = 7 - 3\left(2 - 3x_3 + 3\xi\right) - 5x_3 - \xi$$

$$\text{Thus,} x_1 = 7 - 6 + 9x_3 - 9\xi - 5x_3 - \xi$$

$$x_1 = 1 + 4x_3 - 10\xi$$

Alice can therefore prove the original formula by proving that

$$\left(x_1 = 1 + 4x_3 - 10\xi\right) \text{AND} \left(x_2 = 2 - 3x_3 + 3\xi\right) \text{AND} \left(\xi \text{ is nonzero}\right)$$

To do this, we write Alice's public key $h = g_1^{x_1} \cdot g_2^{x_2} \cdot g_3^{x_3} \cdot h_0^{\alpha}$ as follows

$$h = g_1^{1 + 4x_3 - 10\xi} \cdot g_2^{2 - 3x_3 + 3\xi} \cdot g_3^{x_3} \cdot h_0^{\alpha}$$

The right-hand-side of this equation is the form that Alice wants Bob to verify, but of course she wishes to hide her private key values (i.e., the $x_i$ and $\alpha$) from him. This can be done in the following way.

(i) For each independent exponent in this expression (here, it is $x_3$ and $\alpha$), she wants to hide it using a random value from Bob and a random value that she chooses (so that $x_3$ is replaced by $r_3 = cx_3 + w_3$, and $\alpha$ is replaced by $r_4 = c\alpha + w_4$).

(ii) For the dependent exponents (here, note that the exponents of $g_1$ and $g_2$ depend on $x_3$), she can use the independent variables as needed and choose exponents in $a$ to adjust as necessary (see bullet $iv$).

(iii) If $h$ is raised to the power $c$ (whatever random value Bob chooses), then the exponents on the right-hand-side will be $(c + 4cx_3 - 10c\xi)$, $(2c - 3cx_3 + 3c\xi)$, $(cx_3)$, and $(c\alpha)$. Alice can therefore choose random number $w_3$ to be the exponent for $g_3$, and random number $w_4$ to be the exponent for $g_4$, in $a$. This will result in the desired $r_3$ and $r_4$ exponents for $h^c a$.

(iv) If she chooses the value $(4w_3 - 10\xi w_3)$ as the exponent for $g_1$ in $a$, the resulting combined exponent in $h^c a$ will be $(c + 4cx_3 + 4w_3 - 10c\xi - 10\xi w_3) = (c + 4r_3 - 10\xi(w_3 + c))$. Similarly, if she chooses the value $(-3w_3 + 3\xi w_3)$ as the exponent for $g_2$ in $a$, the resulting combined exponent in $h^c a$ will be $(2c - 3cx_3 - 3w_3 + 3c\xi + 3\xi w_3) = (2c - 3r_3 + 3\xi(w_3 + c))$. Therefore, she can choose $\xi(w_3 + c)$ as her $r$ value (i.e., the value $\xi$ hidden by both $w_3$ and $c$).

---

The proof therefore can be conducted as follows.

<u>Step 1</u>: Alice chooses 2 random numbers $w_3$, $w_4$ and computes $a = g_1^{4w_3 - 10\xi w_3} \cdot g_2^{-3w_3 + 3\xi w_3} \cdot g_3^{w_3} \cdot h_0^{w_4}$. She sends $h$, the CA's signature on $h$, and this random value $a$ to Bob.

<u>Step 2</u>: Bob verifies the CA's signature on $h$ using the *verification equation*. If it is valid, he generates a random number $c$ and sends this to Alice.

<u>Step 3</u>: Alice computes

$$r = \xi\left(w_3 + c\right) \bmod q = \left(7 - x_1 - 3x_2 - 5x_3\right)\cdot\left(w_3 + c\right)\bmod q,$$
$$r_3 = cx_3 + w_3 \bmod q,$$
$$r_4 = c\alpha + w_4 \bmod q.$$

She sends $r$, $r_3$, $r_4$ to Bob.

Bob first confirms that $r \neq 0$ (if so, then he is convinced that $\xi$ must be non-zero). He computes $h^c a$ and checks whether the result is equal to $\left(g_1^{c+4r_3+10r} \cdot g_2^{2c-3r_3+3r} \cdot g_3^{r_3} \cdot h_0^{r_4}\right)$. If so, Alice has proved to Bob that she is the legitimate owner of $h$ and that "NOT($x_1 + 3x_2 + 5x_3 = 7$) AND $(3x_1 + 10x_2 + 18x_3 = 23)$" is true. Bob learns nothing whatever about the actual values of any of her *attributes* $x_i$ or her private number $\alpha$.

*The process for the "issuing protocol form" of h (that is,* $h = \left( g_1^{x_1} \cdot g_2^{x_2} \cdot g_3^{x_3} \cdot h_0 \right)^{\alpha}$,
*as described in Chapter Six) is very similar to the process immediately above, except that Alice will compute and send to Bob*
$a = \left( \left( g_1^{1+4x_3-10\xi} \cdot g_2^{2-3x_3+3\xi} \cdot g_3^{x_3} \cdot h_0 \right)^{-\alpha w} \cdot \left( g_1^{4w_3-10\xi w_3} \cdot g_2^{-3w_3+3\xi w_3} \cdot g_3^{w_3} \right) \right)$ *using a random w, and after receiving c from Bob will send to him c' = (c/\alpha + w) along with r and* $r_3$. *Bob will compute* $h^{c'}a$ *and see if it is equal to* $\left( g_1^{c+4r_3+10r} \cdot g_2^{2c-3r_3+3r} \cdot g_3^{r_3} \cdot h_0^{c} \right)$.
*(Compare with the process presented for this form of h in Section 6.2.1).*

## Combinations

By combining the techniques presented above, it is possible to prove an arbitrarily complex Boolean function of different *attributes* in a credential (using AND, OR, and NOT connectives), as well as to prove ranges in *attributes* without revealing specific values. Brands has also shown how to combine *attributes* from different credentials (even credentials from different issuers!) in a single showing protocol. *Digital Credentials* is therefore extremely flexible as a PET for protecting the privacy of personal information.

## 8.4.2  Enhancements

Beyond Brands' original work (presented in Sect. 8.4.1), there has not been additional activity on proving *properties of attributes* for *Digital Credentials*. On the other hand, for the *anonymous credentials* technology of Camenisch and Lysyanskaya (2001), (2003), (Lysyanskaya 2002) (see a brief description in Section 6.2.2), some research and implementation work has been done. A recent example is the proposed system of Kai Bemmann, et al. (2018) in which, given a public Pedersen commitment $com = g^a h^d \bmod p$, Alice can prove (in zero-knowledge) not only that she knows $a$ and $d$, but also one of the following:

- $a = a^*$, for some public value $a^*$ (an *equality proof*);
- $a \neq a^*$, for some public value $a^*$ (an *inequality proof*);
- $a \in S^*$, for some public set $S^*$ (a *set membership proof*);
- $a^* \leq a \leq b^*$, for public values $a^*$, $b^*$, without revealing the value of $a$ (a *range proof*).

Furthermore, these four types of *attribute property* proofs can be combined in Boolean expressions in a verifier's policy so that Alice can prove, for example,

$$\left( \left( citizenship =^{\cdot\cdot} \mathbf{German}^{\cdot\cdot} \right) \mathbf{V} \left( residence \in \left\{ {}^{\cdot\cdot}\mathbf{Germany}^{\cdot\cdot}, {}^{\cdot\cdot}\mathbf{Austria}^{\cdot\cdot}, {}^{\cdot\cdot}\mathbf{Switzerland}^{\cdot\cdot} \right\} \right) \right)$$
$$\wedge \left( 18 \leq age \leq 25 \right) \wedge \left( status \neq^{\cdot\cdot} \mathbf{student}^{\cdot\cdot} \right)$$

The construction of Bemmann, et al., does not allow arbitrarily complex Boolean expressions of *attributes* (of the form "NOT($x_1 + 3x_2 + 5x_3 = 7$) AND ($3x_1 + 10x_2 + 18x_3 = 23$)", as seen in Sect. 8.4.1), but it does appear to enable many useful verifier policies.

### 8.4.3  Strengths

The ability to prove *properties of attributes*, rather than explicit *attribute values*, in an online transaction with a verifier gives an incredible degree of power, generality, and flexibility to *Digital Credentials*. This is what allows them to hide both the *identity* and the *attributes* of a user, while still giving the verifier precisely the information needed to make an access decision. The bouncer at the entrance to the bar does not need to know Alice's *name*, *home address*, *height*, or *license number* when she shows her driver's license to prove her age. But, in addition to this, the bouncer does not even need to know her actual age (i.e., her *date of birth*); he only needs to ensure that she is "old enough to enter". What he needs in order to make a decision is a *property about her age*, and *Digital Credentials* technology provides exactly this capability.

Proving *properties of attributes* gives Alice the highest level of control over her personal information in online transaction settings.

### 8.4.4  Disadvantages, Limitations, and Weaknesses

There is a clear and compelling use case for being able to prove a property about the *attribute* "age". For example, there are definitely situations in which Alice may wish to prove that she is "over 18" or "over 21" (the often-cited example is when Alice wishes to enter a bar, or purchase alcohol in a liquor store). Similarly, there may be situations in which Alice might need to prove that she is a minor (her age is in the range [0–16]) or that she is a senior (her age is <u>not</u> in the range [0–64]) in order to receive some discounted price on an item or service.

However, it is much more difficult to find use cases (compelling or not) for other types of *attributes*. The ability to prove that your name is not on a blacklist is definitely interesting but, in reality, no airline in the world would see this as sufficient: they will want to know exactly who is boarding the plane! Furthermore, it is quite challenging to find realistic use cases for Boolean expressions of several *attributes* ("*I will prove to you that 3 times my address, minus 5 times my nationality, is equal to 13 times my gold-card status*"). Thus, although this property of *Digital Credentials* is powerful, general, flexible, mathematically interesting, and highly impressive, it is not clear when or where it would be used in many practical real-world environments.

Nevertheless, *Digital Credentials* technology qualifies as a PET that can be used to limit **disclosure** by hiding both the *identity* and the *attributes* of a user in any online transaction.

## 8.5 Summary

The previous five chapters, together with this chapter, have explored the various branches of the privacy tree: limiting **exposure** by hiding the *identity*, hiding the *actions*, or hiding both the *identity* and the *actions*; and limiting **disclosure** by hiding the *identity*, hiding the *attributes*, or hiding both the *identity* and the *attributes*. Each chapter has presented and discussed several PETs that serve as examples of the branch under consideration. For every PET introduced, we have described the technology as it was originally published, some important extensions or enhancements that have been proposed over the years, and a few of its primary strengths and weaknesses/limitations.

This chapter looked specifically at *Hippocratic Databases*, *Platform for Privacy Preferences Project*, *Architecture for Privacy Enforcement using XML*, and *Credential Systems showing properties of attributes*. These technologies hide both the *identity* and the *attributes* of the user.

HDB was inspired by the privacy provision of the *Hippocratic Oath* and was built around ten privacy principles that were distilled from privacy regulations and guidelines from several countries. It is a compelling concept of how individual privacy can be protected in a database setting, but requires further implementation and deployment work in order to fully realize its comprehensive vision.

P3P aims to address privacy concerns in a web browsing setting: a website owner posts a machine-readable privacy policy (written in a standardized format) at a fixed location on his/her site; a client tool (integrated with a web browser application) subsequently downloads the policy, compares it with the user's privacy preferences, and warns the user if there is a mismatch. This PET saw some use in actual websites (and some uptake of an elegant client tool called *Privacy Bird*), but was eventually obsoleted by W3C due to insufficient deployment and implementation support.

The APEX proposal built on P3P technology to address *enforcement* of the website's posted privacy policy. An external auditor, such as a privacy seal company, periodically (and randomly) audits an organization to see whether its internal behaviour matches its advertised privacy policy; if so, the policy can be used as the public key in a *policy-based encryption* scheme and the auditor gives the corresponding private key to the organization. Users that visit the site (because no warning was displayed by the P3P client tool) can encrypt any submitted data using this PBE public key. Thus, only organizations that actually comply with their own advertised policies will obtain plaintext user data.

Finally, the *Credential Systems* introduced in Chapter Six are used in this chapter not to prove explicit *attribute values*, but rather to prove certain properties of the contained *attributes*. Various techniques have been designed to prove arbitrarily complex Boolean functions of credential *attributes*, as well as to prove ranges in *attributes*, without revealing *attribute values*.

Where does our exploration of the various branches of the privacy tree leave us? Why is it useful to know about the privacy tree and about a handful of PETs that reside in various nodes of this tree? The following chapter tackles these questions. We look at how the privacy tree can be used in practice, both in conjunction with the legal infrastructure and in conjunction with specific other technologies that have become prominent in our digital world. The goal is to equip us with the tools and the understanding to properly protect our privacy in whatever corner of the digital world we happen to find ourselves.

**Questions for Personal Reflection and/or Group Discussion**

1. To date, the powerful concept of a *Hippocratic Database* does not seem to have been realized as a single product that can be purchased, or as a single piece of open-source *beta* software that can be downloaded and investigated. Discuss what you think could be done to change this. What would be required in order for a complete (or close to complete) HDB implementation to be made?
2. Showing properties of *attributes* in *Digital Credentials* would be very useful when you want to prove that you are over 18 without revealing your actual age. Can you propose a use case for proving a Boolean function of several of your attribute properties? Is there a situation in which this general and flexible privacy property would be particularly needed?

# References

C. Adams and K. Barbieri, Privacy enforcement in E-Services environments. In *Privacy protection for E-Services*, G. Yee, Ed., Idea Group Publishing, pp. 172–202 (2006)

C. Adams, Y. Dai, C. DesOrmeaux, S. McAvoy, N. Nguyen, and F. Trindade, Strengthening enforcement in a comprehensive architecture for privacy enforcement at internet websites. *Front. Comp. Sci.* 2, 9pp (2020, 4 February)

R. Agrawal and E. Terzi, on honesty in sovereign information sharing. *Proceedings of the 10th international conference on extending database technology*, Munich, Germany, pp. 240–256, (2006, March)

R. Agrawal, J. Kiernan, R. Srikant, and Y. Xu, Hippocratic databases. *Proceedings of the 28th international conference on very large databases*, Hong Kong, 12pp (2002)

R. Agrawal, J. Kiernan, R. Srikant, and Y. Xu, An XPath-based preference language for P3P. *Proceedings of the 12th international world wide web conference*, Budapest, Hungary, pp. 629–639, (2003a, May)

R. Agrawal, A. Evfimievski, and R. Srikant, Information sharing across private databases. *Proceedings of the ACM SIGMOD conference on management of data*, San Diego, California, 12pp, (2003b, June)

R. Agrawal, R. Bayardo, C. Faloutsos, J. Kiernan, R. Rantzau, and R. Srikant, Auditing compliance with a hippocratic database. *Proceedings of the 30th international conference on very large databases*, Toronto, Canada, 12pp, (2004a)

R. Agrawal, J. Kiernan, R. Srikant, and Y. Xu, Order-preserving encryption for numeric data. *Proceedings of the ACM SIGMOD conference on management of data*, Paris, France, pp. 563–574 (2004b, June)

R. Agrawal, P. Bird, T. Grandison, J. Kiernan, S. Logan, and W. Rjaibi, Extending relational database systems to automatically enforce privacy policies. *Proceedings of the 21st international conference on data engineering*, Tokyo, Japan, pp. 1013–1022, (2005, April)

R. Agrawal, D. Asonov, M. Kantarcioglu, and Y. Li, Sovereign joins. *Proceedings of the 22nd international conference on data engineering*, Atlanta, USA, 12pp (2006, April)

K. Bemmann, J. Blömer, J. Bobolz, H. Bröcher, D. Diemert, F. Eidens, L. Eilers, J. Haltermann, J. Juhnke, B. Otour, L. Porzenheim, S. Pukrop, E. Schilling, M. Schlichtig, and M. Stienemeier, Fully-featured anonymous credentials with reputation system. *Proceedings of the 13th international conference on availability, reliability and security*, pp. 1–10 (2018, August )

C.J. Bennett, *Regulating Privacy: Data Protection and Public Policy in Europe and the United States* (Cornell University Press, 1992)

D. Boneh and M. Franklin, Identity-based encryption from the Weil pairing. *Advances in cryptology: Proceedings of crypto 2001*, Springer LNCS 2139, pp. 213–229 (2001)

J. M. Boyer, XForms 1.1. *W3C Recommendation REC-xforms-20091020* (2009, 20 October)

S. Brands, *Rethinking Public Key Infrastructures and Digital Certificates: Building in Privacy* (The MIT Press, 2000)

J. Camenisch and A. Lysyanskaya, An efficient system for non-transferable anonymous credentials with optional anonymity revocation. *Advances in cryptology: Proceedings of Eurocrypt 2001*, Springer LNCS 2045, pp. 93–118 (2001)

J. Camenisch and A. Lysyanskaya, a signature scheme with efficient protocols. *Proceedings of the 3rd International Conference on Security in Communication Networks*, Springer, LNCS 2576, pp. 268–289, (2003, 11–13 September)

R. Chinnici, J.-J. Moreau, A. Ryman, and S. Weerawarana, Web Services Description Language (WSDL) Version 2.0 Part 1: Core Language. *W3C Recommendation REC-wsdl20–20070626* (2007, 26 June)

L. Cranor and R. Wenning, Platform for Privacy Preferences (P3P) Project: Enabling Smarter Privacy Tools for the Web. *W3C P3P Overview* (2018, 2 February)

L. Cranor, M. Langheinrich, and M. Marchiori, A P3P Preference Exchange Language 1.0 (APPEL 1.0). *W3C Working Draft WD-P3P-preferences-20020415*, (2002a, 15 April)

L. Cranor, M. Langheinrich, M. Marchiori, M. Presler-Marshall, and J. Reagle, The platform for privacy preferences 1.0 (P3P1.0) Specification. *W3C Recommendation REC-P3P-20020416* (2002b, 16 April)

L.F. Cranor, P. Guduru, J. Arjula, User interfaces for privacy agents. ACM Trans. Computer-Human Inter. **13**(2), 135–178 (2006a)

L. Cranor, B. Dobbs, S. Egelman, G. Hogben, J. Humphrey, M. Langheinrich, M. Marchiori, M. Presler-Marshall, J. Reagle, M. Schunter, D. A. Stampley, and R. Wenning, The platform for privacy preferences 1.1 (P3P1.1) specification. *W3C Working Group Note NOTE-P3P11–20061113* (2006b, 13 November)

T. Dillard, Hippocratic database and active enforcement. in *Ethical issues and security monitoring trends in global healthcare: technological advancements*, S. A. Brown and M. Brown (Eds.), Medical Information Science Reference (an imprint of IGI Global) , pp. 43–49, (2011)

T. Grandison, C. Johnson, and J. Kiernan, Hippocratic databases: Current capabilities and future trends. in *Handbook on Database Security: Applications and Trends*, M. Gertz and S. Jajodia (Eds), Springer, pp. 409–429 (2008)

M. Kay, XSL Transformations (XSLT) Version 3.0. *W3C Recommendation REC-xslt-30-20170608* (2017, 8 June)

Y. Laura-Silva and W. Aref, Realizing privacy-preserving features in hippocratic databases. *Department of computer science technical reports, Report Number 06–022*, Purdue University, 16pp, (2006)

K. LeFevre, R. Agrawal, V. Ercegovak, R. Ramakrishnan, Y. Xu, and D. DeWitt, Limiting disclosure in hippocratic databases. *Proceedings of the 30th international conference on very large databases*, Toronto, Canada, 12pp, (2004)

A. Lysyanskaya, Signature schemes and applications to cryptographic protocol design. *Ph.D. thesis, Massachusetts Institute of Technology*, Cambridge, MA, USA (2002, September)

B. Markert, Comparison of three online privacy seal programs. SANS Institute Information Security Reading Room (2002)

Regulation: Regulation (EU) 2016/679, General Data Protection Regulation (GDPR). *OJ L 119, 04.05.2016; cor. OJ L 127, 23.5.2018* (2016, 4 May)

E. Rissanen, eXtensible Access Control Markup Language (XACML) Version 3.0 Plus Errata 01. *OASIS Standard Incorporating Approved Errata* (2017, 12 July)

M. Rotenberg, The privacy law sourcebook 2000: United States Law, International Law, and Recent Developments, Electronic Privacy Information Center (2000)

A. Shamir, Identity-based cryptosystems and signature schemes. *Advances in cryptology: Proceedings of crypto 84*, Springer LNCS 196, pp. 47–53 (1985)

H. Von Staden, In a pure and holy way: Personal and professional conduct in the Hippocratic oath (translation by H. Von Staden). *J. Hist. Med. Appl. Sci.* **51**(4), 406–408 (1966)

R. Wenning, Platform for privacy preferences (P3P) project: Background, critics and discussions. *W3C P3P Background* (2018, 2 February)

# Chapter 9
# Using the Privacy Tree in Practice

**Abstract** This chapter discusses how the privacy tree can be used to add privacy protection to real-world environments. This includes using PETs in combination with security technologies, using PETs in conjunction with the legal infrastructure, and using PETs to add privacy to other types of technologies (the specific examples given are software defined networking and machine learning).

**Keywords** Privacy and security · Privacy law · Legal infrastructure for privacy · Privacy and software defined networking (SDN) · Privacy and machine learning (ML)

Having defined and examined the branches of the privacy tree in some detail in the previous six chapters, we are now in a position to consider how the privacy tree can be used in real-world situations.

The three sections of this chapter will discuss the following topics:

- How various PETs in the privacy tree work hand-in-hand with other types of security technologies to achieve privacy;
- How the privacy tree complements the rich legal infrastructure for privacy that exists in many countries around the world; and
- How the privacy tree can be used with other well-known technologies to help Alice identify and achieve her privacy goals.

We begin by looking at how the privacy tree works in conjunction with security technologies.

© The Editor(s) (if applicable) and The Author(s), under exclusive license       209
to Springer Nature Switzerland AG 2021
C. Adams, *Introduction to Privacy Enhancing Technologies*,
https://doi.org/10.1007/978-3-030-81043-6_9

## 9.1   In Conjunction with Security Technologies

The paper by Adams (2006) includes some explanation of how PETs in the privacy tree can be used in combination with various security technologies to achieve the privacy goals of Alice and/or the privacy goals of a holder of Alice's personal information. Figure 9.1 from that paper was reproduced in Chap. 2 of this book; for convenience we include it again here as Fig. 9.1, along with the various labels for the nodes in Level 4 (which are needed for the following discussion).

As a reminder (see (Adams 2006) or Chap. 2), the notation used in the subsequent discussion is defined as follows.

- An *operation tuple* is the pairing of Alice's identity and an action that she performs: $\omega = (\iota, \alpha)$, where $\iota$ is the identity and $\alpha$ is the action. Private operations exist for Alice when unintended entities are unable to discover or infer the tuple $\omega$. Protecting $\omega$ against **exposure** can be done in three ways: a transformation $\tau_\omega(\iota)$ may be applied to hide or remove the identity $\iota$; a transformation $\tau_\omega(\alpha)$ may be applied to hide or remove the action $\alpha$; or a transformation $\tau_\omega(\omega)$ may be applied to hide the full tuple $\omega$.

- Similarly, a *record tuple* is the pairing of Alice's identity and a set of one or more attributes about her: $\rho = (\iota, \bar{a})$, where $\iota$ is the identity and $\bar{a}$ is a collection of attributes. Private records exist for Alice when unintended entities are unable to discover or infer the tuple $\rho$. Protecting $\rho$ against **disclosure** can be done in three ways: a transformation $\tau_\rho(\iota)$ may be applied to hide or remove the identity $\iota$; a transformation $\tau_\rho(\bar{a})$ may be applied to hide or remove the attributes $\bar{a}$; or a transformation $\tau_\rho(\rho)$ may be applied to hide the full tuple $\rho$.

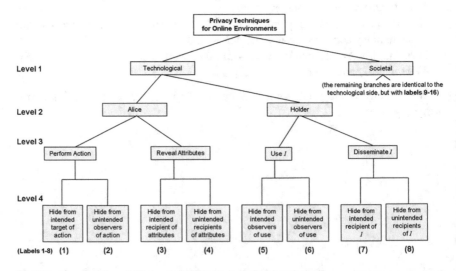

**Fig. 9.1** Classification of (Technological) privacy Techniques for online environments

Looking at the PETs side (i.e., the left side) of the tree in Fig. 9.1, the privacy goals of Alice and of the holder of Alice's personal information $I$ are summarized in the boxes labeled 1–8. As explained in (Adams 2006) (quoted below), privacy enhancing technologies can be combined with security technologies to achieve these goals.

*Label 1*. There are circumstances in which Alice would like to have exposure privacy from an intended target of her operation. For example, she may wish to make anonymous or pseudonymous requests to a Web server and so will use techniques that provide privacy transformation $\tau_\omega(\iota)$ for her operation. Such techniques include Crowds (Reiter and Rubin 1998) and anonymizers of various kinds (see, for example, (Wikipedia 2020)), as well as suitable mix networks (Berthold et al. 2001) and onion routers (Reed et al. 1998) (if identifying information is omitted from the original embedded message). Alternatively, she may be comfortable with letting the server know her identity, but may wish to hide the action she is performing and so will use techniques that provide privacy transformation $\tau_\omega(\alpha)$ for her operation. Such techniques include Private Information Retrieval (PIR) (see (Asonov 2001)), in which, for example, Alice can request and receive records from a database server without the server knowing precisely which records she has requested. There do not seem to be practical situations in which Alice would desire to hide both her identity and her action from the target of the operation, but if such cases arise, Alice may use a combination of the above techniques.

*Label 2*. There are many circumstances in which Alice would like to have exposure privacy from unintended observers (eavesdroppers) of her operations. Privacy transformation $\tau_\omega(\iota)$ may be provided by various anonymizing services, including onion routing and mix networks. Privacy transformation $\tau_\omega(\alpha)$ may be provided by techniques such as embedding Alice's actions in a continuous stream of faked transactions so that any observers are unable to construct an accurate profile of Alice or the group in which Alice is a member (Elovici et al. 2002). Finally, privacy transformation $\tau_\omega(\omega)$ may be provided by techniques such as *IPsec* in *tunnel mode* and OTR Messaging. In all these transformations, if Alice wishes to reveal her identity, action, or both to the operation target (*i.e.*, if she wishes to hide this information *only* from unintended observers of her operation), then she would use encryption technology to protect an internal message containing the relevant information and would then operate on this encrypted message with an outer privacy-preserving transformation. Disabling third-party cookies on the Web browser is another simple example of a $\tau_\omega(\omega)$ technique.

(continued)

*Label 3.* If Alice is deliberately revealing her personal attributes to another entity, there may be circumstances in which she would wish to do so without revealing her identity and so will use techniques that provide privacy transformation $\tau_\rho(\iota)$. For example, she may associate an anonym or pseudonym with this data, or she may ensure that the data is scrubbed of all identifying information prior to revealing it. Note that such a scrubbing operation must take into account the ways in which different attributes may interact to reveal identity (Sweeney 1996). If Alice wishes to hide the attributes themselves (without hiding her identity), privacy transformation $\tau_\rho(\bar{a})$ may be provided by mechanisms in privacy preserving data mining (Du and Zhan 2003), in which Alice can use randomized response techniques to effectively hide her attributes from the intended recipient without compromising the accuracy of statistics computed over the entire population of users. Another example of $\tau_\rho(\bar{a})$ is oblivious polynomial evaluation (Chang and Lu 2001), in which Alice can give data to another entity Bob in such a way that Bob learns nothing about the data and yet is able to compute some function (a polynomial) using that data. As with Label 1, there do not seem to be practical situations in which Alice would desire to hide both her identity and her attributes from the intended receiver of her personal record $\rho$, but if such situations arise, a combination of the above techniques may be used.

*Label 4.* In all realistic situations, Alice would wish to hide her personal information from unintended recipients of this data, even as she reveals it to intended recipients. As with the case of performing an action, she may do this by encapsulating her identity, her attributes, or her tuple $\rho$ in an outer layer that hides the desired information. Privacy transformations $\tau_\rho(\iota)$, $\tau_\rho(\bar{a})$, and $\tau_\rho(\rho)$ may therefore be provided by encryption technology. In particular, for $\tau_\rho(\iota)$ Alice may encrypt her identity using a key shared with the intended recipients and then anonymize or pseudonymize this encrypted string using any appropriate source-hiding technique. For $\tau_\rho(\bar{a})$, in which Alice wishes to hide her attributes from unintended recipients but is not concerned with hiding her identity, secure channel technology such as SSL/TLS is an appropriate technique. The privacy transformation $\tau_\rho(\rho)$ is similar to $\tau_\rho(\iota)$, except that Alice encrypts both her identity and her attributes using the key she shares with the intended recipients before using a source-hiding technique on this encrypted information. Anti-spyware and anti-adware software on Alice's machine also falls into the category of privacy techniques denoted by $\tau_\rho(\rho)$.

*Label 5.* Turning now from Alice to some other entity Harry that is a holder of Alice's personal information $\rho$, there are circumstances in which Harry would like to use $\rho$ in such a way that there are intended observers of this use. For example, an organization may wish to change its business model or service offering in some way as a result of complaints from Alice or other data associated with Alice. However, Harry would like to hide Alice's identity, or

(continued)

her attributes, or both, from the intended observers. The transformations $\tau_p(\iota)$, $\tau_p(\bar{a})$, and $\tau_p(\rho)$ may be provided by inference control techniques. Such techniques are similar to ones used historically in a database context where the goal is to prevent inferences from being drawn from the association of separate pieces of stored data (Denning 1982). Here, the goal is to prevent observers from drawing inferences about Alice's personal information from the observed behaviour of Harry.

*Label 6.* There are circumstances in which the holder, Harry, of Alice's personal information $\rho$ would like to use $\rho$ without leaking anything about $\rho$ to unintended observers of this use. Inference control techniques can again be used to provide the transformations $\tau_p(\iota)$, $\tau_p(\bar{a})$, and $\tau_p(\rho)$. However, in this case, any technology that helps to keep an organization's internal operations secret (*i.e.*, away from prying eyes) can also be a factor in maintaining the disclosure privacy of Alice's personal information. Thus, firewalls, antivirus software, anti-spyware software, intrusion detection systems, and similar security products have a legitimate place within the classification of privacy techniques.

*Label 7.* Many situations exist in which Harry would like to disseminate Alice's personal information to intended recipients while hiding $\iota$ or $\bar{a}$ from these recipients. For example, a company may wish to reveal statistical information about its customer base (such as demographic information, buying patterns, or preference data) to other entities without revealing individual identities or attributes. Privacy transformation $\tau_p(\iota)$ may be provided by techniques for de-identifying data, as are used when the health records of a large number of patients are de-identified for release to organizations for statistical analysis or other research purposes; $k$-anonymity (Sweeney 2002) is one example technique in this category (although it may be infeasible for data sets of realistic size; see the comments at the end of Sect. 6.1.4 of Chap. 6). Privacy transformation $\tau_p(\bar{a})$ may be provided by data randomization techniques (Polat and Du 2003) in which attribute data is perturbed in such a way as to ensure with high probability that observations of individual attributes are incorrect but observations of population statistics are correct. Privacy transformation $\tau_p(\rho)$ does not seem to have a strong requirement in practice, but if there are uses for this, then a combination of de-identifying and data randomizing techniques may be applied.

*Label 8.* As with Label 4, in all realistic situations, Harry would wish to hide Alice's personal information $\rho$ from unintended recipients of this data, even if he might need to reveal it to intended recipients. Again, privacy transformations $\tau_p(\iota)$, $\tau_p(\bar{a})$, and $\tau_p(\rho)$ may be provided by encryption technology (*i.e.*, $\rho$ may be stored in an encrypted form on Harry's computer). In addition, as with Label 6, firewalls, antivirus and anti-spyware software, intrusion detection systems, and similar products can be effective techniques for detecting

(continued)

unwanted intruders and preventing them from retrieving $\rho$ from Harry's system. Another important class of techniques in this leaf of the classification is access control technology. If Harry can properly protect $\rho$ through comprehensive access control tools and thoroughly-tested privacy policy enforcement architectures, then Alice's personal information will be effectively hidden from unintended recipients.

## 9.2   In Conjunction with the Legal Infrastructure

Turning from the PETs side of the tree to the societal side (i.e., the right side) of the tree, we see the role for the legal infrastructure in protecting privacy; see Fig. 9.2.

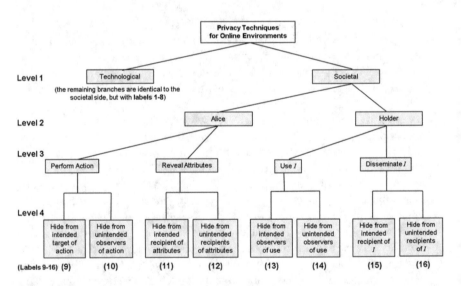

**Fig. 9.2**  Classification of (Societal) privacy techniques for online environments

The paper by Adams (2006) explains it in this way.

On the societal side of the classification, privacy techniques are again conceptually categorized according to what kind of protection they offer $\omega$ and $\rho$. In
this branch of the tree, however, we find that the eight leaves (Label 9 – Label
16) give rise, in practice, to only two classes of techniques, one of which is the
trivial (NULL) class of no external party societal technique. In particular, for
Labels 9 and 11, the only human means that Alice has to protect against exposure and disclosure is to be careful about engaging in activities and revealing
her attributes. If she wishes to keep $\omega$ and $\rho$ private from intended targets or
recipients, she cannot generally rely on other human parties to assist in this
process; the best she can do is to use discretion and to choose carefully regarding whether or not to perform any given operation or reveal any given attribute. This decision can be guided by some knowledge about the potential
recipient entities, such as their organizational structure or procedures with
respect to privacy, their accreditation or certification by recognized privacy
agencies (see, for example, (Office 2000)), their adherence to government
privacy guidelines, their compliance with privacy standards, their confor-
mance with interoperability and "best practices" agreements for privacy, and
the content of any privacy auditor's reports on their operations. In the final
analysis, though, Alice has essentially only herself to rely upon to protect her
exposure and disclosure privacy with respect to intended participants, whether
she is engaged in some operation with an intended target or revealing some
attribute data to an intended recipient.

*Labels 10 and 12.* For the remaining labels in this branch, the class of techniques available to Alice is defined by the existing legal infrastructure. In
particular, for Labels 10 and 12 (in which Alice wishes to limit her exposure
privacy with respect to unintended observers of her actions, and her disclosure
privacy with respect to unintended recipients of attribute data that she reveals),
government-initiated laws regarding the illegality of wiretapping assist Alice
to protect her privacy. This protection may be in the form of a deterrent (a
potential eavesdropper decides not to eavesdrop because of fear of the legal
consequences of getting caught), or may be after-the-fact recourse or retribution when Alice's personal information has been compromised in this way.

Labels 13–16. The legal infrastructure for privacy protection is significantly
more extensive for Labels 13–16 than it is for Labels 10 and 12. Legal mechanisms relevant to the holder of Alice's personal information may be classified
into government-initiated law and contractual obligations. Government-
initiated law governs or constrains a holder's handling of Alice's information
(essentially independently of Alice herself) through the use of privacy-related
laws, regulations, government-imposed guidelines, and so on (see, for exam-

(continued)

ple, Federal 1998; Organization 2013; Lainhart 2018). Contractual obligations, on the other hand, arise from explicit or implicit contracts negotiated
between Alice and the holder that define what the holder can do with Alice's
information (for example, when Alice gives her address information to a store
so that purchased items can subsequently be delivered); the legal infrastructure is brought into the picture only if a dispute or breach of contract occurs.
As with Labels 10 and 12, there may be an element of deterrence here, but the
primary protection offered to Alice is after-the-fact recourse and retribution.

However, there is still a significant role for PETs, even when a full legal infrastructure is in place. This is described by Adams (2006) in the following way.

The classification proposed in this paper makes it clear in particular that there
are areas on the societal side of the tree in which Alice has no real privacy
protection other than her own judgment. Furthermore, even for the areas in
which she has some legal protection, we note that in many cases of privacy
violation there may be no adequate reparation for Alice. Once her personal
information has been used or disseminated inappropriately by a holder, it may
be that Alice cannot be sufficiently compensated for the damages suffered.
The symmetry of the tree in this classification suggests the possibility that a
deficiency in one area may be bolstered by a technique designed to achieve
the same ultimate goal in the other half of the tree. Thus, for example, if Alice
desires disclosure privacy with respect to the eavesdropping of her attributes
by unintended recipients, she can rely not only on the deterrence and after-
the-fact protection of relevant wiretap laws (Label 12), but also on a collection
of technical mechanisms that fit within the corresponding technological
branch (*i.e.*, Label 4). Note that within legal discourse a distinction is drawn
between preventative approaches and remedial ones: tort provides remedy
post-injury while other legal mechanisms, such as injunction, can be used
preventatively. However, in practice, no legal approach is actually preventative. An injunction essentially says, "You are forbidden to do $X$, and if you do
$X$ these bad things will happen to you." But typically nothing physically prevents you from doing $X$ if you are willing to accept the consequences, and so
reliance must then be made on remedial approaches. Technical mechanisms,
on the other hand, are more often preventative in practice: if you do not know
the encryption key, for example, you are quite effectively prevented from seeing data that has been encrypted.

The privacy tree can therefore be a very useful tool for determining which PETs
are most complementary with which legal protections so that the different

techniques can be used together to achieve a particular privacy goal for Alice or for a holder of her information.

## 9.3   In Conjunction with Other Technologies

The privacy tree can also help Alice to determine and achieve privacy goals when she uses other types of technologies (such as communications technologies, computing technologies, storage technologies, and so on). To illustrate this, we look briefly at two technologies that have received widespread attention in recent years: *software defined networking*; and *machine learning*.

### 9.3.1   Software Defined Networking (SDN)

*Software Defined Networking* (SDN) is an approach to network architecture that focuses on decoupling network control (such as routing policies and management functions) from basic network operation (such as forwarding of data packets); see, for example (Benzekki et al. 2017). This concept originated with experiments to separate the control plane and the data plane in public switched telephone networks (PSTNs) in the mid-1990s, but has evolved significantly in both functionality and sophistication since that time.

The *SDN Controller* is a logically-centralized (and perhaps also physically-centralized) entity that has a global view of the network and so can make globally-optimized routing and management decisions. This controller is directly programmable, and so the network components and resources can be programmatically configured as required (quickly, easily, and on-demand).

This programmatic capability is very useful for meeting the needs of *changing traffic patterns* (not client-server, but rather peer-to-peer, with the incorporation of bring-your-own-device (BYOD) as well), *cloud services* (e.g., access to applications, infrastructure, and IT resources whenever needed), and *big data* (with constantly changing network capacity requirements).

Although SDN was primarily designed for efficiency and flexibility in network management and operation, it can also be quite useful in providing some important security services. For example, the SDN architecture can expedite discovery and mitigation of DDoS attacks, as well as botnet and worm propagation: its global view of the network allows collection of full network statistics, which can greatly facilitate anomaly detection. As another example, SDN can be used to implement a "moving target defense" (MTD) by periodically hiding or changing key properties of the component machines (such as assigning virtual IP addresses to hosts, or simulating open/closed ports on random servers) to make a network much more difficult to attack.

Given that the SDN architecture can be used to provide some *security* services, it is worth reflecting on the possibility of *privacy* in SDN. Can privacy be achieved? If so, what kind of privacy, and how can it be accomplished?

Note that anonymity/pseudonymity in network communications can happen at the application layer (e.g., hiding the application-level identity of the user) and at the network layer (e.g., hiding the IP and MAC addresses of the user's machine). It is well known that for true anonymity/pseudonymity (i.e., from the intended recipient as well as from all observers), privacy must be provided at both layers: it doesn't help to hide Alice's name if her IP address is visible in the transmitted data packets, and it doesn't help to hide her IP address in the packets if her name is visible in the transaction messages.

What can be achieved in SDN? Clearly, application-layer protection happens at the application level, and so it must be implemented within the nodes/machines/ devices where the application resides. Therefore, *Digital Credentials*, *anonymous e-voting protocols*, *anonymous payment mechanisms*, and so on (which are implemented at the application layer), can be used as effectively with SDN as with traditional (non-SDN) networks.

On the other hand, by definition, the *SDN Controller* has a global view of the network and is responsible for all routing decisions. Such an architecture is incompatible with *onion routing*, *mix networks*, and similar technologies that must allow user nodes to choose their own paths through the network (e.g., via *routing onions* or randomly-selected sequences of *mixes*). This means that such technologies cannot be used to provide anonymity/pseudonymity protection at the network layer in SDN.

An alternative technology that might seem promising for achieving network-layer privacy is *IPsec in tunnel mode*. This can be used to hide the actual originator and actual recipient of each IP packet (by encapsulating the entire packet in the body of an outer IP packet with a different sender and receiver; see Chap. 5, Sect. 5.1). However, *tunnel mode* can only work if there are nodes in the SDN network that are able to act as gateways to subnetworks which are not in the view of the *SDN Controller* (i.e., subnetworks where IP packet routing is done without the knowledge of the *SDN Controller*); such nodes can then be endpoints for *IPsec tunnel mode* connections.

In real deployments, it is not clear whether these "opaque" subnetworks are a possible (or even an allowable) SDN configuration. (After all, the whole point of the *SDN Controller* is to have a centralized global view of every node in the network!) If this configuration is not allowed, or simply is not used in practice, then there are two options:

- Anonymous/pseudonymous communication is not possible in an SDN architecture (because we can get anonymity/pseudonymity at the application layer but not at the network layer); or

- The *SDN Controller* must be a completely trusted entity with respect to privacy (it will know all senders and receivers since it will see statistics on the activities of every node) and every process in the network must be prevented from observ-

ing both the incoming and outgoing packets of the nodes that initiate and termi-
nate any tunnel connection. (Note that it would be essentially impossible to
guarantee both these conditions in public networks of practical size.)

Where does this leave us with respect to privacy in SDN? From the above discussion we see that completely hiding Alice's *identity* may not be possible in
SDN. However, by using the privacy tree, we discover that hiding Alice's *identity* is
only one of several potential privacy goals. If hiding her *identity* (i.e., obtaining
anonymity/pseudonymity) is not realistically achievable in SDN, Alice can instead
choose to hide her *actions* or her *attributes*, and she can choose to hide these from
intended or unintended observers and recipients. For these other privacy goals, several PETs (including *IPsec in transport mode*, SSL/TLS, *Secure Shell* (SSH), and
many others) may be used, as appropriate.

Thus, with SDN – as with virtually any architecture or technology – it is essential
to investigate carefully (in light of the privacy tree) to see which specific privacy
goals can be achieved. Once this exercise has been completed, users of the technology can decide which of the achievable privacy goals are most important to them
and (again with the aid of the privacy tree) choose the right PETs to deliver the
desired goals.

## 9.3.2  Machine Learning (ML)

*Machine Learning* (ML) – generally considered to be a branch or subfield of
*Artificial Intelligence* (AI) – is the study of computer algorithms that are able to
improve in a fully automated way (i.e., without human assistance). Machine learning algorithms typically build a *model* based on sample data (*training data* followed
by *evaluation/validation data*). The algorithms "learn" from experience and from
the data: they adaptively improve their performance so that the predictions or decisions output by the model become more accurate, or more useful, over time. The
trained model is then used to make predictions or decisions on *new data* that has not
been seen previously. (Note that the model may occasionally need to be retrained
(either automatically or at the decision of the ML expert) to accommodate changes
in the environment that violate the model's current assumptions ("*concept drift*")
and thus degrade model performance.)

Many different techniques and approaches for ML have been explored over the
six decades since the term "machine learning" was originally coined (by Arthur
Samuel in (1959)), but machine learning algorithms are used today in a wide variety
of applications, from anatomy, to banking, to credit card fraud detection, to insurance, to medical diagnosis, to natural language understanding, to sentiment analysis, to user behaviour analytics (just to name a few). Perhaps most relevant to the
scope of this present Chapter is the fact that in a large number of these applications,
the *training data* is, or at least includes, sensitive personal information of the users
that contributed it.

Given that sensitive data is often used in the training of ML models, there has been a growing interest in understanding and protecting user privacy in the context of machine learning. Note that this interest is not purely academic, but is also driven by governmental bodies: the *General Data Protection Regulation* (GDPR) in Europe mandates that projects involving machine learning on personal data must perform a formal *Data Protection Impact Assessment* (DPIA); furthermore, both the *Information Commissioner's Office* in the UK and the *National Institute of Standards and Technology* (NIST) in the US strongly recommend that organizations account for risks to data from machine learning models and comply with data protection regulations (Murakonda and Shokri 2020).

A number of researchers (see, for example, Carlini et al. 2019; Nasr et al. 2019; Shokri and Shmatikov 2015; Shokri et al. 2017; Song et al. 2017) have studied the privacy implications of machine learning, particularly with respect to so-called *membership inference attacks* in which an attacker learns about the presence of particular data in the training set simply by observing the current state of the ML model and/or the outputs of the ML algorithm. It has been found that ML models often incorporate – and sometimes explicitly encode – specific information about some portions of their training data (in fact, it appears that this may be necessary for accurate learning; see (Feldman 2020)). This tends to be more often the case for models with high *capacity*, such as *deep neural networks* but, notably, such models are currently the dominant approach in machine learning work. The existence of particular training data components in the model can be observed in two ways (Murakonda and Shokri 2020).

– *In the parameters of the model.* These parameters store statistically correlated information about specific training data records. Therefore, in a *white-box* setting in which an attacker is able to observe the model parameters, detailed information about certain training set inputs may be learned. (Note that the *white-box* setting is a realistic scenario when an ML model is outsourced to a local company server, for example, that may not be trusted to properly hide its executing software from all observers.)
– *In the predictions or decisions of the model.* These model outputs may display different behaviour on training data than on new data. Therefore, in a *black-box* setting in which an attacker is able to observe only the outputs of the ML algorithm, information about certain training set inputs may be learned. (Note that the *black-box* setting is a realistic scenario when machine learning is offered as a cloud-hosted service by companies such as Amazon, Google, and Microsoft.)

Clearly, it is essential to protect the training data (particularly when this data contains sensitive personal information). An attacker should not be able to infer specific values in the training dataset through observation of the ML model or the ML outputs.

The question, then, is *what can be done to help protect privacy in machine learning applications?* As with *Software Defined Networking* (SDN) in Sect. 9.3.1, we begin with the privacy tree in order to clarify the privacy goals that can be achieved. ML has a training dataset that contains personal information, and so this technology is about *attributes* of Alice, rather than *actions* of Alice. Therefore, we can ignore the portion of the tree that deals with **exposure** and focus instead on the portion that deals with **disclosure**. Furthermore, the sensitive information in this environment is not Alice's identity: what the attacker tries to learn from observing the model or the outputs is data associated with Alice, not Alice's name. The attacker does not want to know whether Alice herself was part of the training set; we can assume that the attacker already knows that she participated in the set of initial users by some external means. Rather, the attacker wants to learn particular information related to Alice: her health condition, or credit card information, or insurance data. Thus, the privacy tree narrows our investigation to techniques that limit **disclosure** by hiding the *attribute*; this is the privacy goal that we seek to achieve in a machine learning application.

Having isolated the privacy goal to be achieved, we can once again use the privacy tree to identify some potential technologies that may be helpful; that is, PETs that perform the transformation $\tau_p(\bar{a})$ (using the notation from Sect. 9.1 above), as well as security technologies that can support this transformation. In the *membership inference attack* that is the focus of this discussion, the attacker wishes to learn something about specific data in the training set. Here, a third party has obtained data from multiple participants and created a training set for the purpose of training the ML model. Thus, the third party is the holder of Alice's information, and this holder would like to use this information while hiding it from intended observers of this use (i.e., those who will see the ML model and outputs in a *white-box* setting and those who will see only the ML outputs in a *black-box* setting). In addition, this holder might retain the training dataset for some period of time and would like to prevent dissemination of this data to unintended recipients.

Therefore, we focus on Labels 5 and 8 from the privacy tree. Label 8 suggests encryption technology for the stored training data, along with traditional computer security techniques such as firewalls, antivirus and anti-spyware software, intrusion detection systems, access control technology, and privacy policy enforcement architectures. Although important (and historically easy to get wrong!), the techniques in Label 8 are familiar and conceptually relatively straightforward. Label 5, on the other hand, suggests the use of inference control techniques similar to those that might be used in a database context. Inference control is a notoriously difficult problem to solve because there are typically so many unknown and unforeseen ways in which an attacker might infer information from a collection of data (including using unanticipated external sources of data) and a collection of queries on that data. The difference in the ML context is that the attacker does not see the training data and cannot make queries on it; instead the attacker tries to make inferences based on observed use of the training data by the ML model.

To minimize the risk of an attacker learning specific values in a dataset through inference, I suggest that the various approaches that are available can be put into two general categories: change the data; and change how the data is used (i.e., change what is done with the data).

– *Change the data.* Changing the data encompasses a set of PETs techniques that are generic (in the sense that they can be applied in many database contexts). These techniques fall into two categories.

  • Modify the *quantity* of data in order to achieve privacy goals without unduly reducing ML output accuracy:

    • Diminish the data: remove errors, obvious outliers, extreme values, or excessively frequent values that may inaccurately bias the overall sample statistics; or
    • Augment the data: collect additional data from other users, or add simulated data to create an overall sample that is more representative of a larger population or that has a more even distribution of statistics (this is analogous to the technique of adding "dummy traffic" in networks to hide sensitive communications).

  • Modify the *quality* of data in order to achieve privacy goals without unduly reducing ML output accuracy:

    • Perturb the data: add random noise to some or all of the data items in such a way that individual data values are unreliable, but statistics across the overall sample are correct; or
    • Dissociate the data from individual user values: use $\varepsilon$-*differential privacy* techniques (see Chap. 7, Sect. 7.3) to formally guarantee that the probability of a given ML output when Alice's data is in the training set is within a multiplicative factor $\varepsilon$ of the probability that the same ML output would be produced if Alice's data was not in the training set, and choose an $\varepsilon$ such that this will be true over all the users that submitted training data.

– *Change how the data is used.* Techniques in this category are not generic, but rather are specific to the particular application under consideration. For the case of machine learning, there are two categories of changes that can be made to the ML model.

  • Modify the *computation* on data in order to achieve privacy goals without unduly reducing ML output accuracy:

    • Adjust weights used in the ML model (for example, in the neurons and edges of an artificial neural network) so that variations in the data have less influence on the computed ML output; or
    • Assign weights to specific data values in the training set so that outliers in the data have less influence on the computed ML output.

  • Modify the *interpretation* of data in order to achieve privacy goals without unduly reducing ML output accuracy:

    • Re-regularize the ML algorithm. In machine learning, *regularization* is a method to vary the complexity of the ML model: a parameter $\alpha$ fine-tunes the coefficients of a function that is used to fit the training data in a regression computation. If the coefficients are reduced too much, the function will behave approximately like a polynomial of significantly smaller degree (ultimately a straight line), resulting in severe underfitting of the data and low accuracy in predictions on any new data. If the coefficients are increased too much, the function will behave like a polynomial of very high degree, resulting in severe overfitting of the data and low accuracy in predictions on new data that differs in any way from the training data. Many regression techniques exist in the literature. *Re-regularization* involves trying different α values for a given regression technique and/or trying different regression techniques in order to construct an ML model that less-closely mirrors the training data while producing acceptably accurate predictions on new data. (Additional discussion on regression and its use in ML regularization can be found, for example, in (Quora 2020) and (Jain 2016).)

For each of the above PET techniques (diminishing data, augmenting data, perturbing data, dissociating data, adjusting model weights, assigning data weights, and re-regularization), there are parameters that can be adjusted. Furthermore, it may be possible to use several of these techniques simultaneously. Extensive experimentation can be done to find suitable values of parameters and an appropriate combination of techniques for a given implementation. The objective is to minimize the risk of a *membership inference attack* while achieving an acceptable level of quality (accuracy, usefulness) in the ML outputs.

As we saw with SDN in Sect. 9.3.1, the privacy tree is helpful in determining which specific privacy goal can be achieved in ML. In addition, the privacy tree can guide us to an applicable collection of PETs to deliver this desired goal.

## 9.4 Summary

This chapter has looked at places and ways in which the privacy tree can be used in real-world environments. It explored the use of PETs in conjunction with other security technologies such as encryption, antivirus software, cookie management, firewalls, intrusion detection systems, access control tools, and privacy policy enforcement architectures. It also looked at the use of PETs in conjunction with the legal infrastructure, particularly in the context of adding preventative techniques to support existing remedial measures. Finally, two examples were given illustrating the use of the privacy tree in conjunction with other types of technologies: *software defined networking* and *machine learning*.

The privacy tree is helpful in determining the privacy goals that can be achieved (as well as those that cannot be achieved) in a given technology or application. Having established the achievable privacy goals, the privacy tree can then help to identify the specific class of PETs (and even suggest specific existing PETs) that can be used to reach those goals. Thus, this tree gives Alice a mechanism to actually attain the privacy she desires much faster than trial-and-error guesswork through the vast array of privacy enhancing technologies scattered across the Internet and the academic literature.

The following chapter will conclude this book by discussing the path forward from where we have now arrived in our PETs journey.

**Questions for Personal Reflection and/or Group Discussion**

1. For each of the *machine learning* PET techniques described in Sect. 9.3.2 (diminishing data, augmenting data, perturbing data, dissociating data, adjusting model weights, assigning data weights, and re-regularization), what are the benefits and drawbacks of using that particular technique? How does improving privacy using that technique affect the accuracy and utility of the ML model outputs? Does using that technique have computational implications?
2. Section 9.3 discussed using the *privacy tree* in conjunction with *software defined networking* (SDN) and *machine learning* (ML). Choose any other technology with which you are familiar and perform a similar analysis. Are you able to identify specific privacy goals for that technology? Can you use the *privacy tree* to select particular types of PETs that would be helpful in achieving those goals? In what ways is the *privacy tree* approach deficient or limited, and what can you do to address this?

# References

C. Adams, A Classification for Privacy Techniques. Univ. Ottawa Law Technol. J. **3**(1) (2006)

D. Asonov, Private information retrieval: An overview and current trends. *Proceedings of the ECDPvA Workshop*, Informatik 2001, Vienna, Austria, (2001, September)

K. Benzekki, A. El Fergougui, A. Elbelrhiti Elalaoui, Software-defined networking (SDN): A survey. Sec. Commun. Networks **9**(18), 5803–5833 (2017)

O. Berthold, H. Federrath, and S. Köpsell, Web MIXes: A system for anonymous and unobservable internet access. in *Designing privacy enhancing technologies*, Springer-Verlag, LNCS 2009, pp. 115–129, (2001)

N. Carlini, C. Liu, Ú. Erlingsson, J. Kos, and D. Song, The secret sharer: Evaluating and testing unintended memorization in neural networks. *USENIX Security Symposium*, pp. 267–284 (2019)

Y.-C. Chang and C.-J. Lu, Oblivious polynomial evaluation and oblivious neural learning. *Advances in Cryptology— Proceedings of Asiacrypt*, pp. 369–384 (2001, 9–13 December)

D. Chaum, Untraceable electronic mail, return addresses, and digital pseudonyms. Commun. ACM **24**(2) (1981)

D. Denning, *Cryptography and data security*. Addison-Wesley, (1982). (See Chapter 6, "Inference Controls")

W. Du and Z. Zhan, Using randomized response techniques for privacy-preserving data mining. *Proceedings of the Ninth ACM SIGKDD International Conference on Knowledge Discovery and Data Mining*, 6pp, (2003, 24–27 August)

Y. Elovici, B. Shapira, A. Maschiach, A new privacy model for hiding group interests while accessing the web. ACM Workshop Privacy Electron. Soc., 63–70 (2002)

Federal: Federal Trade Commission, *Children's Online Privacy Protection Act*, 15 U.S.C. 6501-6506, Pub. L. No. 105-277, Div. C, Title XIII, 112 Stat. 2681-2728, (1998)

V. Feldman, Does learning require memorization? A short tale about a long tail. *Proceedings of the 52nd Annual ACM SIGACT Symposium on Theory of Computing*, Chicago, IL, USA, pp. 954–959, (2020, 22–26 June)

A. Jain, A complete tutorial on ridge and lasso regression in python. *Analytics Vidhya* (2016, 28 January)

S. Kumar Murakonda and R. Shokri, ML privacy meter: Aiding regulatory compliance by quantifying the privacy risks of machine learning. *Privacy Enhancing Technologies Symposium*, HotPETs session (2020)

J. Lainhart, Cybersecurity and privacy enhancements. *American Institute of Certified Public Accountants, issue brief* (2018, 4 June)

M. Nasr, R. Shokri, A. Houmansadr, Comprehensive privacy analysis of deep learning: Passive and active white-box inference attacks against centralized and federated learning. IEEE Symp. Sec. Privacy, 1022–1036 (2019)

Office: Office of the Information and Privacy Commissioner of Ontario and Office of the Federal Privacy Commissioner of Australia, Web Seals: A Review of Online Privacy Programs. *22nd International Conference on Privacy and Personal Data Protection* (2000, September)

Organization: Organization for Economic Co-operation and Development (OECD), OECD Privacy Framework (which includes Guidelines on the Protection of Privacy and Transborder Flows of Personal Data), *OECD Publications Service* (2013)

H. Polat and W. Du, Privacy-preserving collaborative filtering using randomized pertubation techniques. *Proceedings of the third IEEE international conference on data mining*, pp. 625–628, (2003, 12–22 November)

Quora, *What is regularization in machine learning?* (2020)

M.G. Reed, P.F. Syverson, D.M. Goldschlag, Anonymous connections and onion routing. IEEE J. Selected Areas Commun. **16**(4), 482–494 (1998)

M.K. Reiter, A.D. Rubin, Crowds: Anonymity for web transactions. ACM Trans. Inf. Syst. Secur. **1**(1), 66–92 (1998)

A. Samuel, Some studies in machine learning using the game of checkers. IBM J. Res. Dev. **3**(3), 71–105 (July 1959)

R. Shokri, V. Shmatikov, Privacy-preserving deep learning, in *Proceedings of the 22nd ACM conference on computer and communications security*, (2015), pp. 1310–1321

R. Shokri, M. Stronati, C. Song, V. Shmatikov, Membership inference attacks against machine learning models. IEEE Symp. Sec. Privacy, 3–18 (2017)

C. Song, T. Ristenpart, V. Shmatikov, Machine learning models that remember too much, in *Proceedings of the ACM conference on computer and communications security*, (2017), pp. 587–601

L. Sweeney, Replacing Personally-Identifying Information in Medical Records, the Scrub System, in *American medical informatics association proceedings, journal of the american medical informatics association*, ed. by J. Cimino, (Hanley & Belfus, Inc, 1996), pp. 333–337

L. Sweeney, *K*-anonymity: A model for protecting privacy. Int. J. Uncertainty Fuzziness Knowledge-based Syst. **10**(5), 557–570 (2002)

Wikipedia, *Anonymizer (company)* (2020, 7 September)

# Chapter 10
# The Path Forward

**Abstract** This chapter briefly summarizes the previous nine chapters and then contemplates what an appropriate response might be to the information that has been presented. Specifically, it suggests that the first step is to make some decisions (How much privacy do you want? What are you willing to "pay" or to give up in order to attain that level of privacy?). The second step is to take some concrete actions to protect your privacy, and four classes of actions that can be taken by anyone are outlined.

**Keywords** The cost of privacy · Defense-in-depth · Privacy awareness · Data ownership · Privacy research

The previous nine chapters of this book have presented a quick introduction to the world of *privacy enhancing technologies*, PETs. We began in Chap. 1 with a discussion of privacy and gave some rationale for why PETs exist and why they are important. We gave the working definition of "privacy" that is typically used in the context of PETs (and that we assume throughout this book) – *an entity's ability to control how, when, and to what extent personal information about it is communicated to others* – and listed some of the threats to privacy that increasingly occur in our online connected world. Finally, we suggested that there has been a shift in recent years, from mere privacy threats to a literal battle for supremacy over personal data, and we outlined some of the progressively invasive ways that this could affect any single individual. We argued that we are playing hide-and-seek with known and unknown adversaries who want to acquire our personal data, and that the stakes are high because any failure to properly hide the data on our part can have wide-reaching, long-lasting, negative consequences for us.

In Chap. 2 we pointed out that numerous PETs have been proposed, implemented, and deployed over the past four decades. While in some ways this is a very good thing, in practice it can lead to difficulties for someone that wants to use a PET to protect his or her privacy. How can PETs usefully be compared? How can their similarities and differences be assessed? What specific aspect of privacy is each one trying to protect? In short, if you want to use a PET, how can you find the "right tool

© The Editor(s) (if applicable) and The Author(s), under exclusive license
to Springer Nature Switzerland AG 2021
C. Adams, *Introduction to Privacy Enhancing Technologies*,
https://doi.org/10.1007/978-3-030-81043-6_10

for the job"? This chapter discussed the notion of the *privacy tree*, a structured way to classify PETs for the purpose of enabling exactly this kind of comparison and analysis. The tree we adopted for this book suggests two high-level concepts: *exposure* and *disclosure*. Your activities are *exposed* if an observer can link your *identity* to *actions* that you are performing, and your information is *disclosed* if an observer can link your *identity* to some *attributes* about you. PETs achieve privacy by breaking these linkages. Thus, *exposure* can be limited by hiding your *identity*, or hiding your *actions*, or hiding both. Similarly, disclosure can be limited by hiding your *identity*, or hiding your *attributes*, or hiding both. The *privacy tree*, therefore, has six possible leaves (see Fig. 2.3 in Chap. 2).

Chapter 3 examined the first of these leaves, focusing on PETs that protect an individual's *identity*, while leaving the individual's *actions* open to observation by others. This category includes the first PET published in the academic literature: the *mix network* proposed by Chaum. It also includes the *anonymous remailers* (popularized by Helsingius' remailer *anon.penet.fi*) and the *onion routing network* proposed by Goldschlag, Reed, and Syverson. In all these technologies, observers can clearly see that messages are being transported around the network (*actions*), but the senders of these messages (*identities*) are effectively hidden. This chapter discussed the design of these three PETs and presented some strengths and weaknesses of each.

Chapter 4 considered the opposite approach: hiding the *actions* while leaving the *identity* open to observation. Example PETs in this category include *transport layer security* (the widely-used SSL/TLS protocol), *network layer security* (the *IPsec protocol* using what is known as *transport mode*), and the *private information retrieval* (PIR) proposal of Chor et al. In these technologies, observers can see who is talking to whom, or who is making a database query (*identity*), but the content of the conversation or query (*action*) is effectively hidden. This chapter presented these PETs in some detail.

The final leaf in the *exposure* category encompasses PETs that hide both the *identity* and the *actions*. Chapter 5 looked at two example PETs in this leaf: the *IPsec protocol* (this time using a configuration known as *tunnel mode*) and the *Off-the-Record* (OTR) Messaging protocol of Borisov, Goldberg, and Brewer. As explained in this chapter, rather than hiding *identity* using some kind of anonymity technique (as is done in other PETs), OTR proposes to "hide" the *identity* by providing *plausible deniability* ("*you can't prove that I sent this message because literally anyone could have sent it!*"). This is a relatively unique approach to *identity* hiding, but nevertheless allows OTR to fit comfortably in this leaf of the *privacy tree*.

The next three chapters consider the category of *disclosure*. Chapter 6 discusses PETs that limit *disclosure* by hiding the *identity*, even though the *attributes* can be observed by others. The proposal of *k-anonymity* by Samarati and Sweeney does this in a database context: techniques are applied to modify the data in such a way that, for any given collection of *attributes* queried, there are at least $k$ records that match the query (thus, the individuals to whom those records belong are hidden in an *anonymity set* of size $k$). *Credential systems*, on the other hand (as proposed by

Brands and others), are designed for online transaction environments: an individual can release selected *attributes* to a verifier while keeping other *attributes* (particularly including his or her *identity*) unconditionally hidden.

Chapter 7, analogously to Chap. 4, considered the opposite approach: hiding the *attributes* while leaving the *identity* open to observation. The *Ciphertext Policy Attribute-Based Encryption* (CP-ABE) proposal of Bethencourt, Sahai, and Waters encrypts arbitrary data in such a way that only an individual with the correct *attributes* will be able to decrypt it. In this proposal, the *identity* is not protected in any way, but the *attributes* are a part of the individual's *private key* (and are therefore hidden from all observers). In Yao's proposal for *multi-party computation*, again the *identities* of the individuals involved in a joint computation are not protected, but each party's data set (*attribute data*) is kept hidden from all others. Lastly, the ε-*differential privacy* proposal of Dwork et al. ensures that observers of a database query result cannot tell whether a specific individual's data (*attribute*) was included in the computation of the result, even if it is known that this individual (*identity*) may have a record in the database.

As with Chaps. 5 and 8 focuses on the last leaf in the *disclosure* category, which encompasses PETs that hide both the *identity* and the *attributes*. Four example PETs are described in this chapter: the *Hippocratic Database* (HDB) proposal of Agrawal et al.; the *Platform for Privacy Preferences* (P3P) proposal of Cranor et al.; the *Architecture for Privacy Enforcement using XML* (APEX) proposal of Adams and Barbieri; and the *Digital Credentials* proposal of Brands (using a technique in which only *properties of attributes*, rather than explicit *attribute values*, are shown to the verifier). In all these technologies, both *identities* and *attributes* are hidden from unintended observers of database queries and online transactions.

Finally, Chap. 9 took the framework of the *privacy tree*, and the discussion of various PETs that fit into the six leaves of this tree, and examined how to apply this knowledge in real-world situations. We looked at the use of PETs in conjunction with other security technologies to achieve privacy in database or communication network environments. We also considered how PETs can complement the legal infrastructure to create a higher level of privacy protection for individuals. Perhaps most importantly, we showed how an individual can use the *privacy tree* to clarify possible privacy goals when using a given technology of a different kind (i.e., not specifically a security technology), and to highlight possible PETs that can be used to achieve those goals. As concrete examples to illustrate this process, we explored *software defined networking* (SDN) and *machine learning* (ML), discovering how the *privacy tree* can be very helpful in navigating the constraints and possibilities in both these environments.

OK, so we have completed an introduction to the privacy tree and to PETs. What comes next? What is the path forward from here? What, specifically, should you do now? I suggest that the first step is for you to make some decisions. Once that has been completed, the next step is for you to take some actions.

## 10.1   The First Step: Decisions

Privacy, like security, is not something that you can suddenly have by "flipping a switch", or by installing an app (no matter what the vendor of the app might promise!). It is something that requires planning. It is something that requires a detailed understanding of where you are and where you want to be. Furthermore, it requires an explicit roadmap of how you will get to where you want to be. In short, you need to look at your life, your environment, your situation, and make some decisions.

### 10.1.1   Hide-and-Seek (Revisited)

As discussed in Chap. 1, this is hide-and-seek, but it is not a game. The stakes are high. Many, many entities – of every kind and at every level – are looking for your personal data. If you want to hide your data, it will cost you in some way: you may need to do some research, make some choices, use some software that is less "mainstream", install/configure some special tools and applications, forego some "perks", put up with some inconvenience, and avoid some social media platforms and online experiences.

The bottom line is that you will inevitably need to give up something in order to have a more private life. *Ultimately, this means that you need to decide what your privacy is worth to you.* What are you willing to sacrifice in order to have privacy? Is a bit of extra convenience (in the form of saving a few mouse clicks or keyboard taps) really a fair trade for giving your personal information to a website, or will you refuse that offer of convenience? Is a small discount on today's purchase really a reasonable recompense for negative consequences that may persist for some time, or will you decline that offer of a discount?

PETs are a critical and essential piece of the solution but, at the end of the day, protecting personal data requires a lifestyle change. We as a society need to stop glossing over the fact that living our lives in public has privacy ramifications. You personally need to decide whether you are willing to make changes in your online and offline behaviour so that you can reduce the risk of these ramifications.

Lifestyle changes are never easy. They may demand real effort, real time, and real money. But long gone are the days when privacy was a default that came for free. Now, you need to make concrete decisions about how important privacy is to you, and concrete decisions about what you are willing to do to protect it.

## 10.1.2   Defense-in-Depth

Think of a scenario in which a company has important financial information in a particular spreadsheet. Perhaps it is employee salary data, or profit/loss details for each department and product, or economic forecasts regarding a merger that is being considered. Regardless of the scenario, this is company-sensitive information that must be properly protected. The company will almost certainly encrypt this spreadsheet before storing it in the database.

However, in the vast majority of real-world environments, the company will not just encrypt the sensitive record in the database, but will also put access controls in place for the entire database, keep (protected) audit logs of all events that occur across the database server operating system, install intrusion-detection and anti-virus software throughout all computers and networks on-site, configure at least one perimeter firewall, implement security training for all employees, enforce multi-factor authentication for all login and application use activity, purchase insurance against data breaches/loss, and take any other measures that it deems are relevant and useful. This is generally known in the security industry as "defense-in-depth". The idea is that you don't pin all your hopes on a single protection mechanism, but rather use as many protections as you can to minimize the risk of breach as much as possible.

An analogous practice that may have merit in the PETs world is "privacy-in-depth". This is the use of multiple PETs (not just one PET) to achieve a specific desired privacy goal. Thus, instead of just using a single PET to hide your identity, consider the use of one PET to hide your identity, a second PET to hide your attributes, and a third PET to hide both your identity and your attributes. Think about your privacy requirements and goals, and make decisions about when "privacy-in-depth" is both necessary and achievable. Evaluate the costs and benefits of combining "privacy-in-depth" with the security notion of "defense-in-depth" to attain the best protection possible. (As one example of this, see (Willems 2021) for a proposal of an anonymous shopping platform. In this architecture a purchase transaction involves multiple entities: the identity is hidden from some; the data is hidden from others; and both the identity and the data are hidden from still others. PETs and security mechanisms are combined in such a way that collusion is made difficult; thus, no single entity learns both the shopper and the items purchased.)

The focus in this first step is on assessing, appraising, and deciding. How much privacy do you want? What is that amount of privacy worth to you? What are you willing to "pay" (i.e., give up) so that you can attain that level of privacy? What concessions are you willing to make? In what ways are you willing to change your lifestyle or your behaviour? What will you decide to do, or not do, to use, or not use, in order to protect your personal data?

## 10.2   The Next Step: Actions

Having decided that your privacy is something that you want to protect, the next step is to take some concrete actions. But where do you begin? How can you know what you should do as an initial action, then as a second action, then as a third, and so on?

I suggest that there are four classes of actions that can/should be taken. These classes represent increasing degrees of sophistication with respect to privacy, and therefore will require increasing dedication and effort on your part. However, in the first step (above), you have already decided what privacy is worth to you and what you are willing to "pay" to attain a specific amount of privacy. These are the classes of actions you can take to move toward your desired privacy level.

1. The first class of actions you should take has to do with becoming *knowledgeable about your data*. Make yourself <u>aware</u> of what data is personal/private. Think about the implications of what someone else might learn from this data, or do with this data.

   [As one example, Stephen Baker (2008) talks about grocery store loyalty cards and the fact that the store thereby has a record of your grocery purchases for an extended period of time. This may sound inconsequential on the surface, but what could someone learn from looking at nothing at all but your grocery purchases over the course of a year or two? The number of people that live in the house (adults, children, approximate ages, and pets). When someone is sick (based on chicken soup and Tylenol purchases). When someone in the house might be dating (based on better shampoo, mouthwash, and teeth cleaning purchases). When the family is going camping (hot dogs, marshmallows). When you are having company or a party (and how often this happens, which can lead to suppositions about your personality type). Whether you consume a lot of "junk" food or alcohol (and might therefore be a bad health insurance risk). Whether you are susceptible to binges, fads, marketing campaigns, and sale items (which may imply something about your weaknesses or addictive tendencies). And so on, and so on, and so on. The privacy implications from a simple list of groceries can be surprisingly extensive!]

   Think about what it might mean if some personal data was combined with other data about you. Learn about what kinds of data are collected when you do specific activities online and think about which portions of this data are personal (or could become personal if combined or correlated with other information).

   *Increasing your awareness of your personal data is an essential first set of actions and is a necessary prerequisite to all the other classes of actions listed below.*

2. The second class of actions you should take has to do with becoming *knowledgeable about the potential risks*. It is tempting to just think, "Why should I care? Why would anyone be interested in me?", but this is selling yourself short. You need to <u>recognize</u> that your personal data is valuable to others: they want it, and they will expend considerable effort to obtain it. Recognize that if others acquire your personal data, there can be very real and very tangible consequences for you; recognize that you may suffer harm – both explicit and "invisible" (you

don't know why you didn't get the job or the promotion) – if your data is in the hands of others. Recognize, too, that the risk might *not* be that the company holding your data will deliberately misuse it or sell it; the risk is often that their database is breached by an external attacker (in which case your only line of defense is to not give the company your data in the first place; see the next classes 3 and 4). Learn about the possible harms that can occur to you, and perhaps also to your loved ones, when others have your data.

*Increasing your awareness of your potential risks is an essential second set of actions; this is what will motivate you to move to classes three and four.*

3. The third class of actions you should take has to do with constraining the ways in which you *deliberately give away your data.* You need to take explicit steps to <u>guard</u> your personal data. In particular, you need to make informed and conscious choices about the online activities you engage in, about the data you relinquish in exchange for goods and services, and about the data you freely give away in e-mails, on personal websites/blogs/vlogs, and on social media platforms. You have total control over what you put on your own website and Facebook wall; you have total control over what you say in your tweets and Instagram posts. If you are freely giving away personal information and it comes back to hurt you later, you have only yourself to blame.

Make it a habit to restrain yourself in the personal data you give away so that your future is less at risk. Consider using Tor to anonymize your online activities. Consider using browsers that help to protect your privacy by blocking cookies, preventing third-party trackers, and deleting data and search terms upon shutdown. Consider encrypting private data before transferring it to cloud storage. Be cautious about responding to surveys, opinion polls, and questionnaires, (particularly if they are requesting personal information). Be cautious about giving information to telephone and door-to-door solicitors. Be very cautious about transmitting sensitive information (especially passwords) over open Wi-Fi at public places such as coffee shops and airports. Choose to use HTTPS only (or *HTTPS Everywhere*; see https://www.eff.org/https-everywhere) for your Internet connections. Learn to look over TLS certificates when logging into banks, medical sites, and other important services (to confirm that you are really connecting where you want to connect). Have a firewall for your home network. Configure home appliances so that they are not reachable from the Internet, or at least are only reachable via your home firewall. Ensure that personal information is not visible to someone looking inside your parked car. Decide whether you really need remote starting for your car. Refrain from pairing your phone with a rental vehicle (or be sure to unpair it when you return the vehicle). Make use of a paper shredder to destroy your name, address, and other personal details in material that you throw away. And so on, and so on; there are many ways to be careful!

*Constraining the personal data you deliberately release (both online and in the physical world) is critical; it is something we can all do. Restricting what you freely give away is clearly easier than restricting what is taken from you (often without your knowledge or consent); therefore, this third class of actions is highly recommended for everyone.*

4. The fourth and final class of actions you should take has to do with constraining the ways in which you *unintentionally give away your data*. This is all about reclaiming <u>ownership</u> over your personal data. You need to assert authority when dealing with other entities: refuse to share what doesn't need to be shared. It is important to make specific privacy goals and to put protections in place to prevent your data from being taken from you without your knowledge: use PETs that are appropriate for the privacy goals that you have defined.

An essential component of this is to keep track of the status of the PETs you use: replace broken ones; upgrade to more secure versions as they become available. In this process of hide-and-seek, your adversary is continually trying to find ways to acquire your data. PETs are wonderful tools but, just as with the security field, at every conference and in every new journal issue there are proposals for new PETs and descriptions of weaknesses found with existing ones. It is essential to monitor this because if you are inadvertently using a broken PET (or even one that displays vulnerabilities only in the specific circumstances under which you happen to be using it), your adversary will be able to circumvent your protection.

Tracking the numerous PETs-relevant conferences and journals requires effort: it takes work to keep on top of the latest research results because there are so many every year. However, it need not be prohibitively laborious; even if you follow only one conference or online discussion group, you are likely to find out about the most important developments in this field from the top researchers that participate in that forum. In any case, if you are serious about protecting your privacy, it is imperative that you know which PETs (and which versions of PETs) are currently suitable for use. As we mentioned in Sect. 10.1.2, "privacy-in-depth" is an important practice that can help to keep you protected until you find out about, and replace, one of your chosen PETs that is no longer sufficiently strong.

*Constraining the personal data that you unintentionally release is the most sophisticated (and thus the most complex and difficult) class of actions that you can take. However, these actions are the ones that will likely have the most impact in terms of reducing your risk of privacy breach and consequences.*

Four classes of actions, with increasing levels of sophistication, may sound a bit daunting. The last one, especially, may seem like far more effort than you are willing to spend *("Hey, I wouldn't mind a little privacy, but reading dry academic papers and attending technical research conferences is <u>not</u> what I signed up for!")*. This is completely understandable. Nevertheless, it is vital to keep in mind that <u>minimal effort is still better than nothing</u>: any action you can take to make it a bit harder for the adversary to obtain your data means that the adversary might decide to leave you alone. Some adversaries are simply looking for an easy target and anything that requires them to make additional effort will be an effective deterrent, so just do whatever you can. On the other hand, it is also essential to remember that, exactly as with security, <u>maximal effort is not a guarantee</u>: the possibility always exists that, despite everything, some little detail has been missed or some particular assumption did not turn out to be true in your specific situation. Even after tremendous effort on your part, a determined adversary might still find a way to get your data. This is why "privacy-in-depth" should be used in tandem with security's "defense-in-depth": this combination greatly diminishes the adversary's probability of success.

## 10.3  Summary

Although this book has covered much ground, it is important to recognize that this is _not_ (nor was it intended to be) a state-of-the-art survey of the field of privacy enhancing technologies. Furthermore, it is _not_ (nor was it intended to be) a comprehensive in-depth review of any specific PETs. Rather, the goal of this book is to present a framework for understanding PETs (the *privacy tree*), and to provide a relatively high-level introduction to some example PETs in order to illustrate the use and value of this framework. The objective is to describe an approach that facilitates understanding, analysis, comparison, and contrast in the world of PETs.

A second (though no less important!) goal is to get you, the reader, intrigued and excited about PETs! This book was written to convince you that privacy is valuable, that it is in peril, and that there are tools that can help you fight back. Furthermore, it hopefully conveys the fact that correctly designing and implementing these tools is challenging and intellectually stimulating. There is still much room for a lot of fascinating academic and commercial research work in this field.

*The future is now in your hands. Begin by cultivating an attitude of privacy-awareness and letting that guide your daily choices and activities. Learn more about PETs and how they can be used to protect personal information. If at all possible, consider contributing actively to the improvement of existing PETs and to the development of new PETs, for the ultimate benefit of us all.*

*Welcome to the PETs community!*

**Questions for Personal Reflection and/or Group Discussion**

1. Give two examples of data that might seem harmless or unimportant on its own but, when combined with other data, would suddenly become privacy invasive. In what way is this combined data privacy sensitive?
2. Choose any particular online transaction scenario: how can someone find out what personal data is collected (and by whom) in that transaction?
3. List three specific things that you can do to limit the amount of personal information that you deliberately release. For each one, what might you be giving up by limiting this release?
4. What are the top 5 PETs-relevant conferences and journals today? How frequently is new material published at each of these venues? Can someone who is not an academic access this material (is it freely available, or is some kind of fee required), and where can it be accessed? Where can someone find out about, and obtain, open-source implementations of various PETs? If someone only has time to follow one venue for the latest PETs news/research, what venue would you recommend, and why?

# References

S. Baker, *The Numerati* (Houghton Mifflin Company, 2008)

F. Willems, GhostBuy: An All-Steps Anonymous Purchase Platform (ASAPP) based on separation of data, Master's thesis, University of Ottawa, 19 May 2021

# Part I
# Supplemental Chapters

# Chapter 11
# Crypto Primer

**Abstract** This chapter is a brief introduction to the specific cryptographic algorithms, protocols, and concepts that are needed for understanding the PETs described in the previous chapters of this book.

**Keywords** Confidentiality · Integrity · Authenticity · Cryptographic strength · Security proof

*This "crypto primer" is intended to be a brief introduction to the field of cryptographic algorithms and protocols. Cryptology is a fascinating topic that has become increasingly broad and deep, particularly in the past seventy-five years (i.e., the time since World War II). This primer only touches on the specific concepts and tools in cryptology that are directly required for understanding the PETs covered in this book, so if your favourite crypto technique is not mentioned here, that is probably why.*

*If you are interested in learning more about this incredible field, there are many excellent books that may be consulted, including (Katz and Lindell 2015; Menezes et al. 1996; Stallings 2014; Stinson and Patterson 2018; Vaudenay 2005). Note that all these books include good introductions to the underlying mathematics required for this subject, such as information theory, complexity theory, number theory, abstract algebra, and finite fields.*

## 11.1 Terminology

We begin this primer with some essential terminology. **Cryptography** comes from the Greek words "kryptos", meaning *hidden* or *secret*, and "graphein", meaning *writing*. Thus, cryptography has to do with making information (particularly in written or transmitted form) hidden. **Cryptanalysis**, on the other hand, is the *analysis* of that which is hidden (ultimately for the purpose of *uncovering*, *revealing*, or

© The Editor(s) (if applicable) and The Author(s), under exclusive license
to Springer Nature Switzerland AG 2021

C. Adams, *Introduction to Privacy Enhancing Technologies*,
https://doi.org/10.1007/978-3-030-81043-6_11

*understanding* it). These are two sides of the same coin: hiding information and revealing information. **Cryptology** is the combination of these two sides; it is the "study of hiding" or the "study of secrecy"; it is about making and breaking tools to hide information. (Note that in common discussions – and even in many academic papers – the word "cryptography" appears much more often than "cryptology". However, an essential part of cipher design is having cryptanalysts study it for flaws to see if it can be broken, and so both sides of the field are always involved and implied, even if only the word "cryptography" is used. We will adopt this practice here unless there is a special reason to explicitly make a distinction between "cryptography" and "cryptology" in a particular instance.)

Jonathan Katz and Yehuda Lindell (2015) have suggested that, historically, cryptography was seen as an <u>*art form*</u> that dealt only with <u>*secret communication*</u> *for the* <u>*military and intelligence communities*</u>, but that today it has broadened in at least three ways: it is now more correctly seen as a <u>*science*</u> *that helps to* <u>*secure systems*</u> *for* <u>*ordinary people across the globe*</u>. The field is much more formal and rigorous than ever before, with precise definitions, theorems, and proofs (art ➔ science); it protects environments of all kinds, including online business, digital cash, and electronic elections (secret communication ➔ secure systems); and it is used for everything from work and finance, to online games and entertainment (military ➔ ordinary people). In particular (and most relevant to the specific purposes of this book), cryptography is also used to create PETs that protect privacy.

The *tools* of cryptography are **cryptographic algorithms** and **cryptographic protocols**. Cryptographic algorithms are stand-alone techniques that do a single task, such as encrypting data, constructing a digital signature, or generating a key. Cryptographic protocols, by contrast, involve an exchange of messages between two or more participants, and perform distributed functions such as challenge-response authentication, key exchange, or multi-party computation. Cryptographic protocols involve the use of (typically several) cryptographic algorithms, and may include additional data that helps to achieve security such as *nonces*, timestamps, sequence numbers, and message or participant identifiers. We will introduce a number of cryptographic algorithms and protocols in this primer.

Finally, cryptographic tools require *participants* in order for us to understand how they work and model their use in real-world environments. (This is true even for stand-alone cryptographic algorithms, since one entity will normally encrypt data, sign data, and so on, with the intention of sending the result to at least one other entity.) Traditionally, the participants in cryptographic tools are **Alice**, **Bob**, and an **Adversary**. Occasionally other names will be used in academic discourse along with, or instead of, "Alice" and "Bob", and sometimes the Adversary will be given an explicit name (such as "Eve" or "Mallory"). Using human names, rather than generic labels like "Entity 1" and "Entity 2", or "A" and "B", helps to make the use of the tools easier to understand; it also allows, as is common practice in the cryptographic literature, the use of pronouns (he/she/him/her/his/hers) to simplify the presentation and to clarify who is doing what, particularly when describing protocol exchanges. Throughout this book we frequently use "Alice" and "Bob", but other names are sometimes used for variety.

## 11.2   Goals: *Confidentiality, Integrity, Authenticity, Cryptographic Strength*

What are designers trying to achieve when cryptographic tools are used in an environment to support security and/or privacy? I suggest that the designers are normally trying to satisfy a set of *cryptographic properties* (sometimes called *security services*), the most common of which are Confidentiality, Integrity, and Authenticity. **Confidentiality** is about keeping information secret from all but explicitly-intended parties. Secrecy is with respect to the information/data itself, but might also include information about the information (so-called metadata). Thus, "unlinkability" (for example, the inability to learn that two different messages were sent by the same individual, even if the identity of the individual is unknown) can be a desired goal within the umbrella of confidentiality. Similarly, "perfect forward secrecy" (the compromise of the current key does not allow future messages to be read), "backwards secrecy" (the compromise of the current key does not allow previous messages to be read), and "post-compromise security" (the combination of perfect forward secrecy and backwards secrecy) may also be desired goals within confidentiality.

**Integrity** is not about who can see data, but rather it focuses on who can make changes to data. In particular, integrity mechanisms ensure that data has not been modified in any unauthorized way while it was in storage or in transit. This property is sometimes referred to as "data origin authentication": a receiver or user of data can have confidence that the data is exactly as it was when it left the originator (i.e., the source or origin of the data).

**Authenticity** is about knowing who the other party is in an online transaction (i.e., addressing questions such as "Who sent this message?", "Who authorized this procedure?", or "To whom am I sending my data?"). It usually involves an identification step (an identity is claimed) coupled with some corroborating evidence (to prove ownership of the claimed identity). "Non-transferability" may be a desired goal within the umbrella of authenticity: ensuring that Bob, who has valid corroborating evidence of his identity, cannot give this evidence to David so that David can successfully pretend to be Bob in another transaction.

Whatever cryptographic properties are desired in a specific environment or in a specific implementation of a tool, ultimately the designers have the goal of achieving **cryptographic strength** for their cryptographic algorithms and protocols. The tools created and used must be strong enough to thwart/frustrate/foil the Adversary (whose intent is to break the cryptographic properties in order to see data, change data, or impersonate valid users).

## 11.3   Realizing These Goals in Practice

The goals introduced in Section A.2 need to be explored more deeply in terms of how they can be achieved in real-world implementations. In the following subsections, we will discuss each of the four goals in turn: confidentiality, integrity, authenticity, and cryptographic strength.

### *11.3.1   Confidentiality*

Let us imagine that Alice has a situation in which she desires confidentiality: she wants to keep some data hidden from those that should not see it. For example, she has a message that she wants to give to Bob, but she and Bob are separated by some distance and so she must send her message over an open communications channel (such as a local area network, a wireless phone connection, or the Internet). Her message is sensitive (*"Bob, I love you. I cannot live without you for another day!"*); therefore she wants only Bob to see it. In particular, Alice knows that there is an Adversary monitoring the channel (an eavesdropper who we will call Eve): perhaps this is Bob's current partner (who is jealous and distrustful of all Bob's friendships), or Alice's mother (who is always trying to read Alice's communications to see what she is up to), or Alice's nosy little sister (who just wants to read everything in order to be annoying). In any case, Alice wants to transmit her message to Bob while hiding it from Eve.

Alice can use an *encryption algorithm* (sometimes called a *cipher*) to turn her original sensitive message (called *plaintext*) into what looks like unintelligible gibberish (called *ciphertext*). Once she has done this *encryption* or *enciphering* operation, she can transmit the ciphertext over the channel without fear that Eve will learn the message. When Bob receives this ciphertext, he can use a *decryption algorithm* to *decrypt* or *decipher* the gibberish back to the original plaintext and read Alice's message.

Note that the encryption algorithm and the decryption algorithm are not secret. Anyone can know what they are and how they work; specifically, cryptanalysts always assume that Eve will know these algorithms and have copies of them herself. So why can Bob decrypt and recover the plaintext if Eve cannot? It is because the encryption and decryption algorithms take as input an additional parameter aside from the data (i.e., the plaintext or ciphertext): they take a *cryptographic key*. Inputting a key to the encryption algorithm will map a plaintext string to a random-looking ciphertext string. Inputting the corresponding key to the decryption algorithm will recover the correct plaintext from that ciphertext; however, inputting any other key will result in another random string that is not the original plaintext. Hence, Bob (who knows the appropriate decryption key) can decrypt correctly, and Eve (who does not know the key) cannot.

There are two classes of encryption/decryption algorithms. If Bob uses the *same key* to decrypt as Alice used to encrypt, then this is known as a *symmetric algorithm* (and the one key that they both use is known as a *symmetric key*). On the other hand, if they use *different keys* – one key is used to encrypt and a different key is used to decrypt – then this is known as an *asymmetric algorithm*. Naturally, these two keys must be related in some way (since they are doing inverse operations: encryption and decryption), but uncovering their relationship is so mathematically demanding that if Eve saw one of the keys, she would not be able to compute or derive the other key (even with a tremendous amount of computing power at her disposal). This gives rise to the notion that one key could be known by everyone (including Eve!) without endangering the other key in any way. Thus, for example, Alice could encrypt her sensitive plaintext with the key that is known to everyone and send the resulting ciphertext over the channel. Bob, who alone knows the other key, would be able to decrypt and recover Alice's message, but no one else would be able to do this. Asymmetric encryption/decryption algorithms are therefore commonly referred to as *public key encryption/decryption algorithms*, and their respective keys form a *key pair*: a *public key* for the encryption function and a corresponding *private key* for the decryption function.

### 11.3.1.1   Symmetric Encryption Algorithms

A symmetric encryption algorithm takes as input a plaintext and a key, and it outputs a ciphertext (typically each of these is a binary string of a specified length). The corresponding decryption algorithm is an identical (or very similar) process that takes as input the ciphertext and the same key, and it outputs the original plaintext.

*Types of Symmetric Algorithms*

Symmetric ciphers come in two flavours. *Stream ciphers* encrypt one bit at a time (or, in some instantiations, one byte at a time): a single bit of plaintext is masked (using an exclusive-or (XOR) operation) with a single bit of key to create a single bit of ciphertext. Each bit of the key is randomly, or pseudorandomly, generated so that the resulting ciphertext looks like a random string. The identical set of key bits (known as the *key stream*) is used for decryption: each ciphertext bit is unmasked (again using the XOR operation) with the appropriate key bit to recover the corresponding plaintext bit. The *one-time pad* is the most famous of all stream ciphers (and is the only cipher in the world to be unconditionally secure), but other well-known stream ciphers include RC4 ("Rivest Cipher #4", although it is sometimes referred to as "Ron's Code #4", invented by Ron Rivest in 1987; see Section 17.1 of (Schneier 1996)), and ChaCha20 and XSalsa20 (both designed by Daniel J. Bernstein in 2008 and 2011; see respectively (2008), (2011)). Stream ciphers that use a *pseudorandom number generator* (PRNG) take a random key, or *seed*, of a specified size (usually between 128 and 256 bits) and generate a pseudorandom key stream that is the length of the plaintext.

The other flavour for symmetric encryption algorithms is *block ciphers*; these encrypt a set (i.e., a block) of bits at a time. A block size that was commonly used between the mid-1970s and the mid-1990s was 64 bits but, since that time, block sizes of 128 bits or more are typical. The key size for these algorithms is independent of the block size; often it is deliberately chosen to be similar to the block size, but sometimes larger variants are available. Over the history of humankind, countless block ciphers have been designed and used, but some of the most famous are the ciphers that have been standardized by national governments and adopted by huge influential corporations. Prominent examples include the *Data Encryption Standard* (DES, standardized in the US in 1977 with a block size of 64 bits and a key size of 56 bits (FIPS 1977)) and the *Advanced Encryption Standard* (AES, standardized in the US in 2001 with a block size of 128 bits and three official key sizes of 128 bits, 192 bits, and 256 bits (referred to as AES-128, AES-192, and AES-256, respectively) (FIPS 2001)). Note that if the plaintext is longer than the block size of the cipher, then multiple block encryptions will be needed to encrypt the entire plaintext. Techniques for doing this securely are called *modes of operation*; standardized and widely-used modes include *cipher block chaining* (CBC) (Dworkin 2001) and *Galois/counter mode* (GCM) (Dworkin 2007), but several other modes have also been standardized. Modes often use a randomly-chosen block of bits called an *initialization vector* (IV) to bootstrap the process that links these block encryptions together.

*Symmetric Key Derivation*

Whether the symmetric encryption algorithm is a stream cipher or a block cipher, a symmetric key is required as input to the encryption process. In an ideal setting, this key will be created entirely at random (for example, Alice might flip a fair coin 256 times, assigning "heads" to the bit "0" and "tails" to the bit "1" with each successive toss). However, in many real-world environments, the generation of truly random keys is impractical. In such cases, a key may be *derived* from smaller or more memorable inputs (such as Alice's password) using a computational process known as a *key derivation function* (KDF), but the KDF must be carefully designed to ensure that the resulting key cannot be easily guessed or computed by the Adversary (see, for example, (Chen 2009)). An alternative is to spend the effort to create one highly random key (called the *master key*), and then use a KDF to derive subsequent keys from the master key. Thus, the master key is never used for encryption/decryption; it is used only as a high-entropy source for generating other keys.

*Key Distribution*

By the definition of a symmetric cipher, Alice (the one encrypting) and Bob (the one decrypting) must use the same key. Recall that Alice and Bob may be separated by some distance and have only a communications channel between them that is monitored by the eavesdropper Eve. How can they agree on a key to use? This is known as the *key distribution problem* (although note that *key distribution* is sometimes referred to as *key exchange*, *key establishment*, or *key agreement*, with slight differences in meaning based on how the process is carried out). Key distribution might happen once (Alice and Bob agree on a *static key* and then use it indefinitely to protect their communications), or key distribution might happen many times (Alice and Bob agree on an *ephemeral key* and use it to protect only a single message or a single session, and then they need to agree on a new key to protect their next exchange).

A simple method for Alice and Bob to agree on a key is for them to meet offline in a private location: they decide on a key, memorize it, and then go their separate ways. But meeting in person is not always convenient, and may not even be possible in some situations. Whitfield Diffie and Martin Hellman in 1976 proposed a simple, elegant protocol in which Alice and Bob can jointly compute a secret value (that can be used as a symmetric key) by exchanging only public values over an open channel (Diffie and Hellman 1976). Referred to subsequently as the *Diffie-Hellman protocol* (D-H), it can be used in fully ephemeral mode (both exchanged public values are freshly generated with each protocol run), in fully static mode (both exchanged public values are sealed in public key certificates and are reused until the certificates expire), or in ephemeral-static mode (e.g., Alice's public value is new with every protocol run, while Bob's public value remains the same).

*Re-Keying*

It is generally acknowledged to be bad practice to use a key indefinitely. Rather, keys are limited to a specified lifetime whose length depends on the sensitivity of the data to be protected with that key and the potential damage that could occur if the sensitive data was acquired by unintended parties. Thus, some symmetric keys may have a lifetime of at most a few seconds or minutes; others may be used for a few days or weeks; and still others may be used for a longer period of time. In all cases, though, when the lifetime ends, the current key must be replaced with a new key. This is the process of *re-keying*. New key derivation and key distribution steps will typically need to be performed, although key distribution may be as simple as Alice encrypting the newly generated key with the (not-yet-expired) current key, and sending the resulting ciphertext to Bob. (Bob can then decrypt and obtain the new key, and Alice and Bob can begin using the new key and securely discard the old key.)

*Key Partitioning*

There may be situations in which Alice needs to store her key in another location (for example, for backup purposes, so that she can recover the key if she loses her local copy because she does not want to lose all the data that was encrypted with that key). This may be quite feasible if there is a storage server that she trusts completely, but often she has no such server. A possible solution to this problem is a process called *key partitioning*. Alice splits her key into $n$ random-looking pieces (called *key shares*) and gives one share to each of $n$ servers. In this way, no server has to be fully trusted because no server actually holds her key. In fact, Alice can use a technique known as a *secret sharing scheme* to distribute the shares to the $n$ servers and ensure that at least $k$ out of $n$ servers must participate in order to reconstruct the original key (this allows for up to $n-k$ servers to be down/inactive/unresponsive without preventing Alice from recovering her key, while guaranteeing that any coalition of up to $k$-1 servers cannot collude and recover Alice's key without her knowledge). The concept of a secret sharing scheme (and, more generally, *threshold cryptography*) was first explored by George Blakley (1979) and by Adi Shamir (1979).

### 11.3.1.2   Asymmetric Encryption Algorithms

An asymmetric encryption algorithm takes as input a plaintext and a key, and it outputs a ciphertext (typically each of these is a binary string of a specified length, but they may be treated by the algorithm as integers, for example, rather than as simple bit strings). The corresponding decryption algorithm takes as input the ciphertext and a key to output the original plaintext but, in contrast to a symmetric cipher, the decryption key is different from the encryption key.

*The First Asymmetric Encryption Algorithm*

The first public key encryption algorithm (which, through a clever insight, was also the first digital signature algorithm; see Section A.3.3 below) was proposed in 1978 by Ronald Rivest, Adi Shamir, and Leonard Adleman (1978) and was subsequently referred to as the *RSA algorithm*. Whereas symmetric ciphers commonly encrypt by performing binary operations on bit strings (such as XOR, shift, permute, rotate, and so on), RSA encrypts by computing an exponentiation operation on very large integers. Because these computations would quickly result in numbers that are too large to fit in computer memories, all operations are done in a finite field (i.e., modulo a particular integer $n$ known as an *RSA modulus*, which is unique to each user). Thus, for a plaintext message $m$, the corresponding ciphertext $c$ is computed using an encryption key $e$ as $c = m^e \bmod n$. An RSA modulus is the product of two large prime numbers $p$ and $q$ (known only to the specific user that constructed it); the security of the algorithm lies in the difficulty for anyone other than this user to factorize the modulus back into its two prime factors.

Let Alice choose two large prime numbers $p$ and $q$. She does not tell anyone these values. Alice then chooses another number $e$.

Alice computes $n = p \cdot q$. The pair of integers $(e, n)$ are her public key.

Bob encrypts a message $m$ for Alice by computing $c = m^e \bmod n$. He sends $c$ to Alice.

Since 1978, many other public key encryption algorithms have been proposed (with varying levels of efficiency and security). However, none has yet achieved the simplicity and elegance of the RSA algorithm, which is why RSA is usually the first public key algorithm taught in cryptography courses and why RSA is still widely used in deployed cryptographic implementations around the world.

*Key Derivation*

Key derivation for asymmetric ciphers is more involved than key derivation for symmetric ciphers. This is because asymmetric ciphers require a key pair (i.e., a public key and a corresponding private key); these keys need to be related in a particular mathematical way in order for one to decrypt what the other has encrypted. Thus, Alice cannot simply flip a coin a number of times to create her public key, and then flip it several more times to create her private key. Similarly, a KDF for an asymmetric cipher cannot just generate two random-looking strings and call this a key pair.

A KDF must be explicitly designed for a specific intended asymmetric algorithm. Consider the RSA algorithm as an example. Its KDF will take some input from the user Alice (her password, perhaps), randomize it in some way using various sources of entropy from the computer, and use the result as a starting point to search for a prime number, $p$. Additional input (or some defined computation on the original input) will likewise be used as a starting point to search for a second prime number, $q$. A public encryption key $e$ will be selected, and then the private decryption key $d$ will be computed as the mathematical inverse of $e$, with the computation being done modulo $(p-1) \cdot (q-1)$ (that is, $d = e^{-1}$ mod $(p-1) \cdot (q-1)$). The RSA modulus for Alice will be $n = p \cdot q$ and so anyone that can factorize $n$ (to learn $p$ and $q$) will clearly be able to compute Alice's private key $d$ from her public key $e$.

Knowing $p$ and $q$, Alice computes $(p-1) \cdot (q-1)$. She does not tell anyone this value.

Alice computes $d = e^{-1}$ mod $(p-1) \cdot (q-1)$. She does not tell anyone this value: $d$ is her private key.

Alice decrypts $c$ from Bob by computing $c^d$ mod $n = (m^e)^d$ mod $n = m^{ed}$ mod $n = m$.

*Key Distribution*

Key distribution is also different for asymmetric ciphers than it is for symmetric ciphers. Because the encryption key is public (i.e., is known by everyone and is not just a secret value chosen by Alice and Bob in an offline private location), Alice needs to be absolutely certain that this is actually Bob's public key before she uses it to encrypt sensitive data for him. (The danger is that, since all encryption keys are posted publicly, Eve might have substituted Bob's public key with her own public key. Then when Alice uses this key to encrypt and sends the ciphertext, Eve will be able to decrypt it. Bob will not be able to decrypt it, of course, and so Alice will discover that something has gone wrong, but by then it will be too late since Eve will know the plaintext.)

Therefore, in an asymmetric environment, Alice and Bob do not need a private location to share a key, and they do not need the Diffie-Hellman protocol to jointly compute a secret encryption/decryption key from values exchanged over an open communications channel. However, Alice needs a way to ensure that this particular posted public key really belongs to Bob, and Bob needs to ensure that this other particular posted public key really belongs to Alice. There are a number of ways to get this assurance (including having Alice and Bob physically meet in a private location!), but a popular method involves a third party called a *Certification Authority* (CA). The CA digitally signs a data structure that contains an identifier for Bob (e.g., his name, or his e-mail address) and his valid public key. (The CA will need to go through a specified procedure with Bob so that the CA will be convinced that this is truly the correct public key for Bob.) The data structure (known as a *public key certificate*) may contain other pieces of information as well, such as a *validity period*, but the identifier, public key, and CA signature are essential. If Alice has a trusted copy of the CA's public key, then Alice can obtain Bob's certificate from wherever it is hosted (even from an untrusted website), use the CA's public key to verify the signature on the certificate (see the discussion on digital signatures in Sect. 11.3.3 below), and then use the contained public key to encrypt a sensitive message for Bob. Thus, Alice goes from trusting the CA public key to trusting a public key for Bob (without having to interact directly with Bob!). This is why the CA public key is referred to as Alice's *trust anchor*: it is her *basis-of-trust* or *root-of-trust* that allows her to extend her trust to other keys in the environment.

Alice will also have her own public key certificate; if Bob has a trusted copy of the CA's public key, he will likewise be able to use it to extend his trust to Alice's public key. Within a given environment, the CA may issue certificates for many users. Furthermore, the CA will be responsible for the full lifecycle management of all these certificates: creating them, publishing them, revoking them, expiring them, and replacing them. The collection of entities, policies, software, hardware, and procedures for accomplishing these certificate management activities is known as a *public key infrastructure* (PKI): a PKI is what enables secure public-key-based interactions in networked environments (see, for example, (Adams and Lloyd 2003), (Housley and Polk 2001)).

*Re-Keying*

Section A.3.1.1 mentioned that each symmetric key should have a finite lifetime. This is also true for each key pair in an asymmetric environment: Alice's key pair will eventually need to be replaced. The re-keying process will require a new key derivation step and a new key distribution step (certification by the CA of Alice's new public key). As with the symmetric environment, re-keying in an asymmetric environment may be simpler than the initial keying process was: Alice may just send to the CA a certification request that contains her new public key, and sign this request with her current (not-yet-expired) signature key. Since her signing key is still valid, the CA will be confident that this new public key really belongs to Alice and will therefore be able to immediately issue a certificate for it.

### 11.3.1.3   Special Techniques

Under the umbrella of *confidentiality*, there are a number of special techniques that go beyond traditional encryption in some way. In this section, we list the particular special techniques that are used by some of the PETs discussed in this book. Note that most of these techniques use asymmetric algorithms, but broadcast encryption uses symmetric encryption with carefully designed key distribution.

*Broadcast Encryption*

The goal of *broadcast encryption* is to deliver encrypted content over a broadcast channel (such as a television channel) in a way that allows only specific users (such as those that have paid the subscription fee) to decrypt. Because the set of qualified users can change with every broadcast transmission, efficient revocation of some users or groups, without affecting the other users, is essential. Thus, broadcast encryption schemes are sometimes referred to as *revocation schemes*. This field was first introduced by Amos Fiat and Moni Naor in 1993 (1994).

*Attribute-Based Encryption*

With *attribute-based encryption* (ABE), data is encrypted for a *role*, or for anyone with a particular set of *attributes*, rather than for a specific individual. In this way, if a file is encrypted for the "development manager", then if the current manager leaves and is replaced by a new manager, this new person will be able to decrypt the file and read its contents. This can greatly simplify data access in environments that experience significant turnover in personnel but have roles and attributes that remain fairly stable over time across the organization. One difficulty in ABE is guaranteeing collusion resistance: ensuring that multiple users cannot collude to combine their attributes and gain access to data that none of them could individually obtain.

ABE was first proposed by Amit Sahai and Brent Waters in 2005 (2005), but now has been divided into the two subfields of *key-policy attribute-based encryption* (KP-ABE) and *ciphertext-policy attribute-based encryption* (CP-ABE). (The distinction is whether the key or the ciphertext specifies the access policy, and therefore whether the ciphertext or the key holds the actual attributes. See Sect. 7.1 of Chap. 7 for additional details.)

*Identity-Based Encryption and Policy-Based Encryption*

In traditional asymmetric environments, each user has a public key that must be certified (i.e., placed into a public key certificate and digitally signed) by a CA. As discussed in Section A.3.1.2 above, this ensures that an adversary, Eve, cannot replace Bob's public key with her own and gain the ability to read messages encrypted for him. However, certificate management (issuance, publication, revocation, replacement, and so on) is a significant amount of effort for the CA and related entities. In 1984, Adi Shamir proposed the idea that Bob's unique identity (for example, his e-mail address) could actually be his public key: *identity-based encryption* (IBE) (Shamir 1985). If this could be achieved, it would remove the need for certificates: if Alice knows Bob's e-mail address, then she automatically knows his public key and there is no risk that Eve can substitute his public key with her own.

In 2001, Shamir's idea was finally realized (by Dan Boneh and Matt Franklin (2001) and by Clifford Cocks (2001)). Furthermore, in the Boneh and Franklin scheme, the function that maps an identity to a usable public key can take an arbitrary bit string as an input – this gives rise to the possibility that the input can be not just a simple identity, but a full access control policy or privacy policy. Consequently, IBE can trivially be generalized to *policy-based encryption* (PBE) such that Alice can encrypt a document for a set of rules (such as *"development managers requesting this document from inside the company firewall between 9:00 a.m. and 5:00 p.m. on a Tuesday"*) if she desires.

One drawback to IBE/PBE is that, in order for an arbitrary bit string to be mapped to a usable public key, a system authority is needed to generate the corresponding private key for that string. This authority, known as the *private key generator* (PKG), is therefore able to decrypt all ciphertext in the environment (since the PKG creates the private keys for all users) and so it must be a fully trusted entity. Research continues into secure and efficient ways to reduce the trust required in the PKG for IBE/PBE settings.

*Homomorphic Encryption*

*Homomorphic encryption* is a form of encryption in which useful computation can be done on ciphertext without the need to decrypt it first. The result of the computation is in encrypted form and can be decrypted at a later time by someone in possession of the appropriate decryption key. This technique has many applications. For example, it can be used for privacy-preserving outsourced storage and computation: Alice can encrypt and outsource her sensitive data to a commercial cloud environment for processing, and the resulting ciphertext can be sent to Alice (who can decrypt it and obtain her desired answer) without the cloud ever seeing any plaintext.

Homomorphic encryption can be realized using either symmetric or asymmetric cryptography, but asymmetric schemes are more commonly studied. The idea of homomorphic encryption was first proposed by Ronald Rivest, Leonard Adleman, and Michael Dertouzos in 1978 (1978b), but the first construction for a fully homomorphic encryption scheme did not appear until the ground-breaking work of Craig Gentry in 2009 (2009). Since that time, a significant amount of research and implementation has been accomplished in this field.

*Oblivious Transfer*

The final confidentiality technique in this section is not an encryption algorithm, but rather is a protocol between two parties. *Oblivious transfer* allows Alice to give data to Bob without learning what specific data he has received. (This mimics, using cryptography, the well-known "pick a card, any card" game in which Alice holds out a deck of cards to Bob, and he selects a card without her knowing which card he has taken.) The original proposal for oblivious transfer, due to Michael Rabin in 1981 (1981), allowed Alice to give a message to Bob with probability exactly ½, and at the end of the protocol she does not know whether he received the message. In the 1985 version by Shimon Even, Oded Goldreich, and Abraham Lempel (1985), referred to as "1-out-of-2 oblivious transfer", Alice has two messages ($m_0$ and $m_1$), Bob has a bit $b$, and Bob obtains message $m_b$ from Alice (without Alice learning $b$ and without Bob also obtaining $m_{(1-b)}$). The Even, et al., protocol was generalized to "1-out-of-$n$ oblivious transfer" by Gilles Brassard, Claude Crépeau, and Jean-Marc Robert in 1986 (1986) (and different approaches with varying efficiency were proposed subsequently by several others), and then to "$k$-out-of-$n$ oblivious transfer" (see, for example, the 2002 paper by Wen-Guey Tzeng (2002)).

## 11.3.2    Integrity

We now imagine that Alice has a situation in which she desires data integrity: she does not care if an eavesdropper sees the content, but she wants to ensure that Bob receives the data exactly as she sent it (i.e., no one has modified the data in any way before Bob acquires it). For example, perhaps Bob is downloading open-source software from Alice's website. The code itself is not confidential (it is open-source and everyone can see it), but Alice (and Bob!) would like to make sure that this code is not infected with malware as it travels from Alice's server to Bob's desktop. Of course, it is impossible to literally prevent everyone in the world from tampering with the data during transmission (or subsequently during its storage on Bob's hard drive), and so the more correctly-stated goal is to ensure that any change made to the data will be detected with very high probability (so that the changed data will not be accepted as valid).

The general approach for integrity is to create a "tag" (sometimes called a "checksum" or a "fingerprint") of the data that can be transmitted in conjunction with the data. This tag must have the property that (with very high probability) it will change if the data is changed in any way. Alice computes the tag prior to transmission and sends both the data and the tag to Bob (possibly over separate channels, although this is typically not necessary). Upon reception, Bob also computes the tag on the data and compares the result with the tag that he received from Alice. If the two tag values are the same, then Bob can be confident that he has received the original, unaltered, data from Alice.

For this approach to work, it is essential to ensure that an adversary cannot change both the data and the tag before they reach Bob. If we don't need to prevent someone from reading the data, and we don't need to prevent someone from modifying the data (specifically, we just need to detect if it *has* been modified), then the data can be sent completely unprotected and in the clear: all that is necessary is to protect the tag. There are two methods for doing this: one that does not use a key; and one that does use a key.

- *The process of Alice creating the tag (and, similarly, the process of Bob creating his own version of the tag to compare with the tag from Alice) does not use a key.* In this method, the tag must necessarily be protected in some other way. Sending it via a separate channel is one possibility, but more common choices are to have Alice encrypt the tag, or digitally sign the tag, or send both the data and the tag over a separately protected secure channel (such as SSL/TLS). Given that the tag will be "externally" protected, the tag itself is typically created using an unprotected *cryptographic hash function*. A cryptographic hash function (often simply called a "hash function" when the cryptographic context is clear) is a carefully-designed function that has a property called *collision resistance*: any change to its input is highly likely to result in a change to its output (a "collision" occurs when two different inputs map to the same output). Thus, Alice and Bob can each compute tag = *Hash(data)*. The hash function MD5 (*Message Digest #5* (RFC1321 1992)) was used for integrity purposes for many years until cryptographic weaknesses forced a transition to the NIST-standardized *Secure Hash Algorithm* SHA-1 (FIPS 2015), and then to its more secure variants SHA-256, SHA-384, and SHA-512 (FIPS 2015).

- *The process of Alice creating the tag (and, similarly, the process of Bob creating his own version of the tag to compare with the tag from Alice) does use a key.* In this method, the tag is "internally" protected (i.e., its creation uses a key that is known only to Alice and Bob) and so it is not necessary for the tag to be encrypted, signed, sent over a separate channel, or sent with the data over a secure channel such as SSL/TLS. The tool typically used for this is not a cryptographic hash function, but rather a *message authentication code* (MAC) algorithm. A MAC algorithm, like a hash function, provides collision resistance, but requires a symmetric key in its computation (along with a block of "dummy" data, called an *initialization vector* (IV), to initiate the processing). Thus, if Alice and Bob already share a symmetric key, then they can each compute *tag* = $\text{MAC}_{key}(data)$. A number of good MAC algorithms exist, but a commonly-used one is HMAC (*hash-based message authentication code*) which constructs a MAC algorithm out of an underlying hash function (such as SHA-256, to create the MAC algorithm "HMAC-SHA-256") along with a key.

If Alice and Bob use a MAC algorithm to create the tag, or if they use a hash function to create the tag and then protect the tag with symmetric encryption, they will need to use key derivation and key distribution processes to generate and share a symmetric key. Alternatively, if they use a hash function to create the tag and then Alice digitally signs the tag (or encrypts the tag with Bob's public key), then they will need to use key derivation and key distribution techniques that are appropriate for asymmetric settings. Finally, if they use a hash function to create the tag and Alice simply sends the data and tag over a protected channel such as SSL/TLS, then the key derivation and key distribution processes happen automatically during the channel set-up; Alice and Bob will not need to explicitly invoke these processes (but when the data and tag exit the channel at Bob's machine, they are unprotected and Bob will need to take additional steps to protect the tag if he wishes to store them for later verification).

One additional notion relevant to the property of integrity is *delegation*. A frequent example in a business environment is that Alice transfers (delegates) an attribute to Bob (e.g., "authority to approve purchase requisitions") so that he can exercise this in her absence while she is on vacation or on company travel. No confidentiality is required in this situation (since Bob will likely use this attribute in subsequent transactions with others) but the transfer from Alice to Bob must happen with integrity so that Bob receives the precise attribute that Alice desires. Note that when Bob subsequently exercises this attribute, he may need to prove data origin authenticity (i.e., that it originally came from Alice, who legitimately possesses this attribute). Therefore, the tag proving integrity will likely be digitally signed by Alice rather than being protected by any of the symmetric techniques.

### 11.3.3  Authenticity

The third goal that may be of interest to designers using cryptographic tools to support security and/or privacy is *authenticity*. The purpose of authenticity is for Alice to be certain of the identity of the other party in an online interaction; specifically, authenticity is intended to reduce the risk of successful impersonation (i.e., Alice believes that she is interacting with Bob, but the other party is actually Eve). As with the previous goal of integrity, achieving confidentiality may be of little importance for some situations in which authenticity is required.

For Bob to authenticate to Alice, there are two options:

- Bob uses a particular stand-alone *authentication technique*, such as a digital signature or a MAC;
- Alice and Bob engage in an *authentication protocol* in which messages are sent back and forth between them (an example is a *challenge-response entity authentication protocol*: Alice sends some kind of *challenge* to the other party, knowing that Bob is the only person who could produce the correct *response*). Note that an authentication protocol may provide *unilateral* or *mutual* authentication – that is, it may just authenticate Bob to Alice, or it may authenticate Bob and Alice to each other.

With both of the above options, when Bob successfully authenticates to Alice, she is convinced that the other party is Bob. During this authentication procedure (whether it is a single technique or a protocol), Alice will receive certain data from Bob. Depending on the procedure, it may or may not be the case that this collected data would also convince a third party that this is Bob (thus, Alice may be certain that she is interacting with Bob, but she may be unable to prove this to anyone else). For example, Bob's digital signature on a message will be convincing proof to anyone that Bob is the originator. On the other hand, Bob's MAC on a message will convince only Alice: since the MAC uses a symmetric key that is known only to

Alice and Bob, Alice will know that she did not originate the message and so it must have come from Bob, but no third party will be able to determine whether it was Alice or Bob that constructed the message and MAC).

A *digital signature* is a stand-alone authentication technique that uses asymmetric cryptography. To sign a message, Bob computes the hash of the message (using a cryptographic hash function) and operates on the result with his private signature key. Alice (and anyone else who is able to trust Bob's public key by starting with a trusted CA key to verify the relevant public key certificates in a PKI) can then verify the signature on the message using Bob's public verification key. Recall that to "digitally sign the tag" is one of the methods listed in Section A.3.2 to achieve integrity for some data. Thus, if the tag is the hash of Bob's message (i.e., tag = *Hash*(*message*)), his digital signature provides both authenticity and integrity: when Alice receives a message and its signature and she is able to verify the signature using Bob's public key, she (and anyone else) is convinced that Bob is the originator of the message *and* that the message has not been altered in any way since it left Bob.

Because a digital signature provides authenticity and integrity that can be verified by anyone, and because it is a stand-alone technique (i.e., not requiring multiple back-and-forth messages between parties), it has become an essential cryptographic tool for many needs in society (such as e-business, for example, which fundamentally requires that one party is able to submit a signed contract to another party). Consequently, it is not surprising that there are many different algorithms for computing digital signatures, as well as many different types of signatures that have been proposed over the years. Some examples follow.

- The first digital signature algorithm ever proposed is still the most widely known and has been the most widely used around the world. It is the *RSA algorithm* (Rivest et al. 1978a), which was introduced as the first asymmetric encryption algorithm in Section A.3.1.2. The inventors recognized that the public key $e$ and the corresponding private key $d$ are both simply integers less than the RSA modulus $n$, and thus the computation on a message $m$ (i.e., $m^e \bmod n$) could just as easily use the other integer (i.e., $m^d \bmod n$). Since $e$ is a public key known to anyone, it is natural to think of this first computation as an encryption operation; thus, $m^e \bmod n = c$, where $c$ is the ciphertext for the plaintext $m$. Similarly, since $d$ is a private key known only to Bob, we can think of the second computation as a signing operation; thus, $m^d \bmod n = s$, where $s$ is Bob's digital signature on the plaintext $m$. The associated process for the first computation is a decryption operation that can only be performed by Bob (since only he has $d$): $c^d \bmod n = m$. Similarly, the associated process for the second computation is a signature verification operation that can be performed by anyone (since $e$ is public): $s^e \bmod n = m$.

Bob digitally signs a message $m$ by computing $s = m^d \bmod n$.

Given $m$, $s$, and Bob's public key $(e, n)$, anyone can verify his signature by computing $s^e \bmod n = (m^d)^e \bmod n = m^{ed} \bmod n$ and seeing if the result is equal to $m$.

The naïve instantiation of the RSA signature algorithm described in the previous paragraph (as it was proposed in (Rivest et al. 1978a)) suffers from security weaknesses that are fairly easily fixed: rather than operating on the actual message $m$, the operation is on the hash of $m$ which is then padded with a sufficient number of bits to make the string equal to the size of $n$ (i.e., the operation is $[Padding(Hash(m))]^d \bmod n = s$). See (PKCS 2002) for the details of two standardized padding schemes for RSA signatures (PSS and PKCS1-v1.5).

- In 1998, the US National Institute of Standards and Technology (NIST) standardized a signature algorithm that was not able to be used for encryption (i.e., it was possible to create signatures with it, but not ciphertexts). This algorithm is called the *Digital Signature Algorithm* (DSA) and the standard specifying it is named the *Digital Signature Standard* (DSS) (FIPS 1998). This standard was approved for use by all US Federal departments and agencies for the protection of sensitive but unclassified information, but was also made available to any private and commercial organizations that wished to use it for digital signature purposes.
- David Chaum proposed the idea of *blind digital signatures* in 1982 (1983). A blind signature is a variation on a traditional digital signature in that aspects of the computation are hidden from the signer. In particular, (1) the signer Bob computes the signature without ever seeing the actual message that he is signing, and (2) Bob computes the signature without seeing the final signature value itself. Suppose that Bob is a Signing Authority in some environment and Alice is a user who submits a request for Bob to create a signature on some data. Alice employs *blinding factors* (strategically-placed random numbers) in her request so that Bob cannot see the data or the resulting signature value; she can subsequently remove these blinding factors to uncover the true message and signature for her later use. Blind signatures are essential, for example, in a *digital currency* application so that Bob cannot trace the spending of a coin, or in a *digital credential* application (see Sect. 6.2 of Chap. 6) so that Bob cannot trace Alice's credential transactions.
- Given a message and its corresponding signature, the signature scheme is said to be *malleable* if it is possible to efficiently compute a valid signature on a related message without the original signer needing to be involved again (more precisely, without the use of the private signing key). Naturally, there must be tight constraints specifying which particular "related messages" are allowed; otherwise, adversaries will be able to create authentic signatures for arbitrary messages of their own choosing. Malleable signatures were first defined and explored in (Ahn et al. 2012) and (Attrapadung et al. 2012); they have been found to be useful in a number of cryptographic applications, including the construction of *delegatable anonymous credentials* (Chase et al. 2014) and the addition of a multi-show capability to Brands' *digital credentials* (Fan and Adams 2018); see Chap. 6, Sect. 6.2.2 for further discussion.

Finally, it is worth pointing out that authenticity is sometimes combined with some other security function (in order to reduce computation and/or eliminate security flaws compared with doing authentication and the other function separately). Well-known examples of this combined functionality include *authenticated encryption* (AE) and *authenticated key exchange* (AKE). AE provides both confidentiality and authenticity (and therefore integrity) of data in a single block cipher mode of operation. Several AE modes have been proposed, analyzed, and standardized; a popular choice is *Galois/Counter Mode* (GCM) (Dworkin 2007). AKE, on the other hand, provides both key establishment and authenticity in a single protocol. An authenticated version of Diffie-Hellman, for example, mitigates the risk of a *man-in-the-middle* attack (see Sect. 11.3.4.1) during the key exchange between Alice and Bob; the *Station-to-Station* (STS) protocol (Diffie et al. 1992) presents one design of this particular AKE.

## *11.3.4   Cryptographic Strength*

As suggested in Sect. 11.2, cryptographic strength is the foundation for all the other goals that a designer might have: the cryptographic tools must be strong enough to provide confidentiality, integrity, and authenticity. But what does "strong enough" mean? How do we define it; how do we measure it; how do we achieve it? Since the objective is always to thwart or frustrate an adversary, it makes sense to think about our tools relative to, or in light of, the particular adversary that we are most worried about. If we can make it hard for *that* adversary to circumvent our tools, then we can have some confidence that our tools are "strong enough".

### 11.3.4.1   Defining Strength

An *adversary* is an entity that carries out an "attack" on an algorithm, protocol, or system for the purpose of contravening an implicit or explicit security/privacy policy (for example, the adversary may try to learn information that the adversary is not supposed to know, or try to modify information that the adversary is not supposed to modify). For this reason, the adversary is often referred to as an *attacker*. (Note, however, that an attack on a specific cryptographic algorithm or cryptographic protocol is commonly called *cryptanalysis* in the academic literature; in such cases, the attacker may then be called a *cryptanalyst*).

It is useful to carefully consider what the adversary is capable of doing, given the resources that the adversary has at his/her disposal (time, money, computing power, storage space, and so on). This is known as an *attack model* or an *attacker model*. The designers need to create a model of the most powerful/capable/worrisome adversary that they wish to protect their system against. Many different models are possible; a few examples are the following.

- *Passive*: A passive adversary can read data (in transit and/or in storage), perhaps copy it to his own offline storage, and analyze it in an attempt to learn prohibited or confidential information. This analysis can include computation, such as guessing keys or passwords to find a value that will decrypt the data.

– *Active*: An active adversary can read data, but also can modify data in transit or in storage (for example, change the "bits on the wire" so that what Bob receives is different from what Alice sent). An active adversary can also delete messages entirely (so that Bob does not receive them) and inject new messages of the adversary's design (so that Bob receives something even though Alice sent nothing).

– *MITM*: A man-in-the-middle adversary is one that invisibly inserts himself into a conversation between two legitimate users, Alice and Bob, so that Alice thinks she is talking only with Bob and Bob thinks he is talking only with Alice, but the adversary is in between (passively listening to all messages, or actively modifying the conversation). In an *unauthenticated* Diffie-Hellman key exchange, for example, a MITM adversary may be present, so that at the end of the protocol, Alice and Bob believe they share a symmetric key but, in fact, Alice shares one key with the adversary and Bob shares a different key with the adversary.

– *Honest-but-curious*: An honest-but-curious adversary will faithfully perform all required steps, computations, and message exchanges of a protocol but, *in addition*, will do whatever he can to learn information that he is not supposed to know. For example, if an authority gives some data to Bob that has been encrypted for Alice (so that he can send it to Alice at the appropriate time), Bob will transfer the ciphertext to Alice as required/expected, but he may also try to break the encryption in his off hours so that he can learn the hidden plaintext.

– *Fail-stop*: A fail-stop adversary is one who will halt protocol execution at any time of his choosing if he feels that this will give him some advantage over the other party (or parties) in the protocol. For example, if Alice and Bob are jointly computing a function, Bob may choose to halt the protocol as soon as he has learned the function result (particularly if subsequent steps are required in order for Alice to also learn the result).

– *Malicious*: A malicious adversary is one who will arbitrarily deviate from a protocol specification in order to learn confidential information or gain some advantage over other parties. This adversary cannot be relied upon to follow any of the rules or expectations of the protocol.

– *Byzantine*: In a distributed system with multiple communicating nodes, the adversary is byzantine (i.e., there are byzantine nodes, or the system exhibits byzantine behaviour) if some nodes fail (randomly do not communicate) and some nodes act maliciously (deliberately send incorrect or misleading messages), and yet the system as a whole must come to a consensus on a decision. This is considered to be the most general and difficult type of adversary, and so constraints are usually assumed in the attacker model (e.g., "*there are n nodes, at most c of these nodes will collude, at most f of the nodes will fail to communicate, and at most m of the communicating nodes will send misleading messages*").

Once the designers have created their attacker model, they need to design or choose cryptographic tools that can withstand an attacker of that type. If the tools can thwart such an attacker, this is the definition of "strong enough". Clearly, it is essential to get the model right. If the chosen tools are only able to defend against a specific type of attacker but in the deployed system a more powerful attacker shows up (for example, the designers assume a *passive adversary*, but in the real system an *active adversary* begins to act), the tools may be circumvented, allowing the attacker to contravene policy.

### 11.3.4.2   Measuring Strength

If we define cryptographic strength ("strong enough") as something that will resist an adversary of a specific type, how can we measure that strength? How can we say, with some confidence, that an adversary has *this* much power, and that our cryptographic tool requires *more power* than that in order to break it and so the adversary will be thwarted? The answer lies in *computational complexity theory*.

Some cryptographic algorithms (such as asymmetric encryption algorithms and digital signature algorithms) are built on an underlying mathematical problem. Other cryptographic algorithms (such as symmetric ciphers, hash functions, and MAC algorithms) rely on a highly complex mapping between input and output. If an adversary can solve the mathematical problem, or if an adversary can search through the possible inputs to find the one that corresponds to a given output, the algorithm will be broken. Computational complexity theory allows us to estimate the amount of effort that would be required to do such a task. The estimation is typically in terms of the number of "operations" that would need to be computed (where an "operation" might be something simple like an addition or a multiplication, or something contextually defined like a decryption of a ciphertext); this number of operations can then readily be translated into the amount of time it would take ("wall-clock time") on an actual computer.

As a very simple example, suppose that the adversary has a ciphertext and knows that Alice used an encryption algorithm that only takes 1000 possible keys. The adversary can try decrypting the ciphertext with these keys, one by one, until a sensible plaintext results. This search will take 1000 decryption operations at most and so, if the adversary's computer takes 1 second to do each trial decryption, it will take up to 1000 seconds to find the correct key. If, for some precisely-defined setting, we know that the adversary will only have 2 seconds to do this experiment, we might say that this encryption algorithm is "strong enough". On the other hand, if the adversary has 1 hour (i.e., 3600 seconds) to devote to this task, we would conclude that the encryption algorithm is definitely too weak to provide confidentiality for this data.

Computational complexity theory classifies computational problems (i.e., problems that can be solved on a computer by using an algorithm) according to resource usage, and thus gives a way of relating these classes to each other. Importantly, though, it defines *mathematical models of computation* (such as *deterministic Turing machines* and *nondeterministic Turing machines*) that are independent of any specific algorithm, and quantifies the resources needed *with respect to those models*. Resource requirements are typically stated using *big-O notation*, a notation that writes only the highest-order term in an expression and omits all constants and smaller terms (so that, for example, "$f(n) = 3n^3 + 8n^2 + 6n + 5$" would be written as "$f(n) = O(n^3)$"). Therefore the classes that computational complexity theory defines hold true for any given actual implementation using any given actual algorithm: the small performance variations that may come from using a different algorithm, compiler, or operating system are all absorbed under the umbrella of the highest-order term. This approach is very helpful for measuring cryptographic strength because we do not need to know what particular CPU, OS, and algorithm the adversary is using in order to assess the adversary's ability to solve a specific computational problem.

[Note that occasionally *little-O notation* is also used when discussing resource requirements. By definition, "$f(n) = o(g(n))$" means that "$f(n) / g(n)$ tends to zero as $n$ tends to infinity" (i.e., $g(n)$ grows much faster than $f(n)$). Sometimes a term in an expression is written as "$o(1)$". Since "$g(n)$" in this case is a constant (not dependent on $n$), this means that the term itself tends to zero as $n$ grows.]

The following concepts are useful for understanding some of the PETs in this book.

– Classes defined by computational complexity theory (with respect to the resource *time*) for the *deterministic Turing machine model* include

   • *linear*: $O(n)$ (referred to as DTIME)
   • *polynomial*: $O(poly(n))$ (referred to as P)
   • *exponential*: $O(2^{poly(n)})$ (referred to as EXPTIME)

– Classes defined by computational complexity theory (with respect to the resource *time*) for the *nondeterministic Turing machine model* include

   • *linear*: $O(n)$ (referred to as NTIME)
   • *polynomial*: $O(poly(n))$ (referred to as NP)
   • *exponential*: $O(2^{poly(n)})$ (referred to as NEXPTIME)

– A *polynomially-computable function* is one that can be computed using an amount of resources (e.g., *time*, *space*) that is a polynomial in the size of the input to the function. Thus, problems in the computational complexity class P (above) are polynomially-computable.

– A *reduction* is an efficient transformation of one computational problem into another computational problem. If a problem $x$ can be solved using an algorithm for another problem $y$, then $x$ is no more difficult than $y$, and we say that $x$ *reduces to y*.

– A problem $x$ is said to be *hard* for a class of problems $C$ if every problem in $C$ can be reduced to $x$. (In this case, no problem in $C$ is harder than $x$, since an algorithm for solving $x$ can be used to solve any problem in $C$.) As one example, a problem that is *hard* for the class NP is called an *NP-hard* problem.

– A problem that is *hard* for a class $C$ could be in a different class $C'$. However, a problem that is *hard* for $C$, and is in the class $C$, is said to be *complete* for $C$. For example, a problem in the class NP that is *hard* for NP is called an *NP-complete* problem.

Additional background material for computational complexity theory can be found, for example, in (Dean 2016) or Part Three of (Sipser 2012); a brief overview can be found in (Wikipedia 2021).

### 11.3.4.3   Achieving Strength

Having *defined* cryptographic strength and decided how to *measure* it in the previous two subsections, all that remains is to determine how to *achieve* it in practice. An important component of this (as discussed in Sect. 11.3.4.1) is to choose an *attacker model*: what type of attacker are we most worried about, and how much power does that attacker have? However, it was also noted that we can put our system at great risk if we get the attacker model wrong (e.g., we assume a *passive attacker* but an *active attacker* shows up, or we assume an attacker that has only *2 seconds of compute time* but an attacker that has *1 hour of compute time* shows up).

How can we mitigate some of this risk? One option is to always choose the most general type of adversary, but this has the disadvantage that it can lead to unnecessary performance degradation (for example, algorithms and protocols to protect against *byzantine adversaries* may be quite different from, and much slower than, algorithms and protocols to protect against *honest-but-curious* or *fail-stop* adversaries). Furthermore – and somewhat counter-intuitively – this approach can unexpectedly leave aspects of the system unprotected (for example, algorithms and protocols to protect against *byzantine adversaries* will do nothing to thwart a *passive adversary* that monitors the channel between Alice and Bob).

Because of this, the preferred option to mitigate risk is to always assume a *computationally powerful* adversary (regardless of the specific adversary type, or types, chosen). There are two approaches.

– Approach 1. Standard practice in cryptographic settings is to assume that the adversary has significant and impressive computing power (think of a large organization or agency with billions of dollars in budget, thousands of employees, and acres of state-of-the-art supercomputers), but is *polynomially-bounded*. This is a realistic model – the exponent on the polynomial may be quite high and so this represents an enormously powerful adversary. However, it still gives us some hope for security: a sufficiently large instance of any exponential problem will not be solvable by any *polynomially-bounded attacker* (sometimes more loosely referred to as a *computationally-bounded attacker*).

   We therefore base the security of our cryptographic algorithms and protocols on underlying mathematical problems or input space search problems whose solution is believed to require more than polynomial resources. This is called *computational security* (or *computational privacy*). Commonly-used examples of such problems include

- *Factoring* a large number into its component primes,
- Computing the *discrete logarithm* of an integer modulo a prime,
- Computing the analog of the "discrete logarithm" over the group of points on an elliptic curve (*elliptic curve group*) – this gives rise to *elliptic curve cryptography* (ECC), which may be implemented using *standard curves* (e.g., (FIPS 1998), (Brown 2010)) or alternative representations (such as *Edwards curves* (Edwards 2007), (Bernstein and Lange 2007)),
- Determining whether a number is a *quadratic residue modulo n*,
- Computing $g^{xy}$ given only $g^x$ and $g^y$ (all computation done modulo a prime $p$),
- *Finding a symmetric key* that maps a given plaintext to a given ciphertext, and
- Finding the input that corresponds to a given *cryptographic hash function* output value.

- Approach 2. The second approach, used in some cryptographic settings, is to assume no computational limitations whatever for the adversary (the so-called *computationally-unbounded attacker*). That is, we literally assume that the adversary has infinite computing power, infinite time, and infinite memory space. Clearly, such an adversary can solve any computational or search problem, so how can security be achieved? The answer is to ensure that all possible solutions to the underlying problem are equally likely; in this way, the adversary cannot know which candidate solution is the correct one. The adversary has the resources to find every possible answer, but since they are all equally likely to be the right answer, this is no better than finding no answers at all. This is called *information-theoretic security* (or *information-theoretic privacy*): it is information-theoretically impossible for the attacker to break the algorithm or protocol.

  We see this approach used, for example, in a *Pedersen commitment*, $c$, on a value $x$ (Pedersen 1992). The commitment is formed as $c = g^x h^r \bmod p$, where $p$ is a prime, $r$ is a random number, and $g$, $h$ are generators of a $q$-order subgroup of $Z_p^*$, where $q$ is a prime. Because $r$ is random, all candidate guesses for $x$ are equally likely to be correct (in particular, for every possible guess $x'$, there exists a value $r'$ such that $g^{x'} h^{r'} = c$); therefore, even an adversary with infinite resources will be unable to determine $x$ with probability any higher than pure random guessing (which means a probability of essentially zero if the size of $q$ is large).

  As another example, information-theoretic security is used in *zero-knowledge proof of knowledge* (ZKPoK) protocols (often simply called *zero-knowledge proofs* or *zero-knowledge protocols*) (Goldreich et al. 1986), (Goldwasser et al. 1989). As with Pedersen commitments, these protocols employ a random number as a mask so that every guess by the adversary regarding a hidden value is equally likely to be correct.

Both Approach 1 and Approach 2 allow us to achieve cryptographic strength in our tools. Whether we assume the adversary is tremendously powerful but polynomially-bounded, or infinitely powerful (i.e., computationally-unbounded), it is possible for the designer to create/select tools that he is convinced will withstand the attacker. However, it is necessary to go one step further. While it is nice if the *designer* is convinced that his new cryptographic algorithm is strong, it is much more important for the designer to be able to convince *others* (specifically, those who will use this algorithm) that the algorithm is strong. This is the topic of *security proofs* (proofs of cryptographic strength).

## Security Proof

For a cryptographic algorithm or protocol whose security is based on an underlying computational or search problem, the goal of a security proof is to show that breaking the algorithm/protocol (i.e., learning the plaintext or the key) is equivalent to solving the underlying problem. Clearly, if breaking the algorithm is *equivalent to* solving the problem <u>and</u> if the adversary's resources are *insufficient* to solve the problem (even if his resources are infinite), then the algorithm/protocol will be "strong enough" against this adversary.

## Security Proof, Step 1: A Theoretical Model of the Environment

A proof that breaking the algorithm/protocol is equivalent to solving the underlying problem typically uses a *theoretical model* of the environment in which the algorithm/protocol will operate. The *random oracle model* (ROM), for example, assumes that there is a *black box* somewhere in the environment that responds to every unique query with a truly random output (while for any given query, the black box will always respond with the same output for this query). Such a black box (*random oracle*) does not exist in real life, and so a cryptographic hash function is used to instantiate this fictitious black box. Since a hash function is not a perfect imitation of a random oracle, a security proof that relies on the existence of a random oracle might not deliver the "proven" security in an actual implementation. The alternative theoretical model of the environment (that is, the model that does <u>not</u> require a random oracle) is called the *standard model*; security proofs done in the standard model are generally more convincing and, therefore, more widely accepted.

## Security Proof, Step 2: Assumption of Difficulty for Mathematical Computations

Aside from assuming – or not assuming – the existence of specific components in the environment (such as a random oracle), security proofs often make assumptions about the difficulty of performing certain mathematical computations (when this difficulty is not otherwise rigorously known). As one example, consider the assumption that it is difficult to "compute $g^{xy}$ given only $g^x$ and $g^y$ (all computation done modulo a prime $p$)". Despite having been studied for many decades, it is not known with certainty that this task requires more than polynomial resources (in the size of $p$), although many believe that it does. This *computational Diffie-Hellman* (CDH) assumption, and its related *decisional Diffie-Hellman* (DDH) assumption (which says that, given $g^x$, $g^y$, and $g^z$, it requires more than polynomial resources to decide whether $z$ is $xy$ or a random number), forms the basis for many security proofs: "this algorithm is secure if CDH is true", or "this protocol is secure if DDH is true".

A second example of a computational assumption is found in the area of *bilinear maps* (often called *bilinear pairings*). Let $G_1$ and $G_2$ be multiplicative cyclic groups of prime order $p$ and let $g$ be a generator of $G_1$. A *bilinear pairing* $\hat{e}(\cdot,\cdot)$ is an efficiently-computable function of two arguments such that $\hat{e}(g,g) \neq 1$ and, for all $u$, $v$ $\in G_1$ and $a$, $b \in Z_p$, $\hat{e}(u^a,v^b) = \hat{e}(u,v)^{ab}$. (Such pairings have given rise to a very interesting area of research known as *pairing-based cryptography*.) The *decisional bilinear Diffie-Hellman* (DBDH) assumption is defined as follows: given $G_1$, $g$, and randomly-chosen $a$, $b$, $c \in Z_p$, it requires more than polynomial resources to distinguish $\hat{e}(g,g)^{abc} \in G_2$ from a random element in $G_2$. Again, it is not known with certainty that this assumption is true, although many believe that it is; consequently, this assumption has been used in security proofs for cryptographic algorithms (see, for example, (Waters 2010)).

*Security Proof, Step 3: Reduction*

Given an *underlying mathematical computation* that is assumed to be *intractable* (i.e., to require more than polynomial resources, such as factoring, DDH, or DBDH), and given a *theoretical model of the environment* (e.g., the presence or absence of a *random oracle* component), the final step is for the designer to show a *reduction* in this environment from the underlying mathematical computation to the cryptographic algorithm or protocol whose security is to be proved. Such a reduction can in some cases be complex (involving several intermediate steps), but a proven reduction means that an efficient procedure to break this algorithm/protocol will necessarily translate to an efficient procedure to perform the underlying mathematical computation. (Thus, breaking the algorithm/protocol can be considered *equivalent to* solving the underlying mathematical problem.) Since the mathematical computation (e.g., DDH) has been studied for a long time and no one has ever found an efficient way to do it, this means that it is highly unlikely that an efficient method exists to break the algorithm/protocol.

Early and widely-cited reduction proofs of this type include *semantic security* (Goldwasser and Micali 1982), (Goldwasser and Micali 1984) and *indistinguishability of encryptions* under different attacker models (*chosen plaintext attack* (IND-CPA) (Goldwasser and Micali 1984), *chosen ciphertext attack* (IND-CCA) (Naor and Yung 1990), and *adaptive chosen ciphertext attack* (IND-CCA2) (Rackoff and Simon 1992)).

## 11.4 Summary

This primer has been a quick introduction to the terminology, goals, algorithms, and protocols of cryptography that are needed for understanding the PETs discussed in this book. Although it is clearly the "tip of the iceberg" in a vast field of academic, commercial, and governmental research and development, hopefully it will serve to give sufficient background to clarify how these PETs do their job of protecting privacy.

# References

C. Adams, S. Lloyd, *Understanding PKI: Concepts, Standards, and Deployment Considerations*, 2nd edn. (Addison-Wesley, Boston, 2003)

J. H. Ahn, D. Boneh, J. Camenisch, S. Hohenberger, A. Shelat, and B. Waters, Computing on authenticated data. *Proceedings of the Theory of Cryptography Conference*, Springer LNCS 7194, pp. 1–20, (2012, 19–21 March)

N. Attrapadung, B. Libert, and T. Peters, Computing on authenticated data: New privacy definitions and constructions. *Advances in Cryptology: Proceedings of Asiacrypt*, Springer LNCS 7658, 2–6 (2012, December)

D. J. Bernstein, ChaCha, a variant of Salsa20. (2008, 28 January)

D. J. Bernstein, Extending the Salsa20 nonce. (2011, 4 February)

D. J. Bernstein and T. Lange, Faster Addition and Doubling on Elliptic Curves. (2007, 6 September)

G. R. Blakley, Safeguarding cryptographic keys. AFIPS International Workshop on Managing Requirements Knowledge, pp. 313–317, (1979)

D. Boneh and M. Franklin, Identity-based encryption from the Weil pairing. *Advances in Cryptology: Proceedings of Crypto 2001*, Springer LNCS 2139, pp. 213–229, (2001)

G. Brassard, C. Crépeau, and J.-M. Robert, All-or-nothing disclosure of secrets. *Advances in Cryptology: Proceedings of Crypto '86*, Springer LNCS 263, pp. 234–238 (1986)

D. R. L. Brown, SEC 2: Recommended Elliptic Curve Domain Parameters. *Standards for Efficient Cryptography 2 (SEC 2)*, Version 2.0, 37pp, (2010, 27 January)

M. Chase, M. Kohlweiss, A. Lysyanskaya, and S. Meiklejohn, Malleable signatures: New definitions and delegatable anonymous credentials. *IEEE 27th Computer Security Foundations Symposium*, Vienna, pp. 199–213, (2014)

D. Chaum, Blind Signatures for Untraceable Payments. *Advances in Cryptology: Proceedings of Crypto '82*, pp. 199–203 (1983)

L. Chen, Recommendation for key derivation using pseudorandom functions. US National Institute of Standards and Technology, Computer Security Division, NIST Special Publication 800-108, (2009, October)

C. Cocks, An identity based encryption scheme based on quadratic residues. *Proceedings of the 8th IMA International Conference on Cryptology and Coding*, Sepringer LNCS 2260, pp. 360–363 (2001)

W. Dean, Computational Complexity Theory. *The Stanford Encyclopedia of Philosophy* (Winter 2016 Edition), Edward N. Zalta (ed.), 2016

W. Diffie, M.E. Hellman, New directions in cryptography. IEEE Trans. Inf. Theory **IT-22**(6), 644–654 (1976)

W. Diffie, P.C. van Oorschot, M.J. Wiener, Authentication and authenticated key exchanges. Des. Codes Crypt. **2**(2), 107–125 (1992)

M. Dworkin, Recommendation for Block Cipher Modes of Operation: Methods and Techniques. *US National Institute of Standards and Technology, Computer Security Division, NIST Special Publication 800-38A*, (2001, December)

M. Dworkin, Recommendation for Block Cipher Modes of Operation: Galois/Counter Mode (GCM) and GMAC. *US National Institute of Standards and Technology, Computer Security Division, NIST Special Publication 800-38D*, November 2007

H.M. Edwards, A normal form for elliptic curves. *Bulletin of the American Mathematical Society* **44**(3), 393–422 (2007)

S. Even, O. Goldreich, A. Lempel, A randomized protocol for signing contracts. Commun. ACM **28**(6), 637–647 (1985)

J. Fan, C. Adams, Using Malleable Signatures to Allow Multi-Show Capability in Digital Credentials. *International Journal of Sensor Networks and Data Communications* **7**(4), 6 (2018)

A. Fiat and M. Naor, Broadcast encryption. *Advances in cryptology: Proceedings of crypto '93*, Springer LNCS 773, pp. 480–491, 1994

FIPS: Federal Information Processing Standards Publication Series, "Data Encryption Standard (DES)", FIPS PUB 46, 15 January 1977 (reaffirmed as FIPS PUB 46–3 on 25 October 1999)

FIPS: Federal Information Processing Standards Publication Series, Digital Signature Standard (DSS). FIPS PUB 186–1, 15 December 1998 (reaffirmed as FIPS PUB 186–4 in July 2013)

FIPS: Federal Information Processing Standards Publication Series, Advanced Encryption Standard (AES). FIPS PUB 197, (2001, 26 November)

FIPS: Federal Information Processing Standards Publication Series, "Secure Hash Standard (SHS)", FIPS PUB 180–4, (2015, August

C. Gentry, Fully Homomorphic Encryption Using Ideal Lattices. *41ˢᵗ ACM Symposium on Theory of Computing*, pp. 169–178, (2009, May)

O. Goldreich, S. Micali, and A. Wigderson, Proofs that yield nothing but their validity and a methodology of cryptographic protocol design. *Proceedings of the 27th Annual IEEE Symposium on Foundations of Computer Science*, pp. 174–187, (1986, 27–29 October)

S. Goldwasser and S. Micali, Probabilistic encryption & how to play mental poker keeping secret all partial information. *14ᵗʰ Annual ACM Symposium on Theory of Computing*, pp. 365–377, (1982, May)

S. Goldwasser, S. Micali, Probabilistic encryption. J. Comput. Syst. Sci. **28**(2), 270–299 (1984)

S. Goldwasser, S. Micali, C. Rackoff, The knowledge complexity of interactive proof systems. Soc. Indust. Appl. Mathematics (SIAM) J. Comput. **18**(1), 186–208 (1989)

R. Housley, T. Polk, *Planning for PKI: Best Practices Guide for Deploying Public Key Infrastructure* (Wiley, New York, 2001)

J. Katz, Y. Lindell, *Introduction to Modern Cryptography*, 2nd edn. (CRC Press, Taylor & Francis Group, 2015)

A. J. Menezes, P. C. van Oorschot, and S. A. Vanstone, *Handbook of Applied Cryptography*. CRC Press (1996) (5ᵗʰ printing: 2001)

M. Naor and M. Yung, Public-key cryptosystems provably secure against chosen ciphertext attacks. *22ⁿᵈ Annual ACM Symposium on Theory of Computing*, pp. 427–437, (1990, April)

T. P. Pedersen, Non-interactive and information-theoretic secure verifiable secret sharing. *Advances in Cryptology: Proceedings of Crypto '91* , pp. 129–140, (1992)

PKCS: RSA Laboratories, "PKCS #1 v2.1: RSA Cryptography Standard", *RSA Security Inc. Public-Key Cryptography Standards (PKCS)*, (2002, 14 June)

M. O. Rabin, How to Exchange Secrets by Oblivious Transfer. *Technical Report TR-81*, Aiken Computation Laboratory, Harvard University, 20 (1981)

C. Rackoff and D. R. Simon, Non-interactive zero-knowledge proof of knowledge and chosen Ciphertext attack. *Advances in Cryptology: Proceedings of Crypto '91*, Springer LNCS 576, pp. 433–444 (1992)

R. L. Rivest, The MD5 message-digest algorithm. Internet Engineering Task Force (IETF) Request for Comments RFC 1321 (1992)

R.L. Rivest, A. Shamir, L. Adleman, A method for obtaining digital signatures and public-key cryptosystems. Commun. ACM **21**(2), 120–126 (1978a)

R. L. Rivest, L. Adleman, and M. L. Dertouzos, On data banks and privacy homomorphisms. *Foundations of Secure Computation*, Academia Press, pp. 169–179, (1978b)

A. Sahai and B. Waters, Fuzzy identity based encryption. *Advances in Cryptology – Proceedings of Eurocrypt*, Springer LNCS 3494, pp. 457–473 (2005)

B. Schneier, *Applied Cryptography: Protocols, Algorithms, and Source Code in C*, 2nd edn. (Wiley, 1996)

A. Shamir, How to share a secret. Commun. ACM **22**(11), 612–613 (1979)

A. Shamir, Identity-based cryptosystems and signature schemes. *Advances in Cryptology: Proceedings of Crypto 84*, Springer LNCS 196, pp. 47–53 (1985)

M. Sipser, *Introduction to the Theory of Computation*, 3rd edn. (Thomson South-Western, 2012)

W. Stallings, *Cryptography and Network Security: Principles and Practice*, 6th edn. (Pearson, 2014)

D.R. Stinson, M.B. Patterson, *Cryptography: Theory and Practice* (CRC Press, Taylor & Francis Group, 2018)

W.-G. Tzeng, Efficient 1-out-n oblivious transfer schemes. *International Workshop on Public Key Cryptography*, Springer LNCS 2274, pp. 159–171 (2002)

S. Vaudenay, *A Classical Introduction to Modern Cryptography* (Springer, 2005)

B. Waters, "Ciphertext-Policy Attribute-Based Encryption: An Expressive, Efficient, and Provably Secure Realization", *Cryptology ePrint Archive, 2008/290*, 27 June 2008 (Last Revised 2010, 20 December)

Wikipedia, *Computational Complexity Theory*, (2021, 13 March)

# Chapter 12
# Source Material

**Abstract** This chapter amalgamates the references from all the previous chapters in the book. However, as an aid to students and researchers in the field, a hyperlink is added for (almost) every reference to facilitate easy retrieval of the cited material. In addition, a (short) bibliography of recommended reading is provided and pointers to further reading on selected topics are given.

**Keywords** References · Citations · Sources · Publications · Research papers · Bibliography · Recommended reading

*This chapter contains the complete set of references that were cited throughout this book, as well as a short list of recommended books in the privacy field.*

*Most of the references listed below are freely available at the given hyperlinks, but unfortunately some are only "freely" available at institutions (such as many university campuses) that have current subscriptions to the relevant publishers. Every attempt has been made to use truly free sources whenever possible. Note that all hyperlinks were last accessed January-May 2021.*

## 12.1 Full List of Hyperlinked References

1. Carlisle Adams, "A Classification for Privacy Techniques", *University of Ottawa Law & Technology Journal*, vol. 3, no. 1, 2006. (Available at https://crysp.uwaterloo.ca/courses/pet/F07/cache/www.uoltj.ca/articles/vol3.1/2006.3.1.uoltj.Adams.35-52.pdf)
2. Carlisle Adams and Katerine Barbieri, "Privacy Enforcement in E-Services Environments", in *Privacy Protection for E-Services*, G. Yee, Ed., Idea Group Publishing, 2006, pp. 172-202. (Available at https://www.goodreads.com/book/show/17654156-privacy-protection-for-e-services)
3. Carlisle Adams, "Achieving Non-Transferability in Credential Systems Using Hidden Biometrics", *Security and Communication Networks*, vol. 4, no. 2,

© The Editor(s) (if applicable) and The Author(s), under exclusive license
to Springer Nature Switzerland AG 2021
C. Adams, *Introduction to Privacy Enhancing Technologies*,
https://doi.org/10.1007/978-3-030-81043-6_12

269

February 2011, pp. 195–206. (Available at https://onlinelibrary.wiley.com/doi/10.1002/sec.136)

4. Carlisle Adams, Yu Dai, Catherine DesOrmeaux, Sean McAvoy, NamChi Nguyen, and Francisco Trindade, "Strengthening Enforcement in a Comprehensive Architecture for Privacy Enforcement at Internet Websites", *Frontiers in Computer Science*, vol. 2, 4 February 2020, 9pp. (Available at https://www.frontiersin.org/articles/10.3389/fcomp.2020.00002/full)

5. Carlisle Adams and Steve Lloyd, *Understanding PKI: Concepts, Standards, and Deployment Considerations, 2$^{nd}$ Edition*, Addison-Wesley, Boston, 2003. (Available at https://www.amazon.com/Understanding-PKI-Standards-Deployment-Considerations/dp/0321743091)

6. Gagan Aggarwal, Tomás Feder, Krishnaram Kenthapadi, Rajeev Motwani, Rina Panigrahy, Dilys Thomas, and An Zhu, "Anonymizing tables", *Proceedings of the International Conference on Database Theory*, Springer LNCS 3363, 5-7 January 2005, pp. 246-258. (Available at https://link.springer.com/chapter/10.1007/978-3-540-30570-5_17)

7. Charu Aggarwal, "On k-Anonymity and the Curse of Dimensionality", *Proceedings of the 31$^{st}$ Conference on Very Large Databases*, Trondheim, Norway, August 2005, pp. 901-909. (Available at https://dl.acm.org/doi/10.5555/1083592.1083696)

8. Rakesh Agrawal, Jerry Kiernan, Ramakrishnan Srikant, and Yirong Xu, "Hippocratic Databases", *Proceedings of the 28$^{th}$ International Conference on Very Large Databases*, Hong Kong, 2002, 12pp. (Available at http://citeseerx.ist.psu.edu/viewdoc/summary?doi=10.1.1.163.6107)

9. Rakesh Agrawal, Jerry Kiernan, Ramakrishnan Srikant, and Yirong Xu, "An XPath-based Preference Language for P3P", *Proceedings of the 12th International World Wide Web Conference*, Budapest, Hungary, May 2003, pp. 629-639. (Available at https://dl.acm.org/doi/10.1145/775152.775241)

10. Rakesh Agrawal, Alexandre Evfimievski, and Ramakrishnan Srikant, "Information Sharing across Private Databases", *Proceedings of the ACM SIGMOD Conference on Management of Data*, San Diego, California, June 2003, 12pp. (Available at https://www.cs.cornell.edu/aevf/research/SIGMOD_2003.pdf)

11. Rakesh Agrawal, Roberto Bayardo, Christos Faloutsos, Jerry Kiernan, Ralf Rantzau, and Ramakrishnan Srikant, "Auditing Compliance with a Hippocratic Database", *Proceedings of the 30$^{th}$ International Conference on Very Large Databases*, Toronto, Canada, 2004, 12pp. (Available at http://www.sciweavers.org/read/auditing-compliance-with-a-hippocratic-database-137167)

12. Rakesh Agrawal, Jerry Kiernan, Ramakrishnan Srikant, and Yirong Xu, "Order-Preserving Encryption for Numeric Data", *Proceedings of the ACM SIGMOD Conference on Management of Data*, Paris, France, June 2004, pp. 563-574. (Available at https://dl.acm.org/doi/10.1145/1007568.1007632)

13. Rakesh Agrawal and Evimaria Terzi, "On Honesty in Sovereign Information Sharing", *Proceedings of the 10th International Conference on Extending*

*Database Technology*, Munich, Germany, March 2006, pp. 240-256. (Available at https://link.springer.com/chapter/10.1007/11687238_17)

14. Rakesh Agrawal, Dmitri Asonov, Murat Kantarcioglu, and Yaping Li, "Sovereign Joins", *Proceedings of the 22nd International Conference on Data Engineering*, Atlanta, USA, April 2006, 12pp. (Available at https://personal.utdallas.edu/~muratk/publications/joins_icde06.pdf)

15. Rakesh Agrawal, Paul Bird, Tyrone Grandison, Jerry Kiernan, Scott Logan, and Walid Rjaibi, "Extending Relational Database Systems to Automatically Enforce Privacy Policies", *Proceedings of the 21$^{st}$ International Conference on Data Engineering*, Tokyo, Japan, April 2005, pp. 1013-1022. (Available at https://www.researchgate.net/publication/4133542_Extending_Relational_Database_Systems_to_Automatically_Enforce_Privacy_Policies)

16. Jae Hyun Ahn, Dan Boneh, Jan Camenisch, Susan Hohenberger, Abhi Shelat, and Brent Waters, "Computing on authenticated data", *Proceedings of the Theory of Cryptography Conference*, Springer LNCS 7194, 19-21 March 2012, pp. 1-20. (Available at https://www.iacr.org/archive/tcc2012/71940120/71940120.pdf)

17. Chris Alexander and Ian Goldberg, "Improved User Authentication in Off-the-Record Messaging", *Workshop on Privacy in the Electronic Society*, 29 October 2007, pp. 41-47. (Available at https://dl.acm.org/doi/pdf/10.1145/1314333.1314340)

18. Junade Ali, "Validating Leaked Passwords with *k*-Anonymity", *Cloudfare blog*, 2018. (Available at https://blog.cloudflare.com/validating-leaked-passwords-with-k-anonymity/)

19. Olivia Angiuli and Jim Waldo, "Statistical Tradeoffs between Generalization and Suppression in the De-Identification of Large-Scale Data Sets", *IEEE 40$^{th}$ Annual Computer Software and Applications Conference*, 2016, pp. 589-593. (Available at https://ieeexplore.ieee.org/stamp/stamp.jsp?tp=&arnumber=7552278)

20. Annie Antón and Julia Earp, "A Taxonomy for Website Privacy Requirements", *NCSU Technical Report TR-2001-14*, 18 December 2001. (Available at https://www.cc.gatech.edu/~aianton/assets/ataxonomyforwebsiteprivacy.pdf)

21. Annie Antón, Julia Earp, and Angela Reese, "Analyzing Website privacy requirements using a privacy goal taxonomy", *Proceedings of the IEEE Joint International Conference on Requirements Engineering*, Essen, Germany, 9-13 September 2002. (Available at https://ieeexplore.ieee.org/document/1048502)

22. Apple Newsroom, "Apple previews iOS 10, the biggest iOS release ever", *press release*, 13 June 2016. (Available at https://www.apple.com/newsroom/2016/06/apple-previews-ios-10-biggest-ios-release-ever/)

23. Ghada Arfaoui, Xavier Bultel, Pierre-Alain Fouque, Adina Nedelcu, and Cristina Onete, "The privacy of the TLS 1.3 protocol", *Proceedings on Privacy Enhancing Technologies*, vol. 2019, no. 4, October 2019, pp. 190-210. (Available at https://www.sciendo.com/article/10.2478/popets-2019-0065)

24. Dmitri Asonov, "Private Information Retrieval: An Overview and Current Trends", *Proceedings of the ECDPvA Workshop, Informatik 2001, Vienna, Austria, September 2001.* (Available at http://www.dbis.informatik.hu-berlin. de/fileadmin/research/papers/conferences/2001-gi_ocg-asonov.pdf)

25. Nuttapong Attrapadung, Benoît Libert, and Thomas Peters, "Computing on Authenticated Data: New Privacy Definitions and Constructions", *Advances in Cryptology: Proceedings of Asiacrypt*, Springer LNCS 7658, 2-6 December 2012. (Available at https://www.iacr.org/archive/asiac-rypt2012/76580363/76580363.pdf)

26. Stephen Baker, *The Numerati*, Houghton Mifflin Company, 2008. (Available at https://www.amazon.com/gp/product/0618784608/ref=x_gr_w_bb_sout?ie=UTF8&tag=x_gr_w_bb_sout-20&linkCode=as2&camp=1789&creative=9325&creativeASIN=0618784608&SubscriptionId=1MGPYB6YW3HWK55XCGG2)

27. A. Balu and K. Kuppusamy, "Ciphertext policy Attribute based Encryption with anonymous access policy", *International Journal of Peer-to-Peer Networks*, vol. 1, no. 1, October 2010. (Available at https://arxiv.org/ftp/arxiv/papers/1011/1011.0527.pdf) (See also *Quality, Reliability, Security and Robustness in Heterogeneous Networks (QShine 2013)*, K. Singh and A. K. Awasthi (eds), Lecture Notes of the Institute for Computer Sciences, Social Informatics and Telecommunications Engineering, Springer, vol. 115, 2013, pp. 696-705.)

28. Ken Barker, Mina Askari, Mishtu Banerjee, Kambiz Ghazinour, Brenan Mackas, Maryam Majedi, Sampson Pun, and Adepele Williams, "A Data Privacy Taxonomy", *British National Conference on Databases* (BNCOD 2009), Springer-Verlag, LNCS 5588, 2009, pp. 42–54. (Available at https://link.springer.com/chapter/10.1007/978-3-642-02843-4_7; see also http://pages.cpsc.ucalgary.ca/~barker/Publications/Barkeretal2009.pdf)

29. Adam Barth, Anupam Datta, John Mitchell, and Helen Nissenbaum, "Privacy and Contextual Integrity: Framework and Applications", *Proceedings of the IEEE Symposium on Security and Privacy*, pp. 184-198, May 2006. (Available at https://citeseerx.ist.psu.edu/viewdoc/summary?doi=10.1.1.76.1610)

30. Roberto J. Bayardo and Rakesh Agrawal, "Data Privacy through Optimal *k*-Anonymization", *Proceedings of the 21$^{st}$ International Conference on Data Engineering*, April 2005, pp. 217-228. (Available at https://www.cs.auckland. ac.nz/research/groups/ssg/pastbib/pastpapers/bayardo05data.pdf)

31. Amos Beimel, Yuval Ishai, Eyal Kushilevitz, and Jean-Francois Raymond, "Breaking the O($n^{1/(2k-1)}$) Barrier for Information-Theoretic Private Information Retrieval", *Proceedings of the 43$^{rd}$ Annual Symposium on Foundations of Computer Science*, 2002, pp. 261-270. (Available at https://www.computer. org/csdl/proceedings-article/focs/2002/18220261/12OmNxwENMZ)

32. Amos Beimel, Yuval Ishai, and Eyal Kushilevitz, "General constructions for information-theoretic private information retrieval", *Journal of Computer and System Sciences*, vol. 71, no. 2, August 2005, pp. 213-247. (Available at https://www.sciencedirect.com/science/article/pii/S0022000005000309)

33. Amos Beimel and Gihyuk Ko, "Private Information Retrieval", *slides for Applied Cryptography course at Carnegie Mellon University*, ca. 2017. (Available at http://course.ece.cmu.edu/~ece733/lectures/20-pir.pdf)

34. Kai Bemmann, Johannes Blömer, Jan Bobolz, Henrik Bröcher, Denis Diemert, Fabian Eidens, Lukas Eilers, Jan Haltermann, Jakob Juhnke, Burhan Otour, Laurens Porzenheim, Simon Pukrop, Erik Schilling, Michael Schlichtig, and Marcel Stienemeier, "Fully-Featured Anonymous Credentials with Reputation System", *Proceedings of the 13ᵗʰ International Conference on Availability, Reliability and Security*, August 2018, pp. 1-10. (Available at https://dl.acm.org/doi/10.1145/3230833.3234517)

35. Iness Ben Guirat, Devashish Gosain, and Claudia Diaz, "Mixim: A General Purpose Simulator for mixnet", *Privacy Enhancing Technologies Symposium, HotPETs session*, 2020. (Available at https://www.petsymposium.org/2020/files/hotpets/Mixim.pdf)

36. Colin J. Bennett, *Regulating Privacy: Data Protection and Public Policy in Europe and the United States*, Cornell University Press, 1992. (Available at https://www.jstor.org/stable/10.7591/j.ctv2n7hxs)

37. Kamal Benzekki, Abdeslam El Fergougui, and Abdelbaki Elbelrhiti Elalaoui, "Software-defined networking (SDN): a survey", *Security and Communication Networks*, vol. 9, no. 18, February 2017, pp. 5803-5833. (Available at https://onlinelibrary.wiley.com/doi/full/10.1002/sec.1737)

38. Daniel J. Bernstein and Tanja Lange, "Faster addition and doubling on elliptic curves", 6 September 2007. (Available at http://cr.yp.to/newelliptic/newelliptic-20070906.pdf)

39. Daniel J. Bernstein, "ChaCha, a variant of Salsa20", 28 January 2008. (Available at https://cr.yp.to/chacha/chacha-20080128.pdf)

40. Daniel J. Bernstein, "Extending the Salsa20 nonce", 4 February 2011. (Available at https://cr.yp.to/snuffle/xsalsa-20110204.pdf)

41. Oliver Berthold, Hannes Federrath, and Stefan Köpsell, "Web MIXes: A System for Anonymous and Unobservable Internet Access", in *Designing Privacy Enhancing Technologies*, Springer-Verlag, LNCS 2009, 2001, pp. 115-129. (Available at https://link.springer.com/chapter/10.1007/3-540-44702-4_7)

42. John Bethencourt, Amit Sahai, and Brent Waters, "Ciphertext-Policy Attribute-Based Encryption", *IEEE Symposium on Security and Privacy*, Berkeley, CA, 2007, pp. 321-334. (Available at https://ieeexplore.ieee.org/document/4223236)

43. Ola Bini and Sofía Celi, "No evidence of communication: Off-the-Record Protocol Version 4", *Privacy Enhancing Technologies Symposium, HotPETs session*, 27 July 2018. (Available at https://petsymposium.org/2018/files/hotpets/7-bini.pdf)

44. David Bissessar, Carlisle Adams, and Dong Liu, "Using Biometric Key Commitments to Prevent Unauthorized Lending of Cryptographic Credentials", *Proceedings of the 12ᵗʰ Annual Conference on Privacy, Security and Trust (PST 2014)*, Toronto, Canada, 23-24 July 2014. (Available at https://ieeexplore.ieee.org/document/6890926)

45. George Robert Blakley, "Safeguarding Cryptographic Keys", *AFIPS International Workshop on Managing Requirements Knowledge*, 1979, pp. 313-317. (Available at https://www.semanticscholar.org/paper/ Safeguarding-cryptographic-keys-Blakley/32d21ccc21a807627fcb21ea829d 1acdab23be12?p2df)

46. Marina Blanton, "Online Subscriptions with Anonymous Access", *Proceedings of the ACM Symposium on Information, Computer and Communications Security (ASIA CCS)*, Tokyo, Japan, 18-20 March 2008, pp. 217-227. (Available at https://dl.acm.org/doi/10.1145/1368310.1368342)

47. Avrim Blum, Cynthia Dwork, Frank McSherry, and Kobbi Nissim, "Practical privacy: The SuLQ framework", *Proceedings of the 24th ACM SIGMOD-SIGACT-SIGART Symposium on Principles of Database Systems*, 13-15 June 2005, pp. 128–138. (Available at https://dl.acm.org/doi/10.1145/ 1065167.1065184)

48. Avrim Blum, "A brief tour of differential privacy. Your guide: Avrim Blum", *StudyLib*, ca. 2013. (Available at https://studylib.net/doc/16108399/ an-brief-tour-of-differential-privacy-avrim-blum-your-guide-)

49. Avrim Blum, Katrina Ligett, and Aaron Roth, "A learning theory approach to noninteractive database privacy", *Journal of the ACM*, vol. 60, no. 2, Article 12, April 2013, pp. 1-25. (Available at https://dl.acm.org/doi/ pdf/10.1145/2450142.2450148)

50. Dan Boneh and Matt Franklin, "Identity-Based Encryption from the Weil Pairing", *Advances in Cryptology: Proceedings of Crypto 2001*, Springer LNCS 2139, 2001, pp. 213-229. (Available at https://link.springer.com/chapt er/10.1007/3-540-44647-8_13)

51. Paola Bonizzoni, Gianluca Della Vidova, and Riccardo Dondi, "The k-anonymity problem is hard", *International Symposium on Fundamentals of Computation Theory*, Springer LNCS 5699, 2-4 September 2009, pp. 26-37. (Available at https://link.springer.com/chapter/10.1007/ 978-3-642-03409-1_4)

52. Nikita Borisov, Ian Goldberg, and Eric Brewer, "Off-the-Record Communication, or, Why Not to Use PGP", *Workshop on Privacy in the Electronic Society*, 2004, pp. 77-84. (Available at https://dl.acm.org/ doi/10.1145/1029179.1029200)

53. Fabrice Boudot, Berry Schoenmakers, and Jacques Traoré, "A fair and efficient solution to the socialist millionaires' problem", *Discrete Applied Mathematics*, vol. 111, no. 1-2, 15 July 2001, pp. 77-85. (Available at https:// www.sciencedirect.com/science/article/pii/S0166218X00003425?v ia%3Dihub)

54. John M. Boyer, "XForms 1.1", *W3C Recommendation REC-xforms-20091020*, 20 October 2009. (Available at https://www.w3.org/TR/xforms/)

55. Mary Branscombe, "PassProtect tells you if your password has been pwned", *ZDNet*, 25 May 2018. (Available at https://www.zdnet.com/article/ passprotect-tells-you-if-your-password-has-been-pwned/)

56. Stefan Brands, "Privacy-protected transfer of electronic information", *U.S. Patent* (filed August 1993), patent number 5,604,805, issued February 1997.

57. Stefan Brands, *Rethinking Public Key Infrastructures and Digital Certificates: Building in Privacy*, The MIT Press, 2000. (Available at http://www.credentica.com/the_mit_pressbook.html)

58. Stefan Brands, "A Technical Overview of Digital Credentials", *Credentica paper*, 20 February 2002. (Available at http://www.credentica.com/overview.pdf)

59. Gilles Brassard, Claude Crépeau, and Jean-Marc Robert, "All-or-nothing disclosure of secrets", *Advances in Cryptology: Proceedings of Crypto '86*, Springer LNCS 263, 1986, pp. 234-238. (Available at https://link.springer.com/chapter/10.1007/3-540-47721-7_17)

60. Jon Brodkin, "Find out if your password has been pwned – without sending it to a server", *Ars Technica*, 23 February 2018. (Available at https://arstechnica.com/information-technology/2018/02/new-tool-safely-checks-your-passwords-against-a-half-billion-pwned-passwords/)

61. Daniel R. L. Brown, "SEC 2: Recommended Elliptic Curve Domain Parameters", *Standards for Efficient Cryptography 2 (SEC 2)*, Version 2.0, 27 January 2010, 37pp. (Available at http://www.secg.org/sec2-v2.pdf)

62. Jacquelyn Burkell and Priscilla M. Regan, "Voter preferences, voter manipulation, voter analytics: policy options for less surveillance and more autonomy", *Internet Policy Review*, vol. 8, no. 4, 31 December 2019, 22pp. (Available at https://policyreview.info/pdf/policyreview-2019-4-1438.pdf)

63. BusinessWire, "NTT Research Distinguished Scientist Brent Waters and UCLA Professor Amit Sahai Win IACR Test-of-Time Award", *news release*, 9 April 2020. (Available at https://www.businesswire.com/news/home/20200409005689/en/)

64. Jan Camenisch and Anna Lysyanskaya, "An Efficient System for Non-transferable Anonymous Credentials with Optional Anonymity Revocation", *Advances in Cryptology: Proceedings of Eurocrypt 2001*, Springer LNCS 2045, 2001, pp. 93-118. (Available at https://link.springer.com/chapter/10.1007/3-540-44987-6_7; extended version available at https://eprint.iacr.org/2001/019)

65. Jan Camenisch and Anna Lysyanskaya, "A Signature Scheme with Efficient Protocols", *Proceedings of the 3rd International Conference on Security in Communication Networks*, Springer, LNCS 2576, 11-13 September 2003, pp. 268–289. (Available at https://www.researchgate.net/publication/243785819_A_Signature_Scheme_with_Ecient_Protocols)

66. Jan Camenisch, Susan Hohenberger, Markulf Kohlweiss, Anna Lysyanskaya, and Mira Meyerovich, "How to win the clone wars: efficient periodic *n*-times anonymous authentication", *Proceedings of the 13th ACM Conference on Computer and Communications Security*, Alexandria, Virginia, USA, October 2006, pp. 201-210. (Available at https://dl.acm.org/doi/10.1145/1180405.1180431)

67. Jan Camenisch, Maria Dubovitskaya, Peter Kalambet, Anja Lehmann, Gregory Neven, Frans-Stefan Preiss, and Timur Usatiy, "IBM Identity Mixer: Authentication without Identification", *idemix presentation, IBM Research – Zurich*, 12 November 2015. (Available at https://www.zurich.ibm.com/pdf/security/2015-11-12-Idemix-Presentation.pdf)

68. Nicholas Carlini, Chang Liu, Úlfar Erlingsson, Jernej Kos, and Dawn Song, "The secret sharer: Evaluating and testing unintended memorization in neural networks", *USENIX Security Symposium*, 2019, pp. 267–284. (Available at https://www.usenix.org/conference/usenixsecurity19/presentation/carlini)

69. CFIP: The Code of Fair Information Practices, U.S. Department of Health, Education and Welfare, Secretary's Advisory Committee on Automated Personal Data Systems, Records, Computers, and the Rights of Citizens, viii, 1973. (See, for example, https://epic.org/privacy/consumer/code_fair_info.html)

70. Zimo Chai, Amirhossein Ghafari, and Amir Houmansadr, "On the Importance of Encrypted-SNI (ESNI) to Censorship Circumvention", *9th USENIX Workshop on Free and Open Communications on the Internet*, Santa Clara, CA, USA, 13 August 2019, 8pp. (Available at https://www.usenix.org/conference/foci19/presentation/chai)

71. Yan-Cheng Chang and Chi-Jen Lu, "Oblivious Polynomial Evaluation and Oblivious Neural Learning", *Advances in Cryptology— Proceedings of Asiacrypt*, 9-13 December 2001, pp.369-384. (Available at https://link.springer.com/chapter/10.1007/3-540-45682-1_22)

72. Melissa Chase, Markulf Kohlweiss, Anna Lysyanskaya, and Sarah Meiklejohn, "Malleable signatures: New definitions and delegatable anonymous credentials", *IEEE 27th Computer Security Foundations Symposium*, Vienna, 2014, pp. 199-213. (Available at https://ieeexplore.ieee.org/document/6957112)

73. David Chaum, "Untraceable electronic mail, return addresses, and digital pseudonyms", *Communications of the ACM*, vol. 24, no. 2, February 1981. (Available at https://dl.acm.org/doi/pdf/10.1145/358549.358563)

74. David Chaum, "Blind Signatures for Untraceable Payments", *Advances in Cryptology: Proceedings of Crypto '82*, 1983, pp. 199-203. (Available at http://www.hit.bme.hu/~buttyan/courses/BMEVIHIM219/2009/Chaum.BlindSigForPayment.1982.PDF)

75. David Chaum, Jan-Hendrik Evertse, and Jeroen van de Graaf, "An Improved Protocol for Demonstrating Possession of Discrete Logarithms and Some Generalizations", *Advances in Cryptology: Proceedings of Eurocrypt '87*, Springer LNCS 304, 1988, pp. 127-141. (Available at https://link.springer.com/chapter/10.1007%2F3-540-39118-5_13)

76. Liqun Chen, Alberto N. Escalante B., Hans Löhr, Mark Manulis, and Ahmad-Reza Sadeghi, "A privacy-protecting multi-coupon scheme with stronger protection against splitting", *Proceedings of the 11th International Conference on Financial Cryptography and Data Security (FC 2007)*, Springer LNCS 4886, 2008, pp. 29-44. (Available at https://link.springer.com/chapter/10.1007/978-3-540-77366-5_4)

77. Lily Chen, "Recommendation for Key Derivation Using Pseudorandom Functions", *US National Institute of Standards and Technology, Computer Security Division, NIST Special Publication 800-108*, October 2009. (Available at https://nvlpubs.nist.gov/nistpubs/Legacy/SP/nistspecialpublication800-108.pdf)

78. Roberto Chinnici, Jean-Jacques Moreau, Arthur Ryman, and Sanjiva Weerawarana, "Web Services Description Language (WSDL) Version 2.0 Part 1: Core Language", *W3C Recommendation REC-wsdl20-20070626*, 26 June 2007. (Available at https://www.w3.org/TR/wsdl20/)

79. Benny Chor, Oded Goldreich, Eyal Kushilevitz, and Madhu Sudan, "Private Information Retrieval", *Proceedings of the 36th Annual Symposium on Foundations of Computer Science*, 23-25 October 1995, pp. 41-50. (Available at https://ieeexplore.ieee.org/document/492461)

80. Benny Chor, Oded Goldreich, Eyal Kushilevitz, and Madhu Sudan, "Private Information Retrieval", *Journal of the ACM*, vol. 45, no. 6, November 1998, pp. 965-982. (Available at https://www.tau.ac.il/~bchor/PIR.pdf)

81. Clifford Cocks, "An Identity Based Encryption Scheme Based on Quadratic Residues", *Proceedings of the 8th IMA International Conference on Cryptology and Coding*, Springer LNCS 2260, 2001, pp. 360-363. (Available at https://link.springer.com/chapter/10.1007/3-540-45325-3_32)

82. Lance Cottrell, "Mixmaster and remailer attacks", *essay*, 1994. (Available at http://www.obscura.com/~loki/remailer/remailer-essay.html)

83. Lorrie Cranor, Marc Langheinrich, and Massimo Marchiori, "A P3P Preference Exchange Language 1.0 (APPEL 1.0)", *W3C Working Draft WD-P3P-preferences-20020415*, 15 April 2002. (Available at https://www.w3.org/TR/P3P-preferences/)

84. Lorrie Cranor, Marc Langheinrich, Massimo Marchiori, Martin Presler-Marshall, and Joseph Reagle, "The Platform for Privacy Preferences 1.0 (P3P1.0) Specification", *W3C Recommendation REC-P3P-20020416*, 16 April 2002. (Available at https://www.w3.org/TR/2002/REC-P3P-20020416/)

85. Lorrie Faith Cranor, Praveen Guduru, and Manjula Arjula, "User interfaces for privacy agents", *ACM Transactions on Computer-Human Interaction*, vol. 13, no. 2, June 2006, pp. 135-178. (Available at https://dl.acm.org/doi/10.1145/1165734.1165735)

86. Lorrie Cranor, Brooks Dobbs, Serge Egelman, Giles Hogben, Jack Humphrey, Marc Langheinrich, Massimo Marchiori, Martin Presler-Marshall, Joseph Reagle, Matthias Schunter, David A. Stampley, and Rigo Wenning, "The Platform for Privacy Preferences 1.1 (P3P1.1) Specification", *W3C Working Group Note NOTE-P3P11-20061113*, 13 November 2006. (Available at https://www.w3.org/TR/2006/NOTE-P3P11-20061113/)

87. Lorrie Cranor and Rigo Wenning, "Platform for Privacy Preferences (P3P) Project: Enabling Smarter Privacy Tools for the Web", *W3C P3P Overview*, 2 February 2018. (Available at https://www.w3.org/P3P/Overview.html)

88. George Danezis, Roger Dingledine, and Nick Matthewson, "Mixminion: design of a type III anonymous remailer protocol", *Symposium on Security*

*and Privacy*, 2003, pp. 2-15. (Available at https://ieeexplore.ieee.org/stamp/stamp.jsp?tp=&arnumber=1199323&tag=1; see also https://www.mixminion.net/minion-design.pdf)

89. Walter Dean, "Computational Complexity Theory", *The Stanford Encyclopedia of Philosophy* (Winter 2016 Edition), Edward N. Zalta (ed.), 2016. (Available at https://plato.stanford.edu/archives/win2016/entries/computational-complexity/)

90. Dorothy Denning, *Cryptography and Data Security*, Addison-Wesley, 1982. See Chapter 6, "Inference Controls." (Available at https://www.amazon.com/Cryptography-Security-Dorothy-Elizabeth-Robling/dp/0201101505)

91. Damien Desfontaines and Balázs Pejó, "SoK: Differential Privacies", *Proceedings on Privacy Enhancing Technologies*, vol. 2, 2020, pp. 288-313. (Available at https://content.sciendo.com/view/journals/popets/2020/2/article-p288.xml). (The extended version of this paper is "SoK: Differential Privacies: A taxonomy of differential privacy variants and extensions", *arXiv.org*, arXiv:1906.01337v4, 10 July 2020, 58pp. Available at https://arxiv.org/pdf/1906.01337.pdf)

92. Casey Devet, Ian Goldberg, and Nadia Heninger, "Optimally Robust Private Information Retrieval", *Cryptology ePrint Archive*, 22 June 2012. *(Extended version of [Deve12b].)* (Available at https://eprint.iacr.org/2012/083.pdf)

93. Casey Devet, Ian Goldberg, and Nadia Heninger, "Optimally Robust Private Information Retrieval", *21$^{st}$ Usenix Security Symposium*, 8-10 August 2012, pp. 269-283. (Available at https://www.usenix.org/conference/usenixsecurity12/technical-sessions/presentation/devet)

94. Casey Devet and Ian Goldberg, "The Best of Both Worlds: Combining Information-Theoretic and Computational PIR for Communication Efficiency", 14$^{th}$ Privacy Enhancing Technologies Symposium, July 2014. (Available at https://cypherpunks.ca/~iang/pubs/hybridpir-pets.pdf)

95. Claudia Díaz, Stefaan Seys, Joris Claessens, and Bart Preneel, "Towards measuring anonymity", *Proceedings of the Second International Workshop on Privacy Enhancing Technologies,* Springer, LNCS 2482, San Francisco, USA, 14-15 April 2002, pp. 54-68. (Available at https://link.springer.com/chapter/10.1007/3-540-36467-6_5)

96. Whitfield Diffie and Martin E. Hellman, "New directions in cryptography", *IEEE Transactions on Information Theory*, vol. IT-22, no. 6, November 1976, pp. 644-654. (Available at https://ee.stanford.edu/~hellman/publications/24.pdf)

97. Whitfield Diffie, Paul C. van Oorschot, and Michael J. Wiener, "Authentication and Authenticated Key Exchanges", *Designs, Codes and Cryptography*, vol. 2, no. 2, 1992, pp. 107-125. (Available at https://link.springer.com/article/10.1007%2FBF00124891)

98. Terry Dillard, "Hippocratic Database and Active Enforcement", in *Ethical Issues and Security Monitoring Trends in Global Healthcare: Technological Advancements*, Steven A. Brown and Mary Brown (Eds.), Medical Information Science Reference (an imprint of IGI Global), 2011, pp. 43-49. (Available at https://www.igi-global.com/gateway/chapter/full-text-pdf/52358)

99. Roger Dingledine, Nick Matthewson, and Paul F. Syverson, "Tor: The Second-Generation Onion Router", *Usenix Security Symposium*, 2004, 17pp. (Available at https://svn-archive.torproject.org/svn/projects/design-paper/tor-design.pdf)

100. Roger Dingledine, "What is tor used for?", *e-mail to tor-talk chat group*, 3 November 2011. (Available at https://lists.torproject.org/pipermail/tor-talk/2011-November/021997.html)

101. Bolin Ding, Janardhan Kulkarni, and Sergey Yekhanin, "Collecting telemetry data privately", *31st Conference on Neural Information Processing Systems*, Long Beach, CA, December 2017, 10pp. (Available at https://www.microsoft.com/en-us/research/publication/collecting-telemetry-data-privately/)

102. Irit Dinur and Kobbi Nissim, "Revealing information while preserving privacy", *Proceedings of the 22nd ACM SIGMOD-SIGACT-SIGART Symposium on Principles of Database Systems*, June 2003, pp. 202–210. (Available at https://dl.acm.org/doi/10.1145/773153.773173)

103. Mario Di Raimondo, Rosario Gennaro, and Hugo Krawczyk, "Secure Off-the-Record Messaging", *Workshop on Privacy in the Electronic Society*, 7 November 2005, pp. 81-89. (Available at https://dl.acm.org/doi/10.1145/1102199.1102216)

104. Naganand Doraswamy and Dan Harkins, *IPsec: The New Security Standard for the Internet, Intranets, and Virtual Private Networks, 2nd Edition*, Prentice Hall, 2003. (Available at https://www.amazon.in/IPSec-Prentice-Hall-Ptr-Web-Infrastructure/dp/013046189X)

105. Wenliang Du and Zhijun Zhan, "Using Randomized Response Techniques for Privacy-Preserving Data Mining", *Proceedings of The Ninth ACM SIGKDD International Conference on Knowledge Discovery and Data Mining*, 24-27 August 2003, 6pp. (Available at http://www.sciweavers.org/read/using-randomized-response-techniques-for-privacy-preserving-data-mining-42166)

106. George F. du Pont, "The Time Has Come for Limited Liability for Operators of True Anonymity Remailers in Cyberspace: An Examination of the Possibilities and Perils", *Journal of Technology Law & Policy*, vol. 6, 2001, pp. 175-218. (Available at https://web.archive.org/web/20160305043023/http://www.thsh.com/documents/JTLM.pdf)

107. Cynthia Dwork and Kobbi Nissim, "Privacy-preserving datamining on vertically partitioned databases", *Advances in Cryptology: Proceedings of Crypto*, 15-19 August 2004, pp. 528–544. (Available at https://www.iacr.org/cryptodb/archive/2004/CRYPTO/1267/1267.pdf)

108. Cynthia Dwork, Frank McSherry, Kobbi Nissim, and Adam Smith, "Calibrating noise to sensitivity in private data analysis", *Proceedings of the 3rd Theory of Cryptography Conference*, 4-7 March 2006, pp. 265–284. (Available at https://link.springer.com/chapter/10.1007%2F11681878_14)

109. Cynthia Dwork, Krishnaram Kenthapadi, Frank McSherry, Ilya Mironov, and Moni Naor, "Our data, ourselves: Privacy via distributed noise generation", *Advances in Cryptology: Proceedings of Eurocrypt*, Springer LNCS 4004, St.

Petersburg, Russia, 28 May - 1 June 2006, pp. 486-503. (Available at https://www.iacr.org/cryptodb/archive/2006/EUROCRYPT/2319/2319.pdf)

110. Cynthia Dwork, "Differential Privacy", *Proceedings of the 33rd International Colloquium on Automata, Languages and Programming*, Springer LNCS 4052, Venice, Italy, 10-14 July 2006, pp. 1–12. (Available at https://link.springer.com/chapter/10.1007/11787006_1)

111. Cynthia Dwork, "Differential Privacy: A Survey of Results", *International Conference on Theory and Applications of Models and Computation*, Springer LNCS 4978, 2008, pp. 1-19. (Available at https://link.springer.com/chapter/10.1007/978-3-540-79228-4_1)

112. Morris Dworkin, "Recommendation for Block Cipher Modes of Operation: Methods and Techniques", *US National Institute of Standards and Technology, Computer Security Division, NIST Special Publication 800-38A*, December 2001. (Available at https://nvlpubs.nist.gov/nistpubs/Legacy/SP/nistspecialpublication800-38a.pdf)

113. Morris Dworkin, "Recommendation for Block Cipher Modes of Operation: Galois/Counter Mode (GCM) and GMAC", *US National Institute of Standards and Technology, Computer Security Division, NIST Special Publication 800-38D*, November 2007. (Available at https://nvlpubs.nist.gov/nistpubs/Legacy/SP/nistspecialpublication800-38d.pdf)

114. Matthew Edman and Paul Syverson, "AS-awareness in Tor path selection", *Proceedings of the 16th ACM Conference on Computer and Communications Security*, Chicago, Illinois, USA, November 2009, pp. 380-389. (Available at https://dl.acm.org/doi/10.1145/1653662.1653708)

115. Harold M. Edwards, "A normal form for elliptic curves", *Bulletin of the American Mathematical Society*, vol. 44, no. 3, 9 April 2007, pp. 393-422. (Available at https://www.ams.org/journals/bull/2007-44-03/S0273-0979-07-01153-6/home.html)

116. Tariq Elahi, Kevin Bauer, Mashael AlSabah, Roger Dingledine, and Ian Goldberg, "Changing of the guards: a framework for understanding and improving entry guard selection in tor", *Proceedings of the ACM Workshop on Privacy in the Electronic Society*, October 2012, pp. 43-54. (Available at https://dl.acm.org/doi/abs/10.1145/2381966.2381973)

117. Andrew Eland, "Tackling Urban Mobility with Technology", *Google Europe blog*, 18 November 2015. (Available at https://europe.googleblog.com/2015/11/tackling-urban-mobility-with-technology.html)

118. Khaled El Emam and Fida Kamal Dankar, "Protecting Privacy Using k-Anonymity", *Journal of the American Medical Informatics Association*, vol. 15, no. 5, September-October 2008, pp. 627-637. (Available at https://www.ncbi.nlm.nih.gov/pmc/articles/PMC2528029/)

119. Yuval Elovici, Bracha Shapira, and Adlai Maschiach, "A new privacy model for hiding group interests while accessing the Web", *ACM Workshop on Privacy in the Electronic Society*, 2002, pp. 63-70. (Available at https://dl.acm.org/doi/10.1145/644527.644534)

120. Enterprivacy Consulting Group, "A Taxonomy of Privacy", *infographic based on Daniel Solove's "A Taxonomy of Privacy" paper (https://papers.ssrn.com/sol3/papers.cfm?abstract_id=667622)*, ca. 2006. (Available at https://iapp.org/media/pdf/resource_center/A_taxonomy_of_privacy.pdf)

121. Úlfar Erlingsson, Vasyl Pihur, and Aleksandra Korolova, "RAPPOR: Randomized Aggregatable Privacy-Preserving Ordinal Response", *Proceedings of the 21ˢᵗ ACM Conference on Computer and Communications Security*, November 2014, pp. 1054-1067. (Available at https://dl.acm.org/doi/10.1145/2660267.2660348)

122. Shimon Even, Oded Goldreich, and Abraham Lempel, "A Randomized Protocol for Signing Contracts", *Communications of the ACM*, vol. 28, no. 6, 1985, pp. 637-647. (Available at https://cacm.acm.org/magazines/1985/6/10351-a-randomized-protocol-for-signing-contracts/abstract)

123. David Evans, Vladimir Kolesnikov and Mike Rosulek, *A Pragmatic Introduction to Secure Multi-Party Computation*, now publishers inc., December 2018. (Available at https://securecomputation.org/)

124. Jinnan Fan and Carlisle Adams, "Using Malleable Signatures to Allow Multi-Show Capability in Digital Credentials", *International Journal of Sensor Networks and Data Communications*, vol. 7, no. 4, 2018, 6pp. (Available at https://www.omicsonline.org/open-access/using-malleable-signatures-to-allow-multishow-capability-in-digital-credentials-2090-4886-1000160.pdf)

125. Nick Feamster and Roger Dingledine, "Location Diversity in Anonymity Networks", *Proceedings of the ACM Workshop on Privacy in the Electronic Society*, Washington, DC, USA, 28 October 2004, pp. 66-76. (Available at https://dl.acm.org/doi/10.1145/1029179.1029199)

126. Federal: Federal Trade Commission, *Children's Online Privacy Protection Act*, 15 U.S.C. 6501-6506, Pub. L. No. 105-277, Div. C, Title XIII, 112 Stat. 2681-2728, 1998. (Available at https://www.ftc.gov/enforcement/rules/rulemaking-regulatory-reform-proceedings/childrens-online-privacy-protection-rule)

127. Federal: Federal Trade Commission, "In FTC Study, Five Percent of Consumers Had Errors on Their Credit Reports That Could Result in Less Favorable Terms for Loans", *Federal Trade Commission press release*, 11 February 2013. (Available at https://www.ftc.gov/news-events/press-releases/2013/02/ftc-study-five-percent-consumers-had-errors-their-credit-reports)

128. Joan Feigenbaum, Aaron Johnson, and Paul Syverson, "Probabilistic Analysis of Onion Routing in a Black-Box Model", *ACM Transactions on Information and System Security (TISSEC)*, vol. 15, no. 3, article 14, 28pp., November 2012. (Available at https://dl.acm.org/doi/pdf/10.1145/2382448.2382452)

129. Vitaly Feldman, "Does learning require memorization? A short tale about a long tail", *Proceedings of the 52ⁿᵈ Annual ACM SIGACT Symposium on Theory of Computing*, Chicago, IL, USA, 22-26 June 2020, pp. 954-959. (Available at https://dl.acm.org/doi/abs/10.1145/3357713.3384290)

130. Amos Fiat and Moni Naor, "Broadcast Encryption", *Advances in Cryptology: Proceedings of Crypto '93*, Springer LNCS 773, 1994, pp. 480-491. (Available at https://link.springer.com/chapter/10.1007%2F3-540-48329-2_40)

131. FIPS: Federal Information Processing Standards Publication Series, "Data Encryption Standard (DES)", FIPS PUB 46, 15 January 1977 (reaffirmed as FIPS PUB 46-3 on 25 October 1999). (Available at https://csrc.nist.gov/csrc/media/publications/fips/46/3/archive/1999-10-25/documents/fips46-3.pdf)

132. FIPS: Federal Information Processing Standards Publication Series, "Digital Signature Standard (DSS)", FIPS PUB 186-1, 15 December 1998 (reaffirmed as FIPS PUB 186-4 in July 2013). (Available at https://nvlpubs.nist.gov/nistpubs/FIPS/NIST.FIPS.186-4.pdf)

133. FIPS: Federal Information Processing Standards Publication Series, "Advanced Encryption Standard (AES)", FIPS PUB 197, 26 November 2001. (Available at https://nvlpubs.nist.gov/nistpubs/FIPS/NIST.FIPS.197.pdf)

134. FIPS: Federal Information Processing Standards Publication Series, "Secure Hash Standard (SHS)", FIPS PUB 180-4, August 2015. (Available at https://nvlpubs.nist.gov/nistpubs/FIPS/NIST.FIPS.180-4.pdf)

135. Mahdi Daghmehchi Firoozjaei, Sang Min Lee, and Hyoungshick Kim, "O$^2$TR: Offline Off-the-Record (OTR) Messaging", *18$^{th}$ World Conference on Information Security Applications (WISA)*, 24-26 August 2017. (Available at https://seclab.skku.edu/wp-content/uploads/2016/12/wisa17-final28.pdf)

136. Sheila Frankel, *Demystifying the IPsec Puzzle*, Artech House, 2001. (Available at https://doc.lagout.org/network/Demystifying%20The%20IPsec%20Puzzle.pdf)

137. Tore Kasper Frederiksen and Jesper Buus Nielsen, "Fast and maliciously secure two-party computation using the GPU", *Applied Cryptography and Network Security*, Springer LNCS 7954, 2013, pp. 339-356. (Available at https://link.springer.com/chapter/10.1007/978-3-642-38980-1_21)

138. William Gasarch, "A Survey on Private Information Retrieval", *The Computational Complexity Column*, Lance Fortnow (Ed.), ca. 2004. (Available at https://crypto.stanford.edu/~dabo/courses/cs355_fall07/pir.pdf)

139. John Geddes, Rob Jansen, and Nicholas Hopper, "How Low Can You Go: Balancing Performance with Anonymity in Tor", *Privacy Enhancing Technologies Symposium*, 10-12 July 2013, pp. 164-184. (Available at https://www-users.cs.umn.edu/~hoppernj/howlow-pets2013.pdf)

140. Craig Gentry and Zulfikar Ramzan, "Single-Database Private Information Retrieval with Constant Communication Rate", *International Colloquium on Automata, Languages and Programming*, Springer LNCS 3580, 2005, pp. 803-815. (Available at https://citeseerx.ist.psu.edu/viewdoc/download;jsessionid=DEA146CB65362ABE9CBD9A5594EF9ACB?doi=10.1.1.113.6572&rep=rep1&type=pdf)

141. Craig Gentry, "Fully Homomorphic Encryption Using Ideal Lattices", *41$^{st}$ ACM Symposium on Theory of Computing*, May 2009, pp. 169-178. (Available at https://dl.acm.org/doi/10.1145/1536414.1536440)

142. Yael Gertner, Yuval Ishai, Eyal Kushilevitz, and Tal Malkin, "Protecting Data Privacy in Private Information Retrieval Schemes", *Journal of Computer and System Sciences*, vol. 60, no. 3, June 2000, pp. 592-629. (Available at https://www.sciencedirect.com/science/article/pii/S0022000099916896)

143. Shafi Goldwasser and Silvio Micali, "Probabilistic encryption & how to play mental poker keeping secret all partial information", *14th Annual ACM Symposium on Theory of Computing*, May 1982, pp. 365-377. (Available at https://dl.acm.org/doi/10.1145/800070.802212)

144. Shafi Goldwasser and Silvio Micali, "Probabilistic encryption", *Journal of Computer and System Sciences*, vol. 28, no. 2, April 1984, pp. 270-299. (Available at https://www.sciencedirect.com/science/article/pii/0022000084900709?via%3Dihub)

145. Oded Goldreich, Silvio Micali, and Avi Wigderson, "Proofs that yield nothing but their validity and a methodology of cryptographic protocol design", *Proceedings of the 27th Annual IEEE Symposium on Foundations of Computer Science*, 27-29 October 1986, pp. 174-187. (Available at https://ieeexplore.ieee.org/document/4568209)

146. Oded Goldreich, Silvio Micali, and Avi Wigderson, "How to play ANY mental game, or, A Completeness Theorem for Protocols with Honest Majority", *Proceedings of the 19th Annual ACM Symposium on Theory of Computing*, January 1987, pp. 218-229. (Available at https://dl.acm.org/doi/10.1145/28395.28420)

147. Shafi Goldwasser, Silvio Micali, and Charles Rackoff, "The Knowledge Complexity of Interactive Proof Systems", *Society for Industrial and Applied Mathematics (SIAM) Journal on Computing*, vol. 18, no. 1, February 1989, pp. 186-208. (Available at http://crypto.cs.mcgill.ca/~crepeau/COMP647/2007/TOPIC02/GMR89.pdf)

148. David M. Goldschlag, Michael G. Reed, and Paul F. Syverson, "Hiding routing information," in *Information Hiding*, R. Anderson, Ed., New York: Springer-Verlag, LNCS 1174, 1996, pp. 137–150. (Available at https://www.onion-router.net/Publications/IH-1996.pdf)

149. David M. Goldschlag, Michael G. Reed, and Paul F. Syverson, "Privacy on the Internet," *Internet Society INET'97*, Kuala Lumpur, Indonesia, June, 1997. (Available at https://web.archive.org/web/20160103125328/https://www.isoc.org/inet97/proceedings/F7/F7_1.HTM)

150. David M. Goldschlag, Michael G. Reed, and Paul F. Syverson, "Onion Routing", *Communications of the ACM*, vol. 42, no. 2, February 1999, pp. 39-41. (Available at https://cacm.acm.org/magazines/1999/2/7968-onion-routing/fulltext)

151. Oded Goldreich, "Cryptography and cryptographic protocols", *Distributed Computing*, vol. 16, 2003, pp. 177-199. (Available at https://link.springer.com/article/10.1007%2Fs00446-002-0077-1)

152. Shafi Goldwasser and Mihir Bellare, "Lecture Notes on Cryptography", *lecture notes for a week-long course on cryptography taught at MIT over ten*

*summers*, July 2008. (Available at http://cseweb.ucsd.edu/~mihir/papers/gb.pdf)

153. Ian Goldberg, Berkant Ustaoğlu, Matthew D. Van Gundy, and Hao Chen, "Multi-party Off-the-Record Messaging", *ACM Conference on Computer and Communications Security*, 9-13 November 2009. (Available at https://cypherpunks.ca/~iang/pubs/mpotr.pdf)

154. Vipul Goyal, Omkant Pandey, Amit Sahai, and Brent Waters, "Attribute Based Encryption for Fine-Grained Access Control of Encrypted Data", *Proceedings of the 13th ACM Conference on Computer and Communications Security*, October 2006, pp. 89-98. (Available at https://dl.acm.org/doi/10.1145/1180405.1180418)

155. Tyrone Grandison, Christopher Johnson, and Jerry Kiernan, "Hippocratic Databases: Current Capabilities and Future Trends" in *Handbook on Database Security: Applications and Trends*, Michael Gertz and Sushil Jajodia (Eds), Springer, 2008, pp. 409-429. (Available at https://link.springer.com/chapter/10.1007/978-0-387-48533-1_17)

156. Andy Greenberg, *This Machine Kills Secrets: How Wikileakers, Cypherpunks, and Hacktivists Aim to Free the World's Information*, Dutton, 2012. (Available at https://www.amazon.com/This-Machine-Kills-Secrets-WikiLeakers/dp/0525953205)

157. Mike Hamburg, "Ed448-Goldilocks, a new elliptic curve", ePrint archive 2015/625, 30 June 2015. (Available at https://eprint.iacr.org/2015/625)

158. Marcella Hastings, Brett Hemenway, Daniel Noble and Steve Zdancewic, "SoK: General Purpose Compilers for Secure Multi-Party Computation", *Proceedings of the IEEE Symposium on Security and Privacy*, 19-23 May 2019, pp. 479-496. (Available at https://ieeexplore.ieee.org/document/8835312)

159. Johan Helsingius, "Press Release 30.8.1996", 1996. (Available at https://web.archive.org/web/20160303221336/https://w2.eff.org/Privacy/Anonymity/960830_penet_closure.announce)

160. Johannes Heurix, Peter Zimmermann, Thomas Neubauer, and Stefen Fenz, "A Taxonomy for Privacy Enhancing Technologies", *Computers & Security*, vol. 53, September 2015, pp. 1-17. (Available at https://www.sciencedirect.com/science/article/pii/S0167404815000668)

161. Russ Housley and Tim Polk, *Planning for PKI: Best Practices Guide for Deploying Public Key Infrastructure*, Wiley, New York, 2001. (Available at https://www.amazon.com/Planning-PKI-Practices-Deploying-Infrastructure/dp/0471397024/ref=sr_1_1?dchild=1&keywords=housley+polk+pki&qid=1621894993&s=books&sr=1-1)

162. Yan Huang, Jonathan Katz, and David Evans, "Efficient secure two-party computation using symmetric cut-and-choose", *Advances in Cryptology: Proceedings of Crypto 2013*, Springer LNCS 8043, 18-22 August 2013, pp. 18-35. (Available at https://link.springer.com/chapter/10.1007/978-3-642-40084-1_2)

163. Anco Hundepool and Leon Willenborg, "μ- and τ-Argus: Software for statistical disclosure control", *Third International Seminar on Statistical Confidentiality*, Bled, 1996.

164. Russell Impagliazzo and Sara Miner More, "Anonymous Credentials with Biometrically-Enforced Non-Transferability", *Proceedings of the Workshop on Privacy in the Electronic Society*, Washington, DC, USA, 30 October 2003, pp. 60-71. (Available at http://www.sciweavers.org/read/anonymous-credentials-with-biometrically-enforced-non-transferability-144342)

165. David Ingram, "Factbox: Who is Cambridge Analytica and what did it do?", *Reuters*, 19 March 2018. (Available at https://www.reuters.com/article/us-facebook-cambridge-analytica-factbox/factbox-who-is-cambridge-analytica-and-what-did-it-do-idUSKBN1GW07F)

166. Mihaela Ion, Ben Kreuter, Erhan Nergiz, Sarvar Patel, Shobhit Saxena, Karn Seth, David Shanahan and Moti Yung, "Private Intersection-Sum Protocol with Applications to Attributing Aggregate Ad Conversions", *Cryptology ePrint Archive, 2017:738*, 31 July 2017. (Available at https://eprint.iacr.org/2017/738.pdf)

167. Yuval Ishai and Eyal Kushilevitz, "Improved upper bounds on information-theoretic private information retrieval", *Proceedings of the 31ˢᵗ ACM Symposium on Theory of Computing*, May 1999, pp. 79-88. (Available at https://dl.acm.org/doi/10.1145/301250.301275)

168. Aaron Jaggard and Paul F. Syverson, "Onions in the Crosshairs: When the Man really *is* out to get you", *Proceedings of the Workshop on Privacy in the Electronic Society*, 30 October 2017, pp. 141-151. (Available at https://dl.acm.org/doi/pdf/10.1145/3139550.3139553)

169. Aarshay Jain, "A Complete Tutorial on Ridge and Lasso Regression in Python", *Analytics Vidhya*, 28 January 2016. (Available at https://www.analyticsvidhya.com/blog/2016/01/ridge-lasso-regression-python-complete-tutorial/)

170. Markus Jakobsson and Moti Jung, "Proving without knowing: On oblivious, agnostic and blindfolded provers", *Advances in Cryptology: Proceedings of Crypto '96*, Springer LNCS 1109, 1996, pp. 186-200. (Available at https://link.springer.com/chapter/10.1007%2F3-540-68697-5_15)

171. Rob Jansen and Aaron Johnson, "Safely Measuring Tor", *Proceedings of the ACM Conference on Computer and Communications Security*, Vienna, Austria, 24-28 October 2016, pp. 1553-1567. (Available at https://dl.acm.org/doi/10.1145/2976749.2978310)

172. Rob Jansen, Matthew Traudt, John Geddes, Chris Wacek, Micah Sherr, and Paul Syverson, "KIST: Kernel-Informed Socket Transport for Tor", *ACM Transactions on Privacy and Security*, article no. 3, December 2018, 37pp. (Available at https://dl.acm.org/doi/10.1145/3278121)

173. Aaron Johnson, Rob Jansen, Nicholas Hopper, Aaron Segal, and Paul F. Syverson, "PeerFlow: Secure Load Balancing in Tor", *Proceedings on Privacy Enhancing Technologies*, vol. 2, 2017, pp. 1-21. (Available at https://ohmygodel.com/publications/peerflow-popets2017.pdf)

174. Noah Johnson, Joseph P. Near, Joseph M. Hellerstein, and Dawn Song, "Chorus: Differential privacy via query rewriting", *arXiv.com, 1809.07750*, 23 September 2018. (Available at https://arxiv.org/pdf/1809.07750.pdf)

175. Jonathan Katz and Yehuda Lindell, *Introduction to Modern Cryptography, 2nd Edition*, CRC Press, Taylor & Francis Group, 2015. (Available at https://b-ok.cc/book/2483688/1b6af7)

176. Joanna Kavenna, "Interview: Shoshana Zuboff: 'Surveillance capitalism is an assault on human autonomy'", *The Guardian*, 4 October 2019. (Available at https://www.theguardian.com/books/2019/oct/04/shoshana-zuboff-surveillance-capitalism-assault-human-automomy-digital-privacy)

177. Michael Kay, "XSL Transformations (XSLT) Version 3.0", *W3C Recommendation REC-xslt-30-20170608*, 8 June 2017. (Available at https://www.w3.org/TR/2017/REC-xslt-30-20170608/)

178. Batya Kenig and Tamir Tassa, "A practical approximation algorithm for optimal $k$-anonymity", *Data Mining and Knowledge Discovery*, vol. 25, 2012, pp. 134-168. (Available at https://link.springer.com/article/10.1007/s10618-011-0235-9)

179. Aggelos Kiayias, Nikos Leonardos, Helger Lipmaa, Kateryna Pavlyk, and Qiang Tang, "Optimal Rate Private Information Retrieval from Homomorphic Encryption", *Proceedings on Privacy Enhancing Technologies*, vol. 2, 2015, pp. 222-243. (Available at https://content.sciendo.com/view/journals/popets/2015/2/article-p222.xml)

180. Daniel Kifer and Bing-Rong Lin, "Towards an axiomatization of statistical privacy and utility", *Proceedings of the 29th ACM SIGMOD-SIGACT-SIGART Symposium on Principles of Database Systems*, June 2010, pp. 147-158. (Available at https://dl.acm.org/doi/10.1145/1807085.1807106)

181. David A. Knox and Carlisle Adams, "Digital Credentials with Privacy-Preserving Delegation", *Security and Communication Networks*, vol. 4, no. 8, August 2011, pp. 825-838. (Available at https://onlinelibrary.wiley.com/doi/full/10.1002/sec.213)

182. Charles M. Kozierok, *The TCP/IP Guide: A Comprehensive, Illustrated Internet Protocols Reference*, No Starch Press, 2005. (Available at https://www.amazon.ca/TCP-Guide-Comprehensive-Illustrated-Protocols-ebook/dp/B008G30T7W?)

183. Benjamin Kreuter, Abhi Shelat, and Chih-Hao Shen, "Billion gate secure computation with malicious adversaries", *Proceedings of the 21st Usenix Security Symposium*, Bellevue, WA, August 2012, pp. 285-300. (Available at https://www.usenix.org/conference/usenixsecurity12/technical-sessions/presentation/kreuter)

184. Eyal Kushilevitz and Rafail Ostrovsky, "Replication is Not Needed: Single Database, Computationally-Private Information Retrieval", *Proceedings of the 38th Annual Symposium on Foundations of Computer Science*, 1997, pp. 364-373. (Available at http://web.cs.ucla.edu/~rafail/PUBLIC/34.pdf)

185. John Lainhart, "Cybersecurity and Privacy Enhancements", *American Institute of Certified Public Accountants, issue brief*, 4 June 2018. (Available at https://www.aicpa.org/content/dam/aicpa/interestareas/businessindustryandgovernment/newsandpublications/downloadabledocuments/cyber-may2018.pdf)

186. Andrei Lapets, Frederick Jansen, Kinan Dak Albab, Rawane Issa, Lucy Qin, Mayank Varia and Azer Bestavros, "Accessible Privacy Preserving Web-Based Data Analysis for Assessing and Addressing Economic Inequalities", *Proceedings of the 1st ACM Conference on Computing and Sustainable Societies (COMPASS)*, Article no. 48, June 2018, pp. 1-5. (Available at https://dl.acm.org/doi/10.1145/3209811.3212701)

187. Yasin Laura-Silva and Walid Aref, "Realizing Privacy-Preserving Features in Hippocratic Databases", *Department of Computer Science Technical Reports, Report Number 06-022*, Purdue University, 2006, 16pp. (Available at https://docs.lib.purdue.edu/cgi/viewcontent.cgi?article=2664&context=cstech)

188. Kristen LeFevre, Rakesh Agrawal, Vuk Ercegovak, Raghu Ramakrishnan, Yirong Xu, and David DeWitt, "Limiting Disclosure in Hippocratic Databases", *Proceedings of the 30th International Conference on Very Large Databases*, Toronto, Canada, 2004, 12pp. (Available at http://pages.cs.wisc.edu/~vuk/papers/hippoCameraReady.pdf)

189. Ninghui Li, Tiancheng Li, and Suresh Venkatasubramanian, "*t*-Closeness: Privacy Beyond *k*-Anonymity and l-Diversity", *Center for Education and Research Information Assurance and Security (CERIAS) Tech Report 2007-78*, Purdue University, 2007. (Available at https://citeseerx.ist.psu.edu/viewdoc/download;jsessionid=087F7FB0303FB87DBFA4D3C256F7DB5F?doi=10.1.1.158.6171&rep=rep1&type=pdf)

190. Lucy Li, Bijeeta Pal, Junade Ali, Nick Sullivan, Rahul Chatterjee, and Thomas Ristenpart, "Protocols for Checking Compromised Credentials", *arXiv.org*, arXiv:1905.13737v3, 4 September 2019. (Available at https://arxiv.org/abs/1905.13737)

191. Yehuda Lindell, "Fast cut-and-choose based protocols for malicious and covert adversaries", *Advances in Cryptology: Proceedings of Crypto 2013*, Springer LNCS 8043, 18-22 August 2013, pp. 1-17. (Available at https://link.springer.com/book/10.1007/978-3-642-40084-1)

192. Yehuda Lindell, "Secure Multiparty Computation (MPC)", *Cryptology ePrint archive, 2020/300*, 7 March 2020 (last revised 30 January 2021). (Available at https://eprint.iacr.org/2020/300.pdf)

193. Helger Lipmaa, "First CPIR Protocol with Data-Dependent Computation", *12th International Conference on Information, Security and Cryptology*, 2-4 December 2009, pp. 193-210. (Available at https://link.springer.com/chapter/10.1007/978-3-642-14423-3_14)

194. Anna Lysyanskaya, "Signature Schemes and Applications to Cryptographic Protocol Design", *Ph.D. thesis, Massachusetts Institute of Technology*, Cambridge, MA, USA, September 2002. (Available at https://dspace.mit.edu/handle/1721.1/29271)

195. Ashwin Machanavajjhala, Daniel Kifer, Johannes Gehrke, and Muthuramakrishnan Venkitasubramaniam, "l-Diversity: Privacy Beyond k-Anonymity", *ACM Transactions on Knowledge Discovery From Data*, vol. 1, no. 1, article 3, March 2007, 52pp. (Available at https://dl.acm.org/doi/pdf/10.1145/1217299.1217302)

196. Ashwin Machanavajjhala, Daniel Kifer, John M. Abowd, Johannes Gehrke, and Lars Vilhuber, "Privacy: Theory meets Practice on the Map", *Proceedings of the 24th International Conference on Data Engineering*, 7-12 April 2008, pp. 277-286. (Available at https://ieeexplore.ieee.org/document/4497436)

197. Brian Markert, "Comparison of Three Online Privacy Seal Programs", *SANS Institute Information Security Reading Room*, 2002. (Available at https://www.sans.org/reading-room/whitepapers/privacy/comparison-online-privacy-seal-programs-685)

198. Frank McDonough, "Careless whispers: how the German public used and abused the Gestapo", *The Irish Times*, 28 September 2015. (Available at https://www.irishtimes.com/culture/books/careless-whispers-how-the-german-public-used-and-abused-the-gestapo-1.2369837)

199. Alfred J. Menezes, Paul C. van Oorschot, and Scott A. Vanstone, *Handbook of Applied Cryptography*, CRC Press, 1996 (5th printing: 2001). (Available at https://cacr.uwaterloo.ca/hac/)

200. Ralph Merkle, "Secure communications over insecure channels", *Communications of the ACM*, vol. 21, no. 4, April 1978, pp. 294-299. (Available at https://cacm.acm.org/magazines/1978/4/11233-secure-communications-over-insecure-channels/abstract)

201. Adam Meyerson and Ryan Williams, "On the Complexity of Optimal k-Anonymity", *Symposium on Principles of Database Systems*, 14-16 June 2004, pp. 223-228. (Available at https://dl.acm.org/doi/pdf/10.1145/1055558.1055591)

202. Sanjeev Kumar Mishra and Palash Sarkar, "Symmetrically Private Information Retrieval", *Progress in Cryptology: Indocrypt 2000*, 10-13 December 2000, pp. 225-236. (Available at https://link.springer.com/chapter/10.1007/3-540-44495-5_20)

203. Matthew Mohan, "Singapore Police Force can obtain TraceTogether data for criminal investigations: Desmond Tan", *Channel News Asia*, 4 January 2021. (Available at https://www.channelnewsasia.com/news/singapore/singapore-police-force-can-obtain-tracetogether-data-covid-19-13889914)

204. Sara Kendall More, "Secure Group Communication: Self-Healing Key Distribution and Nontransferable Anonymous Credentials", *Ph.D. thesis, University of California, San Diego*, 2003.

205. Sasi Kumar Murakonda and Reza Shokri, "ML Privacy Meter: Aiding Regulatory Compliance by Quantifying the Privacy Risks of Machine Learning", *Privacy Enhancing Technologies Symposium, HotPETs session*, 2020. (Available at https://petsymposium.org/2020/files/hotpets/MLPrivacyMeter.pdf)

206. Moni Naor and Moti Yung, "Public-key cryptosystems provably secure against chosen ciphertext attacks", *22nd Annual ACM Symposium on Theory of Computing*, April 1990, pp. 427-437. (Available at https://dl.acm.org/doi/10.1145/100216.100273)

207. Milad Nasr, Reza Shokri, and Amir Houmansadr, "Comprehensive privacy analysis of deep learning: Passive and active white-box inference attacks against centralized and federated learning", *IEEE Symposium on Security and Privacy*, 2019, pp. 1022–1036. (Available at https://www.computer.org/csdl/proceedings-article/sp/2019/666000b021/19skg8ZskUM)

208. Gregory Neven, "IBM Identity Mixer (idemix)", *presentation given at NIST meeting on Privacy Enhancing Technology*, Gaithersburg, MD, USA, 8-9 December 2011. (Available at https://csrc.nist.gov/csrc/media/events/meeting-on-privacy-enhancing-cryptography/documents/neven.pdf)

209. Helen Nissenbaum, *Privacy in Context: Technology, Policy, and the Integrity of Social Life*, Stanford Law Books, 2009. (Available at https://www.amazon.ca/Privacy-Context-Technology-Policy-Integrity/dp/0804752370)

210. Office: Office of the Information and Privacy Commissioner of Ontario and Office of the Federal Privacy Commissioner of Australia, "Web Seals: A Review of Online Privacy Programs," *22nd International Conference on Privacy and Personal Data Protection*, September 2000. (Available at https://www.ipc.on.ca/wp-content/uploads/Resources/up-seals.pdf)

211. Aleksander Øhrn and Lucila Ohno-Machado, "Using boolean reasoning to anonymize databases", *Artificial Intelligence in Medicine*, vol. 15, no. 3, 1999, pp. 235–254. (Available at https://www.sciencedirect.com/science/article/pii/S0933365798000566?via%3Dihub)

212. OPC: Office of the Privacy Commissioner of Canada, Technology Analysis Division, "Privacy Enhancing Technologies – A Review of Tools and Techniques", *research report*, November 2017. (Available at https://www.priv.gc.ca/en/opc-actions-and-decisions/research/explore-privacy-research/2017/pet_201711/)

213. Organization: Organization for Economic Co-operation and Development, OECD Privacy Framework (which includes Guidelines on the Protection of Privacy and Transborder Flows of Personal Data), *OECD Publications Service*, 2013. (Available at https://www.oecd.org/sti/ieconomy/oecd_privacy_framework.pdf)

214. Lasse Øverlier and Paul F. Syverson, "Locating Hidden Servers", *IEEE Symposium on Security and Privacy*, 2006, pp. 100–114. (Available at https://ieeexplore.ieee.org/stamp/stamp.jsp?tp=&arnumber=1624004)

215. Andriy Panchenko, Asya Mitseva, Martin Henze, Fabian Lanze, Klaus Wehrle, and Thomas Engel, "Analysis of Fingerprinting Techniques for Tor Hidden Services", *Proceedings of the Workshop on Privacy in the Electronic Society*, 30 October 2017, pp. 165-175. (Available at https://dl.acm.org/doi/10.1145/3139550.3139564)

216. Torben Pryds Pedersen, "Non-interactive and information-theoretic secure verifiable secret sharing", *Advances in Cryptology: Proceedings of Crypto*

'91, 1992, pp. 129-140. (Available at https://www.cs.cornell.edu/courses/cs754/2001fa/129.PDF)

217. Fernando Peinado, Elvira Palomo, and Javier Galán, "The distorted online networks of Mexico's election campaign", *El País*, 22 March 2018. (Available at     https://english.elpais.com/elpais/2018/03/22/inenglish/1521710735_571195.html)

218. Andreas Pfitzmann and Marit Hansen, "A terminology for talking about privacy by data minimization: Anonymity, Unlinkability, Undetectability, Unobservability, Pseudonymity, and Identity Management", *Anonymity Terminology document, version v0.34*, 10 August 2010. (Available at http://dud.inf.tu-dresden.de/literatur/Anon_Terminology_v0.34.pdf)

219. Ania Piotrowska, Jamie Hayes, Tariq Elahi, Sebastian Meiser, and George Danezis, "The Loopix Anonymity System", *Proceedings of the 26th USENIX Security Symposium*, Vancouver, BC, Canada, 16-18 August 2017, pp. 1199-1216. (Available at https://www.usenix.org/system/files/conference/usenixsecurity17/sec17-piotrowska.pdf) (See also *arXiv.com, 1703.00536*, 1 March 2017, 16pp.; available at https://arxiv.org/pdf/1703.00536.pdf.)

220. PIPEDA: Personal Information Protection and Electronic Documents Act, S.C. 2000 c.5 (Available at https://laws-lois.justice.gc.ca/eng/acts/P-8.6/FullText.html). See also Stephanie Perrin *et al.*, *The Personal Information Protection and Electronic Documents Act: An Annotated Guide* (Toronto: Irwin Law, 2001).

221. PKCS: RSA Laboratories, "PKCS #1 v2.1: RSA Cryptography Standard", *RSA Security Inc. Public-Key Cryptography Standards (PKCS)*, 14 June 2002. (Available at https://www.cryptrec.go.jp/cryptrec_03_spec_cypherlist_files/PDF/pkcs-1v2-12.pdf)

222. Huseyein Polat and Wenliang Du, "Privacy-Preserving Collaborative Filtering Using Randomized Pertubation Techniques", *Proceedings of The Third IEEE International Conference on Data Mining*, 12-22 November 2003, pp. 625-628. (Available at https://www.semanticscholar.org/paper/Privacy-preserving-collaborative-filtering-using-Polat-Du/fab892a03b74c19af0fb5e5c0222ae5e1a7d8769)

223. Jules Polonetsky and Elizabeth Renieris, "Privacy 2020: 10 Privacy Risks and 10 Privacy Enhancing Technologies to Watch in the Next Decade", *Future of Privacy Forum white paper*, 28 January 2020. (Available at https://fpf.org/blog/privacy-2020-10-privacy-risks-and-10-privacy-enhancing-technologies-to-watch-in-the-next-decade/;     see     also     https://fpf.org/wp-content/uploads/2020/01/FPF_Privacy2020_WhitePaper.pdf)

224. Pavel Pudlák and Vojtěch Rödl, "Modified ranks of tensors and the size of circuits", *Proceedings of the 25th Annual ACM Symposium on Theory of Computing*, 16–18 May 1993, pp. 523–531. (Available at https://dl.acm.org/doi/10.1145/167088.167228)

225. Quora, "What is regularization in machine learning?", 2020. (Available at https://www.quora.com/What-is-regularization-in-machine-learning)

226. Michael O. Rabin, "How to exchange secrets by oblivious transfer", *Technical Report TR-81*, Aiken Computation Laboratory, Harvard University, 20 May 1981. (Available at https://eprint.iacr.org/2005/187.pdf)

227. Charles Rackoff and Daniel R. Simon, "Non-interactive Zero-Knowledge Proof of Knowledge and Chosen Ciphertext Attack", *Advances in Cryptology: Proceedings of Crypto '91*, Springer LNCS 576, 1992, pp. 433-444. (Available at https://link.springer.com/chapter/10.1007/3-540-46766-1_35)

228. Michael G. Reed, Paul F. Syverson, and David M. Goldschlag, "Proxies for anonymous routing", *Proceedings 12th Annual Computer Security Applications Conference*, San Diego, CA, USA, 9-13 December 1996, pp. 95-104. (Available at https://ieeexplore.ieee.org/stamp/stamp.jsp?tp=&arnumber=569678)

229. Michael G. Reed, Paul F. Syverson, and David M. Goldschlag, "Protocols using anonymous connections: Mobile applications," *Security Protocols 5th International Workshop*, Paris, France, 7-9 April 1997, pp. 13-23. (Available at https://link.springer.com/chapter/10.1007/BFb0028156)

230. Michael G. Reed, Paul F. Syverson, and David M. Goldschlag, "Anonymous Connections and Onion Routing", *IEEE Journal on Selected Areas in Communications*, vol. 16, no. 4, May 1998, pp. 482-494. (Available at https://csl.mtu.edu/cs6461/www/Reading/08/Reed-jsac98.pdf)

231. Regulation: Regulation (EU) 2016/679, "General Data Protection Regulation (GDPR)", *OJ L 119, 04.05.2016; cor. OJ L 127, 23.5.2018*, 4 May 2016. (Available at https://gdpr-info.eu/)

232. Michael K. Reiter and Aviel D. Rubin, "Crowds: Anonymity for Web Transactions" *ACM Transactions on Information and System Security*, vol. 1, no. 1, 1998, pp. 66-92. (Available at https://dl.acm.org/doi/10.1145/290163.290168)

233. 2Lisa Rennie, "Top 5 Most Common Errors That Appear on Credit Reports in Canada", *Loans Canada blog*, 2021. (Available at https://loanscanada.ca/credit/top-5-most-common-errors-that-appear-on-credit-reports-in-canada/)

234. Abdelmounaam Rezgui, Athman Bouguettaya, and Mohamed Eltoweissy, "Privacy on the Web: Facts, Challenges, and Solutions", *IEEE Security and Privacy*, November-December 2003, pp. 40-49. (Available at https://www.computer.org/csdl/magazine/sp/2003/06/j6040/13rRUwd9CJP)

*The following set of references are all IETF Request for Comments (RFC) specifications. Note that these are not listed alphabetically by first author because RFCs are invariably referred to in the literature by their RFC number (such as "RFC 1321"), rather than by author. Thus, these have been grouped together logically as "RFC xxxx" (in sequential order) and have been placed between "Rezgui" and "Rissanen".*

235. RFC 1321: Ronald L. Rivest, "The MD5 Message-Digest Algorithm", *Internet Engineering Task Force (IETF) Request for Comments RFC 1321*, April 1992. (Available at https://tools.ietf.org/html/rfc1321)

236. RFC 1825: Randall Atkinson, "Security Architecture for the Internet Protocol", *Internet Engineering Task Force (IETF) Request for Comments RFC 1825*, August 1995. (Available at https://tools.ietf.org/html/rfc1825)

237. RFC 1826: Randall Atkinson, "IP Authentication Header", *Internet Engineering Task Force (IETF) Request for Comments RFC 1826*, August 1995. (Available at https://tools.ietf.org/html/rfc1826)

238. RFC 1827: Randall Atkinson, "IP Encapsulating Security Payload", *Internet Engineering Task Force (IETF) Request for Comments RFC 1827*, August 1995. (Available at https://tools.ietf.org/html/rfc1827)

239. RFC 2246: Tim Dierks and Christopher Allen, "The TLS Protocol Version 1.0", *Internet Engineering Task Force (IETF) Request for Comments RFC 2246*, January 1999. (Available at https://tools.ietf.org/html/rfc2246)

240. RFC 2401: Stephen Kent and Randall Atkinson, "Security Architecture for the Internet Protocol", *Internet Engineering Task Force (IETF) Request for Comments RFC 2401*, November 1998. (Available at https://tools.ietf.org/html/rfc2401)

241. RFC 2402: Stephen Kent and Randall Atkinson, "IP Authentication Header", *Internet Engineering Task Force (IETF) Request for Comments RFC 2402*, November 1998. (Available at https://tools.ietf.org/html/rfc2402)

242. RFC 2403: Cheryl Madson and Rob Glenn, "The Use of HMAC-MD5-96 within ESP and AH", *Internet Engineering Task Force (IETF) Request for Comments RFC 2403*, November 1998. (Available at https://tools.ietf.org/html/rfc2403)

243. RFC 2404: Cheryl Madson and Rob Glenn, "The Use of HMAC-SHA-1-96 within ESP and AH", *Internet Engineering Task Force (IETF) Request for Comments RFC 2404*, November 1998. (Available at https://tools.ietf.org/html/rfc2404)

244. RFC 2405: Cheryl Madson and Naganand Doraswamy, "The ESP DES-CBC Cipher Algorithm with Explicit IV", *Internet Engineering Task Force (IETF) Request for Comments RFC 2405*, November 1998. (Available at https://tools.ietf.org/html/rfc2405)

245. RFC 2406: Stephen Kent and Randall Atkinson, "IP Encapsulating Security Payload", *Internet Engineering Task Force (IETF) Request for Comments RFC 2406*, November 1998. (Available at https://tools.ietf.org/html/rfc2406)

246. RFC 2407: Derrell Piper, "The Internet IP Security Domain of Interpretation for ISAKMP", *Internet Engineering Task Force (IETF) Request for Comments RFC 2407*, November 1998. (Available at https://tools.ietf.org/html/rfc2407)

247. RFC 2408: Douglass Maughan, Mark Schertler, Mark Schneider, and Jeff Turner, "Internet Security Association and Key Management Protocol (ISAKMP)", *Internet Engineering Task Force (IETF) Request for Comments RFC 2408*, November 1998. (Available at https://tools.ietf.org/html/rfc2408)

248. RFC 2409: Dan Harkins and Dave Carrel, "The Internet Key Exchange (IKE)", *Internet Engineering Task Force (IETF) Request for Comments RFC 2409*, November 1998. (Available at https://tools.ietf.org/html/rfc2409)

249. RFC 2410: Rob Glenn and Stephen Kent, "The NULL Encryption Algorithm and Its Use with IPsec", *Internet Engineering Task Force (IETF) Request for Comments RFC 2410*, November 1998. (Available at https://tools.ietf.org/html/rfc2410)

250. RFC 2411: Rodney Thayer, Naganand Doraswamy, and Rob Glenn, "IP Security Document Roadmap", *Internet Engineering Task Force (IETF) Request for Comments RFC 2411*, November 1998. (Available at https://tools.ietf.org/html/rfc2411)

251. RFC 2412: Hilarie Orman, "The OAKLEY Key Determination Protocol", *Internet Engineering Task Force (IETF) Request for Comments RFC 2412*, November 1998. (Available at https://tools.ietf.org/html/rfc2412)

252. RFC 2440: Jon Callas, Lutz Donnerhacke, Hal Finney, and Rodney Thayer, "OpenPGP message format", *Internet Engineering Task Force (IETF) Request for Comments RFC 2440*, November 1998. (Available at https://tools.ietf.org/html/rfc2440)

253. RFC 2633: Blake Ramsdell, "S/MIME Version 3 Message Specification", *Internet Engineering Task Force (IETF) Request for Comments RFC 2633*, June 1999. (Available at https://tools.ietf.org/html/rfc2633)

254. RFC 3546: Simon Blake-Wilson, Magnus Nystrom, David Hopwood, Jan Mikkelsen, and Tim Wright, "Transport Layer Security (TLS) Extensions",*Internet Engineering Task Force (IETF) Request for Comments RFC 3546*, June 2003. (Available at https://datatracker.ietf.org/doc/html/rfc3546)

255. RFC 4301: Stephen Kent and Karen Seo, "Security Architecture for the Internet Protocol", *Internet Engineering Task Force (IETF) Request for Comments RFC 4301*, December 2005. (Available at https://tools.ietf.org/html/rfc4301)

256. RFC 4302: Stephen Kent, "IP Authentication Header", *Internet Engineering Task Force (IETF) Request for Comments RFC 4302*, December 2005. (Available at https://tools.ietf.org/html/rfc4302)

257. RFC 4303: Stephen Kent, "IP Encapsulating Security Payload", *Internet Engineering Task Force (IETF) Request for Comments RFC 4303*, December 2005. (Available at https://tools.ietf.org/html/rfc4303)

258. RFC 4306: Charlie Kaufman, "Internet Key Exchange (IKEv2) Protocol", *Internet Engineering Task Force (IETF) Request for Comments RFC 4306*, December 2005. (Available at https://tools.ietf.org/html/rfc4306)

259. RFC 4346: Tim Dierks and Eric Rescorla, "The Transport Layer Security (TLS) Protocol Version 1.1", *Internet Engineering Task Force (IETF) Request for Comments RFC 4346*, April 2006. (Available at https://tools.ietf.org/html/rfc4346)

260. RFC 4718: Pasi Eronen and Paul Hoffman, "IKEv2 Clarifications and Implementation Guidelines", *Internet Engineering Task Force (IETF) Request for Comments RFC 4718*, October 2006. (Available at https://tools.ietf.org/html/rfc4718)

261. RFC 5246: Tim Dierks and Eric Rescorla, "The Transport Layer Security (TLS) Protocol Version 1.2", *Internet Engineering Task Force (IETF) Request for Comments RFC 5246*, August 2008. (Available at https://tools.ietf.org/html/rfc5246)

262. RFC 5996: Charlie Kaufman, Paul Hoffman, Yoav Nir, and Pasi Eronen, "Internet Key Exchange Protocol Version 2 (IKEv2)", *Internet Engineering Task Force (IETF) Request for Comments RFC 5996*, September 2010. (Available at https://tools.ietf.org/html/rfc5996)

263. RFC 6071: Sheila Frankel and Suresh Krishnan, "IP Security (IPsec) and Internet Key Exchange (IKE) Document Roadmap", *Internet Engineering Task Force (IETF) Request for Comments RFC 6071*, February 2011. (Available at https://tools.ietf.org/html/rfc6071)

264. RFC 6101: Alan Freier, Philip Karlton, and Paul Kocher, "The Secure Sockets Layer (SSL) Protocol Version 3.0", *Internet Engineering Task Force (IETF) Request for Comments RFC 6101*, August 2011. (Available at https://tools.ietf.org/html/rfc6101)

265. RFC 7296: Charlie Kaufman, Paul Hoffman, Yoav Nir, Pasi Eronen, and Tero Kivinen, "Internet Key Exchange Protocol Version 2 (IKEv2)", *Internet Engineering Task Force (IETF) Request for Comments RFC 7296*, October 2014. (Available at https://tools.ietf.org/html/rfc7296)

266. RFC 7858: Zi Hu, Liang Zhu, John Heidemann, Allison Mankin, Duane Wessels, and Paul Hoffman, "Specification for DNS over Transport Layer Security (TLS)", *Internet Engineering Task Force (IETF) Request for Comments RFC 7858*, May 2016. (Available at https://datatracker.ietf.org/doc/html/rfc7858)

267. RFC 8446: Eric Rescorla, "The Transport Layer Security (TLS) Protocol Version 1.3", *Internet Engineering Task Force (IETF) Request for Comments RFC 8446*, August 2018. (Available at https://tools.ietf.org/html/rfc8446)

268. RFC 8484: Paul Hoffman and Patrick McManus, "DNS Queries over HTTPS (DoH)", *Internet Engineering Task Force (IETF) Request for Comments RFC 8484*, October 2018. (Available at https://datatracker.ietf.org/doc/html/rfc8484)

*We now return to listing the references alphabetically by the last name of the first author.*

269. Erik Rissanen, "eXtensible Access Control Markup Language (XACML) Version 3.0 Plus Errata 01", *OASIS Standard Incorporating Approved Errata*, 12 July 2017. (Available at http://docs.oasis-open.org/xacml/3.0/errata01/os/xacml-3.0-core-spec-errata01-os-complete.pdf)

270. Ronald L. Rivest, Adi Shamir, and Leonard Adleman, "A method for obtaining digital signatures and public-key cryptosystems", *Communications of the ACM*, vol. 21, no. 2, February 1978, pp. 120-126. (Available at https://cacm.acm.org/magazines/1978/2/11250-a-method-for-obtaining-digital-signatures-and-public-key-cryptosystems/abstract)

271. Ronald L. Rivest, Leonard Adleman, and Michael L. Dertouzos, "On data banks and privacy homomorphisms", *Foundations of Secure Computation*, Academia Press, 1978, pp. 169-179. (Available at http://people.csail.mit.edu/ rivest/RivestAdlemanDertouzos-OnDataBanksAndPrivacyHomomorphi sms.pdf)

272. Florentin Rochet, Ryan Wails, Aaron Johnson, Prateek Mittal, and Olivier Pereira, "CLAPS: Client-Location-Aware Path Selection in Tor", *ACM Conference on Computer and Communications Security*, 9-13 November 2020, pp. 17-34. (Available at https://dl.acm.org/doi/pdf/10.1145/ 3372297.3417279)

273. Ryan Rogers, Subbu Subramaniam, Sean Peng, David Durfee, Seunghyun Lee, Santosh Kumar Kancha, Shraddha Sahay, and Parvez Ahammad, "LinkedIn's Audience Engagements API: A Privacy Preserving Data Analytics System at Scale", arXiv.*org, 2002.05839*, 14 February 2020 (last revised 16 November 2020). (Available at https://arxiv.org/abs/2002.05839)

274. Marc Rotenberg, *The Privacy Law Sourcebook 2000: United States Law, International Law, and Recent Developments*, Electronic Privacy Information Center, 2000. (Available at https://www.goodreads.com/book/show/1038792. Privacy_Law_Sourcebook_2000)

275. Yossi Rubner, Carlo Tomasi, and Leonidas J. Guibas, "The earth mover's distance as a metric for image retrieval", *International Journal of Computer Vision*, vol. 40, no. 2, November 2000, pp. 99–121. (Available at https://www.researchgate.net/ publication/220659330_The_Earth_Mover's_Distance_as_a_Metric_for_Image_ Retrieval)

276. Amit Sahai and Brent Waters, "Fuzzy Identity Based Encryption", *Advances in Cryptology – Proceedings of Eurocrypt*, Springer LNCS 3494, 2005, pp. 457–473. (Available at https://link.springer.com/chapter/ 10.1007/11426639_27)

277. Pierangela Samarati and Latanya Sweeney, "Protecting privacy when disclosing information: k-anonymity and its enforcement through generalisation and suppression" *SRI International*, 1998. (Available at https://citeseerx.ist.psu. edu/viewdoc/summary?doi=10.1.1.37.5829)

278. Pierangela Samarati, "Protecting respondents identities in microdata release", *IEEE Transactions on Knowledge and Data Engineering*, vol. 13, no. 6, November-December 2001, pp. 1010-1027. (Available at https://ieeexplore. ieee.org/document/971193)

279. Arthur Samuel, "Some Studies in Machine Learning Using the Game of Checkers". *IBM Journal of Research and Development*, vol. 3, no. 3, July 1959, pp. 71–105. (Available at https://citeseerx.ist.psu.edu/viewdoc/summar y?doi=10.1.1.368.2254)

280. Bruce Schneier, *Applied Cryptography: Protocols, Algorithms, and Source Code in C, 2^{nd} Edition*, John Wiley & Sons, Inc., 1996. (Available at https://b-ok.cc/book/609307/380a19?dsource=recommend)

281. Bruce Schneier, *Data and Goliath: The Hidden Battles to Collect Your Data and Control Your World*, W. W. Norton and Company, 2015. (Available at

https://www.amazon.ca/Data-Goliath-Battles-Collect-Control/dp/039335217X/ref=tmm_pap_swatch_0?_encoding=UTF8&qid=&sr=)

282. Andrei Serjantov and George Danezis, "Towards an Information Theoretic Metric for Anonymity", *Proceedings of the Second International Workshop on Privacy Enhancing Technologies,* Springer, LNCS 2482, San Francisco, USA, 14-15 April 2002, pp. 41-53. (Available at https://link.springer.com/chapter/10.1007/3-540-36467-6_4)

283. Andrei Serjantov, Roger Dingledine, and Paul F. Syverson, "From a Trickle to a Flood: Active Attacks on Several Mix Types", *2002 International Workshop on Information Hiding,* Springer LNCS 2578, 2003, pp. 36-52. (Available at https://link.springer.com/chapter/10.1007/3-540-36415-3_3)

284. Adi Shamir, Ronald L. Rivest, and Leonard M. Adleman, "Mental poker", *Technical Report LCS/TR-125,* Massachusetts Institute of Technology, April 1979. (Available at https://apps.dtic.mil/sti/pdfs/ADA066331.pdf)

285. Adi Shamir, "How to Share a Secret", *Communications of the ACM,* vol. 22, no. 11, November 1979, pp. 612-613. (Available at https://dl.acm.org/doi/10.1145/359168.359176)

286. Adi Shamir, "Identity-Based Cryptosystems and Signature Schemes", *Advances in Cryptology: Proceedings of Crypto 84,* Springer LNCS 196, 1985, pp. 47-53. (Available at https://link.springer.com/chapter/10.1007/3-540-39568-7_5)

287. Sharemind, "Track Big Data between Government and Education", *blog post,* 26 October 2015. (Available at https://sharemind.cyber.ee/big-data-analytics-protection/)

288. Abhi Shelat, and Chih-Hao Shen, "Fast two-party secure computation with minimal assumptions", *ACM Conference on Computer and Communications Security,* November 2013, pp. 523-534. (Available at https://dl.acm.org/doi/10.1145/2508859.2516698)

289. Fatemeh Shirazi, Elena Andreeva, Markulf Kohlweiss, and Claudia Diaz, "Multiparty Routing: Secure Routing for Mixnets", *ePrint archive,* 1708.03387v2, 9 November 2017. (Available at https://arxiv.org/pdf/1708.03387.pdf)

290. Vitaly Shmatikov and Ming-Hsiu Wang, "Timing analysis in low-latency mix networks: attacks and defenses", *Proceedings of ESORICS,* 2006, pp. 18-33. (Available at https://citeseerx.ist.psu.edu/viewdoc/summary?doi=10.1.1.64.8818)

291. Reza Shokri and Vitaly Shmatikov, "Privacy-preserving deep learning", *Proceedings of the 22nd ACM Conference on Computer and Communications Security,* 2015, pp. 1310–1321. (Available at https://dl.acm.org/doi/10.1145/2810103.2813687)

292. Reza Shokri, Marco Stronati, Congzheng Song, and Vitaly Shmatikov, "Membership inference attacks against machine learning models", *IEEE Symposium on Security and Privacy,* 2017, pp. 3–18. (Available at https://www.ieee-security.org/TC/SP2017/program-papers.html)

293. Sandra Siby, Marc Juarez, Claudia Diaz, Narseo Vallina-Rodriguez, and Carmela Troncoso, "Encrypted DNS → Privacy? A Traffic Analysis Perspective", *Network and Distributed System Security Symposium*, San Diego, CA, USA, 23-26 February 2020, 18pp. (Available at https://www.ndss-symposium.org/ndss-paper/encrypted-dns-privacy-a-traffic-analysis-perspective/)

294. Michael Sipser, *Introduction to the Theory of Computation, 3rd Edition*, Thomson South-Western, 2012. (Available at https://ca1lib.org/book/2514666/bdba06?regionChanged=&redirect=235695639)

295. Geoff Skinner, Song Han, and Elizabeth Chang, "An information privacy taxonomy for collaborative environments", *Information Management & Computer Security*, vol. 14, no. 4, 1 August 2006, pp. 382-394. (Available at https://www.emerald.com/insight/content/doi/10.1108/09685220610690835/full/html)

296. Daniel Solove, *Understanding Privacy*, Harvard University Press, 2008. (Available at https://www.danielsolove.com/understanding-privacy/)

297. Olivia Solon, "Insecure Wheels: Police turn to car data to destroy suspects' alibis", *NBC News*, 28 December 2020. (Available at https://www.nbcnews.com/tech/tech-news/snitches-wheels-police-turn-car-data-destroy-suspects-alibis-n1251939)

298. Congzheng Song, Thomas Ristenpart, and Vitaly Shmatikov, "Machine learning models that remember too much", *Proceedings of the ACM Conference on Computer and Communications Security*, 2017, pp. 587–601. (Available at https://dl.acm.org/doi/10.1145/3133956.3134077)

299. Yujiao Song, Hao Wang, Xiaochao Wei, and Lei Wu, "Efficient Attribute-Based encryption with Privacy-Preserving Key Generation and Its Application in Industrial Cloud", *Security and Communication Networks*, vol. 2019, Article ID 3249726, 23 May 2019, 9pp. (Available at https://downloads.hindawi.com/journals/scn/2019/3249726.pdf)

300. Alberto Sonnino, Mustafa Al-Bassam, Shehar Bano, Sarah Meiklejohn, and George Danezis, "Coconut: Threshold Issuance Selective Disclosure Credentials with Applications to Distributed Ledgers", *Network and Distributed System Security (NDSS) Symposium*, San Diego, CA, USA, 24-27 February 2019, 15pp. (Available at https://www.ndss-symposium.org/wp-content/uploads/2019/02/ndss2019_06A-1_Sonnino_paper.pdf)

301. Polly Sprenger, "Sun on Privacy: Get Over It", *Wired*, 26 January 1999. (Available at https://www.wired.com/1999/01/sun-on-privacy-get-over-it/)

302. William Stallings, *Cryptography and Network Security: Principles and Practice, 6th Edition*, Pearson, 2014. (Available at https://b-ok.cc/book/5102290/06d4e7?dsource=recommend)

303. STD 79: Charlie Kaufman, Paul Hoffman, Yoav Nir, Pasi Eronen, and Tero Kivinen, "Internet Key Exchange Protocol Version 2 (IKEv2)", *Internet Engineering Task Force (IETF) Internet Standard STD 79*, October 2014. (Available at https://www.rfc-editor.org/info/std79)

304. Douglas R. Stinson and Maura B. Patterson, *Cryptography: Theory and Practice*, CRC Press, Taylor & Francis Group, 2018. (Available at https://b-ok.cc/book/3609574/fce310?dsource=recommend)

305. Yixin Sun, Anne Edmundson, Laurent Vanbever, Oscar Li, Jennifer Rexford, Mung Chiang, and Prateek Mittal, "RAPTOR: Routing Attacks on Privacy in Tor", *Usenix Security Symposium*, 12-14 August 2015, pp. 271-286. (Available at https://www.usenix.org/system/files/conference/usenixsecurity15/sec15-paper-sun.pdf)

306. Yixin Sun, Anne Edmundson, Nick Feamster, Mung Chiang, and Prateek Mittal, "Counter-RAPTOR: Safeguarding Tor Against Active Routing Attacks", *IEEE Symposium on Security and Privacy*, 22-24 May 2017, 16pp. (Available at http://www.ieee-security.org/TC/SP2017/papers/533.pdf)

307. Latanya Sweeney, "Replacing Personally-Identifying Information in Medical Records, the Scrub System" in James Cimino, ed., *American Medical Informatics Association Proceedings, Journal of the American Medical Informatics Association*, Hanley & Belfus, Inc., 1996, pp. 333-337. (Available at https://www.ncbi.nlm.nih.gov/pmc/articles/PMC2233179/)

308. Latanya Sweeney, "Guaranteeing anonymity when sharing medical data, the Datafly system", *Proceedings of the Fall Symposium of the American Medical Informatics Association*, 1997, pp. 51-55. (Available at https://dataprivacylab.org/datafly/paper4.pdf)

309. Latanya Sweeney, "Simple Demographics Often Identify People Uniquely", *Carnegie Mellon University, Data Privacy Working Paper 3*, Pittsburgh, 2000. (Available at https://dataprivacylab.org/projects/identifiability/paper1.pdf)

310. Latanya Sweeney, "*k*-Anonymity: a Model for Protecting Privacy", *International Journal on Uncertainty, Fuzziness and Knowledge-based Systems*, vol. 10, no. 5, 2002, pp.557-570. (Available at https://www.epic.org/privacy/reidentification/Sweeney_Article.pdf)

311. Latanya Sweeney, "Achieving *k*-Anonymity Privacy Protection Using Generalization and Suppression", *International Journal on Uncertainty, Fuzziness and Knowledge-based Systems*, vol. 10, no. 5, 2002, pp.571-588. (Available at https://pdfs.semanticscholar.org/3467/48474a6509d58c5df7b48f0fb0ef50f6a6ff.pdf?_ga=2.258240842.1114057579.1600379732-142626873.1600379732)

312. Paul F. Syverson, Stuart G. Stubblebine, and David M. Goldschlag, "Unlinkable Serial Transactions", *Proceedings of the First International Conference on Financial Cryptography*, Springer-Verlag, LNCS 1318, Anguilla, British West Indies, 24-28 February 1997, pp. 39-55. (Available at https://link.springer.com/chapter/10.1007/3-540-63594-7_66)

313. Paul F. Syverson, David M. Goldschlag, and Michael G. Reed, "Anonymous Connections and Onion Routing", *Proceedings IEEE Symposium on Security and Privacy*, 4-7 May 1997, pp. 44-54. (Available at https://ieeexplore.ieee.org/document/601314)

314. Paul F. Syverson and Stuart G. Stubblebine, "Group Principals and the Formalization of Anonymity", *Proceedings of the First World Congress on Formal Methods in the Development of Computing Systems (FM '99), Volume 1*, Springer-Verlag, LNCS 1708, Toulouse, France, pp. 814-833, 20-24 September 1999. (Available at https://link.springer.com/chapter/10.1007%2F3-540-48119-2_45)

315. Paul F. Syverson, "Sleeping dogs lie on a bed of onions but wake when mixed", *Privacy Enhancing Technologies Symposium, HotPETs session*, 2011. (Available at https://petsymposium.org/2011/papers/hotpets11-final10Syverson.pdf)

316. Paul Syverson, "A Peel of Onion", *Proceedings of the 27th Annual Computer Security Applications Conference*, Orlando, Florida, USA, 5-9 December 2011, pp. 123-137. (Available at https://www.acsac.org/2011/program/keynotes/syverson.pdf)

317. Paul F. Syverson, presentation to *Privacy Enhancing Technologies Symposium, HotPETs session*, on the paper "Oft Target: Tor adversary models that don't miss the mark", 21 July 2017. (Available at https://www.youtube.com/watch?v=dGXncihWzfw)

318. Matthew Traudt, Rob Jansen, and Aaron Johnson, "FlashFlow: A Secure Speed Test for Tor", *arXiv.com, 2004.09583*, 20 April 2020. (Available at https://arxiv.org/pdf/2004.09583.pdf)

319. Wen-Guey Tzeng, "Efficient 1-Out-n Oblivious Transfer Schemes", *International Workshop on Public Key Cryptography*, Springer LNCS 2274, 2002, pp. 159-171. (Available at https://link.springer.com/chapter/10.1007/3-540-45664-3_11)

320. Microsoft, "U-Prove", *research project description*, 25 February 2012. (Available at https://www.microsoft.com/en-us/research/project/u-prove/)

321. Serge Vaudenay, *A Classical Introduction to Modern Cryptography*, Springer, 2005. (Available at https://b-ok.cc/book/437459/24a2f8?dsource=recommend)

322. Jesse Victors, "The Onion Name System: Tor-Powered Distributed DNS for Tor Hidden Services", *Master's thesis, Utah State University, All Graduate Theses and Dissertations 4484*, 2015. (Available at https://digitalcommons.usu.edu/cgi/viewcontent.cgi?article=5517&context=etd)

323. Heinrich Von Staden, "In a Pure and Holy Way: Personal and Professional Conduct in the Hippocratic Oath" (translation by Heinrich Von Staden), *Journal of the History of Medicine and Applied Sciences*, vol. 51, no 4, 1966, pp. 406–408. (Available at https://academic.oup.com/jhmas/article/51/4/404/706022)

324. Ryan Wails, Yixin Sun, Aaron Johnson, Mung Chiang, and Prateek Mittal, "Tempest: Temporal Dynamics in Anonymity Systems", *Proceedings on Privacy Enhancing Technologies*, vol. 2018, no. 3, June 2018, pp. 22-42. (Available at https://www.sciendo.com/article/10.1515/popets-2018-0019)

325. Ryan Wails, presentation to *Privacy Enhancing Technologies Symposium, HotPETs session*, on the paper "CLAPS: Client-Location-Aware Path Selection in Tor" (by Florentin Rochet, Ryan Wails, Aaron Johnson, Prateek Mittal, and Olivier Pereira), 23 July 2020. (Available at HotPETS 2020: CLAPS: Client-Location-Aware Path Selection in Tor - YouTube)

326. Gerry Wan, Aaron Johnson, Ryan Wails, Sameer Wagh, and Prateek Mittal, "Guard Placement Attacks on Path Selection Algorithms for Tor", *Proceedings on Privacy Enhancing Technologies*, vol. 2019, no. 4, October 2019,

pp. 272-291. (Available at https://www.sciendo.com/article/10.2478/popets-2019-0069)

327. Tao Wang and Ian Goldberg, "On Realistically Attacking Tor with Website Fingerprinting", *Proceedings on Privacy Enhancing Technologies*, vol. 4, 2016, pp. 21-36. (Available at https://petsymposium.org/2016/files/papers/On_Realistically_Attacking_Tor_with_Website_Fingerprinting.pdf)

328. Tao Wang and Ian Goldberg, "Walkie-Talkie: An Efficient Defense Against Passive Website Fingerprinting Attacks", *Usenix Security Symposium*, 16-18 August 2017, pp. 1375-1390. (Available at https://www.usenix.org/system/files/conference/usenixsecurity17/sec17-wang-tao.pdf)

329. Watchtower, "About Watchtower Privacy in 1Password", *1Password Support*, 8 October 2020. (Available at https://support.1password.com/watchtower-privacy/)

330. Brent Waters, "Ciphertext-Policy Attribute-Based Encryption: An Expressive, Efficient, and Provably Secure Realization", *Cryptology ePrint archive, 2008/290*, 27 June 2008 (last revised 20 December 2010). (Available at https://eprint.iacr.org/2008/290.pdf)

331. Rigo Wenning, "Platform for Privacy Preferences (P3P) Project: Background, Critics and Discussions", *W3C P3P Background*, 2 February 2018. (Available at https://www.w3.org/P3P/background.html#critics)

332. Alan F. Westin, *Privacy and Freedom*, Ig Publishing, 2015. (This is a new printing of the original 1967 edition of this book, which is now out of print. It is available at https://www.igpub.com/privacy-and-freedom/ or at https://www.amazon.com/gp/product/1935439979)

333. Bernhard Wiedemann, "WhisperSystems/TextSecure Protocol", *GitHub, Inc.*, 2 March 2014. (Available at https://web.archive.org/web/20150107094950/https:/github.com/WhisperSystems/TextSecure/wiki/Protocol)

334. Wikipedia, *Anonymizer (company)*, 7 September 2020. (Available at https://en.wikipedia.org/wiki/Anonymizer_(company))

335. Wikipedia, *Private Information Retrieval*, 13 January 2021. (Available at https://en.wikipedia.org/wiki/Private_information_retrieval)

336. Wikipedia, *Cambridge Analytica*, 16 January 2021. (Available at https://en.wikipedia.org/wiki/Cambridge_Analytica)

337. Wikipedia, *Computational Complexity Theory*, 13 March 2021. (Available at https://en.wikipedia.org/wiki/Computational_complexity_theory)

338. Fabian Willems, "GhostBuy: An All-Steps Anonymous Purchase Platform (ASAPP) based on Separation of Data", *Master's thesis*, University of Ottawa, 19 May 2021. (Available at https://ruor.uottawa.ca/handle/10393/42161)

339. Philipp Winter, Roya Ensafi, Karsten Loesing, and Nick Feamster, "Identifying and Characterizing Sybils in the Tor Network", *Usenix Security Symposium*, 10-12 August 2016, pp. 1169-1185. (Available at https://www.usenix.org/system/files/conference/usenixsecurity16/sec16_paper_winter.pdf)

340. Matthew Wright, Micah Adler, Brian N. Levine, and Clay Shields "Defending anonymous communication against passive logging attacks", *IEEE Symposium on Security and Privacy*, May 2003, pp. 28–41. (Available at https://ieeexplore.ieee.org/stamp/stamp.jsp?tp=&arnumber=1199325)

341. Andrew C. Yao, "Protocols for secure computations", *Proceedings of the 23rd IEEE Symposium on Foundations of Computer Science*, 1982, pp. 160-164. (Available at https://www.computer.org/csdl/proceedings-article/focs/198 2/542800160/12OmNyUnEJP)

342. Andrew Chi-Chih Yao, "How To Generate and Exchange Secrets", *27th Annual Symposium on Foundations of Computer Science*, Toronto, Canada, 1986, pp. 162-167. (Available at https://ieeexplore.ieee.org/document/4568207)

343. Danfeng Yao, Nelly Fazio, Yevgeniy Dodis, and Anna Lysyanskaya, "Id-based encryption for complex hierarchies with applications to forward security and broadcast encryption", *Proceedings of the 11th ACM Conference on Computer and Communications Security*, October 2004, pp. 354-363. (Available at https://dl.acm.org/doi/10.1145/1030083.1030130)

344. Philip Zimmermann, *The Official PGP User's Guide*, MIT Press, 1995. (Available at https://www.amazon.com/Official-PGP-Users-Guide/dp/0262740176)

345. Shoshana Zuboff, *The Age of Surveillance Capitalism: The Fight for a Human Future at the New Frontier of* Power, Public Affairs, 2019. (Available at https://www.amazon.com/Age-Surveillance-Capitalism-Future-Frontier/dp/1610395697/ref=tmm_hrd_swatch_0?_encoding=UTF8&qid=1620832342&sr=1-1)

## 12.2 Hyperlinked Bibliography

*The following are some recommended books that are not specifically/exclusively in the PETs area, but are highly relevant to other critical areas of privacy (such as legal, organizational, and societal considerations).*

Stephen Baker, *The Numerati*, Houghton Mifflin Company, 2008. (Available at https://www.amazon.com/gp/product/0618784608/ref=x_gr_w_bb_sout?ie=UTF8&tag=x_gr_w_bb_sout-20&linkCode=as2&camp=1789&creative=9325&creativeASIN=0618784608&SubscriptionId=1MGPYB6YW3HWK55XCGG2)

J. C. Cannon, *Privacy: What Developers and IT Professionals Should Know*, Addison-Wesley, 2005. (Available at https://www.amazon.com/Privacy-What-Developers-Professionals-Should/dp/0321224094)

April Falcon Doss, *Cyber Privacy: Who Has Your Data and Why You Should Care*, BenBella Books, 2020. (Available at https://www.amazon.com/Cyber-Privacy-Your-Data-Should/dp/1948836920/ref=pd_sbs_23?pd_rd_w=sW2IA&pf_rd_p=3ec6a47e-bf65-49f8-80f7-0d7c7c7ce2ca&pf_rd_r=M73BB13Z4ECRZ6728224&pd_rd_r=1c13a841-9cbf-4df4-b5ef-8fe94a88f02b&pd_rd_wg=457lk&pd_rd_i=1948836920&psc=1)

David H. Holtzman, *Privacy Lost: How Technology is Endangering Your Privacy*, Jossey-Bass (A Wiley Imprint), 2006. (Available at https://www.amazon.ca/Privacy-Lost-Technology-Endangering-Your/dp/0787985112)

Helen Nissenbaum, *Privacy in Context: Technology, Policy, and the Integrity of Social Life*, Stanford Law Books, 2009. (Available at https://www.amazon.ca/Privacy-Context-Technology-Policy-Integrity/dp/0804752370)

James B. Rule, *Privacy in Peril: How We Are Sacrificing a Fundamental Right in Exchange for Security and Convenience*, Oxford University Press, 2007. (Available at https://www.amazon.com/Privacy-Peril-Sacrificing-Fundamental-Convenience-ebook/dp/B00JC5UT4Q/ref=sr_1_1?dchild=1&keywords=james+b+rule+privacy+in+peril&qid=1614291723&s=books&sr=1-1)

Bruce Schneier, *Data and Goliath: The Hidden Battles to Collect Your Data and Control Your World*, W. W. Norton and Company, 2015. (Available at https://www.amazon.ca/Data-Goliath-Battles-Collect-Control/dp/039335217X/ref=tmm_pap_swatch_0?_encoding=UTF8&qid=&sr=)

Daniel Solove, *The Digital Person: Technology and Privacy in the Information Age*, New York University Press, 2004. (Available at https://papers.ssrn.com/sol3/papers.cfm?abstract_id=2899131)

Daniel Solove, *Understanding Privacy*, Harvard University Press, 2008. (Available at https://www.danielsolove.com/understanding-privacy/)

Shoshana Zuboff, *The Age of Surveillance Capitalism: The Fight for a Human Future at the New Frontier of* Power, Public Affairs, 2019. (Available at https://www.amazon.com/Age-Surveillance-Capitalism-Future-Frontier/dp/1610395697/ref=tmm_hrd_swatch_0?_encoding=UTF8&qid=1620832342&sr=1-1)

## 12.3   Further Reading on Selected Topics

*The following are a few books on some of the topics covered in the previous chapters, for those who wish to acquire a greater depth of knowledge in those subjects.*
SSL/TLS:

Eric Rescorla, *SSL and TLS: Designing and Building Secure Systems*, 2000. (Available at https://www.amazon.ca/SSL-TLS-Designing-Building-Paperback/dp/B00HS8KSV8)

IPsec:

Sheila Frankel, *Demystifying the IPsec Puzzle*, Artech House, 2001. (Available at https://doc.lagout.org/network/Demystifying%20The%20IPsec%20Puzzle.pdf)

Naganand Doraswamy and Dan Harkins, *IPsec: The New Security Standard for the Internet, Intranets, and Virtual Private Networks, 2ⁿᵈ Edition*, Prentice Hall, 2003. (Available at https://www.amazon.in/IPSec-Prentice-Hall-Ptr-Web-Infrastructure/dp/013046189X)

Charles M. Kozierok, *The TCP/IP Guide: A Comprehensive, Illustrated Internet Protocols Reference*, No Starch Press, 2005 (Chapter 29). (Available at https://www.amazon.ca/TCP-Guide-Comprehensive-Illustrated-Protocols-ebook/dp/B008G30T7W?)

PIR:

Xun Yi, Russell Paulet, and Elisa Bertino, *Private Information Retrieval*, Morgan & Claypool, 2013. (Available at https://www.oreilly.com/library/view/private-information-retrieval/9781627051538/)

Digital Credentials:

Stefan Brands, *Rethinking Public Key Infrastructures and Digital Certificates: Building in Privacy*, The MIT Press, 2000. (Available at http://www.credentica.com/the_mit_pressbook.html)

ABE:

Dijiang Huang, Qiuxiang Dong, and Yan Zhu, *Attribute-Based Encryption and Access Control*, CRC Press, 2020. (Available at https://www.amazon.ca/Attribute-Based-Encryption-Control-Data-Enabled-Engineering-ebook/dp/B08571VWPL)

MPC:

David Evans, Vladimir Kolesnikov and Mike Rosulek, *A Pragmatic Introduction to Secure Multi-Party Computation*, now publishers inc., December 2018. (Available at https://securecomputation.org/)

DP:

Cynthia Dwork and Aaron Roth, *The Algorithmic Foundations of Differential Privacy*, now publishers inc., 2014. (Available at https://www.amazon.com/Algorithmic-Foundations-Differential-Privacy/dp/1601988184/)

Ninghui Li, Min Lyu, Dong Su, and Weining Yang, *Differential Privacy: From Theory to Practice*, Morgan & Claypool, 2016. (Available at https://www.amazon.ca/Differential-Privacy-Practice-Ninghui-Li/dp/1627054936)

Tianqing Zhu, Gang Li, Wanlei Zhou, and Philip S. Yu, *Differential Privacy and Applications*, Springer, 2017. (Available at https://www.chapters.indigo.ca/en-ca/books/differential-privacy-and-applications/9783319620022-item.html)

HDB:

Tyrone Grandison, Christopher Johnson, and Jerry Kiernan, "Hippocratic Databases: Current Capabilities and Future Trends" in *Handbook on Database Security: Applications and Trends*, Michael Gertz and Sushil Jajodia (Eds), Springer, 2008, pp. 409-429. (Available at https://link.springer.com/chapter/10.1007/978-0-387-48533-1_17)

P3P:

Lorrie Faith Cranor, *Web Privacy with P3P: The Platform for Privacy Preferences*, O'Reilly, 2002. (Available at https://www.amazon.ca/Web-Privacy-P3P-Platform-Preferences/dp/0596003714)

SDN:

Paul Goransson, Chuck Black, and Timothy Culver, *Software Defined Networks: A Comprehensive Approach*, Morgan Kaufmann, 2016. (Available at https://www.amazon.ca/Software-Defined-Networks-Comprehensive-Approach/dp/0128045558)

ML:

Shai Shalev-Shwartz, Shai Ben-David, *Understanding Machine Learning: From Theory to Algorithms*, Cambridge University Press, 2014. (Available at https://www.amazon.ca/dp/B00J8LQU8I?tag=hackr0e1-20&geniuslink=true)

John D. Kelleher, Brian Mac Namee, and Aoife D'Arcy, *Fundamentals of Machine Learning for Predictive Data Analytics: Algorithms, Worked Examples, and Case Studies, 2nd Edition*, The MIT Press, 2020. (Available at https://www.amazon.ca/Fundamentals-Machine-Learning-Predictive-Analytics-dp-0262044692/dp/0262044692/ref=dp_ob_title_bk)

# Glossary

**Access control [7]**  The procedures and functions put in place to restrict access to specific objects or resources

**Access control policy [7]**  A formal specification of the rules governing who is given what kind of access (and under which circumstances) to each protected resource

**Access structure [7]**  When multiple parties need to work together to obtain a resource, an access structure describes who needs to cooperate with whom, and how, in order to access the resource (in **ABE**, the "parties" are attributes)

**Accuracy/correctness of a data set [6]**  A measure indicating whether the data in a data set can be relied upon to be true (as opposed to error-ridden or deliberately falsified)

**Anonymity [3]**  Other entities are unable to determine the identity (i.e., the "real name") of the party that is associated with a particular action or piece of data (see **anonymity set**)

**Anonymity set [6]**  A set of entities that potentially have the same attributes. Thus, **anonymity** means that a given entity is not identifiable (or distinguishable) within a particular anonymity set

**Anonymous credential [6]**  A specific type of **credential system**

**Anonymous remailer [3]**  A PET for sending anonymous e-mail (originally proposed in 1988)

**APEX [8]**  Architecture for Privacy Enforcement using XML (a PET for privacy enforcement proposed in 2006)

**APPEL [8]**  A P3P Preference Exchange Language (an XML encoding for user preferences in P3P environments, proposed in 2002)

---

The following is a glossary of terms and acronyms used in this book. A number in brackets (e.g. "[3]") is a reference to the chapter in which the term is first used.

© The Editor(s) (if applicable) and The Author(s), under exclusive license
to Springer Nature Switzerland AG 2021
C. Adams, *Introduction to Privacy Enhancing Technologies*,
https://doi.org/10.1007/978-3-030-81043-6

**Application proxy [3]**   A service that sits between protected and unprotected networks (an application sends a request to the proxy and the proxy creates its own request and sends it to the recipient; the response is sent to the proxy which then creates its own response and sends it to the application) so that senders and receivers never interact directly and all messages can be completely inspected

**Attribute-based encryption (ABE) [7]**   A type of public key cryptography in which specified attributes are required in order to decrypt the ciphertext into its corresponding plaintext

**Authenticated channel [8]**   A communications channel in which the receiver of a message knows the identity of the sender of that message. The channel has integrity (the message cannot be modified in transit by an adversary), but it may not provide confidentiality

**AWGN [7]**   Additive White Gaussian Noise

**Background knowledge attack [6]**   A security attack in which the adversary has some prior knowledge (or auxiliary knowledge) about the target of his/her attack, which can make the attack more effective

**Black-box setting [9]**   Knowing, or having access to, only the input-output functionality of a system, application, or environment (see also **white-box setting**)

**Broadcast channel [8]**   A communications channel in which a message is sent from one sender simultaneously to multiple receivers

**CAPTCHA [3]**   Completely Automated Public Turing test to tell Computers and Humans Apart (a challenge-response test initiated by a website in order to determine whether the entity visiting the website is a human or a piece of software)

**CP-ABE [7]**   Ciphertext-Policy Attribute-Based Encryption (the **access structure** is specified in the ciphertext, and the private key is a set of attributes)

**Composability property [7]**   Multiple **differentially private** mechanisms can be composed (i.e., used sequentially or in parallel) to create a combined mechanism with a guaranteed level of $\varepsilon$-**differential privacy**

**Contextual integrity [2]**   A theory of privacy in which the "contexts" are social domains (such as health, finance, family, political framework, etc.) and an assessment of the appropriateness of information flow considers the data subject, the sender, the recipient, the type of data, and the transmission principle (consented, coerced, stolen, buying, selling, national security, and so on)

**Credential system [6]**   A PET for minimizing information disclosure in online transactions (proposed in 2000)

**Dark web [3]**   A part of the Internet that is not indexed by traditional search engines and that requires special software, configuration, or authorization to access

**Data minimization [2]**   The practice of limiting the collection of personal information to that which is directly relevant and necessary for accomplishing a specified purpose

**Data perturbation [8]**   The practice of adding "noise" (i.e., random values) to a database so that individual record values cannot be relied upon (because they are incorrect), although aggregate values such as "average" may still be correct

**DDoS [9]**   Distributed Denial of Service

**Deep Neural Network [9]**   An artificial neural network with multiple layers between the input and output layers

**Digital credential [6]**   A specific type of **credential system**

**Disclosure [2]**   The simultaneous acquisition of both the attribute of a user and the identity of that user, by an unintended party

**DNS [3]**   Domain Name Server

**DPIA [9]**   Data Protection Impact Assessment

**EEA [8]**   European Economic Area

**Entry funnel [3]**   The node in an **onion routing network** that takes data from the sender's **application proxy** and **onion proxy**, and passes it to the first of several **onion routers**

**$\varepsilon$-Differential Privacy [7]**   A PET for database privacy proposed in 2006

**EU [8]**   European Union

**Exit funnel [3]**   The node in an **onion routing network** that takes data from the sequence of **onion routers**, and passes it to the receiver's **onion proxy** and **application proxy**

**Exposure [2]**   The simultaneous acquisition of both the action of a user and the identity of that user, by an unintended party

**FTP [3]**   File Transfer Protocol

**Garbled circuit [7]**   A way to "encrypt a computation" such that the output of the computation is revealed, but no information about the inputs or intermediate values is revealed (a garbled circuit is sometimes referred to as a *scrambled circuit*)

**GDPR [8]**   General Data Protection Regulation (a regulation in EU law on data protection and privacy in the **EU** and the **EEA**)

**Guard node [3]**   A specific **onion router** (perhaps one of a very small fixed set of **onion routers**) that will be used as the first **onion router** for Alice's messages (the remaining **onion routers** in her **onion routing network** may be freely chosen). The guard node must satisfy certain criteria in order to minimize the risk of compromise (and, therefore, the risk of anonymity loss for Alice)

**HDB [8]**   Hippocratic database (a PET for database privacy proposed in 2002)

**Hidden services [3]**   Services that can only be accessed through Tor (they are invisible to ordinary Web browsers and search engines)

**Homogeneity attack [6]**   In a set of records having identical **quasi-identifiers**, if the value of the sensitive attribute is always the same, then observers will be able to deduce the value of the sensitive attribute for anyone whose record they know is in that set

**HTML [8]**   Hypertext Markup Language

**HTTP, HTTPS [3]**   Hypertext Transfer Protocol; HTTP over SSL

**IACR [7]**   International Association for Cryptologic Research

**Identifier [6]**   Information (such as a *social security number*) that distinguishes one entity from all others in a set of entities (also referred to as a *unique identifier*)

**IETF [4]**   Internet Engineering Task Force (an international body responsible for the creation and development of Internet standards)

**IM [5]**   Instant Messaging

**Inference attack [6]**   An attacker infers information that he or she should not know, given only information that he or she is allowed to know

**IP [3], IPv4, IPv6 [4]**   Internet Protocol (a communications protocol for transmitting datagrams (packets of data) across networks; the first major version of IP is known as "Internet Protocol Version 4" (IPv4) and its successor is known as "Internet Protocol Version 6" (IPv6))

**IPsec protocol [4]**   IP security protocol (a protocol for protecting IP packets transmitted between devices; it can be operated either in **transport mode** or in **tunnel mode**)

**IRC [3]**   Internet Relay Chat

**Issuing protocol [6]**   An interaction between a user and a Certification Authority (CA) which results in the CA digitally signing a **credential** for the user

*k*-**Anonymity [6]**   A PET for database privacy proposed in 1998

**KP-ABE [7]**   Key-Policy Attribute-Based Encryption (the **access structure** is specified in the private key and the ciphertext is a set of attributes)

**LAN [5]**   Local Area Network

**MAC address [9]**   Media access control address (a unique identifier assigned to a network interface controller for use as a network address)

**Mix network [3]**   A PET for untraceable e-mail proposed in 1981

**ML [9]**   Machine learning

**MPC [7]**   Multi-party computation (a PET that allows multiple entities to jointly compute a function without any party seeing the private inputs of any other party; MPC was proposed in 1986)

**MTD [9]**   Moving target defense (dynamically and constantly changing network configuration in order to increase the difficulty of reconnaissance and intrusion by an attacker)

**NFS [3]**   Network File System

**NIST [9]**   National Institute of Standards and Technology, an agency of the US Department of Commerce whose mission is to promote innovation and industrial competitiveness (in part through standardization of various technologies)

**Nonce [11]**   A contraction for "number used once" (for example, in an authentication protocol, Alice may send to Bob a random number that has not been used before and will not be used again; when Bob returns a signature on this nonce, Alice will be convinced that she is in a live session with Bob)

**NNTP [3]**   Network news transfer protocol (the protocol used to connect to Usenet servers and to transfer newsgroup articles between systems)

**OECD [8]**   Organization for Economic Co-operation and Development

**OCSP [4]**   Online Certificate Status Protocol (a protocol to check the current revocation status of a public key certificate)

**Onion proxy [3]**   The node in an **onion routing network** that receives data from the sender's **application proxy** and prepares it for transmission through the network, or that receives data from the network and prepares it for reception by the receiver's **application proxy**

**Onion router [3]**   A node in an **onion routing network** that receives a message, decrypts the outer layer to reveal the next node, and forwards the internal portion to that next node

**Onion routing network [3]**   A PET for anonymous real-time communications, proposed in 1996

**Operation tuple [2]**   The pair (*identity, action*) that causes **exposure** if known by an unintended party

**OTR [5]**   Off-the-Record messaging protocol (a PET for private messaging in **IM** environments, proposed in 2004)

**Output perturbation [6]**   The practice of adding "noise" (i.e., random values) to query responses from a database so that the correct response values cannot be learned

**P3P [8]**   Platform for Privacy Preferences Project (a PET for creating **privacy policies** proposed in 2002)

**P3P policy [8]**   A **privacy policy** that conforms to the **P3P** specification

**PDP [8]**   Policy Decision Point (in the **XACML** processing model, the PDP is the component that renders an **access control** decision (i.e., "permit" or "deny"))

**PEP [8]**   Policy Enforcement Point (in the **XACML** processing model, the PEP is the component that enforces an **access control** decision which has been made by the **PDP**)

**PET, PETs [1]**   Privacy Enhancing Technology; Privacy Enhancing Technologies

**PGP [5]**   Pretty Good Privacy (a format and protocol for adding encryption and digital signatures to e-mail messages)

**PIN [6]**   Personal Identification Number

**PIR [4]**   Private information retrieval (a PET for database privacy proposed in 1995)

**Point-to-point network [8]**   A network in which there are only two communicating nodes (thus they communicate only with each other)

**Policy reference file [8]**   A statement about what **P3P policy** applies to any given **URI** within a website

**Privacy Bird [8]**   A **P3P** user agent (proposed in 2006)

**Privacy level of a data set [6]**   The maximum probability of re-identification for individuals in the data set

**Privacy policy [1]**   A collection of rules specifying who is allowed to access what data, and what they can do with this data once they have it

**Privacy seal program [8]**   An independent (3rd-party) audit and review of an organization's website and data processing practices in order to assess the organization's website safety and compliance with their publicized **privacy policy**

**Private set intersection [7]**   an example of **MPC** (in which two parties determine whether they have elements in common from their respective private sets)

**Property of an attribute [6]**   information about an attribute that does not reveal its actual value (for example, if the attribute is an integer, a property might be that the attribute is "greater than $x$", or "less than $y$", or "in the range $[x, y]$")

**Pseudonym [3]**   An **identifier** of a party that is not one of the party's "real names"

**Pseudonymity [3]**   The use of pseudonyms as **identifiers**

**PSTN [9]**  Public Switched Telephone Network

**Quasi-identifier [6]**  Attributes (which are not themselves unique **identifiers**) that can be grouped together (possibly with other external information) to re-identify a specific individual

**Query restriction [8]**  Disallowing specific queries, or specific types of queries, from some or all users

**RBAC [7]**  Role-Based Access Control (a form of **access control** in which privileges are assigned to roles (such as "manager" or "system administrator") rather than to individual names/identities)

**Record tuple [2]**  The pair (*identity, attribute*) that causes **disclosure** if known by an unintended party

**RFC [4]**  Request for Comments (an **IETF** standards-track specification)

**SDN [9]**  Software Defined Networking (an approach to network management that enables dynamic network configuration)

**S/MIME [5]**  Secure Multipurpose Internet Mail Extensions (a standardized format and protocol for adding encryption and digital signatures to e-mail messages)

**Sensitivity of a function [7]**  The sensitivity of a database query function $A$ is the amount that $A$ will change if a particular person's data is removed from the database (*global sensitivity* is the maximum possible change, when all individual records are taken into consideration)

**Showing protocol [6]**  An interaction between two entities Alice and Bob in which Alice proves ownership of some attributes in her **credential** to Bob (while hiding all remaining attributes). If the **credential** can only be used in one showing protocol, it is called *single-show*; if it can be used in many showing protocols without diminishing Alice's privacy, it is called *multi-show*

**SMTP [3]**  Simple Mail Transfer Protocol (a standardized communication protocol for e-mail transmission)

**Social engineering [1]**  The art of exploiting social means, rather than technical hacking procedures, to gain access to buildings, systems, or data. In the context of information security, it generally refers to the psychological manipulation of people into performing actions or divulging confidential information (such as a password) that will be of benefit to an attacker

**Social sorting [1]**  The partition of raw data about people into various categories, based on separators such as income, education, race, occupation, social status, geographic residence, and so on

**SOCKS protocol [3]**  Socket service protocol (an Internet protocol that exchanges packets between a client and a server through a proxy server)

**SSH [3]**  Secure Shell (a protocol for operating network services securely over an unsecured network)

**SSL [4]**  Secure Sockets Layer (a protocol to provide communications security over a network; a modified version of SSL was standardized as **TLS**)

**Synchronous network [7]**  A network in which all communications connections are synchronized to a shared clock

**TCP [3]**  Transmission Control Protocol (a connection-oriented service that is typically implemented on top of **IP** in the Internet communications protocol stack)

**TLS [4]**   Transport Layer Security (a protocol to provide communications security over a network; this standardized protocol was based on the earlier **SSL** protocol)

**Tor [3]**   The onion routing (a specific implementation of the **onion routing network**, developed in 2002)

**Traffic analysis [3]**   The process of intercepting and examining messages on a network in order to deduce information from communication patterns

**Transport mode [4]**   A mode of operation for the **IPsec protocol** in which only the packet body is protected (the packet header information is left in the clear)

**Tunnel mode [4]**   A mode of operation for the **IPsec protocol** in which both the packet body and the packet header information are protected

**UDP [4]**   User datagram protocol (a connectionless service that is typically implemented on top of **IP** in the Internet communications protocol stack)

**URL**   Uniform Resource Locator (a reference to a Web resource that specifies its location on a network and a mechanism for retrieving it)

**URI [8]**   Uniform Resource Identifier (a globally unique sequence of characters that identifies a physical or logical resource on a network)

**Utility of a data set [6]**   A measure of how useful a set of data is for achieving a given purpose

**VPN [3]**   Virtual Private Network (a protocol to create a private network connection across a public network connection)

**W3C [8]**   World Wide Web Consortium (an international body responsible for the creation and development of Web standards)

**Website fingerprinting [3]**   The process of collecting sufficient features, information, and traffic from a website to be able to uniquely distinguish it from other websites

**White-box setting [9]**   Knowing, or having access to, the internal structures, workings, and documentation of a system, application, or environment (see also **black-box setting**)

**WSDL [8]**   Web Services Description Language (an **XML**-based language that is used for describing the functionality offered by a Web service)

**XACML [8]**   eXtensible Access Control Markup Language (a human- and machine-readable language for writing **access control policies**)

**XACML policy [8]**   An **access control policy** that conforms to the **XACML** specification

**XML [8]**   eXtensible Markup Language (a text format to enable and facilitate data exchange on the Web)

**XSLT [8]**   eXtensible Stylesheet Language Transformation (a language for transforming XML documents into other XML documents)

# Index

**A**

ABE, *see* Attribute-Based Encryption (ABE)
Acceptable suppression threshold, 114
Access control policy, 145, 190–192, 252
Access controls, 78, 109, 144, 145, 149, 150,
　176–178, 190, 214, 221, 223, 231
Access structures, 145–150, 170
Action analysis, 33
Actions, 2, 5, 25, 29, 32–35, 39, 52, 64, 69,
　75, 79, 81, 82, 89, 95, 96, 98, 99, 105,
　110, 183, 190, 192, 203, 210–212, 215,
　219, 221, 228, 229, 232–235
Active enforcement system, 181
Additive white Gaussian noise (AWGN), 160
Adjustment factors, 147
Advanced Encryption Standard (AES), 42, 73,
　100, 144, 195, 246
Adversary, Adversary model
　active (*see* Malicious)
　byzantine, 259, 262
　covert, 155
　fail-stop, 155, 259, 262
　honest-but-curious, 259, 262
　malicious, 155, 259
　man-in-the-middle, 259
　passive, 47, 62, 155, 258, 260
　semi-honest, 155
AES, *see* Advanced Encryption
　Standard (AES)
After-the-fact protection, 216
After-the-fact recourse, 215, 216
AI algorithms, 9
AKE, *see* Authenticated Key Exchange (AKE)
Alert protocol, 71
Anon.penet.fi, 49–51, 228

Anonym, 212
Anonymity, 22, 27, 28, 44, 45, 47, 49–53, 56,
　58–65, 106, 110, 113, 120, 228
Anonymity set, 111, 118, 137, 139, 228
Anonymity/pseudonymity, 218, 219
Anonymizer architectures, 24
Anonymous
　connections, 33, 54, 55, 57, 58, 60, 61
　credential (*see* Credential system) (*see*
　　Digital credential)
　E-voting protocol, 218
　payment mechanism, 218
　remailers, 39, 49–54, 63, 228
Anti-adware, 212
Anti-spyware, 212, 213, 221
Antivirus, 213, 221, 223
APEX, *see* Architecture for Privacy
　Enforcement using XML (APEX)
Application data protocol, 71
Application protocol, 71
Application proxy, 55–58
Approximate differential privacy, 165
Approximation algorithms, 120
A P3P Preference Exchange Language
　(APPEL), 178, 185, 187, 189, 194, 195
Architecture for Privacy Enforcement using
　XML (APEX), 110, 175, 189–196,
　203, 229
Artificial intelligence (AI), 8, 10, 219
Asymmetric
　algorithms, 251, 260
　ciphers, 248, 249, 260
　encryption algorithms, 42, 248, 256
　(public key) algorithm, 245
Attacker models, 63, 88, 258, 259, 262, 265

© The Editor(s) (if applicable) and The Author(s), under exclusive license
to Springer Nature Switzerland AG 2021
C. Adams, *Introduction to Privacy Enhancing Technologies*,
https://doi.org/10.1007/978-3-030-81043-6

Attackers, 41, 42, 47, 48, 51, 52, 56, 60–62,
   75, 76, 89, 102, 104, 118, 135, 137,
   148, 166, 167, 220, 221, 233, 258–260,
   262, 263
Attacks targeting a specific user, 63
Attribute auditing center (AAC), 149
Attribute values, 110, 113, 116, 117, 125, 126,
   128–133, 135–138, 143, 147, 148, 150,
   196, 202, 204, 229
Attribute-Based Encryption (ABE), 143–146,
   148, 169, 171, 251
   See also CP-ABE, KP-ABE
Attributes, 3, 25, 29, 33–35, 39, 72, 79,
   110–121, 125, 131–137, 139, 144–151,
   170, 175–177, 179, 185, 186, 191,
   196–205, 210, 212, 213, 215, 216, 219,
   221, 228, 229, 231, 251, 255
Audit log information, 145
Audit trail, 177
Auditing framework, 179
Auditing system, 180
Authenticated encryption (AE), 258
Authenticated encryption ciphers, 73
Authenticated key exchange (AKE),
   101–103, 258
Authentication, 54, 70, 71, 75, 76, 78–80,
   100–102, 104, 231, 242, 243,
   254–256, 258
Authentication Header (AH), 76–80
Authentication protocol, 255
Authentication technique, 255, 256
Authenticity, 71, 75, 99, 100, 243,
   244, 255–258
Authorized users, 177, 178
Automated profiling, 9, 10
Autonomous systems (ASes), 62
AWGN, see Additive White Gaussian
   Noise (AWGN)

**B**
Background knowledge attacks, 116, 117, 119
Bandwidth, 45, 48, 61, 63–65
Bandwidth allocation mechanism, 63
Batch issuing protocol, see Showing protocol
Bidirectional anonymity, 59
Big-O notation, 261
   See also Little-O notation
Bilinear maps, 264
Bilinear pairing-based cryptography, 148
Bilinear pairings, 264, 265
Black-box setting, 220, 221
   See also White-box setting
Blind digital signatures, 257

Blinding factors, 131, 257
Blind signatures, 123–125, 138, 257
Block ciphers, 246, 258
Broadcast channel, 156, 251
Broadcast encryption, 145, 251
Border Gateway Protocol (BGP), 62
Byzantine
   failures, 88
   robust PIR, 87


**C**
CA, see Certification Authority (CA)
CAPTCHAs, 62
Cascades, 42–45, 47, 48, 64
Cell-level access control, 179
Certificate management, 250, 252
Certificates, 71, 72, 75, 121–123, 126, 144,
   233, 247, 250, 251, 256
Certification Authority (CA), 100, 122, 123,
   125, 126, 128–136, 250–252, 256
ChaCha20, 245
ChaCha20 stream cipher, 73
Chaining, 51
Challenge-response authentication, 242
Challenge-response protocol, 123
Change Cipher Spec messages, 72, 73
Change Cipher Spec protocol, 71
Checksum, 253
Chief Privacy Officers, 2, 21
Cipher block chaining (CBC), 73, 78, 246
Cipher suite, 71, 72
CipherSpec, 71–73
Ciphertext Policy Attribute-Based Encryption
   (CP-ABE), 143, 144, 146, 148–150,
   169–171, 229, 251
   See also Attribute-Based Encryption
   See also KP-ABE
Ciphertexts, 40–44, 96, 143–146, 148–150,
   153, 169–171, 193, 229, 244, 245, 247,
   248, 250–252, 256, 257, 259, 260,
   263, 265
Circuit scheduling, 63
Classification, vii, 22, 24, 25, 27, 28, 30–33,
   35–37, 62, 213, 214, 216
   See also Privacy tree
Classification of PETs, see Privacy tree
Classification for privacy, see Privacy tree
Classification summary, see Privacy tree
Client authentication, 71
Client hello, 72–74
Client-server interaction, 71, 78, 81
Coding theory, 85, 160
Colluding servers, 88

Collusion resistance, 251
Commitments, 123–128, 132, 133, 138, 198,
    201, 263
    *See also* Pedersen commitment
Communications confidentiality, 70
Communications privacy, 109, 110
Communications protocol stack, 57, 81, 89
Compact policies, 186
Compliance auditing mechanism, 181
Composability property of differential
    privacy, 164
Composition
    concurrent, 156
    modular, 156
    sequential, 156, 167
    universal composability, 156
Computational
    complexity theory, 260–262
    Diffie-Hellman (CDH) assumption (*see*
        Decisional Diffie-Hellman (DDH)
        assumption)
    privacy (*see* Information-theoretic privacy)
    Security (*see* Information-theoretic
        security)
Computational privacy, 83, 86, 88, 262
Computational security, 262
Computationally binding, *see* Computationally
    hiding, *see* Unconditionally binding,
    *see* Unconditionally hiding
Computationally hiding, *see* Computationally
    binding, *see* Unconditionally binding,
    *see* Unconditionally hiding
Computationally-bounded, 83, 89, 132
Computationally-bounded attacker, 40,
    167, 262
Computationally secure PIR (C-PIR), 86,
    87, 89, 90
Computationally-unbounded, 263
Confidentiality, 25, 27, 40, 50, 70, 71, 75, 78,
    79, 89, 101, 103, 104, 149, 151,
    243–253, 255, 258, 260
Congestion control, 58, 63
Consented sharing, 176
Constant pool, 46
Consumer privacy, 23
Contextual integrity, 26, 29
Cookies, 5, 13, 194, 223, 233
Correctness, viii, 115, 151, 153, 155, 163,
    170, 177
Corruption strategies
    adaptive, 155, 167
    proactive, 155
    static, 155
Cover traffic, 58

Covering codes, 84, 85
CP-ABE, *see* Ciphertext Policy Attribute-
        Based Encryption (CP-ABE),
    *see* KP-ABE
C-PIR, *see* Computationally secure
        PIR (C-PIR)
Credential, 121
Credential systems, 110, 120–123, 132,
        135–139, 175, 196–203, 228
    *See also* Anonymous credential
    *See also* Digital Credential
Credential transfer, 132
    *See also* Lending problem
Cryptanalysis, 56, 241, 258
Cryptanalysts, 242, 244, 258
Cryptographic
    algorithms, 36, 64, 71–73, 76, 77, 144,
        150, 156, 158, 241–244, 254, 256, 258,
        260, 262–265
    authentication, 54, 79
    confidentiality, 70, 71, 89, 103, 243, 244,
        255, 258
    hash function, 73, 78, 100, 254, 260,
        263, 264
    hashes, 73, 118, 119, 256
    key, 72, 73, 78, 103, 136, 144, 152, 193,
        242–244, 254, 256, 257, 264
    properties, 64, 89, 103, 243, 254
    protocols, 36, 70, 76, 89, 101, 103–105,
        127, 136, 150, 153, 156, 158, 241–243,
        258, 262–265
    strengths, 118, 243, 244, 258, 260–263
    techniques, 36, 40, 72, 123, 127, 136, 156,
        241, 242, 256
Cryptography, vii, 27, 36, 40, 42, 54, 57, 104,
        241, 242, 249, 252, 253, 263, 265
Cryptology, 241, 242
Curse of dimensionality, 119
Cut-and-choose paradigm, 156
Cypherpunk remailers, 51

**D**
Data
    at rest, 109
    data origin authenticity, 255
    generalizations, 112–114, 119, 138, 180
    holder, 25, 32, 33, 212, 216, 221
    in motion, 109
    minimization, 27–29
    mining, 5, 6, 120
    origin authentication, 243
    ownership, 3, 7, 18, 149, 234
    perturbation, 176

Data (*cont.*)
   privacies, 2, 3, 5, 13, 15, 17, 18, 25, 27–29,
      35, 39, 81, 86, 89, 105, 106, 111, 113,
      114, 116, 118, 139, 143, 145, 149, 164,
      168–170, 175, 176, 179, 181, 184, 188,
      190, 192, 195, 196, 203, 215, 218, 222,
      224, 229, 230, 234, 236
   Protection Impact Assessment (DPIA), 220
   purging, 176
   randomization, 213
   subjects, 25, 26
Data Encryption Standard (DES), 42, 78, 246
Database privacy, 176, 179
Data-link protocol, 71
DBDH, *see* Decisional Bilinear Diffie-
    Hellman assumption (DBDH)
DDH, *see* Decisional Diffie-Hellman (DDH)
    assumption
DDoS attacks, 217
Deanonymize users, 62
Decipher, 244
Decisional Bilinear Diffie-Hellman
    assumption (DBDH), 148, 265
Decisional Diffie-Hellman (DDH)
    assumption, 264
Decryption, 41, 54, 57, 99, 104, 132, 144, 145,
    147–149, 157, 170, 244–246, 248–250,
    252, 256, 260
Decryption algorithms, 54, 244, 245, 248
Decryption operations, 54, 145, 149, 256, 260
Deep neural networks, 220
Defense-in-depth, 231, 235
De-identifying data, 213
Delegatable anonymous credentials, 257
Delegation, 255
Deniability, 27, 99, 101–105
DES, *see* Data Encryption Standard (DES)
*ε-differential privacy*, 16, 110, 143, 158–169,
    171, 182, 222, 229
Differential privacy (DP), 165–168
*ε-differentially private*, 159
Diffie-Hellman (D-H) key exchange
    protocol, 100
Diffie-Hellman key agreement, 72
Diffie-Hellman protocol, 247, 250
Digital
   cash, 242
   Credential (*see* Anonymous credential)
     (*see* Credential system)
   digital currency, 257
   Signature (*see* RSA digital signature)
   trail, 21
Digital credentials, 121–123, 125–128,
    130–133, 136, 139, 196, 201–203, 218,
    229, 257

Digital signature algorithm (DSA), 124, 248,
    256, 257
Digital Signature Standard (DSS), 257
Digital vehicle forensics, 12
Dimensions of DP
   background knowledge, 166
   computational power, 167
   formalism change, 166, 167
   neighbourhood definition, 166
   quantification of privacy loss, 166
   relativization of knowledge gain, 167
   variation of privacy loss, 166
Directory servers, 51, 58
Disclosure-reducing transformation, 35
Disclosures, 25, 34, 35, 39, 110, 118, 143,
    145, 151, 158, 177, 179–181, 184, 188,
    195, 196, 210, 213, 215, 216, 221,
    228, 229
Distinct l-diversity, 116
DOI, *see* Internet IP Security Domain of
    Interpretation for ISAKMP
Domain generalization hierarchy, 114
DP, *see* Differential privacy (DP)
DSA public key, 126
Dummy traffic, 48, 51, 222
Dynamic pool, 46

**E**
Earth Mover's Distance (EMD), 117
Eavesdropper, *see* Unintended observer
Electronic elections, 242
Electronic mail, 22, 39, 40
Elliptic curve groups, 148, 263
E-mail, 40, 44, 49–55, 59, 63, 78, 81, 96, 104,
    132, 193, 250, 252
Encapsulating Security Payload (ESP),
    76–80
Encipher, 244
Encryption, 15, 28, 64, 71, 99, 109, 176, 211,
    229, 248
encryption algorithms, 40, 56, 57, 73, 78, 100,
    244–252, 260
Encryption operation, 256
End-point authentication, 70
End-to-end integrity checking, 59
Entropy l-diversity, 116–118
Entry funnel, 55
Entry guard selection, 61
Entry node, 55, 60
Ephemeral, 58, 73, 102, 247
Ephemeral key, 247
ESP, *see* Encapsulating Security
    Payload (ESP)
Exit funnel, 55

Exit nodes, 60
Exploit tools, 2
Exposure, 25, 34, 35, 39, 70, 77, 81, 98, 110, 210, 215, 221, 228
Exposure privacy, 76, 81, 211, 215
Exposure-reducing transformation, 35
EXtensible Access Control Markup Language (XACML), 190–194
EXtensible Markup Language (XML), 182–184, 186, 187, 190, 191
EXtensible Stylesheet Language Transformation (XSLT), 190–194
Extensions and variants of differential privacy, 166
Extensions for PIR, 87
External observers, 15, 40–42, 89, 116, 118, 137, 143, 196
External recipients, 177


F
Facebook Messenger, 103
Fair Information Practices, 23
Fairness, 151, 156
Fingerprints, 13, 102, 132, 253
Firewalls, 78, 81, 96–98, 191, 213, 221, 223, 231, 233, 252
Free route, 45
Fuzzy-IBE, see Policy-Based Encryption


G
Gaim, 102
    See also Pidgin
Garbled circuit, 152–154, 170
    See also Scrambled circuit
Garbled gate, see Scrambled circuit
Gaussian distributions, 160–162
General communications security protocols, 82
General Data Protection Regulation (GDPR), 195, 196, 220
General database security mechanism, 176
General security mechanism, 144
Generalizations, 26, 113–115, 119, 121, 144, 154, 165, 180, 199
Generic group model, 148
    See also Standard model
Global sensitivity, 164, 169
GTK + AOL Instant Messenger (gaim), see Pidgin
Guaranteed output delivery, 151, 156
Guard nodes, 60, 62


H
Handshake protocol, 71, 72, 75
Hash functions, 73, 78, 100, 126, 254, 256, 260, 263, 264
Hash-based message authentication code (HMAC), 78, 100, 254
HDB, see Hippocratic databases (HDB)
Health data, 110, 111
Helper nodes, 60
Heuristic, 120, 138, 139
Hidden services, 59, 63
Hide the revealed attributes, 196
Hiding
    the actions, 36, 39, 64, 69–90, 95, 98, 105, 109, 203, 228
    the attributes, 36, 39, 105, 109, 110, 118, 143–171, 175, 179, 196, 203, 212, 221, 228, 229
    the identities, 36, 39–65, 69, 74, 82, 98, 99, 109–139, 143, 151, 170, 175, 179, 196, 203, 228, 229
    the identity-action linkage, 105
    the identity-action pair, 36, 95–106
    the identity-attribute linkage, 105, 110
    the identity-attribute pair, 36, 175–205
Hippocratic databases (HDB), 175–182, 196, 203, 205, 229
HMAC, see Hash-based Message Authentication Code (HMAC)
Holder, 4, 25, 33, 35, 210, 211, 213, 215–217, 221
Homogeneity attacks, 116, 117, 119
Homomorphic encryption, 252
Homomorphic encryption algorithms, 86
Hop-by-hop, 46
Host-to-host communications, 97
Host-to-network communications, 97
Human profiling, 7, 9, 16


I
IBE, see Identity-Based Encryption (IBE)
Identifiable individual, 30
Identification, 25, 45, 137, 243
Identifiers, 41, 79, 121–123, 135, 136, 242, 250
Identity
    certificates, 121, 144, 252
    misbinding, 102
    mixer (idemix), 122
    theft, 7, 8, 16
Identity-Based Encryption (IBE), 144, 192, 251, 252
    See also Policy-Based Encryption

IETF, *see* Internet Engineering Task Force (IETF)
IETF Network Working Group, 70
IKE, *see* Internet Key Exchange
IKEv1, *see* Internet Key Exchange
IKEv2, *see* Internet Key Exchange
Internet Key ExchangeIND-CCA, *see*
     Indistinguishability of encryptions
IND-CCA2, *see* Indistinguishability of
     encryptions
IND-CPA, *see* Indistinguishability of
     encryptions
Independence of inputs, 151
*ε-indistinguishability*, 159
Indistinguishability of encryptions, 265
Induced throttling attacks, 63
Inference control techniques, 213, 221
Inference controls, 221
Information
     aggregation, 23, 26, 34
     collection, 6, 23, 28, 33, 34, 76, 145, 176,
          178, 216, 221
     dissemination, 8, 26, 221
     monitoring, 5, 12, 23
     personalization, 23
     privacies, 1–4, 7, 12, 13, 23–26, 29–33, 35,
          36, 39, 64, 74, 86–89, 115, 117, 118,
          120, 135, 148, 151, 158, 160, 163, 166,
          167, 176–179, 181, 185, 187, 189, 193,
          195, 211–213, 215, 216, 220, 221, 227,
          230, 233, 243, 258
     storage, 23, 192, 233
     theoretic privacy (*see* Computational
          privacy)
     theoretic security (*see* Computational
          security)
     theoretically hidden, 83
     theoretically secure PIR, 89, 90
     transfers, 23, 81, 259
Information Theoretically secure PIR, 86–89
Information-theoretic privacy, 83, 86, 263
Information-theoretic security, 131, 135, 137,
     156, 158, 263
Input-output correspondence, 40
Instance hiding problem, 86
Instant messaging, 61, 98, 99, 105
Instant messaging clients, 104
Integrity, 23, 26, 29, 70, 71, 75, 78, 79, 89, 96,
     105, 243, 244, 253–256, 258
Integrity mechanism, 70, 243
Integrity protection, 78
Intended recipients, 25, 33, 35, 43, 47, 50, 55,
     64, 75, 82, 89, 95, 99, 120, 137, 196,
     212, 213, 215, 218
Intended targets, 33, 69, 211, 215

Internet
     Engineering Task Force (IETF), 70, 74, 80
     IP Security Domain of Interpretation for
          ISAKMP, 79
     Key Exchange (IKE), 76, 79, 80
     protocols, 70, 75, 79, 80, 98
     Security Association and Key Management
          Protocol (ISAKMP), 79, 80
Internet IP Security Domain of Interpretation
     for ISAKMP, 79
Internet Key Exchange, 76, 79
Internet Protocol (IP)
     layer, 57, 77, 89
     network, 57
     Security Working Group, 76, 80
Interrogation, 3, 25
Intersection attack, 41
Intractable, 265
Intrusion detection, 213, 221, 223, 231
IP, *see* Internet Protocol (IP)
IPsec, 64, 69, 76–82, 89, 95–98, 105, 211,
     218, 219, 228
IPsec Maintenance and Extensions
     (IPsecME), 80
IPsec-v2, 76–80, 89
IPsec-v2 Architecture document, 97
IPsec-v3, 77, 80, 89, 97
ISAKMP, *see* Internet Security Association and
     Key Management Protocol (ISAKMP)
Issuing protocol, 125, 130, 131, 133, 134, 136,
     138, 201
     *See also* Showing protocol
IT-PIR, *see* Information Theoretically secure
     PIR (IT-PIR)


**K**
K-anonymity, 105, 110–120, 137–139, 180,
     213, 228
K-anonymity requirement, 112
Key
     agreements, 72, 73, 136, 246
     blocks, 73, 149, 254
     derivation, 246
     derivation function (KDF), 152, 153,
          246, 249
     distribution problem, 40, 246
     establishment, 79, 246, 258
     exchanges, 72, 73, 77, 79, 80, 89, 99, 102,
          103, 242, 246, 259
     generation center (KGC), 149
     pairs, 44, 45, 75, 125, 152, 193, 245,
          249, 250
     partitioning, 73, 247

Policy Attribute-Based Encryption
  (*see* CP-ABE)
rotation, 51
stream, 245
Key policy attribute-based encryption
  (KP-ABE), 145, 251
K-minimal generalization, 114, 115
KP-ABE, *see* Key Policy Attribute-Based
  Encryption (KP-ABE)


**L**

Laplacian distribution, 163, 165
Latency, 45, 52, 53, 64, 65
L-diversity, 115–119, 138
Leaky-pipe circuit, 58
Legal infrastructure, 189, 204, 209, 214–217,
  223, 229
Lending problem, 132
  *See also* Credential transfer
Limiting disclosure, 36, 105, 109–139,
  143–171, 175–205, 221, 228
Limiting exposure, 36, 39–65, 69–90, 95–106,
  109, 110, 203
Link padding, 58
Little-O notation, *see* Big-O notation
Load balancing, 61
Loss of confidentiality, 41
Lower-latency mix network, 53
Low-latency anonymity network, 62


**M**

MAC, *see* Message Authentication Code
MAC algorithm, *see* Message
  Authentication Code
Machine learning (ML), 9, 167, 217,
  219–224, 229
Malleable, 134, 135, 257
Malleable signatures, 134, 135, 257
Malware, 15, 99, 137, 253
Man-in-the-Middle (MITM), 76, 258, 259
Man-in-the-Middle (MITM) attack, 102
Marker attacks, 56
Master key, 148, 149, 246
Master secret, 73, 133
Maximum likelihood estimator (MLE), 165
MD5, 73, 78, 254
Membership inference attacks, 220, 221, 223
Mental poker, 151
Message
  authentication code (MAC), 78, 100–102,
    254, 255
  fragmentation, 102

protection technologies, 98
  tracing, 41, 45
Message Authentication Code (MAC), 71, 72,
  78, 101, 102, 218, 254, 255, 260
Millionaires Problem, 103
  *See also* Socialist Millionaires Problem
Minimal generalizations, 114
Minimal query, 178
Minimal required suppression, 114
Minimal suppression, 114
Minimum-cost 2-anonymity, 120
Minimum-cost 3-anonymity, 120
MITM, *see* Man-in-the-Middle (MITM)
Mix
  networks, 36, 39–44, 47–49, 51–54,
    60, 63–65, 82, 110, 134, 211,
    218, 228
  nodes, 40–45, 47, 48, 51, 53, 54, 64, 218
Mixmaster remailers, 46, 51
Mixminion remailers, 51, 52
ML, *see* Machine Learning (ML)
ML algorithm, 220, 222
ML model, 9, 220–224
ML outputs, 220–223
Model outputs, 220, 224
Model parameters, 220
Modified public key, 123, 129
Modified showing protocol, 130
Moving target defense (MTD), 217
MPC, *see* Multi-Party Computation
MPC protocol, *see* Multi-Party Computation
Multi-factor authentication, 231
Multi-level secure relations, 176
Multi-party, 47, 154
Multi-Party Computation, *see* MPC protocol,
  *see* Secure Multi-Party Computationl
Multi-party computation (MPC), 47, 143,
  150–158, 168–171, 229, 242
Multiplexing, 58
Multi-show, *see* Single-show credential
Multi-show credential, 135
  *See also* Single-show credential
Multi-user group chat, 104
Mutual authentication, 75, 255
  *See also* Unilateral


**N**

National Institute of Standards and
  Technology (NIST), 76, 220, 257
Network eavesdroppers, 33
Network layer security, *see* IPsec
Networking protocol, 71
Network-to-network communications, 97

NIST, *see* National Institute of Standards and
    Technology (NIST)
Non-policy-centered approach to disclosure
    protection, 175
Non-transferability, 131, 132, 136, 138, 243
NP-complete, 262
NP-hard, 120, 139, 261


**O**

OAKLEY Key Determination
    Protocol, 79
Oblivious polynomial evaluation, 212
Oblivious transfer, 154, 252, 253
Oblivious transfer protocol, 153, 154
OECD data protection principles, 176
Off-the-Record (OTR), 98–106, 211, 228
Off-the-Record (OTR) messaging, 95,
    98–105, 228
One-time pad, 245
Onion
    proxies, 55, 58
    routers, 54–59, 211
    routing, 16, 53–64, 82, 110, 211, 218
    routing networks, 39, 54–57, 60,
        61, 63, 228
Opaque, 131, 218
Open Whisper Systems, 103
Operation tuple, 34, 210
Order-Preserving Encryption Scheme
    (OPES), 181
OTR, *see* Off-the-Record (OTR)
Otr-dev, 101
Otr-users, 101
Output perturbation, 111


**P**

P3P
    1.0, 182, 183, 185, 186
    1.1, 182, 185, 186
    extension mechanism, 186
    policies, 183–188, 191–195, 203
    user agents, 183–188, 193, 194 (*see also*
        Platform for Privacy Preferences
        Project (P3P))
Packet sniffer, 62
Pairing-based cryptography, *see* Bilinear
    pairing-based cryptography
Passive adversary, 47, 62, 258, 260, 262
Password managers, 119
Path selection algorithms, 61
Payload data, 78, 79
PBE, *see* Policy-Based Encryption (PBE)

Pedersen commitment, *see* Commitment
Pedersen commitment on a biometric, 132
Peer authentication process, 80
Peer Authorization Database (PAD), 80
Perfect forward secrecy, 58, 73, 79, 99, 101,
    104, 243
Performance enhancing mechanisms
    attacks, 63
Personal
    information, 1–4, 6–9, 12–15, 25, 29–33,
        35, 36, 39, 40, 132, 151, 176, 177, 179,
        181, 185, 192, 193, 195, 201, 202,
        210–213, 215, 216, 219, 220, 227, 230,
        232, 233, 235, 236
    privacies, 3, 21, 32, 176, 210, 231
    security, 7, 14, 33, 144, 177, 210,
        211, 213
PETs, *see* Privacy Enhancing Technologies
PET techniques, *see* Privacy Enhancing
    Technologies
PETs community, *see* Privacy Enhancing
    Technologies
Phi-hiding, 86
Physical danger, 7, 16
Pidgin, 102, 104
    *See also* Gaim
PIR, *see* Private Information Retrieval (PIR)
Plaintext, 40, 41, 45, 51, 56, 57, 64, 75, 81, 97,
    147, 149, 203, 244–246, 248, 250, 252,
    256, 259, 260, 263–265
Platform for Privacy Preferences Project
    (P3P), 175, 182–189, 203
Plausible deniability, 106, 228
Policy
    Decision Point (PDP), 191
    Enforcement Point (PEP), 191
    meta-language, 179
    reference file, 185, 189, 193, 194
Policy-Based Encryption, *see* Identity-Based
    Encryption
Policy-based encryption (PBE), 193, 195, 203,
    251, 252
Policy-centered PET, 182
Polynomial time, 120, 155
Polynomially-bounded attacker, 262
Polynomially-computable function, 151–154,
    170, 261
Preference policy, 115
Premaster secret, 72, 73
Pretty Good Privacy (PGP), 98, 99, 104
Principles of a Hippocratic database
    accuracy, 177
    compliance, 177
    consent, 176

limited collection, 177
limited disclosure, 177
limited retention, 177
limited use, 177
openness, 177
purpose specification, 176
safety, 179
Privacy
    advocates, vii, 15, 21
    auditors, 2, 190, 192, 193, 195,
        203, 215
    audits, 28, 189, 190, 192, 193, 203
    bird, 185–187, 189, 203
    breaches, 2, 26, 31, 111, 118, 216, 234
    certification teams, 2
    Commissioners, 2, 21, 28, 220
    communities, 1, 21, 36, 153, 176
    definitions, 3, 4, 16, 18, 25, 27, 29–31,
        110, 117, 144, 165–167, 169, 227
    enforcement, 23, 28, 179, 192, 193,
        195, 203
    goals, 3, 17, 22, 25, 26, 29, 31, 36, 63, 99,
        104, 113, 118, 122, 151, 158, 176, 177,
        184, 204, 209–211, 216, 217, 219–224,
        229, 231, 234, 235, 255
    guidelines, 2, 26, 176, 203, 215
    implications of machine learning, 220
    law, 3, 26, 30, 183, 184, 215
    levels, vii, 1, 2, 8, 22, 27, 28, 31–35, 49,
        63, 75, 111, 114, 118, 120, 122, 134,
        144, 163–165, 168–170, 180, 210, 229,
        231, 232
    metadata, 24, 88–90, 109, 177–179
    metrics, 109, 117
    minefield, 1–18
    policies, 2, 3, 7, 13, 16, 18, 21, 24, 26, 144,
        175–181, 183, 184, 187–190, 192, 193,
        195, 203, 229
    policy enforcement architectures, 214,
        221, 223
    practices, vii, 21, 88, 109, 120, 183–185,
        188–190, 192, 196, 204, 209–224,
        227, 231
    preferences, 176–178, 180, 187, 189, 203,
        213, 229
    preservation, 24
    preserving data mining, 212
    privacy bird user agent, 186
    protection goals, 23, 29
    risks, 8, 16, 74, 75, 81, 89, 104, 106, 111,
        149, 165, 166, 168, 190, 220, 230,
        232–234, 255
    seals, 189, 190, 192, 193, 195, 203
    techniques, vii, 4, 13, 24, 25, 28, 29,
        31–37, 39, 86, 87, 111, 118, 144, 149,
        159, 167, 170, 176, 181, 201, 210–217,
        221–224, 228, 229
    transformations, 192, 211–213, 221
    tree, vii, 17, 21–37, 39, 148, 170, 175, 203,
        204, 209–224, 228, 229, 235
    violations, 3, 4, 6, 26, 29, 216
Privacy enhancing technologies (PETs), vii,
    2–4, 7, 15–18, 21–29, 36, 37, 39, 40,
    53, 61, 63, 64, 69, 82, 88, 89, 95, 96,
    105, 106, 109, 110, 122, 135, 137, 138,
    143–145, 169, 175, 196, 203, 204,
    209–211, 214, 216, 219, 221–224,
    227–232, 234–236, 241, 242, 251,
    261, 265
Privacy threats, 6–9, 227
Privacy-in-depth, 36, 231, 234, 235
Privacy-preserving delegation, 131
Privacy-related laws, 215
Privacy-related system goals, 23
Private conversations, 98, 103, 105
Private information retrieval (PIR), 4, 64, 69,
    82–90, 167, 211, 228
Private key generator (PKG), 149, 193,
    195, 252
Private keys, 42, 45, 55, 72, 99, 100, 122, 123,
    125, 126, 128, 129, 131, 132, 134, 136,
    137, 139, 145, 148–150, 157, 170, 171,
    193–195, 200, 203, 229, 245, 249,
    252, 256
Private Set Intersection (PSI), see Multi-Party
    Computation
Private Set Intersection protocol, see
    Multi-Party Computation
Profiling software, 9, 10
Proofs of cryptographic strength, 264
Properties of differential privacy
    adaptive composition, 167
    composability, 167
    convexity, 167
    convexity axiom, 167
    parallel composition, 167
    post-processing, 167
    post-processing axiom, 167
    sequential composition, 167
Property of an attribute, 121, 196, 198
Pseudonym-credential pair, 133
Pseudonymity service, 44
Pseudonymous, 44, 45, 211, 218
Pseudonymous identifier, 44
Pseudonyms, 22, 27, 39, 44, 133, 212
Pseudorandom number generator (PRNG), 245

Public key
    asymmetric cryptography, 256
    certificates, 72, 75, 100, 122, 123, 126,
        247, 250, 251, 256
    cryptography, 40, 42, 57
    encryption algorithm, 248, 249
    encryption/decryption algorithms, 245
    "fingerprints", 102
    infrastructure (PKI), 75, 122, 126, 250, 256


**Q**
Quadratic residuosity, 86
Quasi-identifier, 113
Query
    interceptor, 179
    intrusion detector, 177, 181
    modifications, 158, 176, 179
    modifier, 179
    restrictions, 176


**R**
Random Oracle Model (ROM), 264
    *See also* Standard model
Randomized response techniques, 212
RC4, 245
RC4 stream cipher, 73
Real-time bidirectional communication, 54
Record
    protocols, 71
    tuples, 34, 35, 210
Recursive (*c-l*)-diversity, 116, 118
Redirect messages, 81
Reference monitor, 149
Refresh protocol, 133
Regularization, 222, 223
Re-identify a specific individual, 111, 119
Re-identify an arbitrary individual, 119
Re-keying, 100, 101, 247, 250
Remote logins, 54, 81
Rendezvous, 47
Rendezvous points, 59
Replay attack, 41
Replay protection, 78
Retention periods, 177, 178, 193
Retention requirements, 5
Revocation schemes, 251
Right-to-be-forgotten, 5
Robust PIR, *see* Private Information Retrieval
Role-Based Access Control (RBAC), 149
Routing
    attacks, 16, 56, 62, 64
    nodes, 61, 218
    updates, 81

RSA
    algorithms, 249, 257
    Digital signature (*see* Digital signature)
    modulus, 133, 248, 249, 256
    public key, 72, 125, 126, 134, 248,
        249, 256
    signature verification operation, 125, 256


**S**
Scrambled circuit, 152, *see* Garbled circuit
SDN, *see* Software Defined
    Networking (SDN)_
SDN Controller, *see* Software Defined
    Networking (SDN)
Secondary use, 25, 26
Second-generation onion router, 55
Secret Conversations, 103
Secret sharing schemes, 154, 247, 248
Secure
    channels, 72, 75, 81, 89, 103, 105, 156,
        212, 254
    connections, 61, 71, 74, 75
    deletion, 106
    E-mail protocol, 99
    Function evaluation (*see* Multi-Party
        Computation)
    MPC, 150, 156, 157
    MPC protocols, 151, 156, 171
    secure connection to a web server, 70
    Shell (SSH), 61, 219
    sockets layer, 70, 71
    systems, 81, 139, 176, 242
Secure/Multipurpose Internet Mail Extensions
        (S/MIME), 98, 99, 104
Security
    Architecture for the Internet Protocol, 76
    association (SA), 77
    gateways, 78
    Proofs (*see* Proofs of cryptographic
        strength)
    services, 60, 77–79, 217, 218, 243
    technologies, 59, 82, 103, 209–214, 221,
        223, 228, 229
Security/privacy versus usability, 139
Semantic security, 86, 265
Sensitive attribute values, 120
Series of mix nodes, 42
Server authentication, 71
Server hello, 72, 74
SHA-1, 73, 78, 100, 254
SHA-256, 73, 254
SHA-384, 254
SHA-512, 254
Shared secret cryptographic keys, 79

Showing protocol, 128–137, 197, 201, *see*
    Issuing protocol
SIGMA protocol, 102, 103
Signal protocol, 103, *see* TextSecure
Signature verification operation, 124, 256
Signing authority, 257
Signing operation, 256
Silent Circle Instant Messaging Protocol
    (SCIMP), 103
Single-show credential, 134
    *See also* Multi-show credential
Single-Use Reply Blocks (SURBs), 51
Skype, 103
SMP, *see* Socialist Millionaires
    Problem (SMP)
Social engineering, 2
Social media, 5–9, 13, 18, 105, 230, 233
Social sorting, 9
Socialist Millionaires Problem (SMP),
    102, 103
    *See also* Millionaires Problem
Socket connections, 54, 55
Software defined networking (SDN), 217–220,
    223, 224, 229
Source routing, 46
Sovereign Information Integration (SII)
    architecture, 181
Spyware, 5
SSL, *see* Secure Sockets Layer (SSL)
SSL/TLS, *see* Secure Sockets Layer (SSL)
Standard model, 148, 264
    *See also* Generic group model
    *See also* Random Oracle Model
Static key, 247
Statistical databases, 158, 168, 176
Store-and-forward messaging architecture, 53
Stratified, 46, 47
Stream ciphers, 104, 245, 246
Super-user, 179
Suppressions, 112–115, 119, 138
Surveillance, 3, 12, 14, 25
Sybil attacks, 62
Sybilhunter, 62
Symmetric
    algorithms, 245, 254, 260
    decryption algorithm, 54, 245
    encryption algorithm, 54, 245
    encryptions, 42, 54–57, 102, 246, 249,
        251, 254
    key, 54–57, 103, 245–251, 254, 255, 259, 263
    key derivation, 100, 246, 247, 249, 250, 254
Symmetrically private information retrieval
    (SPIR), 87
System Authority, 147–150, 171, 252

**T**
Table-level access control, 179
Tag, 133, 253–256
Tamper-resistant smart card technology, 132
Targeted advertising, 4, 6, 8, 11
Taxonomy, *see* Classification
T-closeness, 115, 117–119, 138
TCP/UDP, 81
Technological privacy techniques, *see*
    Classification
TextSecure, 103
    *See also* Signal protocol
Third parties, 3, 6, 8, 14, 18, 25, 27, 64, 69,
    75, 82, 95, 97, 99, 181, 185, 190, 221,
    233, 250, 255, 256
Third party cookies, 211
Threat model for the onion routing
    network, 56
Threats to privacy, 4–8, 16, 227
Threshold cryptography, 150, 157, 195, 248
    *See also* Multi-Party Computation
Timestamps, 41, 242
Timing attacks, 56
TLS, *see* Transport Layer Security (TLS)
Tools of cryptography, 242
Tor
    browsers, 59, 60, 65, 74, 233
    projects, 58
Tracing apps, 13
Trade-off between privacy and utility,
    160, 169
Traffic analysis, *see* Action analysis
Traffic shaping, 58
Training data, 219–223
Training dataset, 220, 221
Transmission Control Protocol (TCP), 48, 58,
    71, 75, 78
Transparency, 81, 89, 98
Transport layer security (TLS), 64, 69–77, 81,
    82, 89, 99, 105, 195, 212, 219, 228,
    233, 254
    1.0, 70, 73, 74, 76
    1.1, 70, 73, 76
    1.2, 70, 73, 76
    1.3, 70, 73, 74, 76
Transport Layer Security; SSL/TLS, *see*
    Secure Sockets Layer
Transport mode, *see* IPsec
Trust anchor, 250
Tunnel mode, *see* IPsec
2-database solution, 84
2-factor authentication, 75
Two-party protocol (2PC), 151, 157
2-server construction, 83–85

Type
  0 remailer(Original anonymous remailer),
    51, 52, 54
  I remailer(Cypherpunk remailer), 51
  II remailer(Mixmaster remailer), 51
  III remailer(Mixminion remailer), 51, 63

U
Unauthorized dissemination of
    personal data, 6
Unconditionally binding, *see* Unconditionally
    hiding, Computationally binding,
    Computationally hiding
Unconditionally hiding, *see* Unconditionally
    binding, Computationally binding,
    Computationally hiding
Unilateral, 75, 255,
    *see* Mutual authentication
Unintended observers, 33, 109, 110, 176, 211,
    213, 215, 219, 229
Unintended recipients, 25, 33, 35,
    212–216, 221
Unintentional release of information, 34
Unique identifiers, 111–113, 137
Unlinkable multi-show credential, *see*
    Single-show credential
Unlinkability, 27, 131–134, 136, 138, 243
Untraceable payment systems, 124
Untraceable return address (URA),
    44, 45, 51
U-Prove, 122
User agents, 183, 185–187, 189, 193, 194
User preferences, 183, 185, 187–190,
    193, 195
Users, 2, 8–10, 16, 21, 22, 25, 28, 29, 39, 42,
    45, 48, 50, 51, 53, 58–64, 69, 70,
    74–79, 81–85, 87–90, 95–98, 101–103,
    105, 109–111, 114, 118, 120, 121, 124,
    125, 132, 133, 136–139, 143–145,
    148–151, 166, 169–171, 175, 177–180,
    183, 184, 186–196, 203, 212, 218–222,
    243, 248–252, 257, 259
Utility of a data set, 114

V
Variable exit policies, 58
Vehicle forensics, 12
Verifiably-secure randomness, 47
Verification equation, 126, 128–130, 197
Virtual private networks (VPNs), 54, 55, 58,
    81, 97, 98
Volume attacks, 57, 58
Voting systems, 124
VPN, *see* Virtual Private Network (VPN)
Vulnerability goals, 23, 29

W
Wearables, 5, 8
Web browsing, 54, 62, 63, 182, 185, 188, 189,
    192, 196, 203
Website fingerprinting attacks, 62, 63
WhatsApp, 103
White-box setting, 220, 221
    *See also* Black-box setting
Wiretap laws, 216
Wiretapper, 62
World Wide Web Consortium (W3C), 182

X
XACML, *see* eXtensible Access Control
    Markup Language
XML, *see* Extensible Markup Language (XML)
XSalsa20, 104, 245
XSLT, *see* eXtensible Stylesheet Language
    Transformation (XSLT)
XSLT stylesheet, *see* eXtensible Stylesheet
    Language Transformation (XSLT)

Z
Zero-knowledge
    proof, 127, 133, 134, 263
    proof of knowledge, 127, 138, 263
    protocol, 132
ZKPoK, *see* Zero-knowledge proof of
    knowledge (ZKPoK)

Printed in the United States
by Baker & Taylor Publisher Services